D0782379

A New World to Be Won

Also by G. Scott Thomas

History
Advice from the Presidents
The United States of Suburbia
The Pursuit of the White House

Demographics
The Rating Guide to Life in America's Fifty States
Where to Make Money
The Rating Guide to Life in America's Small Cities

Sports
Leveling the Field

A New World to Be Won

John Kennedy, Richard Nixon, and the Tumultuous Year of 1960

G. Scott Thomas

PRAEGER

AN IMPRINT OF ABC-CLIO, LLC
Santa Barbara, California • Denver, Colorado • Oxford, England

SOUTH HUNTINGTON
PUBLIC LIBRARY
HUNTINGTON STATION, NY 11746

973.92
Tho

Copyright 2011 by G. Scott Thomas

All rights reserved. No part of this publication may be reproduced, stored in a retrieval system, or transmitted, in any form or by any means, electronic, mechanical, photocopying, recording, or otherwise, except for the inclusion of brief quotations in a review, without prior permission in writing from the publisher.

Library of Congress Cataloging-in-Publication Data

Thomas, G. Scott.
   A new world to be won : John Kennedy, Richard Nixon, and the tumultuous year of 1960 / G. Scott Thomas.
      p. cm.
   Includes bibliographical references and index.
   ISBN 978-0-313-39795-0 (hardcopy : alk. paper) — ISBN 978-0-313-39796-7 (ebook)   1. Presidents—United States—Election—1960.   2. Kennedy, John F. (John Fitzgerald), 1917–1963. 3. Nixon, Richard M. (Richard Milhous), 1913–1994.   4. Presidential candidates—United States—Biography.   5. Political campaigns—United States—History—20th century.   6. United States—Politics and government—1953–1961.   I. Title.
   E837.7.T47   2011
   973.92—dc23   2011021689

ISBN: 978-0-313-39795-0
EISBN: 978-0-313-39796-7

15   14   13   12   11   1   2   3   4   5

This book is also available on the World Wide Web as an eBook.
Visit www.abc-clio.com for details.

Praeger
An Imprint of ABC-CLIO, LLC

ABC-CLIO, LLC
130 Cremona Drive, P.O. Box 1911
Santa Barbara, California 93116-1911

This book is printed on acid-free paper ∞

Manufactured in the United States of America

To Laura, whose birth was undeniably the happiest event of 1960

"It is time for a new generation of leadership, to cope with new problems and new opportunities. For there is a new world to be won."

—*John Kennedy*

"I don't think we'll ever see again—or we've ever seen—a physical campaign involving two young men like Kennedy and Nixon with such enormous physical in-depth campaigning around the country. Goldwater and Johnson didn't put on anything like that. Neither did Eisenhower and Stevenson. But you had two relatively young men with enormous drive, and it was quite a show."

—*Robert Finch*

Contents

Acknowledgments

My personal headlines in 1960 were limited in scope. Chief among them were the start of kindergarten at Oakdale Elementary School in Waukegan, Illinois, and the birth of my future wife in Zeeland, Michigan, almost directly across Lake Michigan. (We wouldn't meet for 23 years, and then in Virginia.)

I remember virtually nothing about events of broader significance, though I do recall accompanying my mom and dad to vote that November. Illinois played a pivotal role in John Kennedy's victory over Richard Nixon, but it's unlikely my parents had any impact on the final margin. My mother was the daughter of a rabidly Republican farmer who subscribed to Colonel Robert McCormick's *Chicago Tribune*. My father was the son of a staunchly Democratic factory worker who revered Franklin Roosevelt. I suspect that their votes canceled out.

These scattered recollections, of course, were of no real help in the preparation of *A New World to Be Won*. But many people and institutions did provide substantial assistance and inspiration along the way. My thanks to them all:

- To the staffs of my local libraries—the Buffalo and Erie County Public Library and the University at Buffalo's Thomas Lockwood Memorial Library—for digging up dozens of books that had migrated to the netherworld known as the closed stacks.
- To the presidential libraries and other institutions that made reference materials available online or through interlibrary loan—the Art Institute of Chicago, Dwight D. Eisenhower

Presidential Library and Museum, Harry S. Truman Library and Museum, John F. Kennedy Presidential Library and Museum, Lyndon Baines Johnson Library and Museum, National Aeronautics and Space Administration, United States Senate Historical Office, and the University of Virginia's Miller Center of Public Affairs.

- To Michael Millman and the good folks at Praeger for their careful and thoughtful handling of my manuscript.
- To my favorite professor at Washington and Lee University, Barry Machado, for proving that history can be a challenging and fascinating subject, not the dry assortment of facts that was dished out in high school.
- And to my wife, Laura, and my daughter, Lindsay, for their endless love and support, as well as their ability to endure an occasionally annoying stream of anecdotes about a certain calendar year. That phase of our lives, at least, is over. I promise.

1

Prologue: The Spirit of Camp David

It was, for Dwight Eisenhower, a case of love at first flight.

Ike—his nickname since boyhood—had endured tedious forms of transportation throughout a military career spanning 37 years, followed by 7 years as president of the United States. He retained unhappy memories of a truck convoy in 1919 that took two months to crawl from coast to coast: of innumerable bumpy, uncomfortable jeep rides; of ponderous, rackety propeller-driven aircraft.

But this was different. Eisenhower's official plane, the *Columbine*, had been replaced by one of the true innovations of the late fifties, a passenger jet. The maiden presidential voyage of the Boeing 707, dubbed *Air Force One,* would carry Ike from Andrews Air Force Base outside of Washington to Germany, France, and Great Britain. It swooshed skyward under a silvery half-moon at 3:57 A.M. on August 26, 1959, heading east.

The president was instantly hooked, pronouncing jet travel "an exhilarating experience." *Air Force One* zipped toward Germany at 540 miles per hour, getting an extra boost from a 50-mile-per-hour tailwind. Eisenhower marveled at the jet's "silent, effortless acceleration and its rapid rate of climb." Long-distance travel, potentially an unpleasant ordeal for a man nearing his 69th birthday, had suddenly become enjoyable.

What awaited Eisenhower was equally surprising. *Air Force One* landed that afternoon in Bonn, the capital of West Germany, the part of Germany that had been occupied by American, British, and French forces at the end of World War II. Bonn was small (population: 140,000), and Eisenhower was the same man who had conquered Nazi

Germany 14 years earlier. There was no reason to expect a thunderous welcome.

But thunderous it was. More than 300,000 Germans jammed the narrow streets of Bonn, wildly cheering the American president and the 83-year-old West German chancellor, Konrad Adenauer. A local newspaper hailed Ike as "The Uncle From America," the only man possessing the blend of benevolence, determination, and strength necessary to guarantee the freedom of West Germany.

Bonn set the tone for the entire trip. More than a million people shouted themselves hoarse for Ike in Paris, which he entered in a convertible alongside French President Charles de Gaulle, himself a World War II hero. The welcome in London was the most enthusiastic of all, drawing the biggest crowds that anybody could remember. Prime Minister Harold Macmillan, who rode with Eisenhower through an endless sea of Britons, kept muttering, "I never would have believed it, I never would have believed it."

The outpouring of affection was a personal tribute to Eisenhower the five-star general, the savior of Western Europe who had driven the Nazi menace from France and Britain—and to Eisenhower the president, the region's current protector against the Soviet Union and its brusque, frightening leader, Nikita Khrushchev.

But Ike sensed something more. The cheers, to him, also conveyed a fervent hope that the coming decade might remain free from strife. "People want peace so much that, one of these days, governments had better get out of the way and let them have it," Eisenhower said to Macmillan after they waved their goodbyes to the enormous crowd.

The European trip had been conceived as an obligation, a perfunctory round of talks with America's allies, reassuring them of the U.S. commitment against the Soviets. But the novelty of jet travel and the exuberance of the German, French, and British people had an unexpected side effect, energizing a man who had grown weary of the presidency.

Eisenhower had entered politics with great reluctance in 1952, defeating another hesitant candidate, Adlai Stevenson, in the presidential election that November. Subsequent health problems and accumulated stress eroded what little enthusiasm he possessed for life in the White House. A heart attack in 1955, a bout of ileitis a year later, and a mild stroke a year after that—all compounded by the daily war of nerves with the Soviets—wore down his spirit.

Doctors advised him to lessen his load, to avoid "irritation, frustration, anxiety, fear, and above all, anger." Ike was baffled. "Just what do you think the presidency is?" he snapped.

Criticism only made things worse. Eisenhower the general was accustomed to having his orders fulfilled without question. Eisenhower the president was second-guessed and sometimes ridiculed by Democrats and intellectuals. They sniped that he wasn't particularly smart or hard-working, that he didn't really understand the dangers facing America, that he had allowed the nation to drift as the fifties drew to a close. "These were the vital years we lost, the years the locusts have eaten," charged John Kennedy, a young Democratic senator from Massachusetts who had his eye on Eisenhower's job.

Most of the accusations were misguided. Ike, in reality, was an ambitious, intelligent, self-disciplined leader. No ineffectual bumbler could have coordinated military operations as complex as D-Day or the final assault on Germany. Richard Bissell, the Central Intelligence Agency's deputy director, was initially surprised to encounter a decisive president who controlled the agenda and issued emphatic commands at closed-door meetings. Historian Fred Greenstein would later call it a "hidden-hand presidency," with Eisenhower as puppet master.

It was the president's *public* style that established his image as an amiable lightweight. Eisenhower was constantly at war with the English language. His sentences were convoluted, his syntax mangled. Some of the chaos seemed deliberate. James Hagerty, the presidential press secretary, once agonized over the best way for Eisenhower to explain a complicated policy decision involving China. "Don't worry, Jim," the president grinned. "If that question comes up, I'll just confuse them."

The grin was what truly mattered. It was the key to Eisenhower's continuing popularity with everyday Americans. Even his critics admitted that the bald, smiling president was a likable guy—everyone's favorite uncle, as the German newspaper had suggested.

And yet, even with the boost he had received in Western Europe, he was a tired man, too. The recently enacted 22nd Amendment prohibited Eisenhower from seeking a third term in 1960, a term he probably could have won with no difficulty. One more year in the White House, and then he would retire to his beloved 192-acre farm near Gettysburg, Pennsylvania. A friend suggested, "You'll be a full-fledged farmer when you get through with your job down in Washington." And Ike flashed that famous grin, momentarily happy. "Brother," he replied, "I hope, I hope."

That, however, was in the future. Eisenhower's immediate concern was 1960, the final chapter of his 45-year career of public service. What could he accomplish in the time that remained? How could he cement his legacy?

The relative ease of jet travel and the eager crowds in Bonn, Paris, and London had given him an answer. He would devote the rest of his presidency to traveling the globe, seeing as many foreign leaders and being seen by as many common men and women as possible, spreading the word that America desired friendly relations with everyone, that it wished to lessen the Cold War tensions that had ensnared the United States and Soviet Union in a nuclear arms race.

Eisenhower had been invited to open the American exhibition at the World Agricultural Fair in New Delhi, India, in December. That, he decided, would be the linchpin for his first mission. White House planners began shoehorning destinations into his itinerary, mapping out an 11-nation, 19-day, 22,370-mile trip that would be the longest undertaken by any president.

Eisenhower approved the whole exhausting schedule from the first stop in Rome to the conclusion in Casablanca. He gave the order to have *Air Force One* fueled and set for departure on December 3. He was ready to meet the people of the world, no matter how arduous the journey. "Such prestige and standing as I have on this earth," he said, "I want to use it."

***

The world's deepest worry in 1959 was the same concern that had overshadowed the entire decade—the fear that the United States and Soviet Union would somehow blunder into a mutually destructive nuclear war.

The mushroom clouds that bloomed over Hiroshima and Nagasaki in August 1945 had been applauded by most Americans. The twin explosions not only compelled Japan's surrender, thereby ending World War II, but also ushered in an era of nuclear monopoly. The United States, as never before in its history, stood as the dominant nation on the planet.

That heady period came to an abrupt end in August 1949 with the astounding news of the Soviets' first atomic detonation. The United

States upped the ante in 1952, producing a hydrogen bomb equal in destructive force to 500 Nagasaki bombs. The Soviets countered with their own thermonuclear device a year later. The two nations spent the rest of the fifties perfecting their systems for launching these fearsome weapons against each other, assembling fleets of jet bombers and arsenals of long-range missiles.

It was madness on a global scale. A June 1959 congressional report estimated the impact of a hypothetical bombardment of 1,500 megatons of Soviet hydrogen warheads, an attack of moderate intensity. It predicted that 20 million Americans would die immediately, and another 22 million would be dead of radiation sickness within two months.

America's anxiety was driven even higher by the erratic personality of the man whose finger rested on the Soviet nuclear button. Nikita Khrushchev was "a crude bear of a man," in the words of Vice President Richard Nixon, who had recently met him. Khrushchev's manners were rough, his language intemperate, his moods mercurial and always readily apparent. "There he goes again. He's either way up here or way down there," his wife, Nina Petrovna, sighed after one of her husband's outbursts. But he was also tough, cunning, and exceptionally skilled at political maneuvering.

Eisenhower and Khrushchev had obvious similarities, beginning with their glistening bald pates. They were of the same generation—the 65-year-old Soviet leader was four years younger than Ike—and they shared small-town roots. Each could trace his political career to military service. Young Khrushchev had been a miner, locksmith, and shepherd when the Russian Revolution erupted in 1917. He cast his lot with the Bolsheviks, the communist forces that would soon seize control of czarist Russia and reconstruct it as the Soviet Union, a self-proclaimed "worker's paradise." His enlistment in the Red Army proved to be a shrewd career move.

The biggest difference between them was education. Eisenhower earned a degree from the U.S. Military Academy. Khrushchev grew up illiterate, unable to read or write until his early twenties, according to some historians. "You all went to great schools, to famous universities—to Harvard, Oxford, the Sorbonne," he once lectured a group of foreign diplomats. "I never had any proper schooling. I went about barefoot and in rags. When you were in the nursery, I was herding cows for two kopeks. And yet, here we are, and I can run rings around you all. Tell me, gentlemen, why?"

Two factors were foremost—his native intelligence and his ruthless ability to get results, no matter the cost in human or economic terms. He rose rapidly in the Soviet hierarchy because he learned quickly, got things done, and did not quail at Joseph Stalin's violent methods. Khrushchev was elected a full member of the Presidium—in essence, the country's board of directors—at 45 years old. He may have been little known in the outside world, but he was well positioned to take charge upon Stalin's death in 1953. He deftly shoved his competitors aside and, within a few months, assumed the position of first secretary, ruler of the Soviet Union.

Most Americans believed that Khrushchev was a dictator, just as Stalin had been. But his grasp on power was precarious. His foes in the Presidium had actually lined up the necessary votes to remove him in June 1957. He simply refused to leave. "But we are seven, and you are four," whined one of the plotters, Nikolai Bulganin. Khrushchev shot back, "Certainly in arithmetic, two and two make four. But politics are not arithmetic." He summoned a larger body, the 309-member Central Committee, to Moscow, where it repudiated the coup and retained him in office. Bulganin soon found himself reassigned to a meaningless job in distant Stavropol.

The biggest problem facing Khrushchev in 1959 was Berlin. The old German capital sat entirely within the boundaries of Soviet-dominated East Germany, 110 miles beyond the West German border, yet the western portion of the city operated as an independent entity. Allied troops—American, British, and French—had been stationed in West Berlin since World War II and had no intention of departing.

Their presence was a symbolic annoyance to Khrushchev, to be sure, but it was the practical consequences that most concerned him. The East German people, insufficiently impressed by the advantages of communism, were fleeing in heavy numbers: 204,000 had escaped in 1958 alone, a substantial percentage of them passing through West Berlin. East German leaders complained that it was impossible to build a strong communist country under such adverse conditions. The outflow of workers had to be stopped. The border had to be secured.

Khrushchev took steps in November 1958 to placate the Kremlin hardliners and East German communists. He condemned West Berlin as a "malignant tumor" and issued an ultimatum to the Western democracies, giving them six months to abandon the city. If they didn't, he pledged to sign a peace treaty with East Germany, ending the legal justification for the Allied presence in West Berlin. "Only madmen," Khrushchev scoffed, "can go to the length of unleashing another world war over the preservation of their privileges as occupiers of West Berlin."

The stage was set for the ultimate Cold War showdown between Khrushchev—angry, boisterous, unpredictable—and Eisenhower's longtime secretary of state, John Foster Dulles—dour, bespectacled, as ardent a saber-rattler as Khrushchev. The president gave Dulles virtually free rein over American foreign policy, a privilege the secretary exercised with grim enthusiasm. "The ability to get to the verge without getting into war is the necessary art," he said. "If you cannot master it, you inevitably get into war. If you try to run away from it, if you are scared to go to the brink, you are lost."

There was no thought of negotiation with Khrushchev, certainly no possibility of capitulation. The world watched with growing anxiety as the Soviet deadline of May 27, 1959—known within the State Department as K-Day—drew inexorably closer. Pessimists envisioned World War III igniting in the same city where the blueprints for World War II had been drawn.

The impasse broke in an unexpected way. Dulles was diagnosed with terminal cancer in February 1959 and weakened quickly. He attempted to run the State Department from Walter Reed Army Medical Center, but finally conceded the inevitable and resigned in April. Khrushchev, meanwhile, grew increasingly vague about Berlin as his deadline loomed and his feet grew colder. The only significant event on K-Day, as it happened, was the funeral of John Foster Dulles.

Relations thawed as summer arrived. Khrushchev hinted to a visiting group of American governors that he might like to visit the United States someday. Eisenhower was already toying with the idea of exchanging visits. "We began to work on this thing," he would recall, "and I gave the subject to two or three of my trusted associates in the State Department." Emmet Hughes, a former Eisenhower aide, was amazed at the speed with which "the clenched fist of Dulles" was replaced by "the outstretched hand of Eisenhower." A formal invitation was quietly sent to Khrushchev on July 11, 1959. The story burst into the headlines when he accepted on August 3.

The resulting trip was as surreal as it was unprecedented. Khrushchev arrived at Andrews Air Force Base on September 15, accompanied by his wife, his 2 daughters, his son, and 63 aides. A troupe of 375 reporters and photographers followed them as they visited everything from Iowa farms and Pittsburgh factories to New York skyscrapers and Hollywood studios.

Demonstrators heckled the Soviet leader at several stops, but audiences also greeted him with smiles and applause. He kissed babies, affixed hammer-and-sickle pins to men's lapels, and shouted hello to everybody he met. "The plain people of America like me," he told Henry Cabot Lodge Jr., the United Nations (UN) ambassador who served as his escort. "It's just those bastards around Eisenhower that don't."

Khrushchev's grand tour culminated in two days of meetings at Camp David, Eisenhower's Maryland retreat. The president and first secretary swapped stories of their experiences in World War II and chatted about current events. There were moments of tension—especially when Khrushchev boasted that he had no fear of nuclear war—but they were surprisingly rare. More important were the concessions the two leaders made. Khrushchev assured Ike that his Berlin ultimatum was no longer in effect. Eisenhower, who had been resisting Soviet and British requests for a summit meeting, now suggested that a four-power summit—the French being the fourth—might be arranged in 1960. Astonished reporters heralded the new "Spirit of Camp David."

The United States and Soviet Union were still enemies, but the success of Khrushchev's visit reinforced Eisenhower's belief that personal diplomacy could bring real peace to the world. Ike was already committed to December's 11-nation grand tour and had begun planning subsequent journeys to Latin America and the Far East—and now he faced the prospect of the greatest trip of all. The date had not been set, but Khrushchev had extended a verbal invitation at Camp David. Eisenhower would soon be flying to Moscow himself.

***

A vice president virtually never blazes a trail in foreign policy—or, for that matter, *any* type of policy. But Richard Nixon, with Eisenhower's approval, had scored an uncommon exception in late July and early August of 1959, visiting the Soviet Union in advance of his boss.

Nixon's official reason for traveling to Moscow was to dedicate the American exhibition in Sokolniki Park, a 78-foot-high geodesic dome that contained a wide array of inventions and products from the United States, including a 6-room model ranch house. The two nations had agreed in 1955 to coordinate a series of cultural exchanges, and this was the first U.S. installment.

But it was the vice president's *unofficial* motivation that was of foremost importance. Nixon would be running for president in 1960, and Sokolniki Park offered an opportunity to prove that he would be a worthy successor to Eisenhower. Ike, somewhat concerned that sparks might fly when the combative Nixon met the mercurial Khrushchev, suggested to his vice president that he maintain "a cordial, almost light, atmosphere" with the Soviet leader.

It was too much to expect. The two men were friendly enough in their closed-door sessions at the Kremlin. But Khrushchev, who was striving mightily (with only mixed success) to improve his country's standard of living, viewed the exhibit in Sokolniki Park, especially the model house, as a capitalist affront.

His feelings boiled to the surface when Nixon led him into the living room. The vice president said that such a home would cost only $14,000 in the United States, making it affordable for an American worker. Khrushchev scoffed that the structure was so flimsy that it wouldn't stand for 20 years. "We build firmly," he said. "We build for our children and grandchildren. We use bricks."

They moved on to the kitchen, featuring an electric dishwasher, electric stove, and refrigerator. "You think the Russians will be dumbfounded by this exhibit. But the fact is that all newly built Russian homes will have this equipment," Khrushchev said with less than complete honesty. He stared glumly at the other gadgets scattered around the room.

"Isn't it better to be talking about the relative merits of our washing machines than the relative strength of our rockets?" Nixon asked. "Isn't this the kind of competition you want?"

"Yes," Khrushchev replied, "that's the kind of competition we want, but your generals say they are so powerful they can destroy us. We can also show you something so you will know the Russian spirit. We are strong. We can beat you." Tension permeated the small kitchen. Khrushchev pressed his thumb against Nixon's chest at one point. Nixon wagged his finger in Khrushchev's face in rebuttal.

The so-called kitchen debate was nothing more than political theater, but Americans loved it. *Time* hailed Nixon's performance as "the personification of a kind of disciplined vigor that belied tales of the decadent and limp-wristed West." The esteemed *New York Times* columnist, James Reston, himself no fan of the vice president, conceded that the

Richard Nixon debates Nikita Khrushchev: "Isn't it better to be talking about the relative merits of our washing machines than the relative strength of our rockets?" (Thomas O'Halloran/Library of Congress)

Moscow trip had been "the perfect way to launch a campaign for the U.S. presidency."

It was yet another example of Nixon making the right move at the right time. He had risen with astonishing speed from an impoverished childhood in Southern California, becoming the most successful young politician to emerge in the wake of World War II. He had touched all the bases—2 terms in the House of Representatives, 2 years in the Senate, nearly 7 years as Ike's vice president—and still was just 46 years old.

Hard work had always been part of his life. Nixon's family owned a lemon grove in Yorba Linda, California, when he was a boy, but the business failed. His parents moved to Whittier, where they operated a tiny gas station and general store. Young Richard rose early to buy produce for the store, spent summers picking crops at nearby farms, and even worked as a barker for a fortune wheel: anything to bring in a few extra dollars.

He also threw himself into his studies, earning a spot in Duke University's prestigious law school. "I'm scared," Nixon confessed to a classmate. "I counted thirty-two Phi Beta Kappa keys in my class. I don't believe I can stay up top in that group." But he did. He graduated third in his class, "not because I was smarter," he later said, "but because I worked longer and harder than some of my more gifted colleagues." His classmates nicknamed him "Iron Butt," testimony to his durability.

Tenacity was the quality that distinguished Nixon's political career from the start. He pursued an investigation into the alleged communist ties of a former State Department official, Alger Hiss, even though other members of the House Un-American Activities Committee were dubious or uninterested. A jury found Hiss guilty of perjury in January 1950, winning Nixon national acclaim. "The conviction of Alger Hiss was due to your patience and persistence alone," former President Herbert Hoover wired him the next day.

The Hiss verdict, Nixon believed, would be his ticket to higher office in 1950. His friends urged caution. He was only 37; there was plenty of time. But he would not be deterred. His victorious campaign against Democrat Helen Gahagan Douglas would go down in history for its nastiness—Nixon insinuating that Douglas voted the communist line, Douglas equating "Nixonism" with Nazism. Each hung a devastating nickname on the other. Douglas would henceforth be remembered as the Pink Lady, Nixon as Tricky Dick.

Nixon had vaulted from the House to the Senate in just 4 years. His next promotion came even faster. Only 18 months elapsed between his Senate oath and his selection as Eisenhower's running mate. Ike was over 60, apolitical, strongly tied to the East and Midwest. Republican strategists sought to balance the ticket with a young, fiercely political Westerner. The choice was easy.

Nixon, by this time, was acknowledged as the golden boy of American politics, rising through the ranks with astounding ease, seemingly unstoppable. His success inspired awe and envy in a former colleague still mired in the House of Representatives. "I was tremendously pleased that the convention selected you for V.P.," John Kennedy wrote Nixon in the summer of 1952. "I was always convinced that you would move ahead to the top—but I never thought it would come this quickly."

The euphoria of Nixon's vice presidential nomination was soon punctured by press reports that he had access to an $18,000 slush fund raised by California businessmen. Nixon insisted that he used the donations to pay for postage, travel, clerical help, and printing costs—nothing more. Democrats howled that he was on the take. Pressure built on Eisenhower to toss him off the ticket. Some of Ike's advisers hinted to Nixon that he should do the right thing and resign.

He went public instead, delivering a half-hour speech on national television, a fascinating blend of pathos and defiance. He briefly defended the fund, but spent most of his time talking aimlessly about his debts and limited savings, his wife Pat's "respectable Republican cloth coat," and his daughters' cocker spaniel, Checkers, which had been a gift from an admirer and which he vowed not to return, no matter how intense the public outcry.

Nor would he leave the ticket. "I am not a quitter," he declared. The resulting wave of public support convinced Eisenhower to keep Nixon as his running mate. The Republican rank and file came to view the young vice president as a hero—applauding his role in bringing Hiss to justice, admiring his courage in making the Checkers speech, and thrilling to his harsh verbal attacks against the Democratic Party.

Nixon used his time well as Ike's second-in-command, speaking to any Republican group that would listen, collecting chits for the big campaign that lay ahead. A Gallup Poll in early 1958 found that two-thirds of the nation's Republicans already supported him for president, even though the election was two-and-a-half years away.

But Nixon was far from the perfect candidate. He lacked the fluidity and grace of a natural politician. He was shy, a loner. His attempts at humor and good fellowship often seemed awkward and forced. "If the time comes when the Republican Party and the voters are looking for an outwardly warm, easygoing, gregarious type, then they will not want the sort of man I am," he admitted to columnist Stewart Alsop in 1958.

Nixon's strident speeches delighted his allies but stamped him as a polarizing figure. His skill with a rhetorical knife was evident from his first national campaign in 1952. He charged that Harry Truman's administration was rife with officials who fronted for "un-American elements, willingly or otherwise." Truman never forgave him, henceforth refusing to appear at any event where Nixon was present. Columnist Walter Lippmann spoke in 1958 for millions of Americans in condemning the vice president as "a ruthless partisan [who] does not have within his conscience those scruples which the country has a right to expect in the president of the United States."

He was, nonetheless, the Republican Party's best campaigner, especially since Eisenhower disdained partisan activity. Nixon had carried the Republican load for six years and was expected to do so again as the 1958 congressional elections approached. Friends, sniffing impending defeat, urged him to beg off. "You're toying with your chance to be president," warned Thomas Dewey, the Republican nominee in 1944 and 1948. "Don't do it, Dick. You've already done enough, and 1960 is what counts now."

Nixon ignored the advice. He pulled out all the old tricks—blasting the Democrats for their "sorry record of retreat and appeasement," criticizing their "defensive, defeatist, fuzzy-headed thinking." But nothing worked. The Republicans were crushed in a landslide, losing 13 seats in the Senate and 47 in the House. The vice president's pessimism grew as he studied the 1958 returns. His administrative assistant, Robert Finch, recalled, "Nixon had grave reservations about whether he could be the candidate or should be the candidate, and whether any Republican was going to have any chance in 1960."

But not every Republican did poorly on the evening of November 4, 1958. Fifty-year-old Nelson Rockefeller—one of *the* Rockefellers, the richest family in America—was elected governor of New York. He unseated the Democratic incumbent, Averell Harriman, by a margin of 573,000 votes, an impressive achievement on what was otherwise a night of unalloyed Democratic triumph. Political columnists immediately anointed him a presidential contender.

Nelson had never been interested in following the typical Rockefeller path. The thought of running a family business or monitoring the family's investments bored him. "No," he said, "that isn't my idea of living a real life." Government was what he truly enjoyed. He capably filled a series of federal posts under Franklin Roosevelt, Harry Truman, and Dwight Eisenhower, ranging from assistant secretary of state to undersecretary of health, education, and welfare. But he wanted a government of his own to run. He set his sights on the governorship.

New York's Republican leaders tried to discourage him. They could not imagine voters accepting a multimillionaire who alternated between 5 residences, including an immense country estate and a 23-room penthouse apartment on Fifth Avenue. Tom Dewey, who had been a three-term governor himself, slapped Rockefeller on the knee, laughed, and said, "Nelson, you're a great guy, but you couldn't get elected dogcatcher in New York." Yet Rocky—the nickname foisted upon him by headline writers—soon proved them wrong. His friendly grin, raspy voice, and rough good looks resonated with the electorate.

Nixon watched with a sense of impending doom. His road to the Republican nomination, once unobstructed, had suddenly become treacherous. Rockefeller added to the vice president's unhappiness by opening a political office in the spring of 1959. Seventy staffers began churning out position papers and press releases.

Nixon gave the word to prepare for battle. The first primary election was slated for March 1960 in New Hampshire, where Rockefeller had attended Dartmouth College. "We were primarily concerned about New Hampshire. Rockefeller obviously had great strength there," Finch said. Nixon's team began laying the groundwork in every primary state from New Hampshire to the vice president's home turf, where the final primary would take place in June. "We anticipated," said Finch, "that it would go all the way through to California."

Rockefeller intensified his schedule as autumn drifted toward winter. He toured New England in November 1959, conceding that Nixon "probably" was the frontrunner for the presidency. He pushed on to the South and Midwest in December, declaring that the race for the Republican nomination would pit the "pros against the people," with himself as the self-appointed champion of the latter.

Rockefeller occasionally criticized the Eisenhower administration in vague terms—"we have seemed too often to lack coherent and continuing purpose"—but he echoed Nixon's positions on most issues. Both men were ardent anti-communists. Both believed in a strong military. Both had liberal records on civil rights—more liberal, in fact, than a large percentage of Democrats.

The big difference was a question of style. Rockefeller, as an affluent, Ivy League scion of the Eastern establishment, found it difficult to stomach the success of a contemporary so socially awkward, so harshly partisan, so relentlessly *middle class* as the vice president. Rocky confessed as much to a friend one day in late 1959, distilling his motivation to nine simple words. "I hate the idea," he said, "of Dick Nixon being president."

***

The Democrats screwed up their courage in early December and ventured a direct attack against President Eisenhower, something they rarely did. "Goodwill tours are an inadequate substitute for solid policies," sniffed the Democratic Advisory Council in advance of Ike's 11-nation trip. No one paid any attention. Eisenhower seemed impervious to political assault, drawing an approval rating of 67 percent in the latest Gallup Poll. He was the epitome of a Teflon president—a generation before that nickname would be hung on Ronald Reagan, and indeed, a year before nonstick Teflon frying pans would hit the market.

The Democrats were correct in a way. Eisenhower had no big plans for his journey. He wouldn't be conducting sensitive negotiations or signing treaties. His primary aim was to see and be seen, to listen and be heard. Waging peace, he called it. "In every country," he said before departing on December 3, "I hope to make widely known America's deepest desire: a world in which all nations may prosper in freedom, justice, and peace—unmolested and unafraid."

The president's official party included his son and daughter-in-law (wife Mamie, not feeling up to the rigors of the trip, would stay home), as well as a platoon of staffers, speechwriters, secretaries, military aides, bodyguards, and jet mechanics. They required a fleet of 5 aircraft: *Air Force One,* a spare 707 jet, 2 turboprop cargo planes, and a chartered jet for the 84 reporters who were tagging along.

The first stop, Rome, was inauspicious. Ike arrived during a heavy rainstorm. Clusters of damp spectators watched his motorcade wind past ancient tombs, catacombs, and churches on the Appian Way. Only 2,000 people awaited him in the Piazza Venezia, huddled under umbrellas. The sun finally peeked out on Eisenhower's third day in Rome, as he paid a call on Pope John XXIII. "You have brought us the sunshine, Mr. President," a Vatican official smiled.

The bright rays were a harbinger. A massive crowd awaited Eisenhower at his next destination, squeezed 20 deep along the lengthy route from the airport to downtown Ankara, the capital of Turkey. An even larger throng of 750,000 welcomed the president to Karachi, Pakistan, which he entered in a carriage drawn by six horses, while tens of thousands of schoolchildren vigorously waved American and Pakistani flags. "I hope you hard-boiled boys were a little bit impressed by this," Ike said to a group of photographers at the end of the route.

But India, everybody agreed, was the pinnacle. Eisenhower landed in New Delhi on December 9. He and India's prime minister, Jawaharlal

Nehru, were supposed to drive 13 miles from the airport to the heart
of the capital city, wave to onlookers along the way, and then settle
down for lengthy discussions.

It wasn't that simple. More than a million people jammed the route,
overflowing the curbs and swarming across New Delhi's boulevards.
A melange of motor vehicles, donkey carts, and even a few camels
added to the bedlam. The chaos more closely resembled a street festival than a parade. The limousine carrying Eisenhower and Nehru
tried to snake through the congestion. Indians pressed against the
open car and showered the two leaders with flower petals. The motorcade inched forward for nearly 2 hours, then ground to a complete halt
for 25 minutes.

Nehru, an avowed pacifist, could take it no longer. He dismounted
from the car and began swinging his walking stick, trying to clear a
path. "This was lively nonviolence," Eisenhower later wrote, though
it proved to be ineffective. A considerable amount of time passed
before police extricated the car. The president was standing a foot deep
in blossoms by the end of the parade.

Nehru was a neutralist, determined to show no favor to either the
United States or the Soviet Union. But that amazing day in New Delhi
moved him to compare Eisenhower, both in historic stature and peaceful intentions, to the revered father of Indian independence, Mohandas
Gandhi. "We have honored you, sir," Nehru told Ike two days later.
"It was because of many reasons, but above all, because you have
found an echo in the hearts of our millions. And I hope and believe
that your coming here will be a blessing to us—and a blessing to all."

***

Eisenhower's absence from the country gave the Democrats an ideal
opportunity to steal a jump on the election season. Twelve hundred
of the party's prominent figures and top contributors gathered at
New York's Waldorf-Astoria Hotel on December 7—ostensibly to celebrate the 75th birthday of Franklin Roosevelt's widow, Eleanor, but
actually to stage a giant anti-Republican pep rally.

Three leading Democratic presidential contenders—all senators—
delivered speeches: young, charismatic John Kennedy of Massachusetts; brisk, well-tailored Stuart Symington of Missouri; loquacious,
effervescent Hubert Humphrey of Minnesota. Yet it was an oldtimer
who stole the show—Adlai Stevenson, a two-time nominee who disavowed interest in the 1960 race, even though the press persisted in

labeling him a candidate. Stevenson told of a man who placed an early morning call to a hotel manager, urgently asking when the bar would open. The manager demanded to know why anyone would seek a bar at such an ungodly hour. The man shouted back, "I don't want to get in. I want to get out!"

It was an uncommon sentiment at the Waldorf that evening. Several governors and senators in the audience were considered prospective presidential candidates, and dozens more believed their own names should be on the list. All, however, adhered to the protocol of the era, which required coyness until half a year or so before the nominating convention. It would later become typical of presidential candidates to declare their intentions two or three years in advance. But the old rules were still in play in 1959. No one had yet announced for the Democratic nomination.

The race, however, was quite obviously underway. Speculation about potential candidates had begun as soon as the final vote in the 1956 election was counted. "Once mentioned, though doubts remain, you are almost immediately convinced," Humphrey later wrote, "The logic of becoming an active candidate is soon overwhelming, at least to yourself."

Humphrey was totally committed by December 1959, traveling all across the country in pursuit of votes. Symington organized a string of campaign clubs that month. Another Democratic aspirant, Senator Lyndon Johnson of Texas, held a series of political rallies in the West and Midwest. "I am not a candidate, and I do not intend to be," he disingenuously told reporters in Des Moines. "I do not say that I would not serve my country if the convention should do the unusual and select someone who isn't a candidate."

Kennedy was the busiest unofficial contender of all, having delivered hundreds of speeches from coast to coast since early 1957. It was clear that the 42-year-old Massachusetts senator—the youngest man in the race—was unintimidated by his elders.

Walt Rostow, a Massachusetts Institute of Technology professor, met Kennedy for breakfast one morning. Rostow suggested that Stevenson might be a formidable opponent in 1960. Kennedy waved him off. Stevenson had already taken two shots and failed. How about Symington? He was intelligent and experienced, Kennedy admitted, but seemed to lack personal drive: "It's not really a job for a lazy man." Humphrey? "I like Hubert," came the answer, "but honestly, I don't think he would make a better president than I would." Johnson?

He was the most talented man of the bunch, Kennedy conceded, but no president had been elected from a Southern state since the Civil War: "It's too close to Appomattox for him to get the nomination."

Kennedy had a few shortcomings as a presidential candidate himself. He lacked natural political skills. His personality was reserved, almost shy. "To stand at a factory gate and shake hands with the workers was never easy for him," admitted Larry O'Brien, one of his Massachusetts operatives. Kennedy consequently spurned rituals that might have won him votes. He refused to socialize with old-line party bosses; or to wear funny hats; or to prominently display his beautiful young wife, Jacqueline, in his campaigns. He tried to appear cool and under control at all times.

Kennedy approached politics without emotion. He was no crusader, despite the mythology that would blossom after his death. He was a rationalist, a pragmatist. He carefully pondered each move, weighing its potential impact on his career. "Kennedy was more cautious than many people realize," said diplomat Dean Rusk, himself a paragon of prudence. Kennedy's professional philosophy, according to author David Halberstam, could be reduced to a maxim: "Better no step than a false step."

It was precisely what might have been expected of a son who had seen his father achieve a position of great influence, only to lose it through carelessness and indiscretion.

Joseph Kennedy Sr. made millions in banking, real estate, movies, liquor importing, and the stock market before accepting a series of positions under Franklin Roosevelt. He served as chairman of the Securities and Exchange Commission and the Maritime Commission, and then was appointed ambassador to Great Britain in 1938. The glamorous post in London raised the senior Kennedy's political profile and his aspirations. He turned his sights to the presidency. Why couldn't *he* be the one who moved into the White House in 1941 when FDR wrapped up his second term and retired to his Hudson Valley estate?

It was at this point, as World War II broke out between Britain and Nazi Germany, that Joe Kennedy made not one, but two false steps. The first was to express doubt that Britain could win. It was rumored that he was anti-Semitic, that he sympathized with some of Hitler's aims. "You have said things about us that we regret to hear," George Murray wrote in the *London Daily Mail*. "They are things which in time, I think, you will regret having said."

That regret was compounded by Kennedy's second mistake, which was to underestimate Roosevelt's political strength and resilience. The president ostracized his defeatist ambassador, forcing his resignation a year after Britain went to war. It was FDR who would win the 1940 election, securing an unprecedented third term.

Joe Kennedy, now a pariah in Washington, had no choice but to transfer his unfulfilled dreams to his eldest son. Everybody agreed that Joseph Kennedy Jr. was the natural politician of the family, possessed of both charm and ambition. The young man launched his career as a delegate to the 1940 Democratic convention (where he cast one of the few votes against Roosevelt's renomination) and made no secret of his desire—his *certainty*—that he would avenge his father's disgrace and win the presidency someday.

The Japanese attacked Pearl Harbor the following year, dragging the United States into the war that Joe Sr. had so fervently hoped to avoid. Joe Jr. and his younger brother, Jack, headed off to fight the Axis. Both would achieve fame—Joe for piloting an explosives-laden plane toward a German submarine pen, Jack for saving 11 crewmembers after his PT boat was split by a speeding Japanese destroyer. The difference was that Jack lived. "It was easy," he once said of becoming a war hero. "They sank my boat."

John Kennedy returned from the Pacific to seek a seat in the House of Representatives in 1946. "When [young] Joe was denied his chance, I wanted to run and was glad I could," he maintained. Skeptics weren't convinced. Joseph Alsop, a political columnist close to the Kennedy family, said, "I don't think he would have bothered with public life if it hadn't been for his father." There was no denying that Old Joe was heavily involved. "I got in touch with people I knew," he said of that first campaign. "I have a lot of contacts." He also threw $50,000 into the House race, substantially more than any of the other 10 candidates had on hand. John Kennedy, a handsome, 29-year-old war hero, was on his way to Washington.

Where he did virtually nothing. "In all my years in public life," said Tip O'Neill, a friend who rose to become speaker of the House in 1977, "I've never seen a congressman get so much press while doing so little work." The House was merely to be a stepping stone to the ultimate prize, the presidency. Jack would avoid Old Joe's mistakes. He would tread cautiously—making no enemies, taking no controversial stands, awaiting a better opportunity.

That chance came in 1952. Kennedy announced his candidacy for the Senate seat held by Henry Cabot Lodge Jr., the Republican incumbent who possessed a prestigious family name and a personal fortune. Lodge, taking victory for granted, channeled his energy into Dwight Eisenhower's presidential campaign. Kennedy stumped tirelessly through more than 300 cities and towns from Boston to the Berkshires, assembling a powerful statewide organization along the way. The Kennedys matched the Lodges dollar for dollar in campaign spending—and then some. Jack carried the state by 70,000 votes.

The new senator seemed to have it all—youth, good looks, money. A rising star of such magnitude was fated to achieve national prominence, and the 1956 Democratic convention proved to be the venue. Kennedy was chosen to narrate a movie on the history of the Democratic Party, which was telecast nationally on the convention's opening night. Adlai Stevenson then asked him to deliver the speech that formally placed Stevenson's name before the delegates for the presidential nomination—more exposure on the TV networks. "He really sparkled at that convention," Humphrey said of Kennedy years later.

But the best was yet to come. Stevenson, with the nomination in hand, defied the unwritten rules of politics and declined to name a vice presidential candidate. He challenged the convention itself to do the job, triggering an overnight scramble by prospective running mates to line up delegate support. This, Kennedy was certain, was his golden opportunity. And, indeed, he almost made it. He came within three dozen votes of the vice presidential nomination before a late flurry of Midwestern and Southern support snatched the honor for Estes Kefauver, a populist senator from Tennessee.

The battle had been exhilarating—the television audience was transfixed by the frantic roll call—but a defeat was a defeat. Kennedy was angry. "He hated to lose anything," recalled aide Kenny O'Donnell, "and he glared at us when we tried to console him by telling him that he was the luckiest man in the world." O'Donnell's reasoning was sound. Stevenson was certain to be crushed by President Eisenhower in November. His running mate, whether Kefauver or Kennedy, would forever be tarred by that loss. It was better for Kennedy to have fallen short of the nomination.

He would never aim so low again. "With only about four hours of work and a handful of supporters, I came within thirty-three-and-a-half votes of winning the vice presidential nomination," Kennedy told

David Powers, his friend and personal assistant. "If I work hard for four years, I ought to be able to pick up all the marbles."

He began traveling extensively, usually with his diligent speechwriter, Theodore Sorensen. Democrats across the country were eager to meet the dashing young senator they had seen on television. Kennedy and Sorensen racked up more than a million air miles the next three years, flying on commercial carriers until 1959, when the Kennedy family acquired a converted Convair with a galley and a bedroom. It was named the *Caroline* after Kennedy's daughter.

Sorensen was instrumental in burnishing the senator's intellectual credentials. He served as primary researcher—some said co-author—of Kennedy's 1956 best-seller, *Profiles in Courage*, which told of senators who had done what they felt was right, defying contrary pressure. "Like JFK's speeches, *Profiles in Courage* was a collaboration, and not a particularly unusual one," Sorensen wrote half a century later. He had pulled together the source material and helped to draft chapters, but it was Kennedy who received sole billing on the title page. "I never felt—not for a moment—that I was wrongfully denied part of the credit," Sorensen said in 2008.

Profiles in Courage won the 1957 Pulitzer Prize under highly unusual circumstances. The Pulitzer jury dutifully read all of that year's nominated books and recommended five finalists to the Pulitzer board, Kennedy's book not among them. But the board rejected all five—an act of rare independence—and presented the award to *Profiles*. It was whispered that Joe Kennedy had indulged in literary wheeling and dealing to achieve the desired result. The senator's mother saw no reason for outrage. "Things don't happen," Rose Kennedy said. "They are made to happen."

And so they are, which is why Jack accelerated his drive for the presidency as 1959 unfolded. He quietly opened a campaign headquarters in Washington; installed his brother-in-law Steve Smith to run it; and dispatched his organizational wizard, Larry O'Brien, into the field. The instructions from the top—from Joe Kennedy himself—were crystal clear. There would be no settling for the vice presidency or a Cabinet post. The only acceptable outcome was victory.

That came as no surprise to anybody familiar with Old Joe and his no-holds-barred approach to life. "Even when we were six and seven years old," recalled Jack's younger sister, Eunice Kennedy Shriver, "Daddy always entered us in public swimming races, in the different age categories so we didn't have to swim against each other. And he did the same thing with us in sailing races. And if we won, he got terribly enthusiastic. Daddy was always very competitive. The thing he always kept telling us was that coming in second was just no good. The important thing was to win. Don't come in second or third—that doesn't count—but win, win, win."

* * *

There were surprising parallels between the lives of Jack Kennedy, who was earnestly seeking power in America, and Fidel Castro, who had recently attained it in Cuba.

Both had grown up in privileged surroundings. Castro was the son of a successful planter, not as wealthy as the Kennedys, but considerably more comfortable than most of his fellow Cubans. Both had been drawn to the Ivy League. Kennedy was a Harvard graduate; Castro had been interested in attending Columbia. And both were attracted to careers in politics. Castro, armed with a law degree from the University of Havana, launched a campaign for a seat in Cuba's Congress in 1952, the same year that Kennedy challenged Henry Cabot Lodge.

Their paths diverged from that point. A former president of Cuba, Fulgencio Batista, made a comeback on March 10, 1952, staging a coup. One of his first acts was to cancel the congressional elections. Castro had suppressed his rebellious streak up to then, willing to play by the establishment's rules, to start a small law practice and enter political life as a junior legislator. But Batista's coup barred even that meager hope for advancement. The enraged Castro soon became one of the dictator's most outspoken critics.

So began an amazing transformation from buttoned-down lawyer to khaki-wearing revolutionary. Castro directed an unsuccessful rebel assault against a regimental headquarters in 1953, served two years in prison, and then sailed into exile in Mexico. "From trips such as this, one does not return," he said in July 1955. "Or else, one returns with tyranny beheaded at one's feet." He chose the latter option, slipping back into Cuba aboard a rickety ship in December 1956, evading Batista's patrols, and establishing a base in the Sierra Maestra. He waged civil war for the next two years.

Victory came on the very first day of 1959. The fearsome Batista—a tyrant who had suppressed free speech, murdered political opponents, and skimmed off millions of dollars from prostitution and gambling rings—abruptly slunk into exile in the Dominican Republic. Castro entered Havana in triumph, proclaiming a new era of freedom.

"Power does not interest me, and I will not take it," he declared. "From now on, the people are entirely free."

The initial reaction from Washington was positive, but Castro was determined to pursue an independent course that inevitably displeased his northern neighbor. He created the National Institute of Agrarian Reform, which was chartered to expropriate large parcels of farmland. It had seized 2.2 million acres by December 1959, establishing 485 state cooperative farms. American companies watched warily. U.S. sugar companies had invested more than $300 million in Cuban cane mills. U.S. oil firms owned Cuban refineries worth $75 million. They feared becoming Castro's next targets.

Cooperative farms and state-owned property, of course, smacked of communism. And that was the great fear—that Castro was a secret communist, a potential ally of the Soviet Union just 90 miles off the Florida coast. Some of his fellow rebels, it was clear, were disciples of Karl Marx. "The Cuban Communist Party," Castro later admitted, "had men who were truly revolutionary, loyal, honest, and trained. I needed them."

But the CIA remained unsure about the orientation of the new leader himself. "There was still some question as to whether he was merely a rather woolly leftist or a disciplined communist," admitted Richard Bissell. The only labels that Castro thought appropriate were *liberator* or *nationalist*. "I hate Soviet imperialism as much as I hate Yankee imperialism," he said at the time. "I am not breaking my neck fighting one dictatorship to fall into another."

That was emerging as a familiar theme in smaller countries and colonies around the globe—a group coming to be collectively known as the Third World. Its member nations yearned for independence. They dreamed of breaking free from the shackles of Cold War politics, of being able to set their own courses into the future, and many were having success.

The UN had already proclaimed 1960 to be the Year of Africa because 16 colonies there, most of them administered by France or Great Britain, were scheduled to gain independence within 12 months. France was proving to be especially generous with its colonial subjects. "You have only to ask for it," Charles de Gaulle graciously told African politicians who hinted at their desire for self-government.

But de Gaulle's benevolence had its limits. France had no intention of freeing its largest African possession, Algeria. Colonization had been almost too successful there—more than 1 million French settlers had put down roots—and that made it difficult to sever ties with the mother country. Algerian nationalists launched a war for independence in 1954, but France resolutely met force with force. De Gaulle bent somewhat in September 1959, offering self-determination to Algeria if the rebels would agree to a cooling-off period of at least four years. They refused, and the fighting went on. Half a million French troops were stationed in Algeria by the end of 1959.

And there were other trouble spots. A prominent one was the Congo, whose Belgian overlords boasted that they could prevent the natives from winning freedom for another half-century. Congolese nationalists led by a fiery ex-postal clerk, Patrice Lumumba, sought to accelerate the timetable, but pro-independence riots landed Lumumba and a fellow rebel, Joseph Kasavubu, in prison in 1959.

The Eisenhower administration had little sympathy for such radical behavior, yet it did offer milder support to black Africans. The United States voted in favor of a November 1959 UN resolution condemning apartheid, the infamous policy of racial separation in the Union of South Africa. Sir Bernard Montgomery, a renowned British field marshal who had worked closely (though not always harmoniously) with Eisenhower in World War II, happened to be visiting Johannesburg at the time of the UN vote. He found Ike's opposition to apartheid "very curious," he told reporters, because the United States "has much the same racial setup [as South Africa] inside its own borders."

Monty had a point. The Supreme Court had outlawed segregation in public schools in 1954; a black boycott had integrated the buses of Montgomery, Alabama, in 1956; and Congress had passed the first civil rights legislation of the 20th century in 1957. Yet the basic facts of American life had not changed for most Negroes, as they were then called. Nearly all schools and buses were still segregated, especially in the South, and the Civil Rights Act had not remedied the situation.

The chasm between American rhetoric and performance perplexed the leaders of Africa's newly independent countries. "We want to stay out of the East-West quarrel; that doesn't interest us," an unidentified official in Guinea told a *New York Times* reporter. "And there's something else you ought to remember. The Negro question in the United States is of more concern to us than any threat of communism in Africa."

***

Thomas Gates had arrived at the Pentagon during the first heady months of the Eisenhower administration, suddenly transformed from a Philadelphia investment banker to the undersecretary of the navy. Nothing in his genteel background prepared him for the rough and tumble of political life, yet he climbed the ranks with impressive skill. He won three promotions in rapid succession, ultimately becoming secretary of defense on December 2, 1959.

Memories of his government service would leave Gates slightly breathless in later years. The intense pressure and dizzying pace were unlike anything he had experienced before or since. "You've got to realize, when I went to Washington in 1954, there were no missiles," he said in 1967, nestled back in his original profession. "There was no aircraft that could fly the speed of sound. There was no atomic power. There was certainly no satellite. The whole thing came, all of a sudden, bunched in there. It came within five or six years—five or six years."

Perhaps Gates was still so shaken that he overstated the rapidity of scientific progress—the first supersonic flight, for instance, had occurred in 1947—but his basic premise was accurate. The Eisenhower years, derided by critics as stagnant and unimaginative, actually coincided with an unprecedented technological revolution. Newspaper readers were bombarded with stories about astonishing new computers, medical vaccines, labor-saving devices, means of communication, modes of transportation, and methods of destruction—all faster and more effective than what had come before.

The most startling advances occurred in the burgeoning field of space travel. It was already becoming common to refer to current times as the "space age," supplanting the postwar appellation of "atomic age," which no longer sounded truly modern. The new era had officially begun on October 4, 1957, when the Soviet Union launched its 184-pound *Sputnik,* the first manmade satellite to orbit the earth. "The United States now sleeps under a Soviet moon," Nikita Khrushchev crowed that evening. Senator Richard Russell gave voice to the fear that gripped most Americans. "*Sputnik,*" he warned, "confronts America with a new and terrifying military danger and a disastrous blow to our prestige."

Only one person in Washington appeared to be unworried. "Now, so far as the satellite itself is concerned," said President Eisenhower, "that does not raise my apprehension one iota." Congressmen and commentators pleaded with him to respond with an equally dramatic accomplishment. One popular suggestion was to develop an American missile that could be blasted all the way to the moon. Ike thought it a ridiculous idea. "We have no enemies on the moon," he scoffed.

Eisenhower's placid reaction to *Sputnik*, more than anything else, would foster his image as a complacent, out-of-touch bumbler—a characterization that many Democrats happily did their best to spread. It didn't help that the first attempt to launch an American satellite on December 6, 1957, was an unmitigated disaster. The Vanguard missile rose briefly from the pad, shuddered a few feet above the ground, and then exploded in an enormous billow of smoke and fire. "U.S. Calls it Kaputnik," laughed the headline in the *London Daily Express*. The *Daily Herald* chimed in, "Oh, What a Flopnik!"

The United States finally joined the space race two months later when it shot *Explorer I* into orbit, yet it seemed unable to make headway. America was an eager competitor, launching 18 satellites before the end of 1959, compared to the Soviets' 6. But the Soviet Union retained three advantages: Its rockets were more powerful, hence more fearsome as potential weapons. It suppressed news of its failed launches, of which there were at least 5, while the United States suffered 19 very public failures prior to 1960. And, most important of all, it achieved several key distinctions, such as first nation in space, first to place a satellite in solar orbit (January 1959), and first to crash a missile on the moon (September 1959). American self-confidence was badly shaken.

But there was reason for optimism. A new federal agency, the National Aeronautics and Space Administration (NASA), committed itself in October 1958 to putting a man in orbit. If the United States could launch and safely retrieve a space pilot—an astronaut, in NASA's lingo—all of the Soviet Union's previous successes would be overshadowed. It seemed to be America's last, best hope.

The hunt for modern-day heroes began immediately. NASA pulled together a list of 324 military test pilots, all between the ages of 25 and 40, all less than 6 feet tall and lighter than 180 pounds, compact enough to squeeze into the tiny Mercury capsule then being designed. Civilian pilots were excluded, even a 28-year-old hotshot, Neil Armstrong, who flew some of the fastest, scariest jets around.

Many of the 324 candidates would have been happy to be passed over, too. They were convinced that astronauts were going to be "spam in a can," mere passengers in a capsule controlled by NASA technicians on the ground. A navy test pilot, Wally Schirra, was so disillusioned that he gave serious thought to backing out of the competition. "Look, Schirra, if you want to go higher, farther, and faster, this is the one way to do it," a colleague told him. That gave him pause. "Okay," Schirra replied, "I'll go along for awhile."

The seven winners who emerged from NASA's vast battery of tests—Schirra among them—were introduced to the American public on April 9, 1959. John Glenn, the oldest of the new astronauts at 37, was also the most self-assured and the most visionary. "The whole project, with regard to space," he said at that opening press conference, "sort of stands with us now like the Wright brothers stood at Kitty Hawk, with Orville and Wilbur pitching a coin to see who was going to shove the other one off the hill."

That sense of impending history enthralled reporters and government officials, who instinctively deferred to America's new space warriors. The astronauts visited Capitol Hill immediately after their press conference and were baffled by their reception. "Here we are, looking around, somewhat awestricken ourselves, and our local representative or senator would come in and salaam practically," Schirra recalled. "I said, 'My gosh, we've joined a whole new world! And we haven't done a damn thing yet!'"

The Soviets were not sitting idly by. Their Vostok capsule was in development, and their search for astronauts—to be known as cosmonauts—began in earnest during the first half of 1959. The mastermind of the Soviet space program, Sergei Korolev, had been invested with the mysterious title of "chief designer." He went looking for pilots about 30 years old, 5-foot-7 or shorter, and lighter than 150 pounds. "Above all," said Korolev, "he should be a man with a smile. He must be brave."

The two countries were working on parallel tracks, each striving to launch a man into space as soon as safely possible—the tail end of 1960, perhaps, or certainly in 1961. Twenty-three thousand military and civilian workers swarmed across Florida's Cape Canaveral, once a barren stretch of swamp, scrubland, and sandspits, to build America's manned spaceflight program. Their Soviet counterparts were even more isolated, constructing a new launch site near the hamlet of Tyuratam in a desolate region of Kazakhstan, where dust storms occurred with dreary frequency and temperatures soared as high as 120 degrees or plummeted as low as minus-40.

Starry-eyed dreamers might speak of reaching the heavens or exploring new vistas or advancing the cause of science, but the men and women of Cape Canaveral and Tyuratam knew the real score. They were engaged in a high-stakes international battle with only two possible outcomes—absolute victory or complete failure. There was nothing else.

***

The first candidate to formally enter the presidential race was Wayne Morse, an irascible Democratic senator from Oregon. The 59-year-old Morse had quarreled with many of his Senate colleagues over the years, including a few likely opponents for his party's nomination. He had repeatedly accused John Kennedy of being an enemy of the workingman, and had once publicly questioned whether Hubert Humphrey was a true liberal.

Morse announced on December 22 that he would run a limited campaign, focusing on primary elections in the District of Columbia, Maryland, and Oregon. He expected to be underfunded. "I would be a candidate with absolutely no money for campaign purposes," he said, "which would be a good thing, because it would give the voters the assurance that I would be on the people's side."

Humphrey boisterously joined the Democratic fray on December 30, pledging to "start out with the props whirling, full steam ahead." He was only 48 years old, yet had represented Minnesota in the Senate for more than a decade. Humphrey, despite Morse's skepticism, was an unabashed liberal who was especially outspoken on the subject of civil rights. He planned to campaign extensively in the primaries, yet could only dream of matching Kennedy's resources. So, in time-honored political tradition, he sought to turn a weakness into a strength, proclaiming himself the candidate for people "who like myself are of modest origin and limited financial means—who lack the power or the influence to fully control their own destiny."

And that was where the Democratic field stood as 1959 drew to a close—two candidates officially in, other possibilities hovering on the sidelines. A reporter in Wichita, Kansas, tried to smoke Kennedy out, asking with light sarcasm if the senator had decided on a contender to support. "I do have a favorite candidate," Kennedy replied. "But until he has the guts to declare he's a candidate, I'm not going to announce my support of him."

These early maneuvers on the Democratic side attracted minimal public attention. It was the impending heavyweight battle between

Nelson Rockefeller and Richard Nixon for the Republican nomination that held the nation's interest.

Rockefeller's unofficial campaign was revving at full throttle by mid-December. The governor traveled through the South and Midwest, conducting several press conferences and public events each day. Position papers and press releases were flowing from his headquarters on West Fifty-fifth Street. His brother, David, and his family's chief financial adviser, J. Richardson Dilworth, were busily soliciting donations from fellow millionaires. (Rocky easily could have paid for his whole campaign himself, but his advisers felt it would have been bad form, almost as if he were writing a personal check to purchase the Oval Office.) A formal announcement of candidacy was surely coming soon.

But all was not well beneath the surface. Rockefeller was greeted with great fanfare wherever he went. He was a celebrity, after all, and a charismatic one at that. But he garnered little support. Nixon had been in the field for years. The vice president had made innumerable appearances in support of Republican candidates for state and local offices, had sent countless letters and Christmas cards to party officials. They enjoyed chatting and having their pictures taken with Rockefeller, but their hearts were with Nixon. Private polls confirmed that the vice president's base was unshakable.

These gloomy tidings did not seep through to the press, which still eagerly anticipated a bitter fight for the Republican nomination. Rockefeller, however, was privately running out of alternatives. He finally—and reluctantly—concluded that his only real option was to exit a race he had never entered, which he did in a 700-word mimeographed statement of withdrawal distributed by his Albany office on December 26. "The great majority of those who will control the Republican convention," it said, "stand opposed to any contest for the nomination." His decision not to seek the presidency was "definite and final."

Rockefeller's announcement, the *New York Times* sputtered, was "unforeseen and almost inexplicable to many observers." Nixon and his team were jubilant. "I remember when I first called Dick and told him, he was incredulous," said Bob Finch. The vice president's road to the Republican nomination was suddenly, blissfully clear.

Rockefeller, for his part, feigned nonchalance. A reporter caught up to him that evening as the governor sipped tea in a Pullman car headed toward Philadelphia, where he would celebrate the holidays with his wife's family. His informal campaign, Rocky said, had been "a very invigorating business" and "great fun." The reporter probed further, asking how he felt about having made such a momentous decision, abandoning—at least for now—his dreams of becoming president. Implied was a second question: What was it like to be chased from the race by a younger man who lacked a personal fortune and whose social status was far from exalted?

Rockefeller refused to rise to the bait. "It was just a decision," he said calmly. And he shrugged his shoulders and smiled.

* * *

It was time for Eisenhower to start home. He jetted from India to Iran, then Greece, where he was hailed by half a million people. "I think he's absolutely getting to love this," a staff member confided to a *Time* reporter. "He doesn't say so, but he'd have to be superhuman not to feel this way."

There was virtually no pomp at Ike's next destination. He had received a tumultuous welcome in Paris in late summer, but this was strictly a working visit. Eisenhower and the other three kingpins of what was known as the Free World—Macmillan, de Gaulle, and Adenauer—gathered on December 19 at the Elysée Palace to seek a consensus on two crucial questions: Should they formally propose a summit meeting to the Soviets? And if so, when should it be held?

Macmillan had long advocated a face-to-face conference with Khrushchev, even though Eisenhower and de Gaulle thought it would be of little value. Political summits, Ike liked to say, were usually as barren as geographical summits. The British leader's persistence occasionally wore on the American president's nerves, causing Eisenhower to grumble in mid-1959 that he would not "be dragooned to a summit."

But that was before the Spirit of Camp David. "The atmosphere seemed better," Ike later explained, "and both President de Gaulle and I believed it best to go along with the idea that a summit might be helpful." An invitation was dispatched to Khrushchev to meet Eisenhower, de Gaulle, and Macmillan in Paris. (Adenauer was excluded because the Soviets refused to recognize West Germany as a sovereign nation.) The summit was tentatively scheduled to begin on April 27, 1960.

And then Eisenhower was off again, paying brief visits to the two countries left on his itinerary, Spain and Morocco, before boarding *Air*

Force One for the final leg of his journey. Awaiting him was the smallest contingent of the entire three-week trip. Mamie Eisenhower, Vice President Nixon, and a few hundred government officials, military officers, and diplomats were the only ones in attendance when the president's jet touched down at Andrews Air Force Base at 11:25 P.M. on December 22. Ike declined to make a speech, noting that he had eaten breakfast in Madrid and lunch in Casablanca, and had landed at 5:25 A.M., Madrid time. He had been awake for nearly 22 hours.

A limousine whisked the president and first lady along Washington's deserted streets to the White House, where a pair of surprises was in store. Several thousand people were waiting in Lafayette Square, all of them cheering, many of them waving sparklers in the frigid air. The crowd was tiny compared to those that had overwhelmed him overseas, but Ike was touched by the personal nature of the greeting. He and Mamie alighted from their car at the White House, where they unexpectedly found four old friends playing bridge on a table in the West Hall.

"Hi," said Alfred Gruenther, a former four-star general who served as president of the American Red Cross. He immediately turned back to the game. "I double," he said. The others paid scant attention until George Allen, a Mississippi businessman and former Democratic Party official, looked up with a quizzical expression. "What's new?" he asked, managing to keep a straight face.

"Looking back over our long journey, we could point to no concrete or specific achievements, nothing to loom large in official records," Eisenhower later conceded. But his trip was nonetheless a major success. It demonstrated the president's strength and vigor, which were especially impressive for someone just 10 months short of his 70th birthday. It dispelled the myth that the United States was unpopular in the Third World. It confirmed Eisenhower's belief that residents of those distant lands had much in common with Americans, especially a hunger for peace. "Their faces are interestingly different and their lands exotic," he concluded, "but their fate and ours are one." And it yielded plans for a full-scale summit conference, which had the potential to greatly reduce international tensions.

Khrushchev, who had long hoped for a summit, eagerly accepted the invitation. He asked only for a change in timing. May 1 was the most sacred day on the Soviet calendar, and he had no intention of missing the festivities. The Western leaders countered by pushing the start back to May 16, 1960. Khrushchev sent word on December 30 that he would see them in Paris. The first secretary told Llewellyn Thompson, the American ambassador to Moscow, that Ike "had simply overwhelmed him with his personality" during his recent trip to America. "If only the president could serve another term," Thompson paraphrased Khrushchev, "he was sure our problems could be solved."

Eisenhower could imagine few nightmares worse than another four years in the White House, but he shared Khrushchev's belief that great progress might be made in the single year he had left. The Democrats dissented. "The real roots of the Soviet-American conflict," Kennedy warned that December, "cannot be easily settled by negotiations." But Eisenhower waved away such negativity, calling himself a born optimist. "I suppose most soldiers are," he said, "because no soldier ever won a battle if he went into it pessimistically."

The people of the world were on his side, Ike firmly believed. He had seen their exuberance and felt their passion—crowds spreading to the horizon in Paris and London, schoolchildren excitedly waving flags as he passed in Pakistan, millions swarming his motorcades in India, tribesmen firing rifles in his honor in Morocco, thousands of his fellow Americans holding sparklers high on a cold midnight in Lafayette Square. Who could fail to be moved by such energy and spirit? Who could possess anything but high expectations and optimism about the challenges that lay ahead in 1960?

It had the makings of a very good year.

2

January: Around the Next Corner

Jack Kennedy finally had a candidate to support.

The senator, deeply tanned after a Jamaican vacation, strode to a podium in the caucus room of the old Senate Office Building shortly after noon on January 2, 1960, and told the audience what it already knew. He was running for president.

"In the past forty months, I have toured every state in the Union, and I have talked to Democrats in all walks of life," he said to the supporters, cameramen, and reporters who packed the room. "My candidacy is therefore based on the conviction that I can win both the nomination and the election."

His confidence was justified. Every Gallup Poll since the start of 1959 had found Kennedy and Adlai Stevenson running neck and neck for the Democratic nomination, with the other potential candidates far behind. Gallup's latest survey, scheduled for release in a few days, would show Kennedy four percentage points ahead of Stevenson, who continued to insist that he would not be launching a third presidential campaign.

And yet there were reasons for concern. Even some of Kennedy's closest friends doubted that anyone just 42 years of age could successfully tackle the world's most demanding job. "It's just that I thought he was too damned young," recalled Charles Bartlett, Washington correspondent for the *Chattanooga Times* and a Kennedy confidant since the late forties. Bartlett privately suggested that Jack wait until 1968 to run for president, but Kennedy dismissed the idea out of hand. He had no great respect for the aging process. "Experience," he once said, "is like taillights on a boat which illuminate where we've been, when we should be focusing on where we should be going."

The liberal faction of the Democratic Party also had misgivings about Kennedy, wondering if his privileged upbringing might prevent him from empathizing with the lower and middle classes. "He smiled, he was charming, but there was no outgoing affection or warmth or even indignation," complained Robert Nathan, who had been a prominent New Deal economist. Kennedy, it was true, did not really understand how difficult life had been for millions of his contemporaries. "I have no memory of the Depression," he admitted to famed Washington reporter Hugh Sidey. "We lived better than ever. We had bigger houses, more servants. I learned about the Depression at Harvard—from reading."

Even more worrisome was the matter of religion. No Catholic had ever been elected president of the United States. Only one had been nominated—New York Governor Al Smith by the Democrats in 1928—and his campaign had subsequently foundered on the religious issue. The Ku Klux Klan threatened him with blazing crosses in Oklahoma and Montana as election day neared, while millions of Americans registered quieter protests on their ballots. The South, which had been solidly in the Democratic camp since the Civil War, repudiated Smith in November, giving a majority of its electoral votes to Herbert Hoover, the first Republican to carry the region since Reconstruction.

The old prejudices endured. The Gallup Poll reported in 1959 that one of every three Southern voters, and one of five in the rest of the nation, refused to vote for a Catholic for president, even one who was highly qualified. Only 47 percent knew at the time that Kennedy was Catholic, but awareness was growing daily. The candidate was determined to put the matter to rest.

"I would think that there is really only one issue involved in the whole question of a candidate's religion," he told the crowd in the Senate's caucus room. "That is, does a candidate believe in the Constitution, does he believe in the First Amendment, does he believe in the separation of church and state? When the candidate gives his views on that question—and I think I have given my views fully— I think the subject is exhausted." Millions would disagree.

Nor was Kennedy able to defuse the controversy surrounding his father. Too many people suspected Old Joe's motives. It didn't help that the senior Kennedy was brazenly willing to spend millions in pursuit of the presidency. "We've come this far," he barked at an early strategy session. "We're not going to let money stand in our way. Whatever it takes, even if it requires every dime I have." Jack publicly made light of his father's relentless ambition, pulling out a phony telegram during a speech to the Gridiron Club's annual dinner in 1958. "Dear Jack," he read to appreciative laughter. "Don't buy a single vote more than necessary. I'll be damned if I'm going to pay for a landslide." Joe failed to see the humor.

Family connections, to be sure, were critically important to Kennedy. One of his brothers-in-law, Steve Smith, had quietly established the campaign's headquarters in Washington's Esso Building in early 1959; and another, Sargent Shriver, was emerging as a political jack-of-all-trades. Kennedy's wife, mother, and sisters stood ready to make public appearances in the months to come, as did his youngest brother, Ted, who had graduated from law school the previous June.

His other surviving brother was handed the most demanding assignment of all. Robert Kennedy would serve as campaign manager, the same role he had played in Jack's 1952 race for the Senate. "Bobby's the best organizer I've ever seen," the candidate enthused. His father chimed in with his unique version of praise. "He's a great kid," Old Joe said. "He hates the same way I do."

It was true. Bobby Kennedy was brash, insensitive, and hot-tempered. "It doesn't matter if I hurt your feelings," he told staffers. "It doesn't matter if you hurt mine. The important thing is to get the job done." His arrogance was legendary. Bobby was only 26 when he barged into the office of Massachusetts Governor Paul Dever in 1952, upbraiding the governor for failing to give top priority to Jack's Senate campaign. Dever angrily shooed the son from his office and then called the father on the phone. "I know you're an important man around here and all that, but I'm telling you this, and I mean it," the governor snapped at Old Joe. "Keep that fresh kid of yours out of my sight from here on in."

Many of Jack's closest supporters also found Bobby difficult to stomach. "I never really liked him," wrote Tip O'Neill, who recalled the younger Kennedy as "a self-important upstart and a know-it-all." Harlan Cleveland, a Syracuse University dean who served as a campaign adviser, considered Bobby "undoubtedly the rudest man I have ever encountered in public life." Even historian Arthur

Schlesinger Jr., who would deify Robert Kennedy after his untimely death, admitted that the campaign manager of 1960 was "a cocky young fellow, opinionated, censorious, rigid, moralistic, prickly, disposed to tell people off and to get into heated arguments."

But Bobby's mixture of audacity and organizational skill would prove indispensable to Jack's pursuit of the Democratic nomination. The party was still controlled in 1960 by a loose network of state leaders. Some were governors, such as David Lawrence of Pennsylvania, Michael DiSalle of Ohio, and Pat Brown of California. Others were stereotypical political bosses, like Richard Daley of Chicago and Carmine De Sapio of New York City. All had initial doubts about Kennedy's electability, worrying that he was much too young and much too Catholic. The latter was a difficult conclusion for a Catholic like Lawrence to reach, but reach it he did. "I was fearful," he later said, "that we would lose Pennsylvania, and that any chance I would have as governor of getting a majority in both houses of the [state legislature] would go skimmering if Kennedy was the head of the ticket."

Jack knew the score. "If it ever goes into a back room," he said, "my name will never emerge." So he, Bobby, and Larry O'Brien opted for a risky strategy. Primary elections were not as common or influential in 1960 as they would later become, but they offered Kennedy his best chance of securing the nomination. He decided to reach out to the voters in a series of primaries, hoping to cement his image as a winner, while quietly ratcheting up the pressure on party leaders. His margin for error was infinitesimal. A loss in any primary, and the bosses' fears would be confirmed. He had to sweep the table.

Two other outsiders, Wayne Morse and Hubert Humphrey, though not Catholic, needed to boost their visibility as Kennedy did. They also decided to travel the primary route, though not happily. "Well, I'll tell you," Humphrey confided to a reporter, "any man who goes into a primary isn't fit to be president. You have to be crazy to go into a primary." The next few months, he knew, would be arduous. Endless days and nights of campaigning through the small towns and union halls of New Hampshire and Wisconsin and West Virginia lay ahead.

The other Democratic hopefuls—older, better-known, Protestant— remained aloof, refusing to announce their intentions, trusting their ties to the party bosses. "The primaries are going to be decisive," Kennedy insisted. "Anybody who wants to be a candidate for president ought to run." But Lyndon Johnson spent most of January in

Washington, pulling strings as the majority leader of the Senate. He broke away for a three-day trip to Chicago and New York City, even speaking to a Catholic men's club in Brooklyn, yet denied he was running for anything. His day job, he said, was challenging enough.

Stuart Symington was more honest about his ambitions. "I certainly would like to be president," he admitted in a January television interview. He sounded like a candidate, promising to "take my campaign into the homes, to the street corners, and to the farms." But he had no intention of becoming ensnared in a primary. Symington hadn't even decided when—or if—he would formally enter the race.

And then there was Adlai Stevenson. The former Illinois governor told anybody who would listen that he was not now—and would not become—a candidate. Nobody believed him. There he was, just behind Kennedy in the Gallup Poll, with millions of fervent supporters demanding another try for the golden ring that had eluded them in 1952 and 1956. How could he possibly say no?

Even Nikita Khrushchev tried to nudge him into the race. Stevenson was puzzled by an invitation to visit the Soviet embassy in Washington on January 16. He was greeted by the ambassador, Mikhail Menshikov, who pulled out a document that obviously had been drafted by Khrushchev and the Presidium. "When we compare all the possible candidates in the United States," the ambassador read, "we feel that Mr. Stevenson is best for mutual understanding and progress toward peace." Then he posed a series of questions: How could the Soviets help Stevenson win the presidency? Should they publicly praise him? Or would it be better if the communist press launched a verbal assault?

Stevenson was horrified. Khrushchev's offer, he told the ambassador, was "highly improper, indiscreet, and dangerous to all concerned." If American reporters ever found out about their meeting, Stevenson said, his career would be ruined. The prospect of such a leak worried him for months to come, though the story would not break in his lifetime.

Stevenson bid a hasty goodbye to Menshikov and hustled into the gathering dusk. What, he wondered, had he possibly done to encourage the Soviets' offer of support? And, for that matter, why were so many of his fellow Democrats still pushing him to run? Should he continue to put them off, or would it be easier to bow to the mounting pressure?

The answers, as always, would not come.

LEXICON: JANUARY 1960

Missile Gap

Democratic senators wailed that the United States was not expanding its nuclear arsenal as rapidly as the Soviet Union. They blamed President Eisenhower, accusing him of turning a blind eye to the resulting "missile gap" in order to save money. "The intelligence books have been juggled," charged Stuart Symington, "so that the budget books may be balanced." The president bristled—as any career military man would—when Democrats charged that he had allowed the nation's defenses to atrophy. "I've spent my life in this," he said, "and I know more about it than almost anybody."

Payola

A House of Representatives subcommittee announced on January 13 that it would investigate surreptitious payments made by record companies to disc jockeys. Most record labels classified "payola" as a standard operating expense, the only way to ensure that their songs received radio exposure. But federal examiners insisted that the practice was fraudulent. "Payola may stink," conceded Alan Freed, perhaps the most famous disc jockey in America. "But it's here, and I didn't start it."

Students for a Democratic Society

The Student League for Industrial Democracy—a sluggish, virtually anonymous organization with a paltry budget of $3,500—adopted the new name of Students for a Democratic Society at a January meeting in Ann Arbor, Michigan. SDS had only three chapters (at Columbia, Yale, and the University of Michigan), but its new president, Alan Haber, set a lofty goal. He pledged to lay the "groundwork for a radical student movement."

Sun City

An ambitious contractor, Del Webb, devised an innovative plan for 20,000 acres of alfalfa and cotton fields northwest of Phoenix. He built a retirement community, strictly limited to residents 50 or older. It was a radically new concept, but was it viable? "We knew we were taking a calculated risk," said Webb, who admitted to nervousness when Sun City opened on January 1, 1960. He had no need to worry. More than 100,000 people swarmed to the site the first weekend. Webb's staff sold so many homes—272 in the first 3 days alone—that it temporarily ran out of contracts.

U-2

An American spy plane had been flying top-secret reconnaissance missions over the Soviet Union since July 4, 1956. The U-2, in the words of Ray Cline, a CIA deputy director, "looked more like a kite built around a camera than an airplane." It was constructed of titanium and other light metals, allowing it to soar as high as 70,000 feet, well beyond the range of any Soviet missile or fighter plane. The U-2's photos unmasked the Soviet nuclear program—proving it wasn't as advanced as the Democrats feared—but Eisenhower steadfastly insisted on secrecy. He refused to make the pictures public.

World Trade Center

David Rockefeller was the polar opposite of his ebullient older brother, Nelson. David was deadly serious and wary of publicity. He was perfectly suited for the life of a banker, which indeed he was, serving as president of Chase Manhattan Bank. The younger Rockefeller was the driving force behind a grandiose plan unveiled on January 26 for the revitalization of New York City's financial district. Its key component was a massive office complex, the World Trade Center, which would rise from a 13-acre site along the East River.

***

Dick Nixon had anticipated a hectic January. He intended to make a big splash with his initial dive—the formal announcement of his presidential candidacy—and then expend every ounce of energy lining up support for the Republican nomination. He would campaign intensively in New Hampshire, Wisconsin, and other primary states. He would meet as many party leaders, wealthy contributors, and convention delegates as possible. He would hustle every single second.

But Nelson Rockefeller's withdrawal had changed everything. Nixon suddenly found himself the only Republican candidate for president, the party's de facto nominee six months prior to the convention. It seemed unnecessary, even wasteful, to gear up his campaign so early when he faced no opposition.

So Nixon veered to the other extreme. He instructed his amiable press secretary, Herb Klein, to issue a brief statement on January 9, coincidentally the vice president's 47th birthday. Klein called reporters into his office and told them that Nixon had "willingly" allowed his name to be placed on the ballot for the New Hampshire, Ohio, and Oregon primaries. And that was that.

The reporters were confused. When would Nixon be making his *formal* announcement? "This will be as formal an announcement as there will be," Klein answered. Wasn't it a strange way to launch a campaign? "I see no necessity to make a formal announcement." When would Nixon hit the road like many of the other contenders? "The vice president has no plans to be in any of these primary states—not even once—as a campaigning candidate."

Nixon now had the luxury of looking ahead to an autumn contest against the Democratic Party's nominee. None of his potential foes had held a job as exalted as the vice presidency. Humphrey and Kennedy, both in their forties, carried the added burden of youth. Nixon, though also on the sunny side of 50, saw a chance to set himself apart. He began seizing every opportunity to emphasize his depth of experience.

The vice president suggested in late January that Eisenhower's successor would need several key qualities—"a man who has judgment, a man who in crisis will be cool, a man who won't go off half-cocked"—and he naturally detected a lone candidate fitting the bill. He buttressed his case with a statistical litany of foreign leaders he had met (47), countries he had visited (54), Cabinet sessions he had attended (163), and private meetings he had held with Eisenhower (173). "I have sat with the president as he made those lonely decisions," he said incongruously.

Bob Finch shifted over from Nixon's vice presidential office to take charge as campaign director. The two men had met on Capitol Hill in the late forties, when Finch served as an aide to a California congressman. He subsequently returned home, rose to become Republican chairman of Los Angeles County, and then headed back East to join Nixon's staff. Finch's sunny disposition and broad streak of idealism contrasted with the vice president's occasionally dark moods and persistent cynicism, yet Nixon had high regard for his aide's political and organizational skills. Finch began hiring staffers, speechwriters, and advance men, including a young advertising executive from Los Angeles, Bob Haldeman, who in turn recommended a classmate from his days at UCLA, John Ehrlichman.

Nixon insisted on a firm foundation. He shot a memo to his manager: "Emphasis should be on organization, rather than on public relations gimmicks." Finch immersed himself in the grunt work of politics—setting up headquarters in all 50 states, raising funds, establishing schedules for research and speeches. The candidate kept close watch, sometimes uncomfortably close. "He saw people when he was in Washington every half-hour," Finch recalled. "He went over his own speeches, rewrote them, nit-picked the schedule, scrutinized everything down to the ethnic appeals."

Nixon was incapable of being truly at ease. Most candidates would have enjoyed the cozy status of his campaign—no immediate opponents, plenty of time for planning and organizational work—but he seemed to be vaguely uncomfortable. The same sense of muted anxiety had been evident throughout his career. He never lacked for something to complain or worry or get angry about.

Like Rockefeller, for instance. The New York governor still sounded like a candidate, still criticized Eisenhower and Nixon, albeit in vague terms. "The Republican Party needs more crusaders," Rocky insisted in January. "I say these things because I am a Republican who is seriously concerned about the future vigor and purpose of my party." Rockefeller didn't utter these inflammatory words at an innocuous event, but at a Republican fundraising dinner with the president and vice president in attendance.

Nixon began to believe that Rockefeller was planning a sneak attack. Perhaps Rocky intended to lay low for a few months and then pop back into the presidential contest, ruining everything. Barry Goldwater, a conservative senator from Arizona, was sure of it. Rockefeller's December 1959 withdrawal, he said, had simply been a change of tactics to temporarily mask his lust for the Republican nomination. "Anyone who says he wouldn't run if it was offered," snapped Goldwater, "is a damned liar."

There also was the matter of the president himself. Eisenhower and Nixon seemed compatible in public, but their relationship was more complex, occasionally even strained, in private. Ike was 22 years— a full generation—older than Nixon. Their backgrounds were starkly different. An elderly military officer who scorned partisanship wasn't likely to have much in common with a young lawyer who considered politics to be both vocation and avocation.

Their biggest misunderstanding had occurred four years earlier, when Eisenhower announced for reelection. A reporter lobbed the standard softball question about his running mate: "Would you like to have Nixon?" Ike was shockingly noncommittal. "It is traditional," he said, "to wait and see who the Republican convention nominates." The press corps, sniffing the unexpected scent of controversy, demanded to know why Ike was withholding the anticipated endorsement of Nixon for vice president. "I am very fond of him," the president replied, "but I am going to say no more about it."

Eisenhower spoke more plainly behind closed doors. He warned Nixon that he would become "atrophied" if he remained vice president for another four years. "You will always be thought of as the understudy to the star of the team," he said, "rather than a halfback in your own right." It would be better, the president suggested, if Nixon acquired valuable administrative experience by tackling a Cabinet position instead, perhaps the top job at the Pentagon or the Department of Health, Education, and Welfare. But, he stressed, the final decision was Nixon's to make. The question dangled for what seemed an eternity—actually two months—before Nixon talked Ike into keeping him on the ticket in 1956. Eisenhower still wasn't totally convinced. "I think he is making a mistake by wanting the job," the president confided to an aide.

Ike and Dick drifted further apart during the second term. Columnist Joe Alsop privately compared the vice president to an anxious heir who had become "utterly distraught because Papa has grown a little senile and spends his time throwing the family fortune out the window." Nixon wanted to expand the military budget and slash taxes. Eisenhower insisted on fiscal restraint—no large increases in appropriations, no big tax cuts. "Dick," he said at a Cabinet meeting, "I hope if someday I surrender this chair to you, I'll be able to give you a balanced budget." Ike did better than that in mid-January, submitting a federal budget with a projected surplus of $4.2 billion. Nixon ground his teeth in frustration, certain that the result would be military decline and economic stagnation.

Few people were privy to the tension between the nation's two highest officials. Most Americans—and most members of the press—thought of them as a happy, unified team. That's why Eisenhower's fancy footwork at his January 13, 1960, press conference came as such a surprise. Reporters fished for an endorsement of the unopposed Nixon, but Ike refused to give it. He suggested instead that several Republicans were worthy of consideration for the presidency: "There is a number of them that, I think, are very, very highly qualified people." It was his 1956 dance all over again.

Eisenhower, in fact, had been secretly searching since 1958 for somebody to challenge Nixon, whom he still considered too callow and too overtly political. Rockefeller, with his penchant for expensive government programs, seemed no better. But Ike was fond of his secretary of the treasury, Robert Anderson. "I'll raise money. I'll make speeches. I'll do anything to help," he told Anderson. The secretary declined to run, so Eisenhower put out feelers to several other Republicans, even Oveta Culp Hobby, his former secretary of health, education, and welfare. "How about a lady 'favorite son'?" Eisenhower asked, a daring suggestion in that masculine age. The answer once again was negative.

Most Republican leaders had already vaulted aboard Nixon's bandwagon, making the president's reticence seem all the more peculiar. Eisenhower, however, would soon have another opportunity to issue a simple endorsement and put the controversy to rest. His next press conference was scheduled for February 3.

The president opened the door a crack on that occasion. "I am not dissatisfied with the individual that looks like he will get it, not by any manner or means," he said. But his refusal to use Nixon's name or even his title was jarring, as was the sentence that followed: "I just simply say there is a number that could be, that could perform the duties of the office with distinction." It was clear that he would not be issuing any endorsement, certainly not this long before the convention. Nixon's nomination, he implied, was far from a sure thing. "We're all human," Ike told the assembled reporters, "and we don't know what is around the next corner."

RISING STAR: PAT ROBERTSON

Everybody assumed that Marion Gordon Robertson would become a lawyer and a politician. His father had set the bar high in both professions. A. Willis Robertson represented Virginia in the United States

Senate from 1946 to 1966, resolutely opposing most programs advanced by his own Democratic Party, especially those that increased government spending or guaranteed civil rights for blacks.

The younger Robertson dutifully headed to Yale, earning his law degree in 1955. But he diverged from the master plan in two significant ways—opting for a career in business and eloping with Dede Elmer, a Northerner and a Catholic to boot. Theirs was a union hardly calculated to please his straitlaced Southern Protestant parents.

Marion and Dede settled in New York, where he worked for W.R. Grace and Company and made an important decision about his name. Marion sounded effeminate, he thought, and M. Gordon was pretentious. He had been nicknamed Pat as a baby because his six-year-old brother liked to tap his cheeks and say "pat, pat, pat," so it was as Pat Robertson that he would seek worldly success.

The early results were discouraging. Pat found his job unfulfilling—"I couldn't see sweating my blood for a big company"—and his personal life little better. He and Dede were avid partygoers, self-described "sophisticated New York swingers." But something was missing. Pat abruptly shifted gears, enrolling in the Biblical Seminary in New York. He graduated in 1959 and moved himself, his wife, and their three children into a decrepit brownstone to do the Lord's work in Brooklyn's gritty Bedford-Stuyvesant neighborhood. "I knew the accommodations would be simple," Dede said. "But this place I never expected."

Bigger surprises were to come. Pat informed her in November 1959 that God had instructed him to buy a bankrupt television station in Portsmouth, Virginia, and switch it to an all-Christian format. The deity had even set the rock-bottom price—$37,000. The fact that Pat had no broadcasting experience was irrelevant. "I didn't own a TV set," he said. "My kids were excited. They thought I was buying a TV. They were disappointed that it was only a station."

Channel 27 had been off the air for months. Rats scampered through its abandoned studios. There was broken glass everywhere. Robertson told the owner, Tim Bright, about his divine mandate to spend no more than $37,000. Bright initially balked, but bowed to God's will on January 11, 1960. "Your boss," he muttered, "sure does know how to drive a business deal." Pat incorporated Channel 27 under the majestic name of the Christian Broadcasting Network (CBN). He opened a corporate bank account, depositing the grand sum of $3. The starting batch of checks cost $6, putting CBN in debt on its very first day.

Money was a constant worry during those early years, but Robertson reached a turning point in 1963, staging a telethon that challenged 700 viewers to donate $10 a month to cover Channel 27's expenses. It was the beginning of *The 700 Club,* which evolved into a nightly talk show, a religious version of Johnny Carson's *Tonight Show.*

Pat, to his own surprise, possessed a natural talent for television. Audiences found his relaxed, folksy manner as host of *The 700 Club* more palatable than the fire-and-brimstone intensity of traditional evangelists. And his entrepreneurial spirit had a positive impact on the bottom line. CBN's annual revenues reached $1 million by 1970 and kept growing. Robertson syndicated *The 700 Club,* launched the CBN Cable Network (later renamed The Family Channel), and founded Regent University.

He belatedly joined his father's profession—though not his party—in 1988. Robertson announced that he had "a direct call and a leading from God" to seek the Republican presidential nomination. He started strong—taking second place in the Iowa caucuses—but was derailed in short order by the successful campaign of George H. W. Bush.

Yet there was no cause for regrets. CBN had made Robertson tremendously influential, a preacher with a worldwide ministry. His business success was equally impressive. Rupert Murdoch bought The Family Channel for a staggering $1.9 billion in 1997. Pat and Dede Robertson lived their senior years on a multimillion-dollar estate, a far cry from their filthy lodgings in Bedford-Stuyvesant.

Pat made no apologies. "Poverty is a curse, not a blessing," he said. "You can be just as holy when you are financially comfortable as you can be when you are poor."

***

A few Americans were preparing for brief flights to outer space as the new year began, but the Mercury astronauts weren't among them. Test pilots and monkeys were scheduled to go first.

A select group of pilots had been assigned to the X-15, a rocket-powered jet that was tucked into the belly of a B-29, ferried to an altitude of 26,000 feet, and set free to roar skyward at a frighteningly steep angle. The X-15 made its supersonic debut in September 1959. Scott Crossfield took the controls on January 23, 1960, for its fourth flight, eager to push the new jet higher and faster. He goosed the X-15 to a sizzling 1,300 miles per hour before touching down in the Southern California desert.

Crossfield's flight was another step toward the air force's goal of developing a rocket ship that could zoom 100 miles above the earth's surface. Test pilots would continue their work as the year progressed, garnering little publicity, but greatly expanding the X-15's capabilities. Joe Walker blazed to a new speed record of 2,111 miles per hour in May 1960, and Robert White reached a record altitude of 131,000 feet— nearly 25 miles—in August. White flew so high that he experienced weightlessness for almost a minute. "This is really fantastic up here," he radioed from the fringe of outer space. He was convinced that the X-15's 100-mile goal was attainable. "I would have no qualms about going higher," he said.

No one cared if NASA's monkeys had qualms. Technicians simply strapped them into foam-lined seats and blasted them beyond the pull of gravity. A rhesus monkey named Sam had lifted off from Wallops Island, Virginia, on December 4, 1959, reaching an altitude of 150,000 feet on his suborbital flight. He was weightless for four minutes. A navy destroyer recovered Sam in the Atlantic Ocean. He seemed unhappy with the whole experience yet otherwise was in fine condition. A second monkey, Miss Sam, rocketed into space in late January. She

The X-15 reaches the fringe of outer space: "I would have no qualms about going higher." (National Aeronautics and Space Administration)

had been trained to pull a lever whenever a light flashed, a task she performed flawlessly except for the short periods when her capsule swiftly accelerated or splashed down.

NASA's seven human astronauts watched their X-15 brethren with envy but took a dim view of flights by monkeys and chimpanzees. Wally Schirra and his colleagues bristled at taunts that Miss Sam was their ideal role model, that they too would earn banana pellets whenever they pulled the correct lever. "We felt we would put man in the loop," Schirra said. "We wanted to replace chimpanzees. We wanted to prove we could fly the vehicle."

That, unfortunately, would have to wait. An operational Mercury capsule would not be available until late 1960, when NASA hoped to launch its first manned flight. The astronauts, in the meantime, trained on simulators. An accelerator known as the Wheel whipped them in a giant circle, subjecting them to gravitational forces more intense than those anticipated during liftoff and splashdown. A converted passenger jet took them to the opposite extreme, flying a ballistic trajectory that simulated weightless conditions. "Everybody was worried about weightlessness," said Robert Voas, a NASA aeromedical consultant. "But that was just the most fun ever. You were Superman. You could jump, and you just flew through the air."

Other simulators were anything but enjoyable. The Panic Box was a tiny cubicle with a control panel that contained a baffling array of gauges, knobs, levers, lights, and bells. If a gauge's reading drifted beyond its normal range, an astronaut was supposed to turn a designated knob or flip an appropriate lever. Lights began flashing if the adjustment wasn't made, followed by ear-splitting sirens. "It really was sensory overload," remembered Scott Carpenter, "because there is so much to watch and adjust, and you don't have a lot of time, and then you've got this red light and the klaxon scaring the bejesus out of you." The astronauts dreaded the Panic Box, though Carpenter's memories softened with age. "It's hilarious," he laughed in 1998, "to see a normally intelligent human being in there, going crazy."

The most sinister simulator of all was MASTIF, the Multi-Axis Space Training Inertial Facility. It was a giant ball, 19 feet in diameter, with a series of 3 gimbals that allowed NASA's trainers to spin their subjects in horizontal circles or cartwheels or head over heels—or all 3 directions at once. The astronaut was armed only with a 3-axis stick shift that fired jets of compressed air to stabilize the gimbals. But MASTIF could whirl as rapidly as 30 revolutions per minute, a speed that few humans could counter. "It was the original vomit machine, I'll tell you," John Glenn said. "That was a gut-buster."

The Soviet Union's spacemen were facing similar challenges, though NASA knew virtually nothing about their practice sessions. The Cosmonaut Training Center opened in Moscow in January, introducing 20 young pilots to a rigorous battery of tests. Cosmonauts were isolated in sensory deprivation cells for hours, sometimes days. They were placed in oxygen starvation chambers, where performance of a simple task was monitored while air was slowly sucked from the room. And they made endless runs on a centrifugal accelerator similar to NASA's Wheel. "My eyes wouldn't shut," said Yuri Gagarin, an especially promising trainee. "Breathing was a great effort, my face muscles were twisted, my heart rate speeded up, and the blood in my veins felt as heavy as mercury."

The American and Soviet training programs were remarkably alike, but U.S. officials were unaware that the space race had grown so close. NASA feared that the Soviets might actually be widening their lead, that they might soon propel the first cosmonaut into orbit, an event potentially more damaging to American prestige than the launch of *Sputnik.*

George Allen, the director of the United States Information Agency, expressed those very concerns to a congressional committee on January 22. (This was a different George Allen, not the bridge player who had greeted the returning president the month before.) "Our space program," he admitted, "may be considered as a measure of our vitality and our ability to compete with a formidable rival."

Eisenhower had always downplayed the space race, often asserting that there was no such thing. Allen not only conceded its existence, but acknowledged that the stakes were extraordinarily large. The United States must push ahead in space, he warned, or prepare for further challenges from an overconfident foe. If the Soviets emerged victorious, Allen warned the congressmen, "the world is in for a good deal of trouble."

QUOTATIONS: JANUARY 1960

"1960 promises to be the most prosperous year in our history."
       —*Dwight Eisenhower, delivering his State of the*
              Union address on January 7. The president

admitted concerns about "nagging disorders"
such as racial inequality, inflation, urban decay,
and the Cold War, but expressed confidence that
the economy would boom and relations
with the Soviets would improve.

"New forms, new energies, new values are straining for expression and release. The Eisenhower epoch—the present period of passivity and acquiescence in our national life—is drawing to a close."

—Historian Arthur Schlesinger Jr., writing
in the January 1960 issue of Esquire.

"Why don't we go completely crazy, and plan on a force of 10,000?"

—President Eisenhower, rejecting a Pentagon
request for an additional 400 intercontinental
ballistic missiles per year, enough to obliterate
the Soviet Union many times over.

"He exudes the self-confidence of a man who senses that he is at the peak of his powers on the world stage, and he is obviously excited by the prospects for realizing his dream of securing the peace."

—New York Times *correspondent Russell Baker,*
writing about Eisenhower's eagerness to
continue his program of personal diplomacy.

"I think the crime I have committed, if any, is that I made a great deal of money in a short time on little investment. But that is the record business."

—Disc jockey Dick Clark, denying accusations
that he received payola. Clark held a financial
interest in 33 companies in the music industry,
including a song publisher, a distribution firm,
a talent management agency, and the manufacturer of
a stuffed kitten known as the Platter-Puss. The
congressional investigation that was launched in
January did not find him guilty him of any wrongdoing.

***

Belgium's smug attitude toward the Congo—its serene confidence that it could retain its colonial jewel for another half-century—vaporized with the arrival of the new year.

King Baudouin, Belgium's 29-year-old monarch, paid a visit to his African territory in the waning days of 1959. "Belgium," he announced, "spontaneously and generously calls the Congo to a near-independence." The prefix *near* was the key to his offer. Baudouin envisioned a lengthy transition to freedom—perhaps 30 years—with the mother country retaining control until the very end.

Joseph Kasavubu turned thumbs down. "We are determined to sacrifice everything if we do not acquire independence in January 1960," he barked. A throng of Congolese nationalists awaited Baudouin in the provincial capital of Stanleyville. Police used tear gas to disperse them, but the tension pervading the colony could not be dispelled. The king began to worry that Belgium might become ensnared in a lengthy, expensive war. The only solution, he abruptly decided, was to wash his hands of the Congo as quickly as possible.

Nearly 100 prominent Congolese were summoned to Brussels on January 20 to make the necessary arrangements. They found Belgian Premier Gaston Eyskens to be surprisingly soothing. "We are all in accord on the essential, the independence of the Congo," he said. It took only a month to draw up the terms of Belgium's capitulation. The Congo would be granted complete, unfettered freedom by the end of June. The transition would take a bit more than four months, stunningly brisk in comparison to the timetables for British and French territories.

Author John Gunther offered a simple explanation for Baudouin's change of heart. "The Belgians," he suggested, "could not face the prospect that the Congo might become an Algeria." It was a valid concern. France's war with Moslem rebels, now dragging into its sixth year, was placing its resources and willpower under tremendous strain. The French were suffering 2,000 casualties and losing $2 billion per year. Popular support for the conflict, once extremely high, had been waning since 1958.

But France's military brass insisted that the war be continued. The army's recent defeats had been profoundly embarrassing—overrun by Hitler's blitzkrieg in 1940, pushed out of the Middle East in 1946, outmaneuvered at Dien Bien Phu in 1954. Major General Jacques Massu, the commander of French forces in Algeria, was determined to write an end to this list of shame.

He was initially supported by Charles de Gaulle, the World War II general who had been elected president of France in 1958. De Gaulle was aloof, arrogant, patriotic to an extreme, and never, ever uncertain. "The only trouble with the general," said one of his cabinet members, "is that he is not a human being." Here, surely, was a man who would stay the course in Algeria, no matter the cost.

But de Gaulle uncharacteristically began to entertain doubts and eventually decided to offer the colony an opportunity to determine its own future. Massu complained bitterly to reporters that the president had betrayed the army. The imperious de Gaulle sacked him on January 22, 1960.

Massu's dismissal outraged the 1 million European settlers who lived in Algeria and wished to remain affiliated with France. Thousands stormed the streets of the colonial capital, Algiers, the next day—tipping cars and fabricating barricades of paving blocks, concrete, wood, and wire. "De Gaulle to the gallows," they shouted. Police fired tear gas in response. The crack of rifle fire was soon heard, followed by bursts from machine guns.

The new French commander, General Maurice Challe, dispatched paratroopers to confront the protesters, but his men refused to block the flow of food, supplies, and weapons through the barricades. Challe explained blandly that he could not order his soldiers to fire on fellow Frenchmen. He blatantly defied de Gaulle's policy of self-determination. "The French army is fighting," Challe insisted, "so that Algeria will remain French once and for all."

Tensions had escalated to an oppressive level in both Algeria and France. A mob now controlled Algiers, while the army appeared to be in open revolt. Rumors began to fly that paratroopers would soon be dropped on Paris to seize control of France itself.

De Gaulle pulled his military uniform from the closet and demanded television time on January 29. "Well, my dear and old country," he said, "here we are together once again, facing a harsh test." He insisted that he would not rescind his offer of self-determination— "the Algerians shall have free choice of their destiny"—and promised to deal harshly with those who stood in his way. He made certain that the latter point was driven home to the recalcitrant troops in Algiers. "If I have put on my uniform today to address you on television," he said, "it is in order to show that it is General de Gaulle who speaks, as well as the chief of state."

It was a remarkable display of will—a single man facing down an entire army. The opposition, which had appeared so menacing just 24 hours earlier, quickly crumbled. A chastened General Challe ordered his forces to seal off the barricades, and the protest dissolved. Workmen hustled in to clear away the rubble, removing almost all evidence of the short-lived revolt within a few days. They were soon followed by crews that covered the streets of Algiers with a layer of smooth, black asphalt.

There would no paving blocks for a second uprising.

3

February: Striding Toward Freedom

Joseph McNeil was frustrated. He and his three friends had been talking for months, making big plans, spinning tales of success, yet they hadn't *done* anything.

McNeil and the others—Ezell Blair Jr., Franklin McCain, and David Richmond—were freshmen at an all-black school, North Carolina Agricultural and Technical College. They had read *Stride Toward Freedom*, Martin Luther King Jr.'s memoir of the 1956 Montgomery bus boycott, and had been inspired by his courage and ultimate success. Their late-night bull sessions pivoted on a single question: how could they use their hero's nonviolent methods to advance the cause of civil rights in the city where they lived, Greensboro, North Carolina?

One promising idea was to seek service at a segregated restaurant, perhaps the lunch counter at F. W. Woolworth, a downtown dime store. They began debating this plan in early January and were still waffling as the month drew to a close. Their collective indecision finally pushed McNeil past his breaking point. He proposed a trip to Woolworth's the very next day, February 1, 1960.

McNeil's resolve convinced McCain, who turned to the others. "Are you guys chicken or not?" he asked. Absolutely not, they replied. They agreed to head downtown the following afternoon.

The four students knew Woolworth's would refuse to serve them, just as Montgomery's bus company had refused to allow blacks to sit in the front rows. But King's boycott and accompanying legal action had eliminated the latter restriction, and the Greensboro Four hoped for similar success, though they lacked a strategy to achieve it. They simply intended to defy a law they considered unjust—and wait to see what transpired.

Their willingness to take a stand was somewhat unusual. The mid-fifties had witnessed a flurry of civil rights activity—the famous school integration case (*Brown v. Board of Education*) in 1954, the Montgomery boycott two years later, and President Eisenhower's use of federal troops to integrate Little Rock's Central High School in 1957. But there had been very little drama since then.

Greensboro seemed an unlikely place to rekindle the spark. It was more enlightened than most Southern cities, having already desegregated its airport, library, buses, and parks. Yet its record was not unblemished. The first black student at Greensboro Senior High School had been pelted with eggs in 1957. The municipal golf course had been closed after blacks dared to play. And restaurants still turned away black customers.

Martin Luther King's four adherents confronted this last barrier at 4:30 P.M. on February 1. Woolworth's had no rule against selling merchandise to blacks, so they made a few purchases—toothpaste, combs, other small articles. Then they took seats at the L-shaped lunch counter, which was not the tiny luncheonette found in many dime stores, but a full-scale dining area that could serve 66 customers.

"I'd like a cup of coffee, please," Blair said.

"I'm sorry," the waitress replied. "We don't serve Negroes here."

"I beg to disagree with you," he replied, gesturing toward the store's retail section. "You just finished serving me at a counter only two feet from here."

She pointed to a separate stand for takeout customers. "Negroes eat at the other end," she said.

"What do you mean?" Blair asked. "This is a public place, isn't it? If it isn't, then why don't you sell membership cards? If you do that, then I'll understand that this is a private concern."

"Well," the waitress shot back, "you won't get any service here." She walked away.

The four students stayed in their seats until the store closed at 5:30. They were scared, though they tried not to show it. They expected police officers to arrive at any moment to cart them off to jail, but none came. "We didn't know what they could do to us," McCain recalled. "We didn't know how long we could sit. Now it came to me all of a sudden: Maybe they can't do anything to us. Maybe we can keep it up."

The store manager, C. L. Harris, a bald man known as Curly, wasn't totally surprised by the sit-in. He had previously asked a Woolworth's executive what to do if his business were targeted by a racial protest. Do nothing, he was instructed, and don't antagonize any customers, white or black. "Let them sit there," he told a waitress on the afternoon of February 1. "Don't say anything else to them."

The same laissez-faire approach was adopted by Greensboro's newspapers—they saw no reason to write about the standoff at Woolworth's—but word spread like wildfire across the North Carolina A&T campus. Thirty-one black students—27 men and 4 women—arrived at 10 o'clock the next morning and took seats at the lunch counter. Most of the men were dressed in coats and ties. The students did classwork as they sat.

Their ranks swelled again on the third day. Protesters now occupied 63 of the 66 seats, and more blacks stood in the aisles, ready to replace anybody who left. Whites began to show up at Woolworth's, too. Three white students from Greensboro College came to express support. Young men of a different persuasion jammed into the store, making derisive comments. The local head of the Ku Klux Klan dropped by to take a look.

An event of this scope was undeniably newsworthy. The *Greensboro Daily News* finally covered the sit-in on February 3, though it gave greater play to a local appearance by the Harlem Globetrotters. The national press also showed its first glimmer of interest. The *New York Times* ran a small story on page 22.

Blacks were doing a better job of spreading the news themselves. North Carolina A&T students excitedly telephoned friends at other all-black colleges across the state, inspiring copycat sit-ins. The ripples from Greensboro rolled into North Carolina's largest city, Charlotte, by February 9, as 150 protesters occupied every seat at 8 lunch counters there. They sat impassively as white waitresses ignored them.

"Of course, this movement here and those in Greensboro, Winston-Salem, and Durham are interrelated, in that they are parts of my race's efforts to secure God-given rights," said Joseph Charles Jones, an organizer of the Charlotte sit-in. "But they are not part of a plan, and were undertaken independently. We did not consult with groups or individuals at the other schools."

Sit-ins spread to dozens of cities in other Southern states by the end of the month, motivated by a common spirit of nonviolence. Each protester in Nashville was handed a mimeographed sheet that stressed the importance of remaining peaceful. It counseled: "Remember the teachings of Jesus, Gandhi, Thoreau, and Martin Luther King Jr." Religion was another unifying thread. Southern blacks adopted an obscure hymn as their rallying song. Americans of all races would soon become familiar with "We Shall Overcome."

Many members of older generations—white and black, Southern and Northern—were uncertain how to react to this new phenomenon. The sit-in movement was unlike anything they had ever seen. Civil rights protesters, up to this point, had demanded access to a wide range of *government* services—attending public schools, riding public buses, swimming in public pools. But the revolution that began in Greensboro was aimed at the *private* sector, insisting that stores and restaurants treat all customers equally.

Most white Southerners, to nobody's surprise, were frightened and angry. Dime-store managers, the first whites affected, did whatever they could to discourage protesters at their lunch counters. They raised the price of coffee. They unscrewed the seats. They roped off the counters so that everyone—white and black—had to stand.

Yet a few breakthroughs occurred. Thirty San Antonio stores integrated their dining areas in late March after store managers, businessmen, and clergymen of both races held a series of meetings. "I feel funny," said a black woman drinking a Coke at a San Antonio lunch counter, "but it's nice of them to serve us." Black students entered the public library in Lenoir, North Carolina, fully expecting the worst, but were treated the same as white patrons. The student newspaper at the all-white University of North Carolina gave editorial support to the protesters.

Many professional journalists in the North weren't as kind. The trumpet of the nation's business establishment, the *Wall Street Journal,* expressed its impatience with sit-ins, as did the *Washington Star.* "There is both a right and a wrong approach to the problem," chided the *Star.* "And these demonstrations are taking the wrong approach."

That, too, was the opinion of Harry Truman, the same man who had based his triumphant 1948 campaign on the strongest civil rights plank in the Democratic Party's history. "If anyone came into my store and tried to stop business," he snapped, "I'd throw him out. The Negro should behave himself and show he's a good citizen."

Officials with the National Association for the Advancement of Colored People (NAACP)—themselves not especially comfortable with sit-ins—were nonetheless certain that their longtime friend had been misquoted. They sent a wire to Truman, seeking reassurance. What they got was more of the same. "I would do just what I said I would," the feisty ex-president replied. "I would say the same thing for all the newspapers and televisions in the country."

If the exchange with Truman wasn't confusing enough, the traditional leaders of the civil rights movement still hadn't resolved their own feelings. James Farmer, a program director with the NAACP, was assigned to analyze the situation. "The NAACP had concentrated upon legal action—though it had done other things, too—and because of that orientation found it difficult to understand any tactic which involved violation even of the local law," he said. This conservative attitude, he added, "did not apply so much to the young, the youth in the NAACP, as it did to the older persons."

Martin Luther King Jr., whose book had inspired the Greensboro Four, was just 31 years old. College students, however, considered him a member of the older generation, a man who had attained fame during their high school years. King, in fact, *did* share many of the views held by old-line civil rights leaders. He, too, had conflicting feelings about sit-ins.

One of King's colleagues, Fred Shuttlesworth, traveled to High Point, North Carolina, 15 miles southwest of Greensboro, on church business in early February. He was there when black students assembled for a demonstration in downtown High Point, one of the first sit-ins to spring up after the initial protest. They were well-dressed and well-mannered, and they exuded a seriousness that greatly impressed him.

Shuttlesworth knew what had to be done. He placed a call to Ella Baker, an organizer with King's Southern Christian Leadership Conference (SCLC) in Atlanta. "You tell Martin," he said, "that we must get with this." Implicit in Shuttlesworth's call was a warning: If King failed to jump on board, his influence—and that of the SCLC—might be permanently diminished.

King heeded the advice and issued a public endorsement. "What is new is that American students have come of age," he said to the protesters all across the South. "You now take your honored places in the worldwide struggle for freedom."

LEXICON: FEBRUARY 1960

Ebbets Field

Two hundred mourners gathered on February 23 at the former home of baseball's Brooklyn Dodgers, Ebbets Field. The Dodgers had stunned the nation by moving to Los Angeles after the 1957 season. New York City decided to knock down the decrepit stadium to make way for a housing project. An iron ball, painted to look like a baseball, smashed through a dugout roof to begin the demolition. The American flag flew upside down from the center field flagpole. It was a simple mistake, said city officials, and not the international sign of distress.

"Man-Computer Symbiosis"

Computers had existed for a generation—the first machines worthy of the name appeared in the thirties—yet only 7,000 were in service by 1960. But behavioral scientist J.C.R. Licklider envisioned great things. "Man-Computer Symbiosis," an article he wrote for an obscure journal, predicted the arrival of personal computers ("thinking centers") and the Internet ("a network of such centers, connected to one another by wide-band communications lines"). Disciples hailed Licklider as the Johnny Appleseed of computers, a sole pioneer planting new ideas that would blossom in the years to come.

Playboy Club

Hugh Hefner had attained a modicum of fame as the publisher of *Playboy,* a strange hybrid that ran pictures of naked women alongside subtle works of fiction. He was selling more than 1 million copies per month by 1960, seven years after *Playboy*'s launch, but he yearned to branch out. Hefner opened his first Playboy Club in Chicago on February 29. The waitresses—always young, always pretty—were known as "bunnies." They helped to make the Chicago operation the world's busiest nightclub by 1962. Other Playboy Clubs quickly sprang up in Miami, New Orleans, New York, and Los Angeles.

Second Industrial Revolution

William Laurence had a knack for coining pithy titles. The Pulitzer Prize-winning science editor of the *New York Times* had dubbed the postwar period the "atomic age," a name that became ubiquitous. Inspiration visited again in 1960. "We are now in the midst," Laurence declared, "of a Second Industrial Revolution." The American way of business, in his opinion, was being dramatically and permanently altered by automation "brought about by the development of self-regulating machines."

Squaw Valley

The eighth Winter Olympics began with great fanfare in Squaw Valley, California, on February 18. The one and only Walt Disney had been hired to inject Hollywood flair into the opening ceremonies, and he surpassed all expectations. The world's athletes were welcomed to the mountain retreat west of Lake Tahoe by an orchestra of 1,285; a chorus of 2,645 singing the Olympic hymn; and an elaborate aerial show featuring fireworks, 2,000 pigeons, and 20,000 balloons. Olympic opening ceremonies had traditionally been simple, relatively sedate affairs. Squaw Valley changed that forever.

Water Pollution

Contamination of America's water supply was not a new problem. "We are a water-drinking people, and we are allowing every brook to be defiled," anthropologist George Bird Grinnell had warned as early as 1900. But few people paid attention until the late fifties. Congress took a small step in February 1960, allocating $90 million for local sewage plants. President Eisenhower vetoed the bill on February 22. Water pollution, he said, was "a uniquely local blight" that should be tackled by local governments, not the federal bureaucracy.

***

The experts in Washington were still trying to figure out what made Fidel Castro tick.

The State Department's Bureau of Intelligence and Research issued a confidential analysis early in the new year, a report that reflected its lingering confusion. It initially suggested that Castro had "a typical Latin temperament," yet later asserted that he belonged to a rarer breed, "a vain egocentric with a decided messianic complex which some observers believe borders on paranoia." President Eisenhower confided to intimates that he thought the Cuban leader was flat-out crazy.

Some of Castro's recent actions had been unorthodox, to be sure, such as his appointment of a radical Argentinian doctor, Ernesto "Che" Guevara, to head the National Bank of Cuba (inspiring puns that it would soon be renamed Che's National Bank). Equally baffling was his apparent lack of concern about the thousands of white-collar Cubans—doctors, engineers, technicians, and managers—who were streaming into exile in the United States. These well-educated refugees jammed every flight from Havana to Miami.

Castro's seizure of foreign-owned property remained the major bone of contention between Washington and Havana. American companies had sunk $850 million into sugar mills, utilities, tobacco plantations, farms, and industries across Cuba. U.S. officials estimated that one-third of these investments had been expropriated by the beginning of February. The other two-thirds were endangered.

Eisenhower struggled to remain calm. His public statements in late January and early February were remarkably measured and reasonable. He pledged not to intervene militarily in Cuba, and he voiced his "real sympathy" for land reform and other "Cuban ideals."

But the president showed a different face in private. "Castro begins to look like a madman," he snapped in a January 25 meeting with his national security advisers. He proposed ringing the island with a naval blockade to prevent importation of food and supplies. "If the Cuban people are hungry," he said grimly, "they will throw Castro out." His staffers scotched the idea. A whole country, they argued, shouldn't suffer for the actions of a seemingly irrational leader. Eisenhower grudgingly agreed.

Further complicating the U.S.-Cuban dispute was the specter of communism, which always inflated the level of anxiety in American politics. Was Castro merely a Cuban nationalist, or was he a Marxist in thrall to the Soviet Union? Everybody in Washington had an opinion, but nobody knew for sure.

Their counterparts in Moscow were equally confused. Nikita Khrushchev salivated over the possibility of establishing a foothold in the Caribbean, yet he was skeptical about Castro's commitment to communist doctrine. He decided to test the waters on February 4, dispatching his deputy premier, Anastas Mikoyan, on a 10-day trip to Havana.

Castro and Mikoyan, who helicoptered to every corner of Cuba, hit it off famously. Any differences between Cuba and the Soviet Union seemed insignificant in comparison to the bond imposed by the United

States, their common enemy. "You Cubans will understand me if I tell you that the imperialists invent more lies about us than they do about you," Mikoyan said. "They try to bury the truth in slime."

Diplomatic relations between the two nations had ceased in 1952, but Mikoyan was empowered to establish new ties if Castro gave evidence of communist sympathies. Khrushchev's deputy, satisfied with what he saw, offered Cuba a $100 million loan, a four-year sugar purchase agreement, and the prospect of exchanging ambassadors within a few months.

It was an impressive victory for Castro, who dreamed of weaning his country from its economic dependence on the United States. The deal with Mikoyan emboldened him to establish a central planning board on February 20, bringing all private enterprise in Cuba under government control. His earlier talk about surrendering power was now forgotten, as was his previous commitment to democracy. "It never functioned in Latin America," he told a Brazilian newsman. "Elections are a myth. The parliamentary system in Cuba reflected the

Fidel Castro tightens his control of Cuba: "Elections now would be a step backward." (Warren Leffler/Library of Congress)

old system, which we are now destroying. Elections now would be a step backward."

Gloom descended on the White House after the Mikoyan-Castro agreement was announced. An internal CIA report conceded in late February that the deal was "a great propaganda victory" for the Soviets. Castro had been unmasked as a communist, or so it appeared, which was the worst outcome that American officials could imagine.

"There is little hope," the CIA analyst concluded, "that we can work out a satisfactory relationship with the Cuban government." The United States was plainly running out of options in the Caribbean.

RISING STAR: BOB NEWHART

It never occurred to George Newhart to question his destiny. The Oak Park, Illinois, native dutifully pursued a bachelor's degree at Chicago's Loyola University, narrowing his focus to three occupations after his graduation in 1952. "I grew up in a world where everybody went to college and got a degree in something," he said. "You were either a lawyer, doctor, or accountant."

Newhart chose the first path without enthusiasm, enrolling in law school. He attended classes in the morning; toiled as a law clerk in the afternoon; and did what he really loved in the evening, performing with a local theater group. It was an exhausting schedule, but George—whose friends called him by his middle name of Bob— refused to scale back his extracurricular activities. "Something had to give," he said, "and it was law school."

That left two options. Medicine demanded even more training than the law, so Newhart became an accountant. His new career, however, seemed mind-numbingly dull. He relieved the drudgery by placing prank phone calls to Ed Gallagher, a friend at an advertising agency. "Sir, it's Mr. Tompkins," he might begin. "We have a problem at your yeast factory. There's a fire." A pause. "Hold on, sir. I have to put you on hold while I run up another floor. The yeast is rising." Gallagher, slipping into the factory owner's role, responded in kind.

Newhart came to consider these calls to be more than a simple diversion. They offered a possible escape from the daily grind. Gallagher had moved to New York, so Bob reworked their act into a series of one-way calls, conveying the other half of his imaginary conversations by repeating key phrases and offering sly observations. He played a security guard reporting a bizarre incident on the Empire State Building: "No, it's not your standard ape." A publicity man polishing Abraham Lincoln's image: "Please read the bio. You were a railsplitter, then an attorney. You wouldn't give up your law practice to become a railsplitter." A colonial secretary puzzled by Walter Raleigh's discovery of tobacco: "You stick it between your lips. Then what do you do with it, Walt? You set *fire* to it?"

A Chicago disc jockey, Dan Sorkin, heard a tape of these routines and invited Newhart to become a guest on his show. Sorkin passed the tape to George Avakian, a talent scout at Warner Brothers. Newhart's wry humor and deadpan delivery intrigued Avakian, who offered an album deal in late 1959. All Warner Brothers needed to do, he said, was tape Newhart's next nightclub appearance.

That posed a problem. Newhart had never done stand-up comedy. His career, such as it was, consisted of phone calls and tapes. Avakian advised him to take the plunge, which is how he landed on stage at the Tidelands Motor Inn in Houston on February 10, 1960, doing two shows with tape recorders rolling. It was his first live appearance as a professional comedian.

Newhart overcame the inevitable jitters. He trotted out Abe Lincoln and other well-practiced routines, and padded the album with new characters. *The Button-Down Mind of Bob Newhart* was released in April with no fanfare. But it began getting radio airplay in a few cities, then in larger markets, and suddenly became a national sensation, catapulting to Number One on the *Billboard* chart, the first comedy recording to reach that rarefied slot.

Major TV shows began fighting to book Newhart as a guest. The producers of a World War II movie offered him a role. And Warner Brothers hustled him back on stage to record *The Button-Down Mind Strikes Back,* which shot to second place on the charts, right behind his other album, which was still Number One.

This explosion from obscurity to international stardom occurred within a few months in 1960. Newhart's star shone even brighter the next year. *The Bob Newhart Show* debuted on NBC in the autumn of 1961—winning an Emmy and a Peabody Award—yet was canceled because of disappointing ratings. Two hugely popular series would follow in the seventies and eighties, establishing Newhart as a TV icon.

Everything about his career—stardom, adulation, wealth—exceeded the grandiosity of his dreams. But what mattered most was that Newhart had attained his original goal. He had found a job he enjoyed.

"On the whole," he laughed four decades later, "I would say that my demise as an accountant was mutually beneficial to all concerned."

* * *

The presidential campaign was finally beginning in earnest, but most voters saw little reason to get excited. The primary election in New Hampshire, the first on the political calendar, was still a month away, and it promised to be dull. Richard Nixon was the lone contender for the state's Republican delegates. John Kennedy of neighboring Massachusetts was, for all intents and purposes, unopposed on the Democratic side.

The first meaningful primary wouldn't come until April, when Wisconsin Democrats would choose between Kennedy and Hubert Humphrey. Geography clearly favored Humphrey, who hailed from neighboring Minnesota. Kennedy grumbled about his opponent's home-field advantage but brightened at the thought of the potential reward. A decisive victory might clear the path to the Democratic nomination. "If I take Humphrey in Wisconsin," he said, "they can't take it away from me."

Kennedy launched his Wisconsin campaign in the arctic darkness of February 16, greeting workers at 5:30 A.M. outside a Madison sausage plant. His motorcade proceeded to tiny Midwestern towns foreign to his urban New England roots—places like Fort Atkinson, Whitewater, Elkhorn, and Lake Geneva—establishing an arduous pattern for the months to come.

Richard Goodwin, a Kennedy aide, recalled sitting in a diner with his boss on another frigid Wisconsin morning. The candidate gestured out the window at a factory gate, where he would soon be shaking hands with the arriving employees. "You think I'm out here to get votes," Kennedy said. "Well, I am. But not just *their* votes. I'm trying to get the votes of a lot of people who are sitting right now in warm, comfortable homes all over the country, having a big breakfast of bacon and eggs, hoping that young Jack will fall right on his face in the snow. Bastards."

The candidate climbed off his stool. "What the hell," he said to Goodwin. "They'll take me if they have to. Let's get started."

The odds against Kennedy weren't as steep as all that. The religious issue, which would bedevil him elsewhere, had the potential to work in his favor in Wisconsin, where more than 30 percent of the voters were Catholic. One of his opponents for the Democratic nomination,

Wayne Morse, alleged that Kennedy's campaign was surreptitiously urging Wisconsin Catholics to vote for their coreligionist. "In my book," Morse wrote in a private letter, "that is an attempt to use religion on one's behalf, and is just as bad as trying to use a man's religion against him."

Nobody expected anything less from the cantankerous Morse, who was widely admired for his outspokenness and independence, and equally despised for his arrogance and sharp tongue. But the Oregon senator, despite being a Wisconsin native, was not on the primary ballot. His campaign was already dangerously short of money.

Humphrey was Morse's polar opposite—upbeat, ebullient, energetic. He exuded confidence as he crisscrossed the state. "I never felt so sure of anything in my life," he said. "I feel like I just swallowed two tons of vitamins." Humphrey professed to be unconcerned about the religious issue. The director of his Wisconsin campaign, Sam Rizzo, insisted that Catholic factory workers would favor his man, a longtime friend of organized labor. "Will it be their bellies or their church?" Rizzo asked. "We think they'll vote their bellies."

Much was made of Kennedy's youth, but Humphrey was only 48 himself. Yet the son of a South Dakota pharmacist had been a national figure for more than a decade, ever since delivering a stirring call for racial equality at the 1948 Democratic convention. "The time has arrived," he had declared, "for the Democratic Party to get out of the shadow of states' rights and walk forthrightly into the bright sunshine of human rights." He won a Senate seat the same year and had been a hero to liberals ever since.

Humphrey's trademark was his all-encompassing enthusiasm, which contrasted sharply with Kennedy's cool self-control. "I only wish I had his gusto, his compassion, or even his sentimentality," Adlai Stevenson said wistfully. But critics insisted that Humphrey carried it too far. "You people always write that I talk on every subject," he jokingly told reporters. "I do—I like every subject. I can't help it."

Humphrey met his match in December 1958 on a trip to the Soviet Union, where he and Nikita Khrushchev talked for eight-and-a-half hours. They discussed everything from U.S.-Soviet relations to their rural childhoods. Khrushchev, toward the end of the marathon, asked Humphrey where he lived. The first secretary walked over to a wall map, picked up a pencil, and drew a big circle around Minneapolis. "That's so I don't forget to order them to spare the city when the rockets fly," he said. Humphrey replied that he was sorry he didn't have similar authority to save Moscow.

Press coverage of his Soviet trip—especially his four-color portrait on the cover of *Life*—greatly elevated Humphrey's national profile. No other presidential candidate but Nixon had spent significant time with Khrushchev. Kennedy had spoken only briefly with the Soviet leader at a Washington reception. Humphrey boasted that his meeting was significantly more important than either of theirs. "I'm the only living American," he laughed, "who has gone to the men's room three times in one day in the Kremlin."

Kennedy envied Humphrey's face time with Khrushchev and his committed base of liberal supporters, but he doubted the Minnesotan could convert these advantages into the Democratic nomination. "Hubert is too hot for the present mood of the people," he told Arthur Schlesinger Jr. "He gets people too excited, too worked up. What they want today is a more boring, monotonous personality, like me."

Many influential Democrats, however, worried that Kennedy was too cool, too detached. The NAACP's Thurgood Marshall urged him that winter to get involved in the battle for civil rights. "I don't think [Kennedy] realized the urgency of it," Marshall said later. Economist John Kenneth Galbraith, a personal friend, remembered Kennedy's lack of interest in farm-related issues. "I don't want to hear about agriculture from anyone but you, Ken," the candidate said. "And I don't much want to hear about it from you, either."

Kennedy faced other problems. There was the controversy about his religion, of course, as well as concerns about his health. War injuries had left him with back pain, causing him to undergo a fusion of spinal discs in 1954 and a bone graft the following year. He also suffered from Addison's disease, a disorder of the adrenal glands that was held in check by cortisone injections. These maladies forced him to be hospitalized nine times in the mid-fifties, endangering his carefully cultivated image of youthful vigor.

Kennedy waved off all questions about his health. His back, he said, did not bother him. He lied even to Schlesinger about his Addison's disease, insisting that he did not suffer from the illness and did not take cortisone. "No one who has Addison's disease ought to run for president," Kennedy told him. "But I do not have it, and have never had it."

He took the same approach to criticism of his youth. Competence, not age, was what mattered, he maintained. Yet millions of American voters remained doubtful. Kennedy approached an elderly woman in a small Wisconsin town during a particularly frosty day in February. She, like so many people he met, made no effort to hide her skepticism when he asked for her support.

"You're too soon, my boy, too soon," she said.

Kennedy, still three months shy of his 43rd birthday, smiled back at the old lady. He had been told the same thing by people of much greater stature—governors, party leaders, even an ex-president—and he would not be dissuaded. "No, this is my time," he replied. "My time is now."

QUOTATIONS: FEBRUARY 1960

"I decided I'd better come home and take care of home, instead of trying to take care of Kenya."
> —*Legendary black lawyer Thurgood Marshall, explaining his hasty return to the United States from London in late February. Marshall had been drafting a constitution for Kenya, a British colony that was preparing for independence. The sudden blossoming of the sit-in movement, however, inspired him to hustle back to defend protesters who had been arrested.*

"I've made a decision about what I'm going to do, and only one person knows about this. It's Hugh Downs [his announcer]. My wife doesn't know about it, but I'll be home in time, and I'll tell her. I'm leaving the *Tonight Show*."
> —*Late-night television host Jack Paar, abruptly quitting in the middle of NBC's* Tonight Show *on February 11. He was angry that network censors had deleted his lame joke about a "water closet" from the previous night's program. They said it was in bad taste. Newspapers across the nation, even the staid* New York Times, *splashed Paar's walkout on their front pages, an unprecedented tribute to the emerging power of television.*

"I don't really need enemies when I have me."
> —*Paar, returning to the* Tonight Show *on March 7. He admitted that his walkout had been childish and emotional, and that he hadn't been able to find a better way to earn $200,000 a year.*

"The Playboy Club is dedicated to projecting the richly roman-
tic mood, the fun and *joie de vivre, t*hat are so much a part of the
publication."
                              —Playboy *magazine publisher Hugh Hefner, opening the*
                                        first Playboy Club in Chicago on February 29.

* * *

The first weeks of campaigning in Wisconsin were reminiscent of the
bygone eras of Warren Harding and Franklin Roosevelt. Jack Kennedy
popping into a barbershop in Lake Geneva, Hubert Humphrey firing
up a Milwaukee crowd with an old-fashioned stem-winder—it was
as easy to imagine them running in 1920 or 1940 as in 1960.

But appearances were deceiving. Recent revolutions in communications, advertising, market research, and transportation guaranteed
that this would be unlike any previous election year. The 1960 campaign would establish a new set of political rules and guidelines that
would endure into the 21st century.

The biggest change was the most obvious. Fewer than half a million American homes owned television sets when Harry Truman
upset Thomas Dewey in the 1948 election. The major TV networks
didn't span the country until their coast-to-coast relay system went
operational in 1951. But the United States was saturated with TV sets
by 1960—more than 45 million of them—and the typical household
watched devotedly.

Television's rapid expansion had ushered in a golden age of advertising, a boon for retailers. The mammoth ad agencies on Madison Avenue skillfully exploited the new medium, building brand awareness
and consumer loyalty on a scale never before seen. They joined forces
with the TV networks to inundate the American public with an endless stream of commercials.

It dawned on Theodore White, a reporter for *Collier's* magazine, that
political campaigns could use these modern techniques to their advantage. He noted in 1956 that Dwight Eisenhower seemed to be an
ideal candidate for the television era. "He was a nationally known, rec-
ognizable brand product," White wrote. "West Point-crafted, money
back if it fails to please, tested in war, tested in peace, reliable, honest,
safe, and look, it makes you smile."

Campaign strategists did not use TV particularly well in 1956.
They typically bought half an hour of airtime for a live telecast of a
candidate's speech, with predictably dull results. But 1960 would be

different. Democratic and Republican technicians were already laying plans for slick documentaries and brisk 60-second commercials, carefully tailoring their messages to the new realities of television. "The slick or bombastic orator, pounding the table and ringing the rafters, is not as welcome in the family living room as he was in the town square or party hall," conceded a Democratic senator in a November 1959 issue of *TV Guide*. The article carried the byline of John Kennedy.

It was easier to generate mass appeal, of course, if a candidate possessed a firm understanding of voters' likes and dislikes—and great strides had been made in that field, too, during the years leading up to 1960.

Opinion polling had been part of the political game for nearly three decades, ever since Herbert Hoover's ill-fated reelection campaign surveyed voters in 14 cities in 1932. George Gallup, Elmo Roper, and other professional pollsters established thriving businesses during the thirties and forties, monitoring the public pulse on behalf of hundreds of clients—not only politicians, but newspapers and corporations as well.

The black year of 1948, however, stripped their wizardry of its mystique. The major pollsters wrote off Truman weeks before the election. Dewey, they predicted, would win the presidency in a landslide, and they had the numbers to back up their claims. But the experts were proven terribly wrong. "I wonder how far Moses would have gone if he had taken a poll in Egypt," Truman cackled after scoring a surprisingly easy victory.

High-profile politicians backed away from polls for a few years after 1948. Truman certainly never commissioned any, and Eisenhower didn't show much interest. But Gallup never lost faith—"no other method will be found, apart from sampling of the kind we do, which is more accurate"—and the next political generation couldn't shake its fascination. The Republican National Committee was commissioning weekly surveys by the late fifties, and every presidential contender in 1960 had a pollster on retainer.

Kennedy was infatuated with polls, making greater use of them than any previous candidate in American history. His campaign conducted dozens of surveys to decide which primaries to enter and then blanketed the chosen states on a regular basis, seeking voters' opinions about candidates, issues, and anything else Kennedy might find useful. "We were not unlike the people who check their horoscope each day before venturing out," said his personal secretary, Evelyn Lincoln.

Richard Nixon didn't match Kennedy's level of fascination with numbers—no politician did, with the possible exception of Nelson Rockefeller—but his polling operation was still high-powered. An astonished Barry Goldwater sat through one of Nixon's briefings. "The presentation was able to give the candidate any answer he wanted," he marveled. "If he wanted to know, 'Why am I weak in southern Pennsylvania?' they could reshuffle the figures and answers, and get it." Nixon and Kennedy, whose Washington offices were close to each other, actually swapped some of their pre-1960 poll results, with their administrative assistants making the exchanges.

The campaign was largely confined to Wisconsin in February, so the candidates still operated on a small scale—riding buses, speaking at Rotary meetings, and going door to door to meet voters. But the evolution of American politics would become evident as 1960 unfolded, as the primaries multiplied, the conventions took place, and the final drive to the White House began. Greater sophistication in the use of television, advertising, and polls—coupled with the new availability of jet travel—would permanently alter the way that men (and eventually women) pursued the presidency.

Theodore White understood this point better than most, having detected the nascent bonds between Madison Avenue and political campaigns in 1956. *Collier's* was no longer in business, so he was on his own. He decided to tag along with the candidates and gather material for a new kind of book. "It would be written as a novel is written," he suggested, "with anticipated surprises as, one by one, early candidates vanish in the primaries until only two final jousters struggle for the prize in November."

The book industry yawned at White's concept of politics as drama. Newspapers still played it straight in 1960, covering the campaign's public events—announcements, speeches, conventions—but rarely peeking behind the scenes or delving into any human aspects of political life. Book publishers saw no reason to deviate. The first three that White approached turned him down before he finally struck a deal with Atheneum.

Just a few days in Wisconsin convinced him that there was a wealth of material. He was amazed by what he was uncovering—grand strategy, intrigue, deception, backstabbing. "It was like walking through a field playing a brass tuba the day it rained gold," he said a decade later. "Everything was sitting around waiting to be reported."

Yet White conceded that the experts in the publishing field were probably right. His book, he told friends, would not be a best-seller. "I know I won't make any money on it at all," he said. His fears sometimes threatened to overwhelm him, as he confessed in a personal memorandum that winter. He had no steady source of income, just a small advance from Atheneum, and his prospects did not seem promising.

"This is a hell of a bad gamble," White wrote. "When I talk the book out, it sounds good. Yet when I am alone, it frightens me."

4

March: The Wind of Change

Albert Zalkind sensed a void in American life, a deficiency the private sector had long ignored. He hustled to his workroom in Arlington, Virginia, to devise a solution.

What the nation truly needed, in Zalkind's opinion, was a pair of mechanical plastic hands that could "repeatedly and rapidly strike each other to simulate a sustained burst of applause." He had never seen such a gadget, so he crafted a set of hands triggered by a windup mechanism. "A device as thus generally constructed has enormous amusement value as a subtle hint to the effect that a person may be talking too much at a party or other gathering," Zalkind wrote in his patent application. Yet his apparatus was not designed merely for derisive clapping. "It can serve as a gift," he suggested, "when it is desired to congratulate someone for a job well done."

The United States Patent Office, convinced of the uniqueness of Zalkind's creation, awarded him patent number 2,931,135 in the spring of 1960. His windup hands joined a flood of innovative products—some frivolous, some life-changing—streaming to the marketplace. The year would bring America its first aluminum cans with peel-off tops, matchless cigarettes, paper clothes, watches that used tuning forks to keep time, home movie cameras that recorded sound, plastic toy blocks called Legos, and hook-and-loop fastening strips known as Velcro.

The Patent Office struggled to keep pace with this burst of inventive spirit. Individuals, corporations, and government agencies filed 84,246 patent applications in 1960, an average of 330 per business day. Patent examiners hadn't experienced such activity since the mid-forties, when filings for war-related inventions had briefly clogged the system.

The onslaught in 1960, for instance, was 30 percent heavier than the flow in 1951, which had averaged 254 applications per day.

The deluge of inventions was attributed to a recently coined acronym, R&D. Modern executives, impatient with the old hit-and-miss system of invention, demanded a methodical approach to the creation of new products. Their spending on R&D—research and development—equaled $12 billion in 1960, more than twice the outlay of $5.2 billion six years earlier. The United States now had more than 5,000 industrial laboratories, dwarfing the total of 290 in 1920, just two generations back.

But R&D—so rational and scientific in concept—was far from perfect in real life. Inventions did not always advance smoothly from their creators' drafting boards to the marketplace, as Chester Carlson could attest. Technicians in a frigid factory in Rochester, New York, were conducting final tests in March 1960 on his brainchild, the world's first automatic plain-paper copying machine. Carlson had battled for three decades to reach this point, never losing faith in his vision of a commercially successful photocopier. The end result, the Xerox 914, was days away from hitting the open market.

Timing had always been Carlson's problem. He graduated from the California Institute of Technology in 1930, the first summer of the Great Depression. The only work he could find was as a patent clerk, a tedious job that required him to retype endless copies of specifications. He had always been an inventor at heart—filling notebooks with more than 400 ideas for new products—so he naturally began to seek an easier way to duplicate the pages piled on his desk.

Carlson experimented at night and on weekends in his Long Island apartment, tinkering endlessly with chemicals and substances. He finally achieved success on October 22, 1938, when he coated a small zinc plate with sulfur, charged it electrostatically by rubbing it with a handkerchief, and exposed it for 10 seconds to a glass slide. He then dusted the plate with lycopodium powder, making the copied image visible, and pressed it against wax paper to print it. He named this new process electrophotography.

The difficult part was over, or so it seemed. Carlson needed only to strike a deal with a company eager to develop commercial applications for his research. He sent letters to 34 firms, including such giants as Eastman Kodak, General Electric, IBM, and RCA. They all said no. "I found," he said, "that my crude little demonstration did not impress them."

Haloid Company finally stepped forward with an initial invest-ment of $10,000 in 1946. Haloid produced equipment that made pho-tographic copies of documents—actual pictures—but its system was time-consuming, expensive, and not particularly popular. The tiny Rochester firm, gambling that Carlson's process might eventually im-prove its profit margin, sank a small fortune into the refinement of elec-trophotography, $3.5 million in the first six years alone.

The new partners hit the market in 1949 with the Model A, a manu-ally operated photocopier that was messy and cumbersome. A skilled operator could make a decent copy every three minutes or so, but typi-cal office workers found the machine impossible to operate. The Model A flopped so badly that it put Haloid's future in danger. The company saved itself by discovering an alternate market for the ill-fated copier, using it to make paper masters for offset printing.

Carlson and Haloid soldiered on. They developed numerous proto-types, fine-tuned the electrophotographic process, and even changed its name. An Ohio State University professor had combined the Greek words for *dry* and *writing* to come up with *xerography,* a linguistic cre-ation that seized the imagination of Haloid's president, Joseph Wilson. He renamed his company Haloid Xerox, eventually jettisoning the first word completely.

The moment of truth was approaching. "We are about to give birth either to our greatest success or to our greatest failure," Wilson told his department heads in the summer of 1959. Analysts anticipated a re-prise of the Model A debacle. IBM considered making an investment in Haloid Xerox's new machine but rejected the idea in the end. The 914 was too big, too slow, and too expensive, said IBM's consultant, who also expressed doubt that American businesses would ever find much use for photocopiers.

Final tests of the 914 were conducted in arctic conditions. It was cheaper to shut off the thermostat at five o'clock in Haloid Xerox's rented facility, so the temperature plummeted as parka-wearing em-ployees toiled into the night. Testers hung sheets of canvas over their copiers, hoping to trap the heat the machines generated. It wasn't until March, several weeks behind schedule, that the company shipped its first 914 to Standard Press Steel, a manufacturer of metal fasteners in Jenkintown, Pennsylvania.

Everybody prepared for the worst, even Chester Carlson, the opti-mist who had persevered for 30 long years. He worried that most of Haloid Xerox's customers would make fewer than 100 photocopies a day, the 914's threshold for profitability. The company estimated that a typical user would initially produce only 40 copies a day, about 10,000 a year. It was banking on a gradual increase in usage as the sixties progressed, eventually generating a return on its investment.

That scenario would prove to be ridiculously conservative. Office workers almost immediately developed an addiction to xerography. Early reports indicated that many customers were making more than 10,000 copies a month. Some were topping 1,000 a day. Haloid Xerox couldn't produce the Xerox 914 quickly enough to meet demand.

"I keep asking myself, 'When are you going to wake up with the dream over?'" Joe Wilson would admit to a reporter the following year. His company, an insignificant cog in Rochester's economy, would mushroom into the nation's 15th largest publicly owned corporation by 1965. "Things just aren't this good in life," Wilson said.

The Xerox machine was undoubtedly the preeminent invention to go public in 1960—*Fortune* hailed it as "the most successful product ever

Joseph Wilson gambles on the Xerox 914: "We are about to give birth either to our greatest success or to our greatest failure." (Xerox Corporation)

marketed in America"—but several significant contenders emerged during the year, including the implantable cardiac pacemaker, the live-virus polio vaccine, the laser, the controlled thermonuclear reaction, and the nonstick frying pan.

The latter was the least dramatic invention of the bunch, though it made the greatest impression on American consumers. Development of the nonstick pan started in 1938, when DuPont chemist Roy Plunkett began experimenting with fluorocarbon gases, hoping to produce a better coolant for refrigerators. He generated a waxy white substance instead. "Initially," he recalled, "I thought I goofed, and that I'd have to start over."

But Plunkett, a meticulous researcher, decided to test the by-product before disposing of it. He discovered that it had a lower coefficient of friction than any solid known to man. Anything that came into contact with polytetrafluorethylene (the compound's chemical name) would slip as if it were gliding on ice.

Weapons manufacturers immediately saw applications. Plunkett's substance, trademarked by DuPont as Teflon, was used by the Manhattan Project, the secret program that developed the atomic bomb. Automotive, food processing, and medical industries eagerly incorporated it in their processes and products after the war. Yet DuPont wasn't satisfied. Sales of Teflon amounted to $28 million in 1960, a pittance for a multibillion-dollar conglomerate. None of its engineers or salesmen could devise an effective way to introduce Teflon to the consumer market, where the really big money was.

A small French cookware company pointed the way. T-Fal coated a skillet with Teflon, dubbed it the Satisfry, and put it on sale for $6.94 in a Macy's store in Manhattan on December 15, 1960. A heavy snowstorm raged outside, but Macy's was inundated with household cooks who were tired of food sticking to their frying pans. The store's supply sold out almost immediately. Neiman Marcus followed Macy's lead and sold 2,000 skillets the first week. Orders for the Satisfry would soar to a million pans a month by mid-1961.

Those early T-Fal skillets were far from perfect. The coating scraped off almost as easily as eggs and bacon did. "Nothing stuck to Teflon," Plunkett said later, "so how the hell did you stick it to the pan?" But DuPont's chemists weren't flustered. They eventually developed a better version of their wonder compound, a substance that bonded more tightly with the skillet and was virtually impossible to scrape off.

Teflon was merely the latest victory for the nation's scientific community, which had registered a stunning series of breakthroughs since World War II, ranging from the cataclysmic terrors of nuclear weapons to the mundane pleasures of television. The American public—slightly jaded by the ceaseless string of innovations—had come to expect no less.

LEXICON: MARCH 1960

Civil Rights Act of 1960

The provisions of the Civil Rights Act of 1960 would soon be forgotten, but memories of the controversy it inspired would linger. The bill was introduced by the Senate's majority leader, Lyndon Johnson, who hoped to attract Northern support for his presidential campaign. Southern segregationists struck back by filibustering, keeping the Senate in continuous session for 125 hours. Members had to sleep on cots near the Senate chamber. Johnson retreated on March 5, joking that "every man has the right to a Saturday night bath." But he soon began searching for another way to get his bill passed.

COMINFIL

The director of the Federal Bureau of Investigation (FBI), J. Edgar Hoover, launched an anti-subversion program in March 1960. The operation, code-named COMINFIL, brought under surveillance a wide range of "legitimate mass organizations" (the FBI's term), ranging from the Boy Scouts to the NAACP. FBI agents were instructed to closely monitor the leaders of these groups, watching for any evidence of previously undetected communist tendencies.

El Viejito Sonriente

President Eisenhower undertook his latest mission of personal diplomacy in late February and early March—a 9-day, 15,560-mile trip to Argentina, Brazil, Chile, and Uruguay. Latin American newspapers dubbed him El Viejito Sonriente, the Smiling Old Man. The crowds were as large and joyous as those that had greeted Ike on his trip to India in December 1959. "There seems to be no word in the English language," he said in Chile, "which would permit me to express the feeling I have for the affection I believe I saw."

Lady Chatterley's Lover

Lady Chatterley's Lover was a notorious novel written by D.H. Lawrence in 1928. Its plot was as simple as it was risqué. Constance marries Lord Chatterley before World War I. The lord marches off to war but returns paralyzed below the waist. His wife takes a series of lovers, eventually running off with one. U.S. authorities banned the book for more than 30 years, citing Lawrence's detailed descriptions of sex acts. But the U.S. Court of Appeals ruled on March 25 that the book had artistic merit and therefore could not be suppressed. *Lady Chatterley's Lover* quickly shot onto the best-seller list.

Operation Pluto

CIA director Allen Dulles dropped by the White House in February with a plan to sabotage Cuban sugar refineries. Eisenhower brusquely rejected the proposal. It was minor league stuff, he said. He told Dulles to come back when he had something more effective in mind. The director returned on March 17 with a four-part plan, code-named Operation Pluto. Its key provision was the creation of "a paramilitary force outside of Cuba for future guerrilla action." Eisenhower gave his hearty approval, and the CIA quietly began recruiting volunteers for its new anti-Castro battalion.

Serial Number 53310761

Elvis Presley was arguably the most famous singer in the world—and indisputably the most famous sergeant in the army. Millions of fans knew everything about him, even his serial number. The 25-year-old superstar had sold 18 million records since 1955, even though his career had been on hold since his military induction in March 1958. Presley was discharged from the army on March 5 at Fort Dix, New Jersey. The train carrying him home to Memphis was mobbed by fans at every stop. His first post-army single, "Stuck on You," soared to the top of the charts in April.

***

John Kennedy detached himself from Wisconsin in early March and hustled east to New Hampshire. He spent four days roaming the Granite State's dreary mill towns and picturesque villages, drumming up support prior to the March 8 primary election, the first of the season.

"Beginning tomorrow," he shouted to an election-eve crowd in Dover, "New Hampshire can fire a shot that will be heard around the country." But the stakes weren't nearly as dramatic as that. Kennedy, the only major Democratic candidate campaigning in the state, was already well-known to New Hampshire voters, many of whom read Boston newspapers and watched Massachusetts television stations. His victory was foreordained.

Only one opponent faced him on the Democratic ballot, Paul Fisher, a pen manufacturer from Chicago. Kennedy considered Fisher a nuisance and held him at arm's length. "The Constitution provides the president must be American-born—an American citizen—and thirty-five years of age," Kennedy said. "These qualifications Mr. Fisher and I have in common." He refused to say anything else about his obscure rival.

Victory came easily. Kennedy drew 43,400 votes, the most ever by a Democratic primary winner in New Hampshire. Richard Nixon did even better on the Republican side with 65,200 votes, topping President Eisenhower's 1956 total by 9,000. Nixon's camp had worried that Nelson Rockefeller would attract considerable write-in support, but only 2,745 voters penciled Rocky's name on their ballots.

The New Hampshire results, despite their general insignificance, convinced one influential politician to commit himself. Eisenhower noted at the Gridiron Club dinner the following Saturday night that somebody else would be sitting in his seat at the 1961 event. The best choice, he said, was just two chairs away, which was where Nixon was sitting.

The Gridiron dinner was supposed to be off the record, but this was big news in Washington, especially since Ike had waffled for months on a Nixon endorsement. Reporters sought official confirmation at the president's press conference on March 16.

"If anyone is wondering whether I have any personal preference or even bias with respect to this upcoming presidential race," Eisenhower replied, "the answer is yes, very definitely." A reporter asked if "bias" meant Nixon. Ike shot back, "Was there any doubt in your mind?" The press corps—which had been very doubtful indeed— roared with laughter.

The Democratic race wasn't as clear cut. Competitors who had by-passed the first primary were quick to disparage Kennedy's walkover. "What has New Hampshire got to do with the price of eggs?" an anonymous Humphrey staffer asked a *Time* reporter. An adviser to Stuart Symington chimed in, "The professionals have been through this before." He pointed out that Estes Kefauver had won the New Hampshire primaries in 1952 and 1956, only to fade badly at both Democratic conventions.

Wisconsin would determine whether Kennedy was a potential nominee or a Kefauver clone. Humphrey was waiting for him there—singing "Solidarity Forever" with union members picketing the J. I. Case Company plant in Racine, handing out copies of his wife's recipe for beef soup, and talking to everybody in sight, even a group of deaf schoolchildren in Delavan.

Humphrey was relying on sheer energy to carry him to victory. Reporters and voters frequently commented on the disparity between his boundless enthusiasm and Kennedy's cool detachment. "I guess it's because Jack's got a feeling he can win," Humphrey said. "Me, I'm not so sure, so I'm going to have some fun."

Kennedy had built a powerful machine in Wisconsin—oiled by his dad's money, run by family members and rich Eastern friends. Humphrey's campaign was disorganized, understaffed, and underfunded. Kennedy could fly across Wisconsin in the family Convair. Humphrey chugged about in an old rented bus. "Come down here, Jack, and play fair," he yelled one day as he watched a plane overhead.

It was a funny line, and the reporters on Humphrey's bus laughed along with the candidate, but frustration lay beneath his humor. Humphrey occasionally lashed out with uncharacteristic bitterness, as when he told a Wisconsin audience that the secret to Kennedy's success was having a rich father. "Let's face it," he said. "I'm not complaining. These are the facts of life."

The Kennedy campaign, for its part, loudly insisted that Humphrey was beholden to the kingpins of organized labor, especially Teamsters boss Jimmy Hoffa. "I have not sought Hoffa's support, and he has not offered it," Humphrey snapped back. "The only time he came into my state recently was to say some unkind things about me." Kennedy's operatives quietly raised questions about the Minnesota senator's lack of a military record. Humphrey was especially sensitive to accusations that he had evaded service in World War II. He had tried to enlist in the army and navy but had been rejected by both because of colorblindness, a double hernia, and scars on his lungs.

Humphrey had no doubt that Robert Kennedy was the source of the rumors and whispers, a belief that strained their relationship for years. "As a professional politician, I was able to accept and indeed respect the efficacy of the Kennedy campaign," Humphrey wrote late in his life. "But underneath the beautiful exterior, there was an element of ruthlessness and toughness that I had trouble either accepting or forgetting."

It was that very toughness, however, that impressed many leading Democrats. They had originally dismissed Jack Kennedy as a callow pretender but were now revising their assessments. His firm backbone, coolness under pressure, and deep pockets, they had to admit, stamped him as presidential material, perhaps the best choice the party had.

Paul Butler, the chairman of the Democratic National Committee, told a group of reporters at a private dinner in mid-March that the race for the nomination might soon be settled. If Kennedy won Wisconsin, Butler said flatly, he would be the nominee. The chairman added that he personally would be "awful unhappy" if either Lyndon Johnson or Adlai Stevenson were nominated at the Los Angeles convention.

These were unwise things for Butler to say—his job required him to be impartial—but they reflected the subtle shift occurring in the Democratic contest in March. Kennedy had now emerged as the clear frontrunner for the nomination. *Time* quoted "one of Wisconsin's most knowledgeable officials" as predicting that the April 5 primary might turn out to be a rout.

"It would not surprise me—in an election held today—if Kennedy swept the state," said the unidentified Democrat. "I don't mean just the popular vote and six or seven [congressional] districts. I mean all ten districts. This may not be true come April, because Hubert has just begun to fight—and he's a good fighter—and he can do nothing from here on in but gain. But it seems to be true now."

RISING STAR: JOHN HOWARD GRIFFIN

Howard Griffin was a bright, free-spirited young man with a skeptical and inquiring mind. Yet there was one tenet of his Texas upbringing that he never questioned, not even after living in France from 1935 to 1941. "We were given the distinctive illusion," he recalled, "that Negroes were somehow different." The inherent superiority of white people seemed obvious.

His attitude didn't change until he served in the army during World War II. A bomb explosion in the Solomon Islands left him blind. "He can only see the heart and intelligence of a man," Griffin wrote of his new condition, "and nothing in these things indicates in the slightest whether a man is white or black, but only whether he is good or bad, wise or foolish."

He pursued his dream after the war, writing books and magazine articles under his full name, John Howard Griffin. He resigned himself to the challenges posed by permanent blindness, yet his eyesight inexplicably returned in 1957. His doctors, as baffled as he, fitted him with a strong pair of glasses.

An unexpected opportunity now presented itself, a chance for Griffin to test the insight he had gained as a blind man. He proposed to alter his skin color and wander across the South, comparing the treatment accorded to him as a black man in communities he had previously visited while white. *Sepia,* a small magazine aimed at black readers, agreed to underwrite the unorthodox experiment.

The racial transformation was guided by a New Orleans dermatologist, who darkened Griffin's skin with an oral medication, oxsoralen, supplemented with ultraviolet rays and vegetable dye. The author also shaved his straight brown hair. A final look in the mirror convinced him that he could pass for black. "The face and shoulders of a stranger—a fierce, bald, very dark Negro—glared at me from the glass," he wrote. "He in no way resembled me."

Griffin hit the road in early November 1959. He spent the next five weeks traveling through Louisiana, Mississippi, Alabama, and Georgia—taunted by whites, denied service in restaurants and hotels, and generally treated not as a second-class citizen, he decided, but as a "tenth-class citizen."

The "nagging, focusless terror" he experienced in Mississippi reminded him of the ceaseless fear that had gripped France after the Nazis seized control. His mind began to ease when he crossed into Alabama, especially after a grandfatherly white man offered him a ride. But their conversation soon drifted onto dangerous ground.

"You got a pretty wife?" the man asked.

"Yes, sir," Griffin responded.

"She ever had it from a white man?"

Griffin had not been black for long, but he knew the appropriate response was to remain silent and keep moving. He continued his frightening odyssey until mid-December, when his pigmentation finally faded. He headed home to Mansfield, Texas, to write a series of articles for *Sepia*.

The first story appeared in March 1960, igniting a media firestorm. *Time* and *Life* called him, as did the wire services and television networks. "I like to see good in the white man," he told a stream of interviewers. "But after this experience, it's hard to find it in the Southern white."

Liberals praised his courage. Segregationists condemned his treachery. Angry residents of Mansfield hanged the newly famous author in effigy. Death threats—by phone and mail—began arriving in Griffin's household. The pressure grew so intense that he decided in August to temporarily move his family to Mexico. "It was too great an injustice to our children to remain," he said.

Griffin expanded his articles into a book the following year, reaching an audience much broader than *Sepia* could command. Hundreds of thousands of white readers, especially those of college age, credited *Black Like Me* with awakening them to the evils of racial injustice. *Newsweek* hailed it as a "piercing and memorable document." *Saturday Review* called it a "scathing indictment of our society."

Griffin remained busy for several years as a lecturer—endlessly recounting the tale of his racial conversion—but he eventually grew tired of the road. He drifted willingly from the spotlight, returning to public attention only upon his death in 1980.

Rumors flew that *Black Like Me* had caused his untimely demise at the age of 60, that oxsoralen had afflicted him with terrible skin cancer. But the truth was much less dramatic. Diabetes and heart disease were prominent among Griffin's several deadly maladies, according to his widow, though cancer was not. "He died," she said wearily, "of everything."

* * *

Unenthusiastic and *reluctant* were the kindest adjectives for Dwight Eisenhower's stance on civil rights. The former general had spent much of his life in segregated surroundings—the army wasn't integrated until 1948, the year he left active service—and he saw no reason to compel others to mingle with different races.

Ike privately expressed sympathy for Southern whites. "These are not bad people," he said to Chief Justice Earl Warren in 1954. "All they're concerned about is to see that their sweet little girls are not required to sit in school alongside some big overgrown bucks." Warren and his Supreme Court colleagues were not persuaded. They ruled shortly thereafter, in *Brown v. Board of Education,* that segregated schools were unconstitutional.

Eisenhower remained on the sidelines during the mid- and late fifties, doing little to contradict Southern politicians who defied desegregation orders. He stirred only when Orval Faubus, the governor of Arkansas, mobilized the National Guard in 1957 to bar black students from Little Rock's Central High School. Eisenhower dispatched paratroopers to integrate the school—not to effect social change, he said, but to uphold federal authority.

It stood to reason that Ike would be offended by the sit-in movement, which had engulfed the South by mid-March. Protesters were not only stirring up racial tension, but were flouting state and local laws—actions certain to incite his anger.

Reporters were consequently amazed when Eisenhower endorsed the sit-ins at his March 16 press conference. "If a person is expressing such an aspiration as this in a perfectly legal way," the president said, "then I don't see any reason why he should not do it." He predicted that the day would come when all Americans were treated equally, "regardless of inconsequential differences [such] as race."

Eisenhower insisted that he had always believed in civil rights, yet had proceeded carefully, aware that equality could not be attained quickly. But white Southerners—who had counted the president as a silent supporter—were stunned by his apparent reversal. South Carolina Governor Ernest Hollings voiced their collective shock when he accused Eisenhower of doing "great damage to peace and good order."

Hollings had reason to worry about such things. More than 1,000 students from two all-black colleges had marched in Orangeburg, South Carolina, the previous day, intending to stage sit-ins at downtown lunch counters. They were stopped by a cordon of police cars and fire trucks. Officers fired tear-gas canisters and sprayed high-pressure fire hoses. They arrested 388 students, herding them to a makeshift stockade alongside the courthouse.

Chuck McDew and James Clyburn were two of the young men milling in the outdoor pen. McDew, an Ohio native who disliked attending South Carolina State College, had been eagerly awaiting the end of the semester, when he would return home for good. But the Orangeburg protest radicalized him. "If there is ever going to be a change in the way this is," he said, "it should be now." Clyburn, who planned to become a Baptist preacher, experienced a similar revelation. He and McDew would go on to play wider roles in the civil rights movement.

Hollings blamed the students for the Orangeburg confrontation. Black protesters, he said, "think they can violate any law, especially if they have a Bible in their hands." He added darkly, "Our law enforcement officers have their Bibles, too."

This portent of racial confrontation—ominous though it was—could not match the bleak reality of life in the Union of South Africa, home to 3 million whites and 11.5 million people with brown or black skins. Restrictive apartheid laws kept the whites in control. "We are not oppressors," said Prime Minister Hendrik Verwoerd. "We are Christians, and we attempt to do what is right." But his definition of proper behavior did not encompass racial equality. "South Africa is white man's country," he declared, "and he must remain the master here."

Verwoerd brooked no opposition. Great Britain's soft-spoken prime minister, Harold Macmillan, arriving the previous month on a goodwill tour, had shocked his host by condemning apartheid. "The wind of change is blowing through this continent," said Macmillan, who added that Great Britain could no longer support her former colony "without being false to our own deep convictions about the political destinies of free men." Verwoerd was curt in reply. "We have problems enough in South Africa," he told Macmillan, "without your coming to add to them."

His biggest problem was the political awakening of the black majority. Two organizations had risen in opposition to apartheid—the moderate African National Congress (ANC) and the militant Pan-Africanist Congress (PAC). Some of the ANC's younger members, rallied by 41-year-old Nelson Mandela, implored their elders to take a harder line against the government, thereby stealing the PAC's thunder. The head of the latter group, Robert Sobukwe, searched for a way to broaden its appeal, hoping to eventually surpass the ANC in total membership.

These conflicting desires, coupled with the intransigence of the Verwoerd government, would soon lead to tragedy.

Sobukwe made his move on March 18, lashing out at South Africa's pass laws, the very backbone of apartheid. Blacks were legally required to carry identification papers at all times. Anybody caught without a passbook was subject to imprisonment. The PAC leader urged blacks to leave their passes at home on March 21 and surrender to the police, flooding the authorities with more paperwork and prisoners than they could handle.

Blacks swarmed to police headquarters across the country, demanding to be arrested. The crowd was especially large in Sharpeville, 30 miles southwest of Johannesburg, where 20,000 blacks encircled the station. Only 20 white policemen were on duty.

The government dispatched air and ground support. Jets buzzed the throng, dipping within 100 feet of the ground. Four armored cars brought in reinforcements. The police silently pointed their guns at the unarmed crowd, then unexpectedly began to fire. Sixty-nine blacks died in a fusillade that lasted two minutes. "My car was struck by a stone," the police commander explained. "If they do these things, they must learn their lesson the hard way."

The Sharpeville massacre brought worldwide condemnation upon the South African government, even inspiring protests by white South Africans. More than 500 students marched at the University of Natal, carrying banners that read "Hitler 1939, Verwoerd 1960."

The leaders of the ANC spent the night debating how to capitalize on this revulsion. Mandela convinced his comrades to shed their moderate past and adopt a radical course. They agreed to publicly burn their passbooks. Oliver Tambo, one of the ANC's top officials, was designated to slip out of the country and establish an exile organization. If his colleagues were arrested, it would be up to him to continue the fight.

Verwoerd quickly imposed a state of emergency. More than 2,000 blacks were detained, Mandela among them, and the ANC and PAC were classified as illegal organizations. Their leaders—the few still at large—scurried underground.

Mandela had previously predicted that apartheid's demise was imminent. South Africa's "hated and doomed fascist autocracy," he said, was "soon due to make its exit from the stage of history." But his optimistic words seemed hollow in the wake of the Sharpeville massacre. The wind of change, at least for the moment, had blown itself out.

QUOTATIONS: MARCH 1960

"I don't especially care if it's constitutional or not."
—*Lee Mingledorff, the mayor of Savannah, Georgia, proposing that civil rights demonstrations be made illegal.*

"Nigger, you better think this over for a few more days, then let me know what you decide."

> *—The registrar in Webster County, Georgia, suggesting that black farmer Willis Wright abandon his attempt to register to vote. The registrar set a pistol on the counter as he spoke. Wright sought advice from a white friend, 35-year-old Jimmy Carter. They agreed that Wright would return to the registrar's office alone, and make it known that Carter, a respected member of the community, had told him to do so. He was allowed to register.*

"The flesh rides herd on the spirit. Soon I must lie down and let Morpheus embrace me."

> *—Everett Dirksen, the theatrical minority leader of the Senate, welcoming the end of the filibuster against the Civil Rights Act of 1960 on March 5.*

"We Like Ike. We Like Fidel Too."

> *—A sign in Rio de Janeiro, Brazil, sending an ambivalent greeting to President Eisenhower during his Latin American trip.*

"Our advertising, our motion pictures, our television, and our journalism are in large measure calculated to produce sexual thoughts and reactions. We live in a sea of sexual provocation."

> *—Attorney Charles Rembar, arguing before the U.S. Court of Appeals that it would be pointless to censor* Lady Chatterley's Lover.

"Certain it is that if the trend continues unabated, by the time some author writes of Lady Chatterley's granddaughter, Lady Chatterley herself will seem like some prim and puritanical housewife."

> *—Judge Leonard Moore, expressing concern about the implications of the* Lady Chatterley *decision. Moore reluctantly agreed with his colleagues that D. H. Lawrence's novel could not be suppressed, yet he was not happy about it.*

* * *

The Wisconsin campaign entered the home stretch in late March. John Kennedy, according to the polls, still held a healthy lead over Hubert Humphrey. But Kennedy knew he wasn't home free. He kept one eye tightly focused on the man he considered his most dangerous opponent, Stuart Symington.

The 58-year-old Symington wasn't on the ballot in Wisconsin. He hadn't even announced his candidacy for president, yet there was no doubt he was running. Harry Truman supported him, and Democratic Party bosses like David Lawrence and Carmine De Sapio considered him their best bet. Surveys by *Congressional Quarterly* and *U.S. News and World Report* found him to be more highly regarded on Capitol Hill and in state party headquarters than any other presidential contender.

Symington *looked* like a president, draping his 6-foot-2-inch frame in smartly tailored suits. He also possessed a rare combination of high-level administrative experience in the private and public sectors—a record considerably more impressive than that of Kennedy, who was 16 years younger.

Symington had made his mark as an entrepreneur, running companies that produced clay goods, radios, industrial steel, and electric fans. He became known as a managerial wizard whose magic touch could revive ailing businesses. It was this reputation, along with his links to fellow Missourian Truman, which earned Symington an appointment as secretary of the air force in 1947. He went on to run for the Senate in 1952—his first campaign for public office—and won by a large margin.

The next logical target was the White House. Truman encouraged his protégé to go for it, but cautioned him to avoid the primaries, which the former president considered a waste of time. Symington took his advice, wooing delegates as an unannounced candidate. But the strategy wasn't working. Kennedy and Humphrey were attracting all the press coverage, pushing him into the shadows.

The Missouri senator finally dialed his mentor's home and suggested it might be time for a formal announcement. Truman agreed. Symington officially joined the field the very next day, March 24, in the same room where Kennedy had made his entrance in January.

Many of his friends, however, began to wonder if Symington's announcement meant anything. He was a surprisingly lethargic campaigner, reserving plenty of time in his schedule for rest and relaxation. "I believe that in his heart of hearts, he never craved the presidency the way so many others do," said Clark Clifford, a fellow Truman appointee. "To be sure, he wanted to be president, but he was not willing to go to any and all lengths to achieve his goal."

Similar things were said about the party's presidential nominee in 1952 and 1956, 60-year-old Adlai Stevenson, who was still considered a prospective candidate. The former Illinois governor grumbled constantly about the demands of campaigning. Other hopefuls had industriously crisscrossed the nation the previous summer, but not Stevenson. He had escaped on a lengthy European cruise. "All is sun and sea, crumbling castles and iced wine, laughter, reading, sleeping— and eating," he reported to friends.

His biggest problem was a reputation for indecisiveness. Jokes made the rounds about Stevenson's inability to choose. One of these fictional tales involved a speaking engagement, where he was told he had just five minutes before his turn at the podium. "Do I have time to go to the bathroom?" Stevenson asked an aide, who assured him he did. That merely led to another question: "Do I *want* to go to the bathroom?"

Yet Stevenson's eloquence and wit had won him millions of supporters. They remembered his 1952 pledge to "talk sense to the American people" and his graceful concession speech after losing to Eisenhower. "Governor, you educated the country with your great campaign," a woman told him that night. Stevenson merely laughed. "A lot of people," he said, "flunked the course."

His loyal fans were now demanding a third campaign, a challenge that Stevenson rejected unequivocally. Yet there was reason to believe he could be persuaded. A key factor was his dislike for Kennedy, whom he considered inexperienced and arrogant. "That young man, he never says please, he never says thank you," Stevenson told friends. "He never asks for things. He demands them."

All Stevenson needed, his backers decided, was an emphatic push. James Doyle, the former chairman of Wisconsin's Democratic Party, began assembling a campaign team. Mike Monroney, a senator from Oklahoma, threw his weight behind the cause, as did Eleanor Roosevelt. She casually dismissed Kennedy, Humphrey, and the other active candidates as not being of Stevenson's caliber. "The Democrats," she said, "have a lot of good vice presidential material."

The Draft Stevenson Committee—unauthorized by its candidate— opened its headquarters in New York on April 11. Reporters hounded Stevenson for his reaction. What would he do if the Democratic convention drafted him as its nominee? "If I said I'd accept a draft, I'd be courting it," he said. And if not? "If I said I would not," he laughed, "I'd be a draft evader." A happy press corps had its headline, and the Stevenson committee still had reason to hope. Its candidate had not completely shut the door.

No such doubts seemed to plague Lyndon Johnson, the 51-year-old senator from Texas. A friend remembered Johnson exclaiming as a young congressman in the thirties, "By God, I'll be president some-day!" He had always been a man in a hurry—reaching the House of Representatives in 1937 at the age of 28, coming within 1,300 votes of winning a Senate seat 4 years later, finally edging his way into the Senate by an 87-vote margin in 1948. The latter campaign—rife with fraud on behalf of both Johnson and his opponent, Coke Stevenson—would earn the new senator the nickname of "Landslide Lyndon," an appellation he despised.

The secret to Johnson's rapid advancement was his deftness in currying favor with political elders. He became a protégé of two congressional giants—Sam Rayburn, the speaker of the House; and Richard Russell, the South's most respected senator. Those connections paid off repeatedly.

Senate Democrats needed a new floor leader in 1953, with Russell the clear favorite to fill the job. But he passed. "I think Lyndon is entitled to a promotion," he said. Johnson, still only 44, became the youngest and liveliest leader in Senate history. He carried the status of every bill in his head—who would vote aye, who was opposed—and could predict any roll call with uncanny accuracy. If he wanted a bill passed, he pulled out all the stops to convert recalcitrant colleagues. "Well, he'd argue with them, he'd promise them benefits," said A. Willis Robertson of Virginia. "And then he'd threaten the hell out of them."

The presidency was now in Johnson's sights, but formidable barriers stood between him and the White House. His intense schedule, horrible eating habits, and chain smoking had brought the inevitable heart attack in 1955—so severe that doctors originally estimated his odds of survival at 50-50. Whispers about his health still dogged him five years later, as did concerns about his Southern heritage. Zachary Taylor had been the last resident of the South to be elected president, 112 years in the antebellum past. "Johnson always told me that no Southerner would ever be nominated for president on the Democratic ticket in his lifetime," said an aide, Jack Valenti.

The Texas senator consequently seemed to be of two minds about the 1960 race. He lusted after the presidency, yet believed the fates were solidly against him. "He would authorize the establishment of a campaign headquarters, and then refuse to allow it to do anything," recalled another aide, George Reedy. "He would authorize his staff to draw up campaign proposals, and then forbid any action." He steadfastly refused to make a formal announcement, saying that his job as Senate majority leader was keeping him busy enough.

Some of his supporters, however, began to worry that he lacked the gumption to pursue the job of his dreams. "I didn't know that he wasn't going to do one thing himself, because nobody can get out and do all the work for a man," groused a former vice-chairwoman of the Democratic National Committee, India Edwards, whose frustration grew as she tried to line up convention delegates for Johnson that spring. "And according to the way I looked at it, he didn't do a thing in 1960 to help himself. Absolutely nothing."

5

April: Paper Tigers

The Constitution decrees that an "actual enumeration" of the nation's population must be conducted "within every subsequent term of ten years," a requirement that came due on April 1, 1960. The U.S. Census Bureau dispatched an army of 170,000 workers that morning. They carried identical 14-pound cardboard satchels as they rang every doorbell in every city, town, village, and hamlet from Lubec, Maine, to Adak, Alaska.

These enumerators gathered basic information about the people at each address. Every fourth household was subjected to a so-called "long form" that was considerably more intrusive, even asking what time the residents awoke and how many TV sets they owned. The chief breadwinner at 1600 Pennsylvania Avenue in Washington dutifully reported that his house had running water, flush toilets, and 132 rooms. The only permanent residents, said Dwight Eisenhower, were himself, his wife, and her maid.

The census of 1890 was considered the most significant event in the history of American demography. It had identified a generally continuous string of white settlements from one coast to the other, providing the first statistical evidence that the frontier had disappeared and the young nation had matured. The census of 1960 would prove to be equally important, documenting another seismic shift in the country's demographic balance. "The fact of a new era was plain," historian Eric Goldman wrote about the data collected on April 1. "The leadership of the town or the merely urban American was waning."

Big cities clearly were on the decline. The core communities of 14 of the nation's 15 largest metropolitan areas had shrunk since 1950.

The city of Detroit lost 180,000 people during the 10 years leading up to 1960, while New York City dropped by 110,000 people, St. Louis by 107,000, and Chicago by 70,000. The sole exception was Los Angeles, a sprawling, chaotic city that defied the classic model of urban development.

Closer inspection of the new data pinpointed two reasons for this decay. Immigration had always been the driving force behind the growth of America's major cities, but the flow of immigrants had slowed. America had only 9.7 million foreign-born citizens in 1960, the lowest number in the 20th century. Race was also a factor. The influx of Southern blacks to Northern cities had triggered an opposite response that was becoming known as "white flight." Negroes accounted for 54 percent of the residents of Washington, D.C., in 1960, making it the first city in American history with a black majority.

Rural areas were also losing population. Nearly a quarter of all Americans had lived on farms as recently as 1940, but modern machinery had greatly reduced the manpower required for agriculture. Only 9 percent of the nation's citizens were farmers as of 1960, the first time that figure had ever fallen below 15 percent.

Yet the country, as a whole, was prospering, even though big cities and small farms were struggling. America's population, propelled by the Baby Boom, had soared from 150.7 million in 1950 to 179.3 million in 1960—an eye-popping gain of 19 percent in a single decade. The country was adding 7,836 people every day, 326 every hour.

Two-thirds of this increase was occurring in the new promised land—suburbia—which offered young white families a bountiful supply of modern homes, freedom from urban congestion, and a soothing lack of racial diversity. Six million people moved from cities to suburbs during the fifties—the greatest mass exodus in American history—and they quickly added millions and millions of babies to the population.

"To build the vast girdle of suburbia about each of our withering cities," marveled Theodore White, "has required a national exertion greater than that of clearing the wilderness; housing has thus become our largest single industry." Nineteen million new homes had sprouted on the American landscape since World War II, mostly in suburbia. City dwellers typically rented apartments, duplexes, or row houses, but the suburban ethos required a family to hold title to a freestanding house. The nation's homeownership rate topped 60 percent in 1960, the first time that had ever happened.

Life was different in the suburbs in other ways. Many dads spent so much time commuting to and from jobs in the distant city that they became curiously disengaged from family life, at least during the workweek. Adlai Stevenson clucked that suburbia was producing "a strange half-life of divided families and Sunday fathers."

Organized activities for children—unheard of in the city—helped to fill the void. Stay-at-home moms doubled as chauffeurs, shepherding their kids to an endless round of Boy Scout and Girl Scout meetings, Little League games, and swimming lessons. "If the theory of evolution is still working," suggested a *Time* article, "it may well one day transform the suburban housewife's right foot into a flared paddle, grooved for easy traction on the gas pedal and brake."

A second demographic change—one nearly as important as the blossoming of suburbia—was confirmed by the 1960 census. The two dominant sections of the country, the Northeast and Midwest, were losing their demographic momentum, while the most sparsely settled sections, the South and West, were picking up speed.

Only 6 Northeastern and Midwestern states surpassed the national growth rate of 19 percent between 1950 and 1960, but 13 Southern and Western states did so. Florida led the country with a population increase of 79 percent, followed by Nevada at 78 percent and Arizona at 74 percent. Northern growth rates were anemic by comparison—Illinois at 16 percent, New York at 13 percent, and Pennsylvania at 8 percent.

There were several reasons for this shift toward the Sunbelt, as the South and West would collectively become known. Perhaps the most important factor was the wider availability of air conditioning, which made tropical or desert climates tolerable for transplanted Northerners. Window-mounted air conditioners that cooled a single room had been difficult to obtain prior to 1950, but annual production rose to 3 million units by 1960.

The growth of the South and West was also fueled by a new restlessness. Hundreds of thousands of retirees headed to the Sunbelt after World War II, as did military veterans seeking a fresh start. Northeasterners and Midwesterners—both young and old—no longer seemed as firmly rooted to their hometowns. The 1960 census found that 30 percent of adults were living in a state other than the one in which they had been born. The comparable figure in 1940 had been 23 percent.

Northern industries and retail chains were also drawn to the Sunbelt. They found the growing population base attractive, to be sure, but also liked the lower wages, smaller taxes, and lack of union activity. Ralph McGill, the liberal editor and publisher of the *Atlanta Constitution*, believed that this influx of Northern capital and executive skill would prove to be the South's salvation. Southern merchants and managers, he wrote, had largely "gone to seed." The best hope for the region's revitalization lay with "executives, young and old, who [have] poured into the South to direct the new assembly and production plants and the burgeoning retail business."

Not everybody agreed with McGill's analysis—many white Southerners hated the North for stirring up the dangerous issue of civil rights—but there could be no doubt about the demographic trend illuminated by the census. The South was definitely on the rise again.

LEXICON: APRIL 1960

Brasilia

Brazil transferred its capital on April 21 from the coastal metropolis of Rio de Janeiro to Brasilia, a new inland city. The scope of the four-year project was mind-boggling: 60,000 workers had been employed in Brasilia's construction, 1.6 billion cubic feet of earth had been moved, and 600,000 trees had been transplanted. Its futuristic buildings, designed by Oscar Niemeyer, seemed to have been transported from the 21st century. "You will not say that you have seen similar things anywhere else," Niemeyer boasted. Visitors could not disagree.

Channel Tunnel

Plans were first drawn in 1802 for a tunnel beneath the English Channel, though drilling didn't begin until the 1880s. British generals scuttled the project, contending that an invading army could swarm through the tunnel. There the matter stood until April 20, 1960, when a multinational consortium announced a $280 million project to connect France and Great Britain with three channel tunnels. Leo d'Erlanger, chairman of the Channel Company, pledged to make "a last, glorious effort to try and get this through." Thirty-four years would pass before the project was completed.

Gateway Arch

A design competition was held in 1948 for the Jefferson National Expansion Memorial, a park envisioned for the Mississippi River shoreline in St. Louis. Eero Saarinen's soaring 580-foot stainless steel arch—later expanded to 630 feet—was the winning entry. His notes casually described his creation as "symbolizing the gateway to the West, the national expansion, and whatnot." Progress was agonizingly slow. The site for the Gateway Arch wasn't cleared until 1957, and it took another three years to line up funding. Work on the Arch's subfoundation finally began in 1960.

Pay TV

Readers who settled down with the *New York Times* on April 1 learned that Zenith Radio Corporation and RKO General Incorporated were joining forces to test a new concept called "pay TV." The two companies planned to scramble the signal of Channel 18 in Hartford, Connecticut, and transmit commercial-free movies, sports, and cultural programming. Subscribers would rent decoding boxes to unscramble the picture. The major networks were not pleased. "If the pay system develops," grumbled Robert Sarnoff, NBC's president, "free television, as we know it, would face disintegration."

Smog

Los Angeles had been enveloped by an acrid, yellowish-gray cloud for more than a decade. Everybody called it "smog"—a linguistic merger of smoke and fog—but the name was inaccurate. The real culprits were hydrocarbons and nitrogen oxides emitted by factories and automobiles. California's state legislature fought back on April 6. It passed the nation's first anti-smog law, requiring the installation of devices to reduce automotive emissions. "In three to four years, we'll rarely have smog," predicted Smith Griswold, the director of the Los Angeles County Air Pollution Control District.

Tiros I

The earliest satellites were drones whose only task was to float through space. *Sputnik,* for all of its notoriety, did little more than beep. But the newest satellites were designed to be useful. *Tiros I,* which was launched on April 1, was built to monitor the weather. Its two cameras transmitted pictures to NASA's ground stations, where meteorologists were able to observe something they had never seen before, large-scale cloud patterns. "Hurricanes spawned anywhere over vast oceanic areas can be detected much earlier than ever before," crowed Francis Reichelderfer, the chief of the Weather Bureau.

Lyndon Johnson is among the onlookers as a NASA project manager explains the wizardry of Tiros I: "Hurricanes . . . can be detected much earlier than ever before." (Warren Leffler/Library of Congress)

***

John Kennedy's family was even busier than the census enumerators during the opening days of April. Mother Rose and her daughters hosted receptions from one end of Wisconsin to the other. Campaign manager Robert entertained service clubs and farm cooperatives with tales of his investigations of labor racketeers. Youngest brother Ted gamely made the first ski jump of his life in front of an enthusiastic crowd.

"I feel like an independent merchant competing against a chain store," moaned Hubert Humphrey, whose father had struggled to keep the family drugstore open during the Great Depression. The Kennedys intended to drive Humphrey from the race. A rout in the April 5 primary would not only send him crawling back to the Senate but would also force Lyndon Johnson, Stuart Symington, and Adlai Stevenson to think twice before gearing up their presidential campaigns.

The Wisconsin primary was actually 10 contests in one—separate elections for convention delegates in each of the state's 10 congressional districts—and the Massachusetts senator was hoping for a sweep. Ben Bradlee, a *Newsweek* reporter, asked him to make a public prediction. Kennedy declined to be so bold, though he did offer to write his forecast on a slip of paper and seal it in an envelope, provided that Bradlee did the same. The senator dropped the envelopes into a drawer on his plane.

The primary was several days in the past before the men encountered each other again. Bradlee asked about the envelopes, and Kennedy dug them out. "Kennedy 7, Humphrey 3," read the reporter's slip. The candidate's prediction had been even more upbeat: "JFK 9, HHH 1."

But election night didn't go according to plan.

Humphrey surprised everybody by seizing an early lead. He led by 6,500 votes at 9 p.m., as Kennedy glumly watched the returns in his Milwaukee hotel suite. The balance gradually shifted, with Kennedy eventually winning by 109,000 votes, but the crucial district-by-district tallies didn't go nearly as well. Humphrey defied the pundits by carrying 4 of 10. Democratic Party leaders noted that Kennedy's weakest performances came in the 4 districts with the heaviest concentrations of Protestant voters.

"There was a terrible sense of gloom in our headquarters on election night as the results came in," recalled Larry O'Brien. "Kennedy was pacing and shaking his head and biting his fingers—all the nervous habits he possessed. We watched Humphrey on television talking about the moral victory he had won. I felt sick."

Kennedy's family members and friends, steeped though they were in politics, found it difficult to decipher the conflicting statewide and district results. "What does it mean?" asked one of his sisters.

"It means that we've got to go to West Virginia in the morning and do it all over again," the candidate replied unhappily. "And then we've got to go on to Maryland and Indiana and Oregon and win all of them."

Humphrey's aides, anticipating the worst in Wisconsin, had been gently nudging him in recent days to face the inevitable. If he couldn't beat Kennedy in one of Minnesota's neighboring states, they said, his prospects were unlikely to be better someplace else. They thought he should withdraw.

But that was before the votes were counted. Humphrey now began to entertain the notion that he could win the Democratic nomination. "I must say," he later admitted, "that I may have become a little intoxicated with the belief that it was an outside possibility."

The upcoming West Virginia primary intrigued him. Organized labor was strong there, and the state was heavily Protestant—two factors in his favor. Financial considerations also affected his thinking. "I paid a thousand-dollar filing fee in that state and decided, by cracky, I couldn't get the thousand dollars back," he said. "I'd better go on in and make the race."

So it was settled. Kennedy and Humphrey would battle again on May 10 in West Virginia. "I was going to try and get a ride with Jack on his plane," Humphrey laughingly told reporters, "but he thought I ought to catch the next bus." The Minnesota senator actually borrowed $2,000 from a friend and flew to Charleston, the state capital.

West Virginia was a strange place for a high-level political showdown. It was a rural, impoverished state in an urban, increasingly affluent country. Joe Kennedy had argued strenuously that there was no reason for his son to enter such an atypical primary. "It's a nothing state," he sputtered, "and they'll kill him over the Catholic thing."

But Jack disagreed. He and his advisers saw no evidence of a substantial anti-Catholic bias in West Virginia. Several Catholics had been elected, without controversy, to the current state legislature. Al Smith, the epitome of the urban Catholic politician, had won the very same West Virginia primary en route to the 1928 Democratic presidential nomination.

A private report reinforced Kennedy's confidence. His pollster, Louis Harris, had conducted an extensive survey in West Virginia earlier in the year. It showed Kennedy leading Humphrey by 40 percentage points, precisely the type of landslide that had eluded him in Wisconsin. He looked forward to finishing off his tenacious opponent once and for all.

Kennedy's enthusiasm, however, would soon wane. Harris conducted another poll in mid-April to see if anything had changed. Humphrey, by then, had earned positive publicity for his Wisconsin comeback, and public awareness of Kennedy's Catholicism had grown substantially. The result was a turnaround of dramatic proportions. Harris's new survey showed Humphrey ahead by 20 points.

Kennedy, who had not yet arrived in West Virginia, placed an urgent call to aide Kenny O'Donnell, who was already in Charleston.

"Tell me, Kenny," said the candidate, "is there any way we can win down there?"

"Yes," said O'Donnell. "You can convert."

West Virginians' latent distrust of Catholics seemed to be as strong as Old Joe had predicted. Even longtime residents of the state were amazed. Raymond De Paulo, the general manager of a commercial bakery in Beckley, West Virginia, was a volunteer with the Kennedy campaign. He encountered unexpected resistance from close friends—Baptists and Methodists—who expressed horror at the prospect of a Catholic president. "I asked what their objections were," said De Paulo, himself a Catholic. "Well, they didn't want this country run from Rome."

It was an assertion that was being heard more and more frequently—not only in West Virginia, but throughout the country. Even Harry Truman was warning that Catholics did not believe in the separation of church and state, that their ultimate allegiance was to the Vatican. "You don't want to have anyone in control of the government of the United States who has another loyalty, religious or otherwise," the ex-president said darkly.

Jacqueline Kennedy tried to make light of the situation. "I think it is unfair for Jack to be opposed because he is a Catholic," she told friends. "After all, he's such a poor Catholic." Her husband's first impulse was to ignore the controversy—a strategy that clearly wasn't working. Everything, in fact, suddenly seemed to be going wrong. Kennedy's energy was lagging, and his voice was beginning to fail. Surrogate speakers, including 28-year-old political neophyte Ted Kennedy, were pressed into service at several stops.

The candidate finally bowed to reality on April 19 in Wheeling, West Virginia, deciding to confront the religious issue head-on. "I am a Catholic," he told the crowd in Wheeling. "But the fact that I was born a Catholic, does that mean I can't be president of the United States? I'm able to serve in Congress, and my brother was able to give his life, but we can't be president?" He moved on to Fairmont the same day, asking, "Is anyone going to tell me that I lost this primary forty-two years ago when I was baptized?"

His opponent was riding high. "Here Comes Humphrey," declared a huge sign on the Minnesota senator's bus. He brought hope to people accustomed to unemployment and poverty. Boarded-up windows on abandoned homes and businesses were mocked as "Eisenhower curtains" in West Virginia, but Humphrey promised to let the sunshine in. His administration, he pledged, would create jobs and show real compassion for the poor. It would focus on problems at home, not abroad. "The next time you take a trip, don't go just to India," he publicly challenged the incumbent president. "Stop off in West Virginia."

The Democratic contenders who had bypassed West Virginia were watching with keen interest. Robert Byrd, a young senator who supported Lyndon Johnson for president, exhorted his fellow West Virginians to vote for Humphrey. It was the only way to stop Kennedy, he said. "If you're for Adlai Stevenson, Senator Stuart Symington, Senator Johnson, or John Doe," Byrd warned, "you better remember that this primary may be your last chance."

Kennedy began showing the strain. He snapped to reporters that Humphrey was a "hatchet man" who was "being used" by Johnson and Symington. Humphrey shot back, "He's acting like a spoiled juvenile." The uncharacteristic crack in Kennedy's cool facade confirmed the reversal in the polls. Humphrey had all the momentum.

But there were some things he didn't have. Money, for instance. It was customary for candidates in West Virginia to spread cash around—stipends to key volunteers, donations to Democratic county leaders, "walking around" money to voters. Herb Waters, a Humphrey staffer, explained the concept to his underfunded boss one April night.

"Well, what does this entail?" Humphrey asked. "What do we have to do?"

"Frankly," Waters said, "it means money."

"How much?"

The aide shrugged. "I don't know, but I've told the appropriate people we're prepared to put up $25,000. I felt we had to make the offer."

Humphrey was dumbfounded. It seemed an impossibly large sum. "What," he finally asked, "was the response?"

Waters shook his head. "I was laughed out of the office," he said.

RISING STAR: ISAAC STERN

He was no child prodigy—the music didn't come quite that easily—but Isaac Stern was always willing to work. The six-year-old boy began taking violin lessons in 1926, just five years after his family arrived in California from Ukraine. He practiced diligently and quickly became proficient.

The rich tone emanating from his violin set Stern apart from the other students at the San Francisco Conservatory of Music, as did his vigorous, almost frenetic, bowing style. He hit the big time at age 17 with his New York debut at Town Hall, though the critics were underwhelmed. "I didn't know what to do," Stern recalled. "Finally I said to myself, 'Damn it, I want to play!' So I came back to New York the next year and got rave reviews, and maybe I didn't even play as well."

His core philosophy had been validated. Hard work, once again, had been rewarded. An emboldened Stern plunged deeper into his music. He was playing at least 150 dates a year by the mid-fifties, already recognized as one of the world's greatest violinists—and undoubtedly the busiest. "I have begged him not to play so much," his manager, Sol Hurok, moaned. "I tell him, 'The less you play, the longer you will play.' It does no good."

One of Stern's favorite venues was New York's Carnegie Hall, the 5-level, 2,800-seat auditorium that had been America's ultimate concert stage from its opening night in 1891, when Pyotr Ilyich Tchaikovsky had taken the podium. Playing Carnegie Hall remained the goal of young classical musicians the world over. Stern had appeared 51 times by 1959 and was scheduled to return on December 6 of that year.

He assumed it would be his final visit. The grand old building had fallen into disrepair. There hadn't been a renovation or even a major cleaning since 1948. Its major tenant, the New York Philharmonic, planned to flee 9 blocks uptown to the magnificent Lincoln Center for the Performing Arts being constructed on West Sixty-fifth Street. Carnegie Hall was to be demolished in the late spring of 1960 and replaced by a 44-story skyscraper.

"Everyone was sympathetic," Stern later wrote. "No one knew what to do." Instinct told him that hard work was the only answer. He invited fellow musicians and politically connected laymen to his apartment in mid-January to form the Citizens' Committee to Save Carnegie Hall.

Stern had brought them together, the group's members decided, so Stern should lead them. He plunged into negotiations with Mayor Robert Wagner and state legislators as the deadline loomed. They slowly cobbled together a plan. The city would buy Carnegie Hall for $5 million, and a nonprofit corporation would be created to operate the facility. Governor Nelson Rockefeller signed the appropriate state legislation on April 16, 1960, and the city gave its assent 12 days later. The historic structure had been saved from the wrecking ball.

The busiest man in classical music intended to return to his every-day life, but events conspired against him. The board of the new Carnegie Hall Corporation met on May 23 to choose a president. Stern was elected. He supervised a top-to-bottom renovation of the build-ing that summer. The dirty exterior was steam cleaned. The interior was painted white with gold trim. Every fixture was scrubbed and shined in preparation for the auditorium's grand reopening, a New York Philharmonic concert on September 27, 1960.

The guest soloist that night was Stern himself—his 53rd appear-ance on the famous stage. The audience greeted him with the lon-gest standing ovation that anybody could remember. It seemed to go on forever, palpable evidence of New York's gratitude for his initia-tive and persistence. "I actually felt my knees shaking," he recalled. "Stage fright was hardly unfamiliar to me, but I had never before felt it to that degree."

Stern's work ethic did not lessen after 1960. Sony issued a collection of his recordings in 1995, six years before his death. It took 44 com-pact discs to hold all of his music. But he also pursued a second career as an activist. He became a driving force behind the National Endow-ment for the Arts, a mentor to dozens of promising young musicians, and president of the Carnegie Hall Corporation for 41 years.

"The struggle to save Carnegie Hall was a watershed event in my life," he conceded. It had taught him how to work with others toward a common goal, how to use his skill and fame to effect social change, how to truly make a difference. "Nothing," said Isaac Stern, "was ever the same for me after Carnegie Hall."

***

Half a year had passed since the world's tallest airliner, Nikita Khru-shchev's TU-114, set a homeward course from Andrews Air Force Base to Moscow. Yet the world had not forgotten. The cautious optimism that blossomed after Khrushchev's visit with President Eisenhower—the Spirit of Camp David—remained strong in April.

The United States and Soviet Union still had differences and dis-agreements. They competed in outer space, suspected each other's intentions in Cuba, and bickered in Geneva, Switzerland, where dis-armament talks droned on. But the period since late September 1959 had been the most peaceful six months of the Cold War. And there was reason to believe that harmony would continue, perhaps even grow, in the years to come.

The summit meeting in Paris was only a month away, and President Eisenhower's trip to the Soviet Union was just two months off. Preparations for both were in full swing. The foreign ministers of the United States, Great Britain, and France met in Washington in mid-April to coordinate their plans for the summit. A smiling Secretary of State Christian Herter met reporters at the end. "A very satisfactory meeting," he said.

Khrushchev anticipated a similar outcome for Eisenhower's visit in June. The first secretary had drawn up an elaborate itinerary—a state dinner in the Kremlin; a special performance of the Bolshoi Ballet; and excursions to Leningrad, Kiev, and Irkutsk. Khrushchev told the American ambassador, Llewellyn Thompson, that he would be glad to add any destination Ike wished to see, even areas that were officially restricted, "despite the fact that as a military man, the president is an especially dangerous person." There were rumors that Khrushchev was taking golf lessons so that he might play a few holes with his distinguished guest.

Yet this good fellowship did not warm the hearts of Allen Dulles and his subordinates in the CIA. They still had a job to do—keeping tabs on the Soviet military—and they believed the president was hampering their efforts. Eisenhower had refused to allow any U-2 flights over Soviet territory since Camp David, a ban that Dulles disputed without success. The president insisted the stakes were simply too high. "If one of these aircraft were lost when we are engaged in apparently sincere deliberations," he explained, "it could be put on display in Moscow and ruin [my] effectiveness."

But Dulles would not be deterred. He assured Eisenhower of two things—first, a new flight was absolutely essential for American intelligence; and second, the Soviets still lacked the wherewithal to shoot down the U-2. The president finally consented to a single flight on April 9.

The mission was productive, yet it greatly angered Khrushchev. "It's as though they flew over laughing at our efforts," he later wrote. The resumption of overflights made him look foolish to the hardliners in the Kremlin. "He'd been telling obviously all the other leaders that Eisenhower was a good, solid guy, and you could trust him," said Charles Bohlen, who had served as American ambassador to

Moscow in the mid-fifties, "and then—whambo—this plane comes over, and this shook a lot of Khrushchev's authority in the Soviet Union."

The timing was unfortunate. Khrushchev was already taking heat from Presidium members who disapproved of massive troop reductions that he had announced in January. His East German headache was worsening, too, with the flow of refugees to West Berlin reaching its highest level in seven years. And now the Chinese—long his faithful followers—compounded these problems by publicly challenging Khrushchev's authority.

The Soviets and Mao Zedong had been staunch allies since the twenties, two decades prior to Mao's 1949 triumph in the Chinese civil war. The two countries signed a treaty of "friendship, alliance, and mutual security" on Valentine's Day in 1950, and thereafter portrayed themselves as international lovebirds, though there was never any doubt that the Soviets were the dominant partner in the relationship.

But tensions sprouted behind this facade of amity. Mao grew to believe that the Soviets were soft. He demanded that they deal forcefully with the United States, which he mocked as a "paper tiger," his favorite epithet for capitalist nations. "This paper tiger," Khrushchev reminded him, "has nuclear teeth." Mao was not persuaded. The Soviets, he said, should give atomic weapons to China. "If the imperialists unleash war on us, we may lose more than 300 million people," he conceded. "So what? War is war. The years will pass, and we'll get to work producing more babies than ever before." Khrushchev, unhappily aware that China outnumbered the Soviet Union by 400 million people, had no intention of turning his belligerent neighbor into a nuclear power.

There also was a personal component to this philosophical dispute. Mao derided Khrushchev as a spineless bureaucrat, "a time-server." He enjoyed maneuvering his Soviet counterpart into embarrassing situations, as when he staged a meeting in a Beijing pool in 1958. "He's a prizewinning swimmer," Khrushchev wailed, "and I'm a miner." The first secretary, for his part, mocked Mao as "a lunatic on a throne," and compared him to the discredited Joseph Stalin. "He treated the people around him like pieces of furniture," Khrushchev wrote, "useful for the time being, but expendable."

This petulance remained below the surface until April 16, 1960, when *Red Flag*, a Beijing newspaper, published an article commemorating the ninetieth anniversary of Vladimir Lenin's birth. The story was not so bold as to attack Khrushchev or the Soviets by name, yet it did condemn their apparent desire to live in peace with the United States. "The imperialist system will not crumble by itself," *Red Flag* warned. It suggested that atomic war might be the most effective means to defeat the Americans: "The victorious people would create very swiftly a civilization thousands of times higher than the capitalist system and a truly beautiful system for themselves."

Capitalist leaders—accustomed to viewing the Soviets and Chinese as a communist monolith—were taken aback by their ideological dispute. China's willingness to speak its mind, even in muted language, had the potential to alter the balance of power more dramatically than any other event since the Korean War. Mao obviously was worried that his Soviet counterpart might succeed at the summit. If Khrushchev and the capitalists achieved peaceful harmony in Paris, Mao appeared willing to break off in a pugnacious direction.

The Soviet-Chinese dispute would escalate as 1960 progressed. Khrushchev attacked Mao by name at a June meeting of world communist leaders in Bucharest, Romania. Mao, he said, was "oblivious of any interests other than his own, spinning theories detached from the realities of the modern world." And, Khrushchev being Khrushchev, he couldn't resist a crude insult, ridiculing Mao as "a Buddha who gets his theory out of his nose." The Chinese representative, Peng Zhen, snapped back that the Soviet leader was "patriarchal, arbitrary, and tyrannical."

The Soviets canceled industrial, technical, and scientific assistance to China three weeks after the verbal fireworks in Romania, abruptly recalling 1,400 Soviet engineers and their families. Six hundred contracts and projects came to a screeching halt. The Chinese accused the Soviets of ripping up blueprints, leaving factories half finished, and stealing the results of joint research projects.

Much of this was unknown to American officials at the time. The Bucharest quarrel had taken place behind closed doors, and the Chinese had been informed by a diplomatic note—not a public announcement—that their aid was being cut off. But details leaked soon enough. *Time* learned of the withdrawal of Soviet technicians six weeks after Moscow issued the order, though it failed to grasp the story's true dimensions. "The official explanation," the magazine dutifully reported, "is that the Soviet experts are leaving after the expiration of their contracts." Its headline, on the other hand, perfectly depicted the sudden frost that had descended on the communist world. The Soviet

Union and China, according to *Time,* could now be called "The Frigid Friends."

QUOTATIONS: APRIL 1960

"It is still much more effective to build instruments to make scientific observations than it is to support and maintain a man comfortably and helpfully in a spacecraft."
> *—James Van Allen, a pioneer in the study of extraterrestrial radiation, expressing his preference for unmanned satellites. He conceded, however, that astronauts might be superior in some ways. "There are many more subtle things that a man could report," he admitted, "such as, 'Gee whiz, I have a terrible headache,' or, 'I have just vomited all over the cabin.'"*

"They were very definite about not wanting ever to seem anxious, fearful, naive, immodest, irreverent, unkind, angry, jealous, or in any way uncertain that the whole enterprise was going to come out just fine."
> *—Loudon Wainwright, an editor with* Life, *describing the Mercury astronauts' insistence on being portrayed in heroic terms. The astronauts collectively sold the magazine the exclusive rights to their personal stories but retained veto power over the content of all articles.*

"He was as restive and as full of asperity and hot temper as he could be. The whole thing was irritating the hell out of him."
> *—Harry McPherson, an aide to Lyndon Johnson, describing his boss's unhappiness with the slow progress of the Civil Rights Act of 1960. Johnson finally maneuvered the bill through the Senate on April 8, after allowing Southerners to water down its key provisions.*

"Dick, here is my sword. I hope you will give it back to me so that I can beat it into a plowshare for the spring planting."
> *—Joseph Clark, a senator from Pennsylvania, speaking to the South's elder statesman, Richard Russell, after the Civil*

Rights Act was approved. Clark considered the vote a
reverse Appomattox—a triumph for segregationists—
because the bill had been rendered ineffective.

* * *

Republicans were starting to worry as April drew toward its close. President Eisenhower had promised that 1960 would be "the most prosperous year in our history," but his vision had not materialized. Economists were now detecting the first signs of a recession. Many of them placed the blame on Ike for insisting on a balanced budget.

Richard Nixon argued in private that it was time to "prime the pump" by loosening credit and increasing military spending. The vice president was haunted by a premonition that the recession might reach full flower around election day. Angry voters would be sure to punish the representative of the incumbent administration—namely, him. But Eisenhower ignored his suggestions. The president was determined to keep the budget in balance.

The quiet nature of Nixon's campaign also concerned many Republicans. The Democrats, with their contentious primaries, landed on the front page every day, while Nixon flitted around in virtual anonymity. Republican leaders pushed him to become more visible. John Bricker, the party's vice presidential nominee in 1944, sent a sharply worded note in April, which Nixon parried. "It would be unwise to start intensive campaigning at this point," he replied. "I feel very strongly that the time to be fresh and strong, both mentally and physically, is the month before election."

Nixon enjoyed the rare luxury of being able to look ahead to the fall campaign. Nobody was contesting him for the Republican nomination, and the odds were heavily against anybody who might jump into the race at this late date. Yet the party's two extreme wings, unexcited about Nixon, continued to hope for a miracle.

Conservatives had several reasons for dismay. They disapproved of the vice president's commitment to civil rights. They were worried—the kitchen debate with Khrushchev aside—that he might be too soft on the Soviets. Nixon had recently promised to "keep open every possible channel of communication" with Moscow, a pledge that right-wingers considered dangerously close to appeasement. And he appeared to lack the typical Republican enthusiasm for major corporations and moneyed interests. "I was basically for small business," Nixon would admit a quarter-century later. "I never was for big business. My source of strength was more Main Street than Wall Street."

Such ambivalence was unacceptable to the party's staunchest conservatives. They preferred plainspoken Barry Goldwater, a 51-year-old senator from Arizona, who had codified his philosophy in *The Conscience of a Conservative*, a book published in March. The federal government, Goldwater charged, was "a vast national authority out of touch with the people, and out of their control." Washington, in his opinion, needed to keep its nose out of people's business. "My aim is not to pass laws," he declared, "but to repeal them."

Goldwater was refreshingly blunt for a politician. He grew up as a self-described "spoiled well-off kid" in a prominent Arizona family and later worked for the department store chain that his grandfather had founded. His greatest distinction as a businessman came when he designed men's underwear decorated with large red insects—ants in the pants. *Women's Wear Daily* hailed him in 1939 as a "creative merchandising dynamo."

The Republican Party, desperately in need of a candidate, approached Goldwater about running for the Senate in 1952, largely because of his family name. He harbored no expectations of winning—his opponent was the Senate's majority leader, Ernest McFarland—but he scored an upset on the same night that his party elected a new president. "It was the Eisenhower victory that carried me in," Goldwater said. "I couldn't have made it without him."

Yet the new senator was no fan of Ike's moderate brand of Republicanism. Goldwater blasted Washington's involvement in social services ("the recipient of welfarism mortgages himself to the federal government") and civil rights ("the Constitution does not permit any interference whatsoever by the federal government in the field of education"). And he demanded a more forceful stance against the Soviets ("we must try to make the communist world free"), even if American commanders had to use nuclear weapons.

Goldwater established himself as the Republican Party's leading conservative by the late fifties. Fellow believers encouraged him to run for president. An unofficial campaign committee, Americans for Goldwater, sprang up in mid-1959. The prospective candidate didn't disavow the group, but he didn't help it, either. He was convinced that Nixon would be the nominee.

The publication of *The Conscience of a Conservative* in March 1960 would cast doubt on his modest calculations. The book became a best-seller, stunning everybody involved, especially the author. Goldwater received another shock when he delivered the keynote address at the South Carolina Republican convention on March 26, shortly after his book reached stores. The convention immediately voted to support him—and not Nixon—for the Republican nomination.

"Hell, I'm not looking for them," Goldwater sputtered after South Carolina's 13 delegates pledged their votes to him. "I'm not running for president. I'm backing Nixon." Louisiana and Arizona jumped on the Goldwater bandwagon before the end of the April. The senator discouraged these offers of support—"I never wanted it," he later said of the 1960 nomination—but he understood the frustration that lay behind them. Nixon had been drifting "far to the left," he wrote that spring to a fellow Arizona Republican, William Rehnquist, and "we must employ means to get him back on the right track."

Goldwater's unwillingness to run came as a great relief to Nixon's camp, but Nelson Rockefeller was not as cooperative. The New York governor's December withdrawal had baffled Nixon and his campaign director, Bob Finch—"to this day, I don't know why Rocky didn't run," Finch would say 25 years later—and they watched nervously for signs of his reemergence.

Their worst fears seemed to be confirmed when Rockefeller returned from a Venezuelan vacation in early April, jauntily telling reporters that he would not rule out being drafted by the Republican convention. "I'd cross that bridge if it came," he said. The party's liberal wing—declining in numbers, though still a potent source of campaign funds—rejoiced at this expression of interest by its hero.

Rockefeller was a mass of contradictions. He bored audiences as a public speaker, yet displayed an energetic, charismatic personality when dealing with people individually, slapping backs and yelling "hiya" as they pressed to meet him. He was as liberal on domestic affairs as most Democrats, and matched their ability to spend government money, too. "I like you, Nelson," Tom Dewey once said, "but I don't think I can afford you." Yet Rockefeller was as fiercely anti-communist as most conservatives.

It was easy to see how such a man might be politically dangerous to Nixon. Rockefeller became even more threatening on April 22, when he delivered a scathing speech in Philadelphia. The nation, he charged, was adrift, and it was time for a "bold, new approach" to world leadership. His speech sounded very much like a condemnation of the Eisenhower-Nixon team and a call for a fresh face on the

Republican ticket. Pundits began to speculate that Rocky would soon throw his hat into the presidential ring.

Richard Nixon—whatever his inner turmoil—watched these developments with outward calm. The rush of publicity for the Democratic contenders, the surge of enthusiasm for Goldwater, the abrupt intrusion of Rockefeller—all of these things were unfortunate, but they were to be expected in politics. Nixon still held the advantage, especially with the Paris summit less than a month away. Eisenhower's diplomatic successes were bound to give his vice president a welcome boost.

Yet nothing was certain. Nixon knew that the six months between the summit and the election would be a roller coaster—up one day, down the next. "Anyone who does not recognize that we were in for the fight of our lives must be smoking opium," he lectured an audience in Lincoln, Nebraska. "I believe we will win. But we must expect this to be one of the closest and hardest-fought campaigns in America's political history."

6

May: Spoiling for a Fight

One more flight was all that Allen Dulles wanted: one more U-2 mission over the Soviet Union. The angle of the sun was shifting as days grew longer in the Northern Hemisphere, making it difficult for the spy plane to snap pictures of Soviet missile bases. The window for high-altitude photography would soon close, not to reopen for several months. The CIA director asked President Eisenhower to authorize a final run.

Ike hesitated. "We don't want to have that thing up there while the summit's on," he said. He knew that the overflights infuriated Nikita Khrushchev. But Dulles promised the U-2 would be back in its hangar before the four world leaders gathered in Paris on May 16. Eisenhower approved a single flight for April 25.

Francis Gary Powers—a 30-year-old CIA pilot called Gary by his wife, Frank by everybody else—was tapped for the mission. Powers had left Virginia's Appalachian fringe in 1951 to enlist in the air force, rising to the rank of captain. He was vague about his reasons for resigning his commission in 1956, saying only that the opportunities would be better for him as a civilian pilot. His new job paid $30,000 a year, four times what he had earned in the military.

Money was important to Powers, who had seen precious little of it in Appalachia. A CIA officer, James Donovan, considered him the perfect man for a top-secret assignment as dangerous as a U-2 overflight. "Powers was a man who, for adequate pay, would do it," Donovan said, "and as he passed over Minsk, would calmly reach for a salami sandwich."

His family and friends were equally unconcerned. Frank had told them about his cushy job flying a NASA weather plane in Turkey. They were blissfully unaware that it was a CIA cover story, that he was actually preparing to fly 3,800 miles from a base near Peshawar, Pakistan, to Bodo, Norway, crossing a broad swath of the Soviet Union en route.

Clouds hung low over the flight path on April 25, so Powers bided his time. The dreary weather persisted until May 1, when the sun finally shone over his primary objectives. Eisenhower, despite his misgivings, gave the go-ahead for the mission. The U-2 roared skyward from Peshawar at 6:26 A.M.

The initial stage of the flight was uneventful. Powers zoomed over Tyuratam, home of the Soviet space program. His seven cameras fired into action. The U-2's automatic pilot began to sputter—an annoyance, not a serious problem—so he took manual control. He set course for Sverdlovsk.

That's when he heard a dull thump. The U-2 was abruptly illuminated by a brilliant orange flash. It began spinning wildly. Powers didn't know what had happened—a missile had exploded near the jet, firing shrapnel into its fuel lines and shearing its wings—but the plane was obviously doomed. He unfastened the cockpit's canopy and worked his way free.

The Soviets had been firing at U-2 overflights since 1958 without success. The radar officer who was tracking Powers's flight saw flakes of "snow" on his screen, indicating the jet might have been destroyed. He instinctively dismissed the possibility. "The target has discharged chaff," the officer shouted, "and is performing an evasive maneuver."

But Powers—parachuting toward enemy territory—decided not to evade his destiny. The CIA had given him a small poison needle. He briefly reached for it as he drifted toward earth but felt no desire to commit suicide. He landed in a field east of the Ural Mountains, where villagers disentangled him from his parachute and asked if he was all right. He responded in a language they didn't understand. "Are you Bulgarian?" one villager asked. Another had a different thought, writing "USA" on the dusty window of a car. Powers nodded. The Soviet state police, the KGB, were called to take him away.

Khrushchev was notified as he watched a May Day parade at the Kremlin. The CIA passed the unhappy news to a presidential aide, Andrew Goodpaster, who placed a call to his boss. The U-2, said Goodpaster, "is overdue and possibly lost."

Eisenhower and his advisers saw no reason for concern. The pilot, of course, had to be dead. The U-2, a fragile mechanism, had almost certainly disintegrated. If the Soviets made any announcement, they would only embarrass themselves by revealing how easily and repeatedly their airspace had been violated. The president decided to wait for Khrushchev to make a move. Perhaps the affair could be kept quiet.

The Soviet leader made his own calculations. "Father told me right away of his plan," his son, Sergei, later wrote. "He had decided to play hide-and-seek with the Americans." Khrushchev revealed the "bandit flight" in a May 5 speech to the national legislature, the Supreme Soviet, yet was careful to place the blame not on Eisenhower but on "Pentagon militarists." It was the first the world had heard of the U-2. The White House immediately conceded that a NASA weather plane might have strayed into Soviet airspace. It promised an investigation.

The president remained hopeful that the issue could be finessed, but his optimism was punctured a few hours later. Jakob Malik, the Soviet deputy foreign minister, attended a reception at the Ethiopian embassy in Moscow. A guest asked if the Soviets intended to file a formal protest over the U-2 incident. "I don't know for sure," Malik responded. "They're still questioning the pilot." The stunned American ambassador, Llewellyn Thompson, overheard Malik's slip. Thompson hustled back to his embassy. The wire he sent to Washington was labeled "Most Urgent."

Khrushchev had no choice but to return to the Supreme Soviet on May 7. "When I made my report two days ago," he grinned, "I deliberately refrained from mentioning that we have the remnants of the plane—and we also have the pilot, who is quite alive and kicking." The legislators cheered wildly. Khrushchev mocked the CIA's phony cover story ("Allen Dulles is no great weatherman"), held up a picture of Powers's poison pin ("the latest achievement of American technology for killing their own people"), and showed the photos the U-2 had snapped ("I must say that our cameras take better pictures").

Yet the Spirit of Camp David had not been extinguished, not totally. The first secretary again speculated that Eisenhower had been unaware of the U-2 mission. "I still believe," he said, "that those who met me [during his U.S. trip] want peace and friendly relations with the Soviet Union."

The president decided it was time to come clean. Dulles argued against accepting responsibility, as did Harold Macmillan, but Ike saw no other way. He publicly admitted on May 9 that the over-flights had been occurring for years, and that he had approved every single one. He defended the U-2 program as a justifiable risk to obtain valuable information about Soviet military capabilities and intentions. "No one," he said, "wants another Pearl Harbor."

The remnants of the U-2 went on display in Moscow's Gorky Park on May 10. Khrushchev toured the exhibit and then answered questions from several hundred journalists. What did he think of Eisenhower's statement? "Impudence," he spat, "sheer impudence." Would he still welcome the president to the Soviet Union in June? "Put yourself in my place and answer for me," he replied. "I am a man, and I have human feelings." Could the crisis be resolved? "You understand that if such aggressive actions continue, this might lead to war."

Khrushchev left for Paris four days later. He decided during the flight that he would demand an apology from Eisenhower. If one was not forthcoming, he would scuttle the summit he had so eagerly sought. "My anger," he later wrote, "was building up inside me like an electric force which could be discharged in a great flash at any moment."

A U-2 is disguised as a weather plane to support the Eisenhower administration's cover story: "No one wants another Pearl Harbor." (National Aeronautics and Space Administration)

Khrushchev informed Charles de Gaulle of his two preconditions—an American apology and punishment of the U.S. officials who had conceived Powers's mission—and de Gaulle passed the word to Eisenhower when the latter arrived in Paris. Ike had always thought of Khrushchev as an actor playing a part, and was inclined to dismiss the new demands as innocent bluster. But his advisers sensed that the summit was doomed. Defense Secretary Thomas Gates declared a state of alert on May 16, hours before the opening session. American soldiers, sailors, and airmen manned their battle stations, as the world waited to see what would happen in Paris.

De Gaulle called the summit to order at the Elysée Palace that morning. A red-faced Khrushchev, pulling out a large sheaf of papers, immediately demanded the floor. He launched into a blistering tirade against the United States and its Cold War policies. Eisenhower's trip to the Soviet Union, he announced, was hereby canceled. "Conditions have now arisen," Khrushchev said, "which make us unable to welcome the president with the proper warmth which Soviet people display toward fond guests."

Eisenhower watched impassively, though his face turned crimson. He slid a note to Christian Herter, his secretary of state. "I'm going to take up smoking again," it said.

Khrushchev worked himself into such a frenzy that he began shouting. De Gaulle told him to lower his voice. "The acoustics in this room are excellent," the French president said. Khrushchev briefly complied, yet continued to vent his outrage. "I have been overflown," he wailed, his volume heading toward its previous levels, and his host cut him off again.

"Yesterday," de Gaulle said, "that satellite you launched just before you left Moscow to impress us, overflew the sky of France eighteen times without my permission. How do I know that you do not have cameras aboard which are taking pictures of my country?"

Eisenhower grinned. Khrushchev, momentarily abashed, responded in a curious manner for a self-professed atheist. "As God sees me," he said, "my hands are clean."

The other leaders eventually had opportunities to speak. The overflights had been suspended, Eisenhower said, and "are not to be resumed." He trotted out the Pearl Harbor analogy again, stressing that the U-2's missions were not aggressive in nature. Macmillan chimed in that everybody at the table, including Khrushchev, employed spies. "Espionage," said the prime minister, "is an unpleasant fact of life."

But Khrushchev was in no mood to be concede these points. "I was all worked up, feeling combative and exhilarated," he later said. "As my kind of simple folk would say, I was spoiling for a fight." There had been no apology and no punishment of American underlings. His only option, he said, was to leave. And so he did. "Only *my* face is ruddy," he exulted after stalking out. "Eisenhower's is white. And Macmillan's has no color."

The other three leaders stayed at the table for a few minutes, talking among themselves, but there clearly was no point. De Gaulle touched Eisenhower on the elbow as they left the palace. "Whatever happens," the French president said, "we are with you."

It remained for Khrushchev to write the coda to this briefest of summits, which he did at a bizarre two-and-a-half-hour press conference on May 18. More than 3,000 reporters and photographers crowded into the Palais de Chaillot. They were jammed everywhere—standing in the aisles, sitting on windowsills, even squatting on top of phone booths. The air in the hot, noisy room was gray with cigarette smoke.

Khrushchev was at his energetic best. He gestured vigorously, repeatedly pointed his finger at his audience, and even swung his fists in uppercuts on one occasion. "To hear President Eisenhower, it would seem that the question of whether U.S. military planes will or will not fly over [the Soviet Union] depends on him and him alone," he shouted. "Just think—what presumption! Now he says they will not overfly—what magnanimity! This is to be decided by us and us alone. We shall shoot such planes down."

Eisenhower also exhibited flashes of his famous temper, though only in private. The face he displayed in public was typically stoic, occasionally disappointed. The only course for America now, he said, was to "tighten our belts, put our chins up a little higher, and if we can, be more eloquent in telling the story that we have."

It would not be that simple. Both sides were embarrassed—the Soviets by the weakness that four years of overflights had revealed, the Americans by the rhetorical abuse they had endured in Paris. The hard-liners in both countries insisted that national pride must be restored, that all talk of the Spirit of Camp David and peaceful coexistence must be forgotten. The Cold War was dialed up to full intensity.

Both leaders would pay a steep price for the follies of May. Khrushchev would henceforth be dogged by opponents—both Soviet and Chinese—who accused him of displaying atrocious judgment at Camp David and an unsteady hand during the U-2 crisis. Eisenhower would be castigated by domestic critics for the rest of his term. James Reston, writing in the *New York Times,* delivered the ultimate blow: "Mr. Eisenhower was responsible, directly or indirectly, for the greatest series of humiliating blunders suffered by the United States in a decade."

Eisenhower had envisioned the final year of his presidency as the capstone of his career, the foundation of his permanent legacy. He had been confident that his travels around the globe would burnish America's image and enhance the prospects for peace, but the summit had done neither. He had staked everything on personal diplomacy, and he had lost.

The president voiced these unhappy thoughts to his science adviser, George Kistiakowsky, late in the month. Eisenhower "began to talk with much feeling," his aide later wrote, "about how he had concentrated his efforts the last few years on ending the Cold War, how he felt that he was making big progress, and how the stupid U-2 mess had ruined all his efforts."

The president's term had eight months to run, but he no longer looked ahead with optimism. Eisenhower seemed to believe that his time had run out, that he had no more options to pursue. "He ended very sadly," Kistiakowsky wrote of their talk. "He saw nothing worthwhile left for him to do now until the end of his presidency."

LEXICON: MAY 1960

Fallout Shelters

Nelson Rockefeller wanted to require every New York homeowner to build a fallout shelter. Legislators balked at the $1.5 billion price tag, but Rocky insisted his plan offered the best hope of surviving an onslaught of Soviet missiles. "I would rather face political suicide," he said, "than have our country or state wiped out by a nuclear attack." He even pushed his idea on the famed Indian pacifist, Jawaharlal Nehru, when the latter visited New York in 1960. "He talked to me about nothing but bomb shelters," said a dazed Nehru. "Why does he think I am interested in bomb shelters?"

Mossad

"It was my job to catch our Jewish enemies like fish in a net and transport them to their final destination," bragged Adolf Eichmann, who supervised the execution of 6 million Jews during World War II. Eichmann mysteriously vanished after Nazi Germany's defeat. Israel's intelligence agency, the Mossad, finally discovered him in Argentina, posing as an autoworker named Ricardo Klement. Mossad agents kidnapped Eichmann on May 11, setting the stage for a dramatic trial in 1961. "Jews are not sheep to be slaughtered," declared Israel's premier, David Ben-Gurion, "but a people who can hit back."

Petroleum Deficit

Construction of the 41,000-mile interstate highway system began in 1956. Nearly 10,000 miles were completed by 1960. "The nation, invited by the new highways to become guzzlers of gasoline," wrote Theodore White, "learned to drive five miles for a six-pack of beer or a pound of butter." The United States had been a net exporter of petroleum until the fifties, but the increase in demand shifted the balance. America exported 71 million barrels in 1960 but imported 293 million the same year. The result was a massive petroleum deficit of 222 million barrels.

Operation Alert

The timing was coincidental, yet strangely prescient. A national civil defense drill, Operation Alert, was conducted on May 3. The White House already knew of the U-2 crisis, though everybody else would remain in the dark until Khrushchev's revelation two days later. The country assumed a war footing at 2:15 P.M., Eastern time. Cabinet members were helicoptered to a top-secret command post in Virginia. TV stations went off the air, businesses closed their doors, factories stopped production, and schoolchildren filed into shelters. America remained eerily quiet for the next half-hour.

Union Miniere du Haut Katanga

The news from the Congo was ominous. Fifty-seven people were killed in election-related violence in May. Outbound flights were packed with white settlers desperately fleeing before indigenous blacks took control on June 30. Recruiting new engineers from Belgium had always been a simple task for the colony's largest mining company, Union Miniere du Haut Katanga, but its pool of candidates was suddenly bone dry. The shortage of skilled labor was a serious problem, since the Congo produced 69 percent of the world's industrial diamonds, 49 percent of its cobalt, and 9 percent of its copper.

USS *Triton*

The new USS *Triton* was the world's largest submarine, 447 feet in length and 7,750 tons in displacement. Its skipper, Captain Edward Beach, anticipated an easy shakedown voyage, but his orders from the Pentagon were decidedly more ambitious. *Triton* slipped away from Connecticut on February 16, destined to become the first sub to circumnavigate the globe underwater. It surfaced off the Delaware coast on May 10 after cruising 41,500 miles in 84 days.

***

His son urged him to enter the Indiana primary, but Stuart Symington opted not to accelerate his lethargic pursuit of the Democratic presidential nomination. Harry Truman and Frank McKinney, an Indiana native who had once headed the Democratic National Committee, advised Symington to stay clear. "We didn't go into Indiana," son Jim recalled. "I think Frank McKinney said don't bother, because this is one place that Kennedy won't make it."

It was an inaccurate prediction. Symington's decision left a virtually clear field for the May 3 primary. Jack Kennedy pulled 80 percent of the vote, yet his aides were vaguely troubled. "I couldn't help wondering what kind of vote Stu Symington might have gotten in the Indiana primary if two fringe candidates had received 20 percent," admitted Larry O'Brien.

The focus shifted back to West Virginia, where things were not going well. Pundits agreed that Kennedy was still trailing Hubert Humphrey, and the margin might be too big to erase in the final week before the May 10 election. Kennedy, betraying no evidence of discouragement, intensified his efforts.

Franklin Roosevelt was still revered in West Virginia. Old Joe Kennedy, of all people, had the brainstorm of inviting FDR's son, Franklin Jr., to join Jack's team. It didn't matter that the patriarchs of the Roosevelt and Kennedy families had been bitterly estranged; nor that the late president's widow, Eleanor, questioned Jack's fitness for the nation's highest office. All that mattered was winning. The younger FDR held thumb and forefinger close together as he told West

Virginia audiences, "My daddy and Jack Kennedy's daddy were just like that." Reporters groaned, yet audiences ate it up.

FDR Jr., who had served six years in Congress, demonstrated real skills as a political attack dog. "A vote for Humphrey is a wasted vote," he said repeatedly, and he once went further than that. "He's a good Democrat," Roosevelt said of the Minnesota senator, "but I don't know where he was in World War II." John Kennedy quickly apologized. The slur, he said, had been extemporaneous, though Humphrey was unconvinced. He suspected Bobby Kennedy of engineering the slander.

Catholicism remained the biggest issue. Kennedy appeared on statewide television two days before the primary to reiterate his allegiance to the United States. Every president, he noted, took an oath to uphold the Constitution, which stipulated the separation of church and state. "If he breaks his oath," Kennedy went on, "he is not only committing a crime against the Constitution, for which the Congress can impeach him—and should impeach him—but he is committing a sin against God." He raised his hand from an imaginary Bible. "A sin against God," he repeated, "for he has sworn on the Bible."

Kennedy's message was transmitted to every corner of West Virginia, generously lubricated by a stream of cash. O'Brien solicited the support of county Democratic organizations in exchange for financial contributions, a process known as slating. "Once I confirmed that our slating arrangement was firm," he wrote, "I would hand over our agreed-upon share of the expenses, and we would take off for the next stop." The money came from a suitcase that O'Brien's secretary, Phyllis Maddock, kept under her hotel bed.

Such arrangements were common not only in West Virginia, but in Jack Kennedy's previous campaigns. His election to Congress in 1946, as Tip O'Neill recalled, was greased by $50 handouts, ostensibly in exchange for help at the polls. "They didn't really care if these people showed up to work," O'Neill said. "They were simply buying votes, a few at a time, and fifty bucks was a lot of money." Estimates of the largesse in West Virginia ranged widely. Investigative reporter Seymour Hersh concluded in 1997 that Kennedy spent $2 million to $4 million in advance of the primary. O'Brien always insisted the real figure was less than $100,000.

The total—whatever it might have been—outstripped the meager sum at the disposal of Kennedy's opponent. "I can't afford to run through this state with a little black bag and a checkbook," Humphrey complained. His aides felt the momentum shifting. Rein Vander Zee, his West Virginia campaign coordinator, was spreading cash around, too, but not enough to be effective. "I knew something was way wrong," he later said of the race's final days. "The Humphrey signs were down, and Kennedy signs were up."

Yet the press was unanimous in predicting a Humphrey victory. The *Wall Street Journal*'s forecast had the Minnesotan taking 60 percent of the vote. Kennedy, preferring not to await defeat in Charleston, returned home to Washington. He attended a movie on the evening of May 10, leaving the theater as the first totals were being released 250 miles to the west.

A telephone call from an excited Bobby Kennedy brought news of a landslide, though not the one that had been predicted. Jack was up by 20 percentage points. His last-ditch strategy had worked to perfection—the use of Franklin Roosevelt Jr., the neutralization of the religious issue, the extravagant distribution of cash. Kennedy's margin reached 84,000 votes by the end of the night. He won all but 7 of the state's 55 counties.

Kennedy hustled to the airport to join the celebration in Charleston. Humphrey, meanwhile, was facing facts. He gazed at a blackboard covered with election returns, joined by Joseph Rauh, the vice chairman of Americans for Democratic Action, the nation's preeminent liberal organization. "It was incredible," Rauh said. "We were losing sixty-forty almost everywhere." He remembered the episode as "one of the most excruciating, painful moments of my life, because it was over."

It was, indeed. Humphrey withdrew from the race that evening. "The truth is that I was whipped not only by money and organization but, more particularly, by an extraordinary man," he would say magnanimously toward the end of his life. But his supporters were bitter. His wife, Muriel, reacted with distaste when Bobby Kennedy kissed her that night. Aide Max Kampelman made no secret of his unhappiness. "All of us who were for Humphrey were rather sour about the process," he said, "particularly about West Virginia, where we had reason to believe that the election had been stolen by the Kennedys."

The candidates who had remained on the sidelines spoke bravely. "This primary will not be any more decisive than Wisconsin," said Symington. Lyndon Johnson chimed in, "The nation can start judging on the basis of merit." But the bandwagon was rolling. Two primaries followed on the heels of West Virginia, and both went Kennedy's way. He won 70 percent of the vote in Maryland on May 17, then took 51 percent in Oregon on May 20. His chief opponent in both elections was Wayne Morse, whose campaign had lacked money and energy from the very start.

The latter defeat humiliated Morse, coming in his home state. He dropped out of the race that night, offering an endorsement that was typically brusque and uncharitable. "I'll hold my nose and vote for him, even campaign for him," he said of Kennedy, "because even he is better than Nixon, and that's the best I can say for him."

Oregon was the final contested primary of the season. Kennedy had run in seven. Not all of his performances had been impressive—he had faced token opposition in New Hampshire, Indiana, and Nebraska (the latter election occurring the same day as West Virginia), while the Wisconsin outcome had been a mixed bag at best—but he had won all seven. He had swept the table. The formidable challenge awaiting him was to take those seven victories and somehow cash them in for the Democratic nomination.

RISING STAR: DIANE NASH

Mississippi was hell on earth for black people in the twenties, and its toxic blend of racism and poverty grew more oppressive during the Depression. Thousands of blacks—Leon and Dorothy Nash among them—escaped to Northern cities, desperately seeking better lives. The Nashes made their way to Chicago, where Dorothy gave birth to a daughter in 1938.

Diane Nash enjoyed a pleasant childhood, rarely encountering racial discrimination. She excelled in the classroom and entered the 1956 Miss Illinois competition, winning runner-up honors at the regional level. It was her beauty—light complexion, unruly black hair—that first drew the attention of her male classmates at Fisk University in Nashville, where she transferred from Howard University in 1959. "She was one of God's beautiful creatures," raved John Lewis, "just about the most gorgeous woman any of us had ever seen."

A young man invited Nash to the Tennessee State Fair a few days after her arrival. The segregated washrooms at the fairgrounds shocked her, as did her date's passive acceptance of discrimination. She discovered that Nashville was not Chicago, that she was not welcome at many stores and most restaurants. "I came to college to grow and expand," she said, "and here I am, shut in."

A black minister, James Lawson, was quietly training black students to defy the city's segregation laws. Nash joined their ranks. The group intensified its preparations after the Greensboro sit-in on February 1. Lawson hastily scheduled the first Nashville protest for February 13. "I remember thinking [that] I'm only twenty-two years old," Nash recalled. "What do I know? What am I doing?"

The first three sit-ins proceeded without incident, but the police briefly jailed Nash and 80 other protesters on February 27. The arrests galvanized the movement. More than 3,000 blacks packed the streets on April 19 for a march to City Hall, the biggest demonstration yet. Mayor Ben West, who awaited the throng, sought a common bond in religion. "Let us pray together," he said. But he could not sidestep a confrontation. Nash pushed toward the microphone as the prayer came to an end, and asked the mayor whether he supported racial discrimination.

It was a dangerous question. West faced a largely black audience, yet he owed his job to white voters who scorned racial equality. He chose to answer forthrightly. "I appeal to all citizens," he said, "to end discrimination, to have no bigotry, no bias, no hatred."

Nash shot back, "Then, Mayor, do you recommend that the lunch counters be desegregated?"

West looked at Nash and then at the mass of protesters. He replied with a single, unexpected word—"yes"—before adding that he lacked the power to force store owners to comply. But the cheering audience heard only the first word. "Integrate Counters—Mayor," screamed the headline in the *Nashville Tennessean.*

Nash's impromptu query had punctured the white establishment's solid front. Six downtown stores—reeling because of a black boycott and sensing that further resistance would be futile—agreed to integrate on May 10, 1960. It was one of the first great victories for the civil rights movement in the South.

Most Fisk students returned to their books, but Nash moved on to Rock Hill, South Carolina, where she was jailed after requesting service at a segregated soda fountain. "The Chaucer classes," she said, "became unbearable after Rock Hill." She dropped out of Fisk, dedicating herself to the battle for racial equality.

Her passion inevitably drew her to the center of the action, to Mississippi, the state her parents had fled a generation earlier. A pregnant

Nash—she had married a fellow activist, James Bevel, in 1961—was arrested in 1962 and threatened with two-and-a-half years in prison. "Since my child will be a black child born in Mississippi," she replied, "whether I am in jail or not, he will be born in prison." The judge decided that no good could come from putting a pregnant woman behind bars, no matter her color. He suspended her sentence.

Nash drifted from the headlines after that, though she spoke out for civil rights into the 21st century. Her long-ago visit to the Tennessee State Fair, she admitted, had triggered a chain of events that turned her world upside down, but it had also brought an unequaled sense of fulfillment. "It's a satisfaction," she said, "that has to do with the fact that my living has made a difference on the planet. And I love that. I really do."

***

The Baby Boom—to the amazement and occasional displeasure of the elderly and the middle-aged—had transformed American society within a single decade.

Children and teenagers had become ubiquitous by 1960, while men and women in their twenties jammed colleges and the job market. Reverence for the old had been supplanted by a preoccupation with the young. It seemed fitting that the year's presidential candidates were unusually youthful. Humphrey and Kennedy both celebrated birthdays that May, respectively turning 49 and 43. Vice President Nixon was 47 years old.

The previous month's census quantified the trend. Fifty-three million youngsters—ranging from newborns to 13-year-olds—were now scampering around America. They constituted 30 percent of the nation's population, up from 25 percent 10 years earlier. Elementary and secondary schools were bursting at the seams with 41.8 million students, an increase of nearly 12 million in 8 years. Colleges were educating an all-time record of 6.4 million young adults in 1960, and their enrollment was expected to soar to 9 million by 1970.

Politicians cited these statistics as proof of the nation's vigorous spirit and dynamic economy. Paul Goodman, however, was quite willing to express a contrary opinion. The 58-year-old Goodman wrote poetry, novels, and nonfiction books about subjects as diverse as psychology and urban planning. His latest cause was the troubled youth of America, especially males in their teens and twenties. "The young men are angry and beat. The boys are juvenile delinquents," he wrote. "These groups are not small, and they will grow larger. Certainly they are suffering."

Goodman's book on this subject, *Growing Up Absurd*, was published to great controversy in 1960. Devotees hailed it as an instant classic of cogency and style. Critics assailed it for being alarmist and occasionally unintelligible. But there was no disputing the author's passion. Goodman asserted that young males were enmeshed in a "deepening crisis of boredom." He envisioned youthful rebellion as the inevitable result. The poor and uneducated would likely turn to crime and vandalism, but the spirited and intelligent might decide to challenge the system directly. The latter prospect did not displease him. Goodman claimed to be "heartened by the crazy young allies" who dared to question authority. "Perhaps the future," he wrote, "may make more sense than we dared hope."

This prediction seemed incongruent with the sedate behavior of the younger generation throughout the fifties, but a mid-May protest in San Francisco fit Goodman's pattern. The House Un-American Activities Committee arrived to investigate the Communist Party's dealings—both real and imaginary—in California. The student newspaper at the University of California urged students to picket the opening day of hearings on May 12, and about 1,000 did so. The crowd outside City Hall grew considerably larger—and more restive—the next day. A scuffle broke out when students tried to get seats in the hearing room but were turned away.

Subsequent details were fuzzy. Police officers accused students of rushing at them, led by an activist who grabbed a patrolman's billy club. Student leaders claimed they had been milling peacefully outside the hearing room when the police suddenly attacked. The authorities unreeled high-pressure fire hoses and washed most of the protesters down the marble steps of City Hall. "We won't move. We won't move," chanted a few dozen students who resisted. But they were soon dragged to the bottom of the stairs, hastened by police nightsticks. Sixty-four protesters were arrested.

Critics had no doubt where to place the blame. "Many Americans point to the strength of our nation and say, 'It can't happen here,'" harumphed J. Edgar Hoover. "The communist success in San Francisco in May proves it *can* happen here." He was off the mark. The sit-in movement that began in Greensboro had inspired not only black protesters but thousands of their white contemporaries. The latter, however, realized that their efforts were trivial in comparison to the battle being waged by black students against racial injustice. The San Francisco protest was an early attempt by young whites to exhibit a similar level of involvement.

Students for a Democratic Society, the fledgling radical organization, staged a three-day conference on civil rights in early May at the University of Michigan, an obvious attempt to piggyback on the success of the Greensboro movement. Nothing of substance occurred at the session, though a few idealistic students were drawn to the cause, including Tom Hayden, the newly named editor of Michigan's student newspaper.

The 20-year-old Hayden, who was wrapping up his junior year, decided to head west in the summer of 1960, drawn by what he had heard of the San Francisco protests. The University of California's Berkeley campus, as he later wrote, was "already known as the Mecca of student activism," and he felt the urge to make a pilgrimage. It proved to be a life-changing trip. Hayden experienced a political rebirth while hanging around the university for several weeks—"I got radicalized"—and he committed himself to fusing like-minded students into a single powerful organization.

"What Berkeley did was define my politics, and turn me on to the idea of student power," Hayden recalled 20 years later. He returned to Michigan for his senior year, "very exhilarated" by what he had seen in California. His life's work, he had decided, would be political, not journalistic, in nature.

QUOTATIONS: MAY 1960

"What is it—a new German submarine?"
> —*Edward Beach, skipper of the USS* Triton, *expressing confusion after being asked what he thought of the U-2.* Triton *had been running under radio silence when Francis Gary Powers was shot down.*

"This is an exhibit hall? We've got 110 urinals we just installed. What in the hell are you going to exhibit?"
> —*A West Virginia contractor, scoffing at the cover story for a bunker being built in 1960 under the Greenbrier, a luxury resort. Greenbrier officials said they planned to stage shows there, but the facility was actually a top-secret*

> *fallout shelter for the Senate and House of Representatives.*
> *It had 1,100 bunk beds, decontamination showers, a*
> *crematorium, and a TV studio with murals of the*
> *Capitol and White House as backdrops.*

"We talk casually about moving a man to the moon and back. Yet we can't move the man to work and back so he can build the missile."

> —*Sam Taylor, the head of Los Angeles's traffic department,*
> *bemoaning the gridlock afflicting local freeways. The city's*
> *first expressway, the Arroyo Seco Parkway (later renamed*
> *the Pasadena Freeway), had opened 20 years earlier with a*
> *planned capacity of 45,000 cars per day, yet was jammed*
> *with 70,000 vehicles on a typical day in 1960.*

"The beast is in chains."

> —*A Mossad agent, sending a coded message to David*
> *Ben-Gurion after the May 11 capture of Adolf Eichmann.*
> *Eichmann was smuggled out of Argentina nine days*
> *later on El Al, Israel's national airline. Agents dyed their*
> *prisoner's hair gray and applied makeup to make him*
> *appear older. They dressed him in an El Al uniform—*
> *complete with the Star of David on his cap—and then*
> *administered a sedative. Airport guards waved*
> *him through without a search.*

* * *

The Democratic candidates were uncertain how to proceed after the collapse of the summit. Attacking the grandfatherly Eisenhower had never been politically profitable, yet they wondered if this time might be different. Perhaps the U-2 crisis had deflated Ike to the status of mere mortal, putting him—at long last—on the same political level as everybody else in Washington.

The first Democratic marksman to take aim was Adlai Stevenson, who ridiculed the president for handing Khrushchev "the crowbar and sledgehammer to wreck this meeting." He soon had cause for regret. James Farley, a former chairman of the Democratic National Committee, rushed to the Republican president's defense. Farley accused Stevenson of trying "to sledgehammer and crowbar another disastrous nomination for himself as the apostle of appeasement."

Further proof of Eisenhower's strength was provided by the first post-summit Gallup Poll, which pegged the president's approval rating at 65 percent, 3 points higher than the reading on May 1, the day Frank Powers had hoisted himself into the U-2's cockpit.

That settled the matter. A frontal assault on Eisenhower was out of the question. It made more sense for Democratic hopefuls to portray themselves as the sternest of anti-Soviet hawks. Henry Jackson, a Democratic senator and Kennedy supporter, summed up the conventional wisdom. "The public," he said, "is going to expect a tough, tough line."

Jackson's man forgot this sage advice during a campaign stop in St. Helens, Oregon, shortly after the summit's demise. A high school student asked Kennedy how he would have handled the U-2 crisis. The candidate noted Khrushchev's two stipulations. "First, that we apologize. I think that might have been possible to do," said Kennedy. "And that, second, we try those responsible for the flight. We could not do that."

Kennedy hastened to minimize the damage, ordering an aide to phone a clarification to the *Portland Oregonian*. The senator meant to say "express regrets," not "apologize," the staffer told the newspaper's editor. Could the *Oregonian* possibly change the wording before running the story? The editor could not be persuaded and published the original quote.

The other contenders piled on with gusto. Johnson added a new line to his speeches. "I'm not prepared to apologize to Mr. Khrushchev. Are you?" he bellowed at his audiences. "Noooooooooooo!" they shouted in reply. Vice President Nixon charged that Kennedy's "naive" comments were proof of his inexperience. No president, said Nixon, should ever apologize "for trying to defend the United States."

The press had recently anointed Kennedy as the frontrunner for the Democratic nomination. He had appeared to be unstoppable, a juggernaut roaring out of West Virginia. But the U-2 affair raised new concerns about his youth and immaturity. Johnson and Stevenson met on May 16 and agreed that the dynamics of the race had changed. Kennedy could still be defeated.

Nixon, unopposed for the Republican nomination, tried to sidestep the controversy as best he could. There might even be a silver lining, he suggested to his party's congressional leaders. "In retrospect, years from now, people may still criticize the president for his initial statements," he said. "But they will recognize it was a great achievement to get as much information as we have from the U-2."

The congressmen were impressed by Nixon's lack of bitterness. A successful summit, followed by a triumphant tour of the Soviet Union by Eisenhower, would have greatly helped Ike's Republican heir. That alluring scenario had vaporized, yet the vice president remained sanguine, and with good reason. The Associated Press reported on May 24 that Nixon had lined up endorsements from more than half of the delegates to July's Republican convention in Chicago. The nomination, for all intents and purposes, was in the bag.

That was why Nelson Rockefeller's subsequent actions seemed so peculiar. Rocky now spied an opportunity—one his fellow politicians could not perceive—to exploit the U-2 debacle. He issued a vaguely condemnatory statement on May 23. "The crudity of Soviet conduct," he said, "gives neither reason nor excuse for denying that some aspects of American conduct, immediately prior to the conference, demand examination of their purpose and prudence."

The chairman of New York's Republican Party, Jud Morhouse, fanned the flames by confiding to reporters that Rockefeller was thinking about running for president. The governor added more fuel by asking his state's 96 Republican delegates to delay any endorsement of Nixon. They dutifully agreed to remain uncommitted until the convention.

Rockefeller held a press conference on May 25—ostensibly to clarify the situation—but he merely added to the confusion. He would not be mounting a traditional campaign for president, he said, yet if the Republican convention called him to duty, he would answer affirmatively. His dissatisfaction with Nixon was obvious.

"Drafts come very seldom in this country," he said. "But if a draft should come, I would be greatly honored, and I would accept." This was much stronger than his April remark about dealing with the bridge when the time came. He had now decided to cross.

A reporter slyly asked the governor if he was planning to "sit by an open window waiting for a draft."

"No," Rockefeller replied lamely. "The office is air-conditioned." He let loose with a rasping laugh, and everybody in the room joined in. It was hard to tell exactly what was happening—or why—but one thing was clear. The Republican race was becoming a whole lot more interesting.

7

June: Off Again, On Again

Lyndon Johnson dropped the pretense as May faded into June. He still refused to formally announce his candidacy—an insistence that baffled even his closest allies—but he finally began acting like an honest-to-God presidential contender. The new Johnson made his debut at a reception in Idaho, where the state's Democratic delegates bluntly expressed their frustration with his coyness. "We don't want to bet on a horse that's going to stay in the paddock," one man snapped. "Are you a candidate?"

Johnson smiled. "You're damned right I am," he drawled.

"Then I'm with you," the local politician replied, thrusting out his hand.

The only question was whether he had waited too long. The Democratic convention in Los Angeles was just six weeks away, and Jack Kennedy was doing everything possible to secure the nomination on the first ballot. Johnson, who had seemed a formidable candidate at the beginning of the year, now appeared weaker, less intimidating. Harry McPherson bemoaned his boss's sloppiness, "the bases not touched, none of the groundwork that Kennedy had laid." Hubert Humphrey, still nursing wounds from West Virginia, didn't see how Johnson could be nominated. "I knew that Kennedy had this tremendous forward movement and publicity," he said. "It was inevitable he was going to be the nominee."

Yet Johnson showed no signs of discouragement. He asked the speaker of the House, fellow Texan Sam Rayburn, to open his national campaign headquarters in Washington on June 2. Rayburn assured reporters that Johnson would arrive in Los Angeles with "a very

minimum of 500 votes," roughly two-thirds of the 761 delegates required for victory. An advertisement with a bold headline—"Who Shall
Lead Us?"—was placed in 19 major newspapers the following Sunday,
imploring readers to write or wire Johnson's office "to urge him to become an active candidate."

Johnson's only option was to tear Kennedy down while building
himself up. He escalated his attacks, reserving his sharpest ridicule
for Kennedy's U-2 blunder. The Democratic nominee, Johnson said,
"must be a man who will not go off the deep end because Khrushchev
says you must apologize to me." He told an audience in Des Moines
that the times demanded a president with experience, "a man with a
little gray in his hair."

The two senators had served together since 1953, though few on
Capitol Hill considered them equals. Johnson was the vaunted majority leader of the Senate, one of the hardest workers in Washington.
Kennedy was a backbencher who rarely burned the midnight oil. The
51-year-old Johnson found it difficult to take his younger colleague
seriously. "Now I realize you're pledged to the boy," he told Tip
O'Neill, who represented Kennedy's old district in the House. "But
you and I both know he can't win. He's just a flash in the pan, and he's
got no record of substance to run on."

Their disparities in age and experience were compounded by the
dissimilarity of their upbringings. "They had come from totally different backgrounds," said George Smathers, a senator from Florida. "Kennedy—affluent, Eastern top-college, Harvard, prep schools,
everything. Johnson—down there in the backwoods of Texas, went
to some little school nobody had ever heard of, had to work his way
up." Smathers believed they secretly disliked each other, despite
their public professions of goodwill. Their staffs certainly did little
to hide their mutual disdain. Kennedy's aides mocked Johnson as an
uncouth oaf. Johnson's people dismissed Kennedy as a pretentious
upstart.

One of the widest gaps was in their breadth of political appeal. Kennedy had proven to be the party's most popular presidential candidate in the East, Midwest, and West. Johnson, try as he might, attracted
very little delegate support outside of his native South. India Edwards,
speaking to a group of Minnesota Democrats, promised them that Johnson would be a president for the entire country, a true liberal. "Well, the
delegates just put their heads back and screeched," she said. "It was the
funniest thing they had ever heard."

Southerners, on the other hand, flocked to the first serious candidate that their region had produced in generations. Kennedy had been trying since January to lure Southern delegates into his tent, only to watch hundreds drift to Johnson. He voiced his frustration to the governor of North Carolina, Luther Hodges, who had long been friendly with Kennedy, yet was supporting Johnson.

"Well, I'm doing this, senator, because of prejudice," Hodges explained.

"What kind of prejudice?" Kennedy asked.

"The prejudice of the North against a Southern candidate," Hodges replied, "because we've been written off, so to speak, for a hundred years."

Kennedy gave thought to writing off the South himself. Michigan's powerful governor, Mennen Williams, endorsed him on June 2, and New York chipped in a sizable bloc of delegates. Perhaps he could attract enough votes outside the South to lock up the nomination. "I don't want to have to go hat in hand to all those Southerners," Kennedy told Arthur Schlesinger. He was wary of alienating Northern voters, especially blacks, by appearing to be too cozy with segregationists. "It's absolutely fatal to have Southern support," he went on. "I want to be nominated by the liberals. I don't want to go screwing around with all those Southern bastards."

Kennedy, however, wasn't especially liberal. He described himself in various ways—"a moderate Democrat who seeks to follow the national interest" or "a Northern Democrat with some sense of restraint" or "a pragmatic liberal"—yet never used the L-word in its undiluted form. He spoke disdainfully of liberals in private, ridiculing them as indecisive and weak. But the left wing of the Democratic Party controlled the votes he needed, so he tacked in its direction. His lack of interest in the civil rights movement gave way to a new enthusiasm for sit-ins. "It is in the American tradition to stand up for one's rights," he said in June, "even if the new way is to sit down."

Kennedy's biggest fear was that Adlai Stevenson—still the hero of millions of liberals—might become a candidate at the last minute, deadlocking the Democratic race. If that happened, Johnson or Stuart Symington could fill the void and seize the nomination. Kennedy hoped to persuade Stevenson to stay on the sidelines, so he visited the former nominee's home in Libertyville, Illinois, in late May.

It did not go well. Kennedy sought an endorsement, but Stevenson parried the request. He must remain neutral, he said. They talked awhile longer, yet settled nothing. Kennedy had arrived in Libertyville unsure of Stevenson's intentions. He departed a few hours later, unhappily convinced that the older man was quietly angling for the nomination. Stevenson's close aide, William Blair, drove Kennedy to the airport. "Guess who the next person I see will be," said Kennedy, "the person who'll say about Adlai, 'I told you that son of a bitch has been running for president every moment since 1956.'"

Blair knew the answer. "Daddy," he said.

Eleanor Roosevelt had reached the same conclusion, though she was pleased, not angry. "We need a more mature man with more knowledge of the world in the next four years," she said, formally endorsing Stevenson for president on June 9. Reporters asked why she would back somebody who wasn't running. "I think you will find it clear," she said, "that Mr. Stevenson is a candidate." The squire of Libertyville took issue with her characterization, then waffled when a reporter read back his denial over the phone. "Oh, dear," Stevenson said, "I suppose that will get me into it with Eleanor, won't it?"

The former first lady agreed to serve as honorary chairman of the Draft Stevenson Committee, which was housed in a former USO center in Manhattan and now had 7,000 volunteers. A five-story banner—"Stevenson-for-President Headquarters"—dominated the front of the building. Bedlam reigned inside—jangling phones, shouted commands, hurried meetings. It seemed just like a real campaign headquarters. All it lacked was a candidate.

A quarter of a million voters signed pro-Stevenson petitions in June, yet he continued to play it cool. "I had no idea that there was such an extensive grassroots support and confidence in me still," he said. But Stevenson knew much more than he let on. Aide Newton Minow communicated regularly with the leaders of the draft committee. "We disavowed it, but we always kept in touch with it," Minow later said. "Often [Stevenson] played dumb and innocent when he really knew all about something. In 1960, he kept saying that he didn't want to run. But he was interested."

LEXICON: JUNE 1960

Arnie's Army

Arnold Palmer had won six tournaments so far in 1960, establishing himself as the world's best professional golfer. His legions of fans—

"Arnie's Army"—expected him to dominate the U.S. Open in Denver. Yet he struggled badly, entering the final round on June 18 in fifteenth place. Palmer rallied to stage the greatest comeback in golf history, outdueling icon Ben Hogan and amateur Jack Nicklaus for the Open title. He tapped in his final putt, yanked the visor from his head, and joyously flung it like a boomerang. The photo made the front pages of newspapers everywhere.

Japan-United States Security Treaty

Japan chafed under a treaty it had been compelled to sign with the United States in 1951. The pact granted America unfettered rights to garrison its troops in Japan. A more lenient agreement was negotiated in 1960, and President Eisenhower planned to fly to Tokyo for its implementation in late June. But dissidents staged a series of violent anti-American protests, forcing the Japanese government to call off the ceremony. Eisenhower was greatly discouraged by the cancellation, coming as it did on the heels of the failed summit. He announced that he would make no more trips as president.

Psycho

Only 2 movies from 1960—released on successive days in mid-June—would make the American Film Institute's 1998 list of the 100 greatest motion pictures. One was Alfred Hitchcock's first horror thriller, *Psycho,* which was more dependent on shock than suspense. Most critics initially hated *Psycho,* but audiences flocked to see it, triggering a reassessment that eventually elevated the movie to classic status. "I remember the terrible panning we got when *Psycho* opened," Hitchcock said ruefully. "My films went from being failures to masterpieces without ever being successes."

Salt and Pepper

An approaching era of judicial activism was heralded on June 4, when U.S. District Court Judge Whitfield Davidson issued a school desegregation order for the second-largest city in the South. Davidson's plan was limited in scope, a so-called "salt and pepper" approach that would integrate only a few Dallas schools as of September 1961, yet it went much further than the white establishment cared to go. Similar orders dangled over Atlanta and New Orleans. The latter was commanded to admit black first graders to all-white schools in September, just three months hence.

The Apartment

"I want to be truthful," said Billy Wilder. "But if I have to choose between truth and entertainment, I will always choose entertainment." The director skillfully juggled those impulses in his June 15 release, *The Apartment*, blending broad humor with serious commentary about the struggle for success. Jack Lemmon, a rising Hollywood star, infused the movie with a mixture of amiability and zaniness. *The Apartment* went on to win Academy Awards for best screenplay, best director, and best picture. It joined *Psycho* on AFI's list of the 100 greatest films.

Toonder and Lightning

Ingemar Johansson began the year as boxing's heavyweight champion. The relatively unknown Swede had won the title in 1959 by knocking out Floyd Patterson. Their rematch took place on June 20 at New York's Polo Grounds. Johansson promised to unleash his "toonder and lightning" punch, but he could not fend off the challenger's rapid jabs. Patterson scored a fifth-round knockout, becoming the first dethroned heavyweight champ to regain his crown. Johansson—the last white man to hold the undisputed heavyweight title in the 20th century—began his slide into obscurity.

* * *

Business had never been better for the nation's tobacco companies. Their assembly lines were rolling the largest quantity of cigarettes ever produced—506 billion in 1960, up from 392 billion 10 years earlier. Six of every 10 American men puffed away on a regular basis, as did one-third of women. Half of all 18-year-olds had already acquired the habit. Smokers across the United States were buying 960,000 cigarettes every minute, 16,000 every *second*.

Yet success had not come easily. Naysayers had been contending since the early fifties that cigarettes were unhealthy, perhaps even fatal. The tobacco companies did their best to counter such negativity, annually sinking more than $200 million into advertising. But *Reader's*

Digest did not carry ads and therefore had no qualms about publishing a sensational story in 1954 that established a plausible link between smoking and lung cancer.

Sales began to dip after the *Digest* hit newsstands. The tobacco industry struck back with filtered cigarettes. Filters, it claimed, would protect smokers against any dangers that tar or nicotine might pose. Consumers—happily reassured—began inhaling more deeply than ever. Filtered cigarettes had accounted for 1 percent of industry sales in 1952, a share that ballooned to 50 percent by 1960. The chairman of R. J. Reynolds Tobacco Company, Bowman Gray, predicted that the public would soon dismiss the cancer scare completely. "People are hearing the same old story," he said, "and the record is getting scratched, the needle stuck."

Oscar Auerbach would have agreed with him. Auerbach was a pathologist who studied lung diseases at the Veterans Administration hospital in East Orange, New Jersey. He and his team analyzed more than 1,500 cadavers in the late fifties. They found cell abnormalities in the lungs of 4 percent of nonsmokers, 11 percent of occasional smokers, and 99 percent of pack-a-day smokers. Auerbach became convinced that cigarettes damaged smokers' airways, caused cell mutations, and greatly increased the odds of contracting lung cancer.

But he found it virtually impossible to spread his message. Most doctors and scientists seemed to be skeptical or totally uninterested. "I had to wade through clouds of smoke," Auerbach recalled. "It seemed as if 90 percent of doctors were smoking then." The American Cancer Society also appeared hesitant to take a stand. Cynics noted that millions of the society's contributors were smokers.

The numbers, however, were too compelling to ignore forever. Lung cancer was claiming twice as many victims in 1960 as it had in 1950. The percentage of Americans dying from heart disease was also on the rise. Was smoking really the cause, or was some undetermined factor to blame? More and more researchers were arriving at the same conclusion as Auerbach.

The World Health Organization, a branch of the United Nations, formally listed cigarettes in April 1960 as a major cause of lung cancer. The American Heart Association followed with its own report on June 6, tying smoking to heart ailments. The latter story hit especially hard because it reversed conventional wisdom. The association had rejected a cause-and-effect relationship in 1956 but now admitted that its earlier stand had been in error. "The data strongly suggest that heavy cigarette smoking may contribute to or accelerate the development of coronary heart disease or its complications," said Carlton Ernstene, the association's president.

Even the American Cancer Society came around in 1960. Its president, Warren Cole, pulled no punches in an October address marking the end of his term. "How they cause it we still don't know," he said, "but the case against such carcinogens as occur in cigarette smoke is so strong that it seems certain now that some 20,000 lives a year are the cost the American public pays for this practice."

Scientists were trying to document another controversial link in 1960. The Food and Drug Administration had ruled the previous December that "the role of cholesterol in heart and artery diseases has not been established," but Ancel Keys disagreed. Keys, a physiologist at the University of Minnesota, was conducting a three-year study of eating habits in the United States and other countries. He published his initial findings in a book, *Eat Well and Stay Well*, which hit the best-seller list during the year.

High cholesterol counts were indeed dangerous, Keys concluded, and so was obesity. His proposed remedies were simple—strenuous exercise and a healthy diet. "People should know the facts," he said. "Then if they want to eat themselves to death, let them." His research persuaded the American Heart Association to acknowledge, for the first time ever, the potential dangers of cholesterol.

Yet millions of people rejected these new scientific conclusions, refusing to make any changes in the way they lived. Peter Steincrohn, a medical doctor and newspaper columnist, spoke for them in *Mr. Executive: Keep Well, Live Longer*, a self-help manual that arrived at bookstores in the fall.

Steincrohn began with an indisputable premise—"the prematurely sick or dead executive is a failure"—but his suggestions differed dramatically from those proposed by Auerbach, Keys, and the other oracles of the new wave. Steincrohn's recipe for good health featured such ingredients as leisurely lunches and afternoon naps. He endorsed moderate consumption of liquor because "it promotes appetite and amiability."

Exercise, on the other hand, was to be avoided if at all possible. Nine holes of golf, perhaps, but no more than that. Steincrohn shuddered at the very thought of working up a sweat. "Many get away with it," the author clucked, "but many get away with Russian roulette, too." Let the nutrition-and-exercise crowd say what it will. He preferred to take another nap.

RISING STAR: ROBERT BURNS WOODWARD

Robert Burns Woodward married two women and fathered four children, but he was never an attentive husband or parent. Both wives found him impossible to live with, and his kids rarely saw him. Woodward's scientific specialty was his only passion. "I'm just fascinated by chemistry," he once said. "I am in love with it."

This intense attraction had existed since childhood. Woodward set up a basement chemistry lab before turning 10—not a child-sized kit with a few test tubes and beakers, but a full-blown laboratory. He was said to have performed every experiment in Ludwig Gattermann's *Practical Methods of Organic Chemistry*—the manual used by German graduate students—before reaching his teens. This legend, he admitted, was "substantially true."

World War II broke out when Woodward was 24, yet he was not drafted. His work as a Harvard faculty member was simply too valuable. America's supply of quinine—an antimalarial drug and ingredient in the manufacturing process for lenses—had been cut off by Japan's conquest of the Dutch East Indies. Woodward and a partner, William Doering, set out to create synthetic quinine. They devised a complicated series of chemical conversions that yielded success in 1944.

Woodward focused next on cortisone, which was perpetually scarce because it could be derived only from the bile of slaughtered animals. He replicated the steroid in his lab in 1951, enabling the production of cortisone in unlimited amounts, happy news indeed for sufferers from rheumatoid arthritis and rheumatic fever. The *New York Times* hailed him as the winner of "the greatest international race in modern chemistry."

Woodward was already on the hunt for new challenges, eager to pit his considerable talents against nature's secrets. "The structure known, but not yet accessible by synthesis," he said, "is to the chemist what the unclimbed mountain, the uncharted sea, the unfilled field, the unreached planet, are to other men." He decided to tackle his biggest project yet, seeking to unlock the inner workings of chlorophyll, the molecule that enables plants to obtain energy from sunlight. Generations of researchers had tried to find the key. All had failed.

Woodward and his 17-member team toiled through the latter half of the fifties, developing subtle chemical tricks to replicate the elusive molecule. They worked their way through a complex series of 55 steps, finally achieving victory in June 1960 with the production of a microscopic amount of chlorophyll—six hundred-thousandths of an ounce.

The *New York Times* applauded Woodward's newest breakthrough as "electrifying" and "one of the greatest triumphs in chemistry." *Time* expressed awe for the "chemical witch's brew" that he had devised. The magazine bestowed its ultimate honor upon Woodward, naming him its Man of the Year for 1960, along with 14 fellow pioneers in other scientific fields. "They are representative of all science," wrote *Time*, "with its dependence on the past, its strivings and frustrations in the present, and its plans, hopes and, perhaps, fantasies for the future."

Woodward's status as one of the world's most celebrated scientists was sealed with the 1965 Nobel Prize for chemistry. "It is sometimes said that organic synthesis is at the same time an exact science and a fine art," said Arne Fredga, a member of the award committee. "Here nature is the uncontested master, but I dare say that the prizewinner of this year, Dr. Woodward, is a good second." The Nobel panel cited his wide range of chemical syntheses, though it gave the greatest weight to his 1960 success with chlorophyll.

One final triumph lay ahead. Twelve years of painstaking labor culminated in the replication of vitamin B-12 in 1972, a synthesis even more impressive than chlorophyll. But Woodward's obsessive lifestyle—the endless hours in the lab, the decades of smoking, the complete lack of exercise—took its inevitable toll. He suffered a fatal heart attack in 1979 at the age of 62.

His personal life was admittedly unsuccessful, but it could safely be said that Woodward died happy. "For almost fifty years now," he wrote shortly before the end, "I have been involved in an affair with chemistry. It has been throughout a richly rewarding involvement, with numerous episodes of high drama and intense engagement, with the joys of enlightenment and achievement, with the special pleasures which come from the perception of order and beauty in nature—and with much humor."

***

The television networks were constantly searching for something—*anything*—that might boost their ratings and revenues. Quiz shows proved to be a happy solution in the mid-fifties. Audiences loved the intensity of programs like *Treasure Hunt, Break the $250,000 Bank,* and *Twenty-One.* The latter required two contestants to answer questions on a wide range of topics, some remarkably difficult. "The show was straight," recalled producer Albert Freedman, "but it was so dull, the sponsor wanted to take it off the air. They had to control it."

"To control" meant "to fix"—to choreograph *Twenty-One* to make it suspenseful, to slip answers to contestants in advance, to handpick the eventual winners. The show's co-creator, Dan Enright, had no qualms. "I was determined to be successful no matter what it cost," he said, "and I was greedy."

Enright struck it rich in November 1956 with a mild-mannered English instructor from Columbia University. Charles Van Doren demonstrated an impressive breadth of knowledge on *Twenty-One,* breezing through subjects as disparate as baseball, classical music, and fairy tales. He won $129,000 during a 14-week streak. The show's ratings skyrocketed, and Van Doren landed on the cover of *Time,* an honor normally reserved for national and world leaders.

But the web of deceit slowly unraveled. Several contestants had been forced by the producers of *Twenty-One* and other quiz shows to lose, to give incorrect answers to questions they easily could have handled. They were understandably angry, and some began to talk. A Manhattan grand jury launched an investigation in 1958, with a congressional panel on its heels.

Van Doren's moment of truth arrived on November 2, 1959, in an overcrowded, overheated committee room on Capitol Hill. He admitted being coached by *Twenty-One* staffers prior to each show. "I was involved, deeply involved, in a deception," he said in a hollow voice. "I would give almost anything I have to reverse the course of my life in the last three years." Columbia immediately requested his resignation.

And that was the end of the quiz-show scandal—or so the networks hoped. But the district attorney of Manhattan, Frank Hogan, had no intention of letting them off the hook so easily. He alleged that contestants on *Twenty-One* and other programs had lied to investigators, "a very serious matter" that he vowed to rectify.

Hogan's pressure yielded results. Vivienne Nearing, a New York lawyer who had dethroned Van Doren on *Twenty-One,* came forward on June 3, 1960, to confess to perjury. She admitted that the show's producers had supplied her with answers in advance, a fact she had previously denied. Nineteen contestants followed her to the grand jury room that summer, with Van Doren testifying on July 28. Such a

Charles Van Doren (right) and Vivienne Nearing speak with *Twenty-One* host Jack Barry in 1957: "I was involved, deeply involved, in a deception." (Orlando Fernandez/Library of Congress)

"great number" of witnesses had lied in earlier appearances, Hogan announced, that the investigation might drag into autumn.

Network executives were disheartened by this news. They searched desperately for ways to counteract the negative publicity and redeem their reputations. One concept they batted around was a series of televised debates between the Democratic and Republican presidential nominees, an updated version of the previous century's famed Lincoln-Douglas debates.

But a formidable barrier loomed. If ABC, CBS, and NBC gave airtime to the major party nominees, Section 315 of the Communications Act would require them to provide "free and equal" time to all 14 minor party candidates. The networks asked Congress to suspend this provision for the rest of the year—thereby legalizing one-on-one debates—and the Democratic and Republican floor leaders complied with bipartisan haste. The Senate gave its approval on June 27, and the House soon followed suit.

It seemed likely that Richard Nixon would be one of the two debaters. He remained the odds-on favorite for the Republican nomination, even though Nelson Rockefeller was doing his best to confuse the situation. Rocky traveled in early June to North Dakota, where an election was being held to fill an empty Senate seat. Nixon's campaign director, Robert Finch, dispatched aide John Ehrlichman to keep tabs.

"I had decided before arriving in Fargo," Ehrlichman wrote, "that I would not lie to anyone about my identity or what I was doing there, if I was directly asked." Nobody posed the question. Rockefeller staffers thought he was a local Republican, and the Dakotans assumed he was from New York. The Nixon aide attended receptions, made small talk with Rockefeller's wife (who was clearly bored by campaigning), and even drove a car in the governor's motorcade. Ehrlichman sent back a six-page report about the politicians Rocky met, the speeches he made, and the way the press treated him. "Reporters mainly easy on NR," he wrote with distaste. "Didn't bore in as they do with RN."

The good vibrations in North Dakota convinced Rockefeller to ratchet up the pressure on June 8. He accused Nixon of being deliberately vague, of campaigning "with a banner aloft whose only emblem is a question mark." Rockefeller demanded that the vice president clarify his positions prior to the Republican convention. "The path of leadership," he said, "does not lie along the top of a fence."

It was Rockefeller's boldest attack to date, yet he baffled reporters by refusing to take the next logical step. "I was not a candidate yesterday, and I am not today," he told them. Well, then, would he be endorsing Nixon anytime soon? "I hadn't planned to," he said.

Rockefeller, in fact, was not sure what to do. He asked Eisenhower on June 10 if he should announce his candidacy. Ike advised against it. If Rockefeller joined the race after withdrawing six months earlier, the president said, voters would consider him indecisive. They would say he was, in Eisenhower's phrase, "off again, on again, gone again, Finnegan." It was better to sit this one out and wait for 1964 or 1968.

Rocky, however, couldn't help himself. He had previously announced that he would not attend the Republican convention, yet he now switched course. He would go to Chicago, he said, to fight for changes in the party platform. Few voters paid attention to platforms, those bland composites of political rhetoric and clichés. But Rockefeller declared that the 1960 Republican platform, then being assembled by a party committee, was so "seriously lacking in strength and specifics" that he had no choice but to speak out.

He held his tongue, however, when a San Francisco lawyer, William Brinton, established the Draft Rockefeller Committee on June 29. Brinton had offered to desist if Rocky wished. "We got neither approval nor disapproval," he said of his conversations with the governor's aides. "They said, in effect, 'You're on your own,' and that was all right with us."

Nixon withstood this political agitation calmly, at least in public. If Rockefeller remained silent on the issues, the vice president said, "he would not be being true to himself, and I think would not serve either the party or the country." Yet Nixon agonized in private about Rockefeller's accusations that the nation had grown weaker and had lost its sense of purpose. "What Rocky is saying about defense can have a big impact," he told Republican congressional leaders. "We cannot allow this charge of weakness to stand." It was essential to coax Rockefeller aboard Nixon's bandwagon or, at the very least, to get him to shut up.

A concerted attempt was made on June 26. Rocky joined the other 49 governors for their annual conference at a lodge in Montana. They discussed a broad range of issues—from the St. Lawrence Seaway to medical care for the elderly—yet still found time for politics. Harold Handley, the governor of Indiana, passed along a piece of paper. It was an oath pledging "full and loyal support" to Nixon. Every other Republican governor at the conference had already signed. Surely, Handley suggested innocently, Rockefeller wanted to sign, too.

Rocky put on his glasses, read the oath, and smiled wryly. "You guys," he said, "are some artists, aren't you?" He slowly folded his glasses, paused a moment, and slid the paper back to Handley. The space for his signature remained blank.

QUOTATIONS: JUNE 1960

"Allow me."

> *—Yuri Gagarin, volunteering to be the first cosmonaut to squeeze into the Soviet Union's new Vostok capsule. Gagarin and 19 colleagues were introduced to the tiny wingless ball in June. Their trainer asked if anybody wished to try out the pilot's seat. The other cosmonauts deferred to self-assured Gherman Titov, the odds-on favorite to fly the first Soviet space mission. But Gagarin jumped ahead of Titov, and slid into the capsule.*

"We're going to do everything we can. We'll use every means we can."

> —*Jimmie Davis, governor of Louisiana, vowing to defy a federal court order to desegregate the public schools in New Orleans.*

"If we behave like a banana republic, we shall get and deserve the economic rewards characteristic of a banana republic."

> —*Malcolm Bryan, president of the Federal Reserve Bank of Atlanta, telling a Rotary Club luncheon that it would be a mistake for that city to delay integration.*

"For God's sake, do something. My business is going to pot."

> —*Curly Harris, manager of the Greensboro Woolworth's, begging Mayor George Roach to resolve the city's racial impasse. The previous year had been the best in the store's history, but sales had dropped 20 percent so far in 1960, and profits had plummeted 50 percent. Blacks refused to shop at Woolworth's as long as its lunch counter was segregated. Many whites were afraid to go there as long as the sit-ins continued.*

"He had invested all [his] amassed political capital in the two great chances—one in Paris, one in Tokyo. Now it was spent— all of it."

> —*Former presidential aide Emmet Hughes, remarking on President Eisenhower's unhappiness after his Japanese trip was canceled.*

***

Paul Goodman might predict the imminent emergence of his "crazy young allies," but revolutionary spirit was in an embryonic stage on most college campuses in 1960. The majority of students still accepted the establishment line without question.

That was certainly true at the University of Illinois, where the student newspaper, the *Daily Illini,* published an editorial that deplored "excessive necking" at campus parties. Leo Koch, a 44-year-old biology professor, considered this stance absurd, both for its obsequious tone and its ignorance of reality. He composed a letter to the editor.

"With modern contraceptives and medical advice readily available at the nearest drugstore, or at least a family physician," Koch wrote, "there is no valid reason why sexual intercourse should not be condoned among those sufficiently mature to engage in it without social consequences and without violating their own codes of morality and ethics." The university's president, David Dodds Henry, accused the professor of encouraging immoral behavior, which was grounds for immediate dismissal. Koch fought for his job for the next three years—"I am a biologist, and I think I know something about sex"—but he would not regain it.

The Koch case was tallied as a victory for the status quo, yet it was a hollow triumph. Most young Americans scorned the puritan ethic, despite the *Daily Illini*'s contrary viewpoint. A landmark study by biologist Alfred Kinsey had found that two-thirds of college students were engaging in premarital sex in 1948, and societal restraints had loosened considerably since then. Hugh Hefner's success with *Playboy* was proof of that, as was a decision by the University of California at Los Angeles to open coeducational dormitories in September 1960, the first on any American campus. Male and female students would be housed on separate floors but would otherwise have easy access. "We are not planning to set up flamethrowers or machine guns at strategic passes," joked Byron Atkinson, a UCLA dean.

Margaret Sanger, 81 years old, was pleased with this evolution of American mores, though it was still too slow for her tastes. Sanger believed that women—married or not—should be able to enjoy sex without the possibility of pregnancy, unless they truly wished to give birth. She had dedicated her life to contraception—opening America's first birth control clinic in 1916 (and serving 30 days in jail for doing so), smuggling diaphragms into the country during Prohibition in shipments of contraband gin, and founding the group that would become Planned Parenthood.

Sanger sought out a Massachusetts endocrinologist, Gregory Pincus, in 1951, imploring him "to rally the world of science" to develop a safe and effective female contraceptive. She then enlisted the financial support of Katherine McCormick, heiress to the McCormick reaper fortune. The new patron offhandedly wrote an initial check for $40,000, with an additional $3 million to come.

Pincus recruited two partners—M.C. Chang, a longtime colleague, and John Rock, the chief of gynecology and obstetrics at Harvard Medical School. They set out to combine synthetic hormones into a single pill that would trick a woman's reproductive system into functioning as if she were already pregnant. Rock had devoted his career to the opposite pursuit—helping childless couples conceive—but he considered excessive fertility a problem of equal severity. "Nature," he said, "never intended a woman to be pregnant over and over again." Skeptics asked how he squared this belief with his devout faith in Catholicism, given the church's opposition to birth control. "I separated biology from theology quite early in my life," he replied, "and never confused them again."

Pincus's team, aided by liberal infusions of McCormick's cash, developed an oral contraceptive, Enovid, by 1954. Its next step was to conduct human trials, the only path to eventual approval by the Food and Drug Administration. Pincus recruited 221 volunteers in Puerto Rico. Not one became pregnant during the first eight months. Equally important was the fact that 85 percent of the women who stopped using the pill became pregnant within four months, proof that Enovid did not induce infertility.

The FDA was persuaded—but only partially—by this trial run. It approved Enovid in 1957 for a limited purpose: the treatment of menstrual problems. "Even that much came about, in part, because the medical director of the FDA was a friend of mine," said Irwin Winter, director of clinical research at G.D. Searle and Company, the pharmaceutical firm that produced the new pill. Searle didn't dare ask the FDA to clear Enovid for contraceptive use. The Catholic Church's opposition was assumed to be an insurmountable obstacle.

The FDA inadvertently resolved Searle's dilemma by requiring the firm to affix a label to each container, warning that Enovid prevented ovulation. "It was like a free ad," Winter said. Half a million women sought prescriptions for Enovid by 1959, and a large share obviously desired contraception. How many millions would join them if the FDA gave its full approval? The company nervously begin laying the groundwork in 1959.

"We were going into absolutely unexplored ground in terms of public opinion," said James Irwin, Searle's policy counselor. "My fear was that this would provoke an avalanche of letters." He planted stories about Enovid's birth control powers in *Reader's Digest* and *Saturday Evening Post* and braced himself for a violent backlash. Nothing happened. "We got quite a surprise," he admitted. Searle was now emboldened to take the final step, applying for approval of Enovid as the first pharmaceutical contraceptive.

The formal hearing was held in Washington on a bitterly cold day in December 1959. The FDA's reviewer, Pasquale DeFelice, admitted to a feeling of intimidation. "There I was," he said, "a thirty-five-year-old, qualified but not yet board-certified OB-GYN man. Standing before me was John Rock, the light of the obstetrical world."

The two men would recall the hearing differently—Rock remembering it as a tense debate of moral issues, DeFelice as a straightforward discussion of scientific minutiae. But both were aware of what was at stake. "I knew what was going to happen once we licensed it," DeFelice said. "I knew that birth control pills would be flying out the windows. Everybody and her sister would be taking it." DeFelice was tempted to buy Searle stock after the hearing but decided it would be unethical. He passed up a chance to become rich.

The FDA dragged its feet for five months. "Even though the pill had been through more elaborate testing than any drug in the FDA's history, there was a lot of opposition," said DeFelice. There were no significant side effects, no health risks. "But," he said, "we were in no hurry to put the FDA stamp of approval on it." That didn't come until May 9, when the agency announced that Enovid would be legally available for contraceptive purposes as of June 23, 1960. "Approval was based on the question of safety," John Harvey, the FDA's associate commissioner, said timidly. "We had no choice as to the morality that might be involved."

The significance of the ruling escaped the nation's newspapers. The *New York Times* buried a 149-word story on page 75 the next morning. Margaret Sanger, living outside Tucson, Arizona, learned of the decision only when her son spotted a five-paragraph item in the local paper. Women of childbearing age, however, soon grasped its importance. Enovid was expensive—$10 for 20 pills—yet 400,000 women sought contraceptive prescriptions within a year. The number shot up to 2.3 million by 1963.

Searle marketed Enovid not merely as a health aid but as a source of freedom. Its magazine ads depicted the mythological princess Andromeda, suddenly unshackled from the rock to which she had long been bound. Millions of women were persuaded. The birth rate plummeted 24 percent between 1960 and 1970. The typical woman of 1960 could expect to give birth to 3 or 4 children during her lifetime, but the average dropped to 1.8 children for the adult female of the mid-seventies.

Most observers focused on Enovid's demographic impact, but Clare Boothe Luce saw a broader picture. Luce was a world-renowned playwright, journalist, and politician—fields that few women entered in

1960, let alone in the thirties, when she had gotten her start. The scarcity of female artists and professionals, she predicted, would soon be changing. The pill would release women from the all-encompassing demands of ever-expanding families, allowing them to pursue their creative and intellectual interests. "Modern woman is at last free," Luce said, "as a man is free, to dispose of her own body, to earn her living, to pursue the improvement of her mind, to try a successful career."

8

July: The New Frontier

July—at long last.

Both political parties had been mired in confusion since January, and key questions remained unanswered as 1960 reached its midpoint. Could a candidate as young as Jack Kennedy win the Democratic presidential nomination? Was Lyndon Johnson a formidable contender or a paper tiger? Would Adlai Stevenson jump into the race at the 11th hour? Did Dick Nixon have the Republican nomination locked up? Or could Nelson Rockefeller snatch it away?

Nobody knew the answers at the start of July, but the month would bring clarity. Democrats were already streaming toward Los Angeles, where their convention would convene from the 11th through the 15th. Republicans would gather two weeks later—July 25 to 28—in Chicago. The national tickets of both parties would be settled before August arrived.

The growing likelihood of Kennedy's nomination worried the old guard of the Democratic Party. Harry Truman called a press conference on July 2. The country, he said, needed a candidate "with the greatest possible maturity and experience," and Kennedy lacked both. The ex-president addressed the young senator through the television cameras. "May I urge you to be patient?" he asked. Truman would have failed his own test back in 1945, when he reached the White House after just 10 years in the Senate and 82 days as vice president. Kennedy had served in Congress for 13½ years.

The frontrunner issued his formal response on July 4. "Mr. Truman regards an open convention as one which studies all the candidates, reviews their records, and then takes his advice," Kennedy joked before turning serious. He questioned the performance of the aging men who had called the shots since World War II—"who is to say how successful they have been in improving the fate of the world?"—and suggested that they yield the stage. "It is time for a new generation of leadership, to cope with new problems and new opportunities," he said. "For there is a new world to be won."

Lyndon Johnson announced his candidacy a day later, insisting that the demands of Senate business had delayed his formal entry into the presidential race. "Someone has to tend the store," he said publicly, though he was more caustic in private. "Jack was out kissing babies," he snapped, "while I was passing bills, including his bills." Johnson offered something for everyone—pledging a fresh approach to the nation's problems, yet placing great emphasis on his two-and-a-half decades as a Washington insider. "If [the president] himself is not seasoned and is inexperienced in making government work," Johnson maintained, "he becomes a weak link in the whole chain of the free world."

This thinly veiled slap at his young opponent came a day after Kennedy had planted his own barb. The Massachusetts senator stressed the need for "strength and health and vigor" in the White House, noting ominously that four of the seven presidents in his lifetime had suffered heart attacks.

Johnson, himself a heart attack survivor, felt the sting. Two of his aides, John Connally and India Edwards, responded with their own press conference, accusing Kennedy of having serious health problems himself, the most severe being Addison's disease. Their allegation was accurate, though Kennedy's aides parried it. Ted Sorensen assured a reporter than his boss did not receive cortisone injections to keep Addison's in check, when in fact he did. Sorensen would later admit that Kennedy took "more pills, potions, poultices, and other paraphernalia than would be found in a small dispensary."

The stage was set for a no-holds-barred scrap between two powerful, charismatic men who clearly did not like each other. Both insisted that it would be all or nothing in Los Angeles, that they would not accept anything less than the presidential nomination. Johnson recommended that the vice presidency go to "a young man who needs training." Kennedy was equally adamant. "Once you say you're going to settle for second," he said, "that's what happens to you in life, I find."

The convention was being held at the Los Angeles Memorial Sports Arena, a spacious hall that had been dedicated the previous year by Vice President Nixon. Kennedy had not yet sealed the deal when he arrived there. He remained short of the 761 votes required for the nomination. "Going into Los Angeles, we had continuing question marks," Larry O'Brien admitted. "We weren't locked in."

Johnson was having problems, too. His inability to line up Northern support was symptomatic of his campaign's ineffectiveness, yet a rare Kennedy mistake offered one last reason for hope. Kennedy's staff dispatched form letters to the Democratic chairmen of influential states, requesting face-to-face meetings with their delegations. There was no reason to contact the Texas Democrats, who unanimously supported Johnson, but a letter was sent accidentally. Johnson seized on the opportunity, challenging Kennedy to debate him in front of the Texas delegates on July 12. Kennedy agreed, asking only that the Massachusetts delegation be allowed to attend, too.

Jack Valenti, a Johnson aide, recalled the "glee" that pervaded his boss's camp when Kennedy rose to the bait. A massive television audience—including the delegates from the other 48 states—would finally be able to compare the candidates directly. The parliamentary master would surely destroy his young rival in rhetorical battle.

Johnson went on the attack from the beginning. He ridiculed Kennedy's record on civil rights and farm legislation, saying that he, Johnson, was a better friend to minorities and farmers. Kennedy blandly replied that he could think of no issue on which the two men truly disagreed. Johnson launched into a diatribe against unnamed senators who shirked their duties. "I assume," Kennedy laughingly interjected, "that he was talking about some of the other candidates and not about me." He congratulated Johnson for his "wonderful record in answering those quorum calls" and conceded his legislative superiority. "So I come here today full of admiration for Senator Johnson," Kennedy said, "full of affection for him, strongly in support of him—for majority leader."

The Johnson campaign, for all intents and purposes, came to an end that Tuesday afternoon, buried by his opponent's wit and poise. "Kennedy just massacred him," Valenti recalled sadly. "It wasn't even close." Johnson privately admitted it was all over. "It is going to be Kennedy by a landslide," he said.

Kennedy wasn't quite so certain, not yet. His big concern now was Adlai Stevenson, who had been greeted at Los Angeles International

Lyndon Johnson makes a last-ditch stand at the Los Angeles convention: "It is going to be Kennedy by a landslide." (Warren Leffler/Library of Congress)

Airport the previous Saturday by 7,000 supporters. The former nominee continued to disavow interest in the presidency, but Eleanor Roosevelt arrived in Los Angeles to sing his praises, Hubert Humphrey formally endorsed him, and a thousand pro-Stevenson demonstrators ringed the Sports Arena before the convention's first session. Their hero was overwhelmed by this outpouring of enthusiasm. He was especially delighted when he spotted a pregnant woman toting a sign that said "Stevenson is the Man."

Candidates traditionally stayed away from convention halls, but Stevenson insisted he was merely a delegate from Illinois. He headed inside. His fellow delegates roared when he reached the floor. Arthur Schlesinger, who was there to support Kennedy, called it "the first massive outburst of honest emotion in the convention." Few politicians could resist such mass adulation. Stevenson capitulated later that day, agreeing to mount a last-minute campaign for the nomination. "To me, it was just heartbreaking," said Newton Minow, a longtime Stevenson aide. "Just what we didn't want. We did it, anyway." Minow and his colleague, William Blair, were certain their boss had no chance of being nominated. But Stevenson hastily set out to visit delegations and line up as many votes as he could.

The roll call could not be held until the candidates' names were formally submitted to the convention on July 13—a protracted, dreary procedure. It was 8 o'clock when Eugene McCarthy, a senator from Minnesota, strode to the podium to nominate Stevenson. "Do not turn away from this man," he implored the delegates. "Do not reject this man. He has fought gallantly. He has fought courageously. He has fought honorably." The applause swelled as McCarthy reached his conclusion. "I submit to you a man who is not a favorite son of any one state," he shouted. "I submit to you a man who is the favorite son of fifty states—Adlai E. Stevenson of Illinois."

McCarthy's final words unleashed a torrent of emotion. Delegates ripped state banners from their stands and paraded around the hall. They were joined by a brass band and 2,000 Stevenson fanatics who streamed into the Sports Arena. Neophytes suddenly believed that Stevenson could steal the nomination. Ben Bradlee, covering his first convention for *Newsweek,* had convinced his editors to put Kennedy on the front of that week's magazine, all but anointing him as the nominee. He now knew he had chosen the wrong man. "Halfway through the Stevenson demonstration," he recalled, "I figured that I'd blown it through naivete and inexperience." But his bureau chief, Ken Crawford, snapped him back to reality. "Just look at the delegates, Bradlee," he barked. "They're not demonstrating."

It was true. Most delegates were still in their seats, not snake-dancing down the aisles. Bobby Kennedy had quickly phoned his operatives on the floor. "Stand firm," he told them. "Don't any of you join that parade. This thing is sewed up. We've got the votes." The cheering continued—a last tribute to the hero who had kept the Democratic faith through the Eisenhower fifties—but it would not alter the outcome. The arena finally quieted when the lights were turned off, half an hour after McCarthy had ignited the frenzy.

And then it was time to vote.

Alabama and Arkansas went for Johnson, staking him to an early lead. California proved to be a muddle, with Kennedy and Stevenson splitting the lion's share of its votes. Delaware and Georgia gave Johnson their unanimous support. Casual observers were surprised by the tightness of the race. It was not the blowout they had been led to expect.

But Kennedy's months of campaigning in the East and Midwest began to pay off. Illinois, Indiana, Iowa, and Kansas went heavily his way. Then came clean sweeps of Maine, Maryland, and Massachusetts, followed by more than 80 percent of Michigan's delegates. Kennedy was now leading Johnson by more than 200 votes, with Symington and Stevenson far behind. The only question was whether the Massachusetts senator could win the nomination on the first ballot. Windfalls from New York, Ohio, and Pennsylvania tacked another 236 votes onto his total. Johnson's 61 Texas delegates could not stem the tide. The roll call wound its way to Wyoming, the very last state in alphabetical order.

Kennedy needed 11 votes for victory. His staff's final tally showed only 8½ supporters in the Wyoming delegation. But the candidate, leaning toward his television set, spotted his youngest brother, Ted, standing next to Wyoming's chairman. Both sported huge smiles. "This could be it," Jack said, and indeed it was. Wyoming cast all 15 votes for Kennedy. The nomination was his.

Johnson snapped off the television in his suite. "Well, that's that," he told his family. "Tomorrow we can do something we really want to do. Go to Disneyland, maybe." He dictated a clever telegram to Kennedy that played on his own initials—"LBJ now means Let's Back Jack"—and went to bed.

Johnson's schedule was so empty that he could speak wistfully of Disneyland, but Kennedy faced two important obligations before leaving Los Angeles. He had to pick a running mate by Thursday evening—just 18 hours off—and then deliver his acceptance speech in the vast Memorial Coliseum on Friday.

The smart money was on Stu Symington for vice president. Bobby Kennedy had been assuring liberals and labor leaders that the man chosen for the second spot on the ticket would be a "Midwestern liberal." But his brother was beginning to rethink the situation. Kennedy had done very well in 3 of the 4 sections of the country, but only 13 Southern delegates—a mere 3 percent—had backed him. The Democratic platform's forthright stand on civil rights—"the time has come to assure equal access for all Americans to all areas of community life"—was another matter of concern. The platform would surely lure votes for Kennedy from liberals and blacks, but it was anathema to the white South. He needed a running mate who could ease his burden.

Kennedy signaled his new direction at breakfast. "Dave," he said to his personal assistant, David Powers, "wasn't that a nice telegram

Lyndon sent last night?" Larry O'Brien and other advisers were soon summoned to Kennedy's Biltmore suite. They arrived shortly after six o'clock, anticipating a full-scale meeting to discuss vice presidential possibilities. They were told instead that Kennedy had made up his mind. Johnson was his man.

Bobby, as O'Brien recalled, was "not at all enchanted" with the selection. Nor was another aide, Kenny O'Donnell, who confronted the nominee directly. "I'm forty-three years old," Kennedy shot back. "I'm the healthiest candidate for president in the United States. You've traveled with me enough to know that. I'm not going to die in office. So the vice presidency doesn't mean anything." Other advisers saw wisdom in the decision. Johnson was popular with white Southerners, yet had championed civil rights. "Johnson was the logical person to ask," concluded Ted Sorensen.

Precisely what happened the rest of that Thursday will never be fully known. Schlesinger threw up his hands in 1965—"the confusion of that afternoon defies historical reconstruction"—and the ensuing decades have not brought clarity. What *is* known is that Kennedy called Johnson at 8 A.M. to ask for a meeting, which took place at 10. Kennedy made the offer, and Johnson asked for a couple of hours to think it over. His eventual answer was positive. "I had no right to say that I would refuse to serve in any capacity," Johnson later explained.

Bobby Kennedy, who would feud with Johnson for the rest of his life, always contended that the invitation to join the ticket was a mere formality, a polite gesture toward the man who had finished second on the presidential roll call. "The idea that [John Kennedy] would go down and offer him the nomination in hopes that he'd take the nomination is not true," he insisted five years later. But Sorensen claimed the offer was genuine: "It would be inaccurate to say that he was hoping Johnson would say no." The nominee himself was cryptic. "The whole story will never be known," Jack once told his press secretary, Pierre Salinger. "And it's just as well that it won't be."

It had been a long, difficult convention. A visibly tired John Kennedy took the podium at the Memorial Coliseum on July 15 to formally accept the nomination. His voice was unusually high. His delivery was choppy, rushed, occasionally strident.

Kennedy's speech was a strange hybrid—one part political attack, one part rhetorical flourish. He blasted Richard Nixon for endorsing policies "as old as McKinley," for uttering "generalities from Poor Richard's Almanac," for showing "charity toward none and malice for all." These mundane gibes were married with a lofty call for a new generation of leadership. "The old era is ending," Kennedy said. "The old ways will not do." He unveiled a name for his program—the New Frontier—the successor to Franklin Roosevelt's New Deal and Harry Truman's Fair Deal. "The New Frontier sums up not what I intend to offer the American people, but what I intend to ask of them," he said. "It appeals to their pride, not to their pocketbook. It holds out the promise of more sacrifice, instead of more security."

Kennedy's words were more compelling on paper than in the half-empty Coliseum. Richard Nixon, watching on television a continent away, was not impressed. Kennedy seemed unimposing, unsure of himself, almost fragile. Yes, Nixon decided at that moment, he would be glad to debate his opponent on television. And yes, he would most definitely defeat him.

LEXICON: JULY 1960

Federal Hazardous Substances Act

President Eisenhower signed the Federal Hazardous Substances Act into law on July 12. It required containers of poisonous, corrosive, and flammable chemicals to display warning labels. The concept of government-mandated warnings was an innovation that would be extended in coming decades to products as diverse as cigarettes and vinyl blinds. George Wheatley, the president of the American Academy of Pediatrics, acknowledged the significance of this first step. "This law," he said, "now adds a new dimension to health protection."

Gipsy Moth III

Five competitive sailors departed from Plymouth, England, in mid-June, aiming their sailboats toward America. The best-known racer was 58-year-old Francis Chichester, a lifelong adventurer who had gained public attention in 1929 by flying solo from Great Britain to Australia. He piloted the 39-foot *Gipsy Moth III* to victory, reaching New York on July 21. His elapsed time of 40 days, 11 hours, and 30 minutes was a new record for a solo crossing of the Atlantic Ocean. The final competitor wouldn't reach Long Island until August 24.

Polaris

The idea of shooting a missile from a concealed submarine first occurred to the Germans during World War II, but a workable system wasn't devised until 1960. American engineers believed a concentrated blast of air could propel a 15-ton Polaris missile through the water and into the atmosphere. The navy ran its first test on July 20. The submerged USS *George Washington* fired a Polaris 1,150 miles from the Florida coast into the distant reaches of the Atlantic Ocean. Skipper James Osborn dispatched a message to President Eisenhower: "Polaris—from out of the deep to target. Perfect."

RB-47

An American RB-47 spy plane crashed on July 1 in the frigid Barents Sea near the Soviet Union's northern border. Nikita Khrushchev revealed nine days later that the plane had been shot down by a Soviet fighter jet. Two American survivors were in custody. The United States, backed by CIA radar data, maintained that the RB-47 had been over international waters, though the Soviets insisted it had violated their airspace. Eisenhower braced for repercussions, but none came. "Fortunately," he wrote, "the RB-47 episode took its place as but another expression of the ugly Soviet pattern of the day."

Supreme Military Tribunal

Francis Gary Powers gradually disappeared from the headlines after the Paris summit collapsed. The CIA pilot was held incommunicado in a Moscow prison, where Soviet agents interrogated him for 61 days. The U.S. ambassador, Llewellyn Thompson, did what little he could. His embassy filed four visitation requests, but the Soviets did not reply to any of the notes. The Supreme Military Tribunal finally announced on July 18 that it would adjudicate the case. Powers would stand trial for espionage on August 17, his 31st birthday.

The Long Season

Thirty-year-old Jim Brosnan of the Cincinnati Reds was an average pitcher, but his writing ability made him an atypical baseball player.

Brosnan kept a breezily cynical diary in 1959, which was published the following July as *The Long Season*. Most sports books prior to 1960 were hagiographic, but Brosnan broke the mold. He revealed that players disliked sportswriters, scanned crowds for attractive female fans, sometimes broke the game's rules, and loved a good prank. Jimmy Cannon, an influential sports columnist, hailed *The Long Season* as "the greatest baseball book ever written."

***

American interests had controlled almost all of Cuba's oil production as recently as 1958, along with 90 percent of the country's mines, 80 percent of its utilities, and 50 percent of its railways. But Fidel Castro was slowly breaking America's economic grip. He confiscated plantations and factories as spring eased into summer, even taking 7,000 U.S.-owned parking meters in Havana. No compensation was offered. One American proprietor was charged $30 for staying in his former hotel the night after it had been seized.

The ill will worsened on June 29, when Cuba expropriated Texaco's oil refinery after the American company refused to process Soviet crude. Refineries owned by Standard Oil and Royal Dutch Shell were nationalized on July 1. Next on Castro's agenda were American-owned sugar mills, valued at $200 million. "There will never be another foreigner on our land," he boasted.

Seizure of the refineries was the final straw for President Eisenhower. The United States had originally agreed to purchase 750,000 tons of Cuban sugar during the latter half of 1960. Eisenhower slashed that total to 40,000 tons on July 6—costing Cuba $92.5 million—and hinted that the quota would drop to in 1961. The massive reduction, Ike said, was in response to Cuba's "deliberate policy of hostility toward the United States." It amounted to a declaration of economic war.

Castro was furious. "If we can lose our sugar quota, part of our quota, they can lose part of their investments," he raged. "If we can lose all our sugar quota, they can lose all their investments." He ordered 600 American-owned companies to submit their operating records to the Cuban government, an obvious prelude to nationalization.

Mere diplomacy could not resolve a disagreement of such intensity, especially after Nikita Khrushchev intervened on July 9. The Soviet leader denounced the Eisenhower administration for "planning perfidious and criminal steps against the Cuban people." He offered to help Cuba resist. "If need be," he said, "Soviet artillerymen can support the Cuban people with their rocket fire." The CIA began monitoring Soviet exports to Cuba, alert for shipments that might contain components for missile bases.

Khrushchev's accusation was prescient—the United States was indeed planning military action against Castro—but no evidence has ever surfaced that the first secretary knew about Allen Dulles's scheme. CIA trainers were already at work in Guatemala, preparing a few dozen anti-Castro guerrillas to infiltrate their homeland. "The concept," said Richard Bissell, Dulles's second-in-command, "was that U.S. personnel would train twenty to thirty Cubans, that this would be a very select cadre, and that their role in turn would be to train a considerably larger number of guerrilla warriors." This small force would join existing rebels in Cuba's Escambray Mountains to foment a revolution, a carbon copy of the plan that Castro had employed to seize power.

Skeptics inside the Eisenhower administration doubted that lightning could strike twice. They argued that the Escambray rebels were badly outmanned and that Castro was stockpiling large quantities of arms. The only solution, these critics suggested, was to greatly expand the invading force. "It began to appear less and less possible to build a strong guerrilla movement in Cuba," Bissell conceded.

Eisenhower had his own concerns. He met with Dulles and Bissell on August 18 to discuss Operation Pluto, the Cuban plan he had approved in March. Ike expressed disappointment with the CIA's lack of progress. He was particularly unhappy that the agency had been unable to fuse the various strains of anti-Castro refugees into a single Cuban government-in-exile, his prerequisite for any invasion. "Boys," the president said impatiently, "if you don't intend to go through with this, let's stop talking about it."

Bissell, feeling the pressure, searched for a way to get quick results. He pondered alternatives. Why not simply kill Castro? If the Cuban leader were assassinated, perhaps his government would fall of its own weight. Bissell began batting the idea around in late August with Sheffield Edwards, the director of the CIA's Office of Security. Edwards suggested that they ask the Mafia to do the job. Gangsters had been making a fortune in Havana until Castro tossed them out. Their assassins would merely appear to be seeking revenge. Nobody would suspect that they were acting on behalf of the White House.

Bissell and Edwards took their proposal to Dulles in September. The three men spoke in vague terms about what would be done. Dulles nodded his assent. It was all very circumspect. "I knew it was serious," Bissell said. "I knew these were Mafia leaders, and I knew they were in a position to make very damaging revelations about the agency. But we thought it was all under control."

The CIA's Technical Services Division, meanwhile, began working on Cuban gimmicks of its own. No concept was deemed too bizarre for serious consideration—spraying Castro's broadcasting studio with a chemical that would induce erratic behavior, dusting his shoes with thallium salts that would cause his beard to fall out, contaminating his cigars with toxins that would disorient or kill him. Agents began to flesh out each of these brainstorms, preparing for possible implementation.

The mood at the CIA improved, though Richard Helms, the agency's director of operations, dissented from the widespread optimism. Helms watched sourly as the Cuban project branched out in a dozen different directions. The whole thing was "harebrained," he said. It was badly planned and way too risky. He stayed as far from the scheming as he could.

Agents plotting Castro's demise frequently brought their questions to Helms. He waved them all away. "I have nothing to do with this operation," he always said. Helms left the clear impression that if he were in charge, Operation Pluto would be scrapped immediately. But he wasn't running the show yet—he wouldn't become the CIA's director until 1966—so the work went on.

RISING STAR: HARPER LEE

People assumed that Nelle Harper Lee must be the daintiest of Dixie flowers. She grew up in the sleepy Alabama town of Monroeville during the twenties and thirties, and possessed such a prim and proper name. How could she be anything but a quiet, reserved lady—a genteel Southern belle?

Yet that wasn't Nelle, not at all. She had been very much the tomboy in her younger days. A childhood friend, Truman Capote, used her as the model for Idabel Tompkins, a character in his first novel, *Other Voices, Other Rooms,* which was published in 1948. "I want so much to be a boy," he had Idabel say.

Nelle blossomed into a feisty, independent woman—except when dealing with her father. A.C. Lee wanted her to join his legal practice, so she dutifully attended the University of Alabama, though her heart wasn't in it. She and Capote had enjoyed writing stories on an Underwood typewriter that A.C. had given them, and she longed to emulate his success as an author. She wrestled with this dilemma until 1949, when she left law school—one semester shy of graduation—and headed to Manhattan.

Life in the big city was difficult. Lee worked as a bookstore clerk and airline ticket agent, writing short stories at night. She struggled for eight years, refusing even to approach an agent with her material, which she considered woefully inadequate. A gift from friends Michael and Joy Brown extricated her from this rut in 1956. "You have one year off from your job to write whatever you please. Merry Christmas," said the note they gave her. Lee gratefully accepted their money—she insisted on calling it a loan—and quit her job with British Overseas Airways.

The Browns' generosity freed Lee to begin a novel about Atticus Finch, a dignified attorney in Maycomb, Alabama, who was raising 2 children, 10-year-old son Jem and 6-year-old daughter Scout, in the midst of the Depression. Theirs was an insular world, at least until Finch was appointed to defend a black man charged with raping a white woman, a controversial assignment in the segregated South.

There could be no doubt that Atticus was A.C. Lee inflated to mythological proportions—a man of infinite patience and unusual tolerance—or that Scout was young Nelle; or that Dill, the effeminate boy next door, was Capote. The J.B. Lippincott publishing house offered Lee a contract in October 1957. She and her editor, Tay Hohoff, labored the next two years to convert the rough manuscript into a polished book.

"Don't be surprised, Nelle, if you sell only two thousand copies—or less," warned Hohoff as the publication date neared. The caution was unnecessary. *To Kill a Mockingbird* hit bookstores in July 1960—Nelle had decided to be identified on the cover as Harper Lee—and flew onto the best-seller list. A few critics sniped that Atticus was too good to be true, or that the story was simplistic, but the popular reaction was overwhelmingly positive. Lee won the Pulitzer Prize in 1961. Her book was made into a movie starring Gregory Peck the following year.

What would she do for an encore? A note came in the mail in July 1961: "Dear Nelle: Tomorrow is my first birthday, and my agents think there should be another book written soon to keep me company. Do you think you can start one before I am another year old?" It was signed by The Mockingbird. Lee seemed willing, though no manuscript was forthcoming. "I hope to goodness that every novel I do gets better and better," she told an interviewer in 1964. She spoke optimistically about becoming "the Jane Austen of south Alabama."

But there would never be a second book. Nobody knew for sure— Lee declined interview requests after 1964—but her desire for privacy seemed to have overcome her dreams of a Southern *Pride and Prejudice*. She kept her New York apartment, yet lived most of the year in Monroeville with her sister. Nelle was often seen around town, though she declined to discuss *To Kill a Mockingbird* in social situations and would leave the room if strangers talked about it.

Reporters continued to pester Lee for interviews half a century after publication of her novel, now acknowledged to be an American classic. Much of her time, she complained, was wasted in writing back to decline their requests. A listener suggested that she compose a form letter for such cases, an idea that made plainspoken Nelle Harper Lee smile. It would be a brief letter, she said. Two words would suffice: "Hell, no."

***

Belgium completed its hasty retreat from the Congo on June 30, independence day for the world's newest nation. The Congolese government had a fragile, slapdash quality. Patrice Lumumba and Joseph Kasavubu hadn't hammered out a power-sharing agreement until six days before independence. Hundreds of key executive posts had not been filled. The new parliament lacked even a simple urn, so legislators were forced to deposit their voting slips into a wastebasket.

None of this mattered to Belgium's King Baudouin, who delivered a condescending speech at the independence ceremonies in the capital city of Leopoldville. "Don't replace the structures that Belgium hands over to you until you are sure you can do better," he lectured the Congolese. The king defended Belgium's colonial policies—considered indefensible by much of the world—and challenged the natives to prove they could run the country as effectively. "It is now up to you, gentlemen," he said, "to show that you are worthy of our confidence."

Kasavubu, the new president, followed with a bland, conciliatory speech. But Lumumba, the Congo's prime minister, was in no mood to accept Baudouin's version of history. Belgium, he declared, was not a benefactor. It was reluctantly granting independence to a race it considered inferior. "We have known ironies, insults, blows that we endured morning, noon, and evening because we are Negroes," Lumumba charged. He pledged that the Congo would rise above Belgium's "cruel and inhuman" legacy to become "the center of the sun's radiance for all of Africa."

Baudouin took the speech as a personal insult—as Lumumba undoubtedly intended—and decided to depart immediately. His ministers pleaded for more than an hour, finally convincing him to stay for the remainder of the celebration. The rest of the day passed without incident. Happy Congolese filled the streets, chanting, "Independence! Independence!" Huge celebratory bonfires burned from one end of the country to the other.

The optimism didn't last long. Belgium had not bothered to teach natives the craft of military administration, leaving the Congo no alternative but to retain Belgian officers for its new army. This angered the black rank and file, which mutinied on July 6, less than a week after independence day. The country was swept by rumors, often unfounded, of white men being beaten and white women being raped. Belgian civilians fled to the airports in Leopoldville, Stanleyville, and Elisabethville. Roughly 29,000 European whites had been living in the Congo on independence day. Only 3,000 remained by July 10.

Belgium's premier, Gaston Eyskens, warned against overreaction. "These are the minor growing convulsions of a young nation," he said. But a substantial number of his constituents demanded immediate military intervention. Eyskens reluctantly dispatched paratroopers to the Congo on July 8. The soldiers easily regained control of their old turf.

Their key objective was Elisabethville, the provincial capital of Katanga. Most of the Congo's incredible mineral wealth was concentrated in that part of the country, the base for the Belgian-owned mining conglomerate, Union Miniere du Haut Katanga. The provincial premier, Moise Tshombe, was no fan of the Congo's central government—"the Katanga cow will not be milked by Lumumba's serpents"—but retained kind feelings for the mother country. Tshombe announced on July 11 that Katanga would set its own course as an independent nation. Belgian troops established themselves as his protectors.

The Congo had disintegrated with breathtaking speed. Lumumba sought to stave off a complete breakdown of civil authority. "It took me just five seconds," he said, "to decide that the only place to go was the United Nations." The UN agreed on July 14 to send a 6,000-man peacekeeping force, staffed with soldiers from Sweden, Ireland, and several African nations. The Belgian command willingly gave way to the UN in most instances, though it declined to yield the white section of Leopoldville to black African troops, waiting instead for white Swedes—and it refused to leave Katanga at all.

Lumumba needed more help than the UN could provide. He traveled to the United States in late July, urgently requesting military and economic support. Secretary of State Christian Herter was favorably impressed, but his undersecretary, C. Douglas Dillon, most definitely was not. "He was a person that was gripped by this fervor that I can only characterize as messianic," Dillon said. "He was just not a rational being." The latter view resonated with Eisenhower, who considered Lumumba a dangerous radical and an incompetent administrator. "Rarely has a government proved in so short a time its lack of ability to govern," Ike said. There would be no U.S. aid.

Lumumba soon struck a deal with the Soviet Union, bringing 1,000 Soviet technicians—including 300 military advisers and a cache of weapons—to the Congo. This new partnership horrified Kasavubu and the chief of staff of the Congolese army, Joseph Mobutu, who wanted nothing to do with communism. And it convinced the United States that Lumumba was a communist himself. The CIA, which gave the prime minister the code name of Stinky, began contemplating methods of deodorization.

Eisenhower accelerated this process—wittingly or unwittingly—at a National Security Council meeting on August 18, launching into a rant about Lumumba's Soviet ties. The president's exact words were not recorded, but Allen Dulles began plotting Stinky's assassination. He sent a cable to the CIA's agent in Leopoldville on August 26. The elimination of Lumumba, Dulles wrote, was an "urgent and prime objective."

Richard Bissell insisted that Ike had sanctioned Lumumba's removal. "He would have preferred if it could be done in the nicest possible way," Bissell said, "but he wanted it done and wasn't prepared to be too fussy about how it was done." But Eisenhower's aides argued that the president was averse to assassination. They accused the CIA of seeking a scapegoat for its various failures. "Bissell was in on the plot against Castro," said Andrew Goodpaster, "and I think he was just trying to spread the blame around in implicating the president." A Senate committee concluded in 1975 that there was "ambiguity and lack of clarity in the records" about Eisenhower's intentions in the Congo.

A CIA scientist arrived in Leopoldville in late September 1960 with what was later described as "toxic biological materials." The poison was to be squirted into Lumumba's food or toothpaste. But 1960 was not the CIA's year—the U-2 had been shot down, the anti-Castro program was floundering—and the agency's bad luck held true in the Congo.

Joseph Mobutu, not yet 30 years old, moved more decisively than the CIA. He staged a coup on September 14. "We are bringing a truce to politics until the end of the year," he announced. "During this revolutionary period, we will try to achieve a political agreement between the factions." It would not be easy. Kasavubu was still technically the president, though Mobutu was now the dominant force in Leopoldville. Lumumba retained authority in the northern city of Stanleyville. And Tshombe, backed by the Belgians, continued to assert the independence of Katanga.

The CIA came to realize that it could not unravel this Gordian knot. Slipping a toxic substance into Patrice Lumumba's toothpaste could not restore order to the new nation. The logical alternative was to give Mobutu a chance to unify the country, perhaps with Kasavubu's help. The agency's man in Leopoldville abandoned his plans. He surreptitiously took the container of poison to the Congo River and tossed it in.

QUOTATIONS: JULY 1960

"It is pointless to search for a culprit in this situation. Unlike the veteran parent, we cannot say simply, 'I don't care who did it—you pick it up.' We must all pick it up together."
—*Walsh McDermott, a noted researcher at Cornell University Medical College, recommending a unified response to America's worsening problems with air and water pollution. A growing number of scientists and laymen were demanding collective action by governments, industries, and private individuals to save the environment.*

"I really enjoyed it tremendously, It was fascinating to me what the ballplayers actually said to each other during games, in the bullpen, or after games. It really revealed them as personalities.

What were these guys like? How did they think? What do they talk about?"

—Jim Bouton, a minor league baseball player, raving about Jim Brosnan's The Long Season. *Bouton was destined to reach the majors in 1962 and to write a much racier baseball book,* Ball Four, *in 1970.*

"I don't want to ever have to push that fire button. That doesn't mean I wouldn't—any time. If I have to launch them, I'll launch them. This is no canoe club we're running. But the big value of this ship is that if the Russians realize what we have here, it ought to deter them."

—Commander James Osborn, skipper of the USS George Washington, *discussing the strategic importance of the $3.5 billion Polaris missile program.*

"What news of the others?"

—Francis Chichester, shouting to the boat that greeted him off the coast of Long Island on July 21. The five competitors in the transatlantic sailing race were forbidden to communicate with each other—or anyone else—so he had no way of knowing that he was in the lead.

***

The Republican convention was nearly at hand, and Richard Nixon had not yet solved his biggest problem. Nelson Rockefeller still refused to endorse him—even though there were no other candidates—and the governor continued to belittle the party's platform. It was especially weak, Rocky said, on the crucial issues of national defense and civil rights. Nixon, who had endured Rockefeller's ill-disguised condescension for more than a year, had finally expended his patience. He decided to act.

The vice president telephoned Eisenhower's former attorney general, Herbert Brownell, and asked him to arrange a private appointment. Rockefeller was in a prickly mood when he took Brownell's call. He insisted upon three ground rules: Nixon would have to personally request the meeting; it must be held at the governor's 32-room Manhattan apartment; and Rockefeller would decide what, if anything, would be announced once the two men had wrapped up their business.

Nixon agreed to the stipulations, slipping off to New York on the evening of July 22 without notifying his aides. His first order of business was to ask Rockefeller to join him on the Republican ticket, but Rocky declined, as Nixon had known he would. The two men then turned their attention to the platform.

Rockefeller had prepared a list of recommended changes, and he and Nixon went through them until 4:30 the following morning. Rockefeller conceded several points—abandoning, for example, his demand for health insurance for the elderly—but he held firm on defense and civil rights. His intransigence posed no problem for Nixon, who privately agreed with the governor. The vice president, too, preferred to take a tougher line against the Soviets than Eisenhower had, and he had no qualms about a stronger endorsement of racial equality. The trick was to reword both planks in a manner that would not offend either the president or the Republican Party's right wing.

Nixon and Rockefeller hammered out an agreement as dawn approached. They were imprecise about defense spending, pledging "increased expenditures," but shying away from a dollar figure. "There must be no price ceiling on America's security," they wrote. They were more explicit about civil rights, replacing a vague plank with a version that Nixon hailed for dealing "specifically and not in generalities with the problems and with the goals that we desire to reach." The two men changed 14 planks in all. The resulting document would become known as the Compact of Fifth Avenue.

Rockefeller released details at 5 A.M., igniting a furor in Chicago, where the platform committee had just released its 10,000-word declaration of Republican principles. Enraged committee members asked how they could possibly incorporate wholesale changes only two days before the convention. Barry Goldwater, voicing the anger of his fellow conservatives, blasted the Compact of Fifth Avenue as the "Munich of the Republican Party," a capitulation to the party's liberal wing. Eisenhower was equally livid at the suggestion that he had allowed the nation's defenses to atrophy.

The press depicted the Compact of Fifth Avenue as the vice president's surrender to a superior political force. But Nixon saw it differently. He acknowledged that his aides, had they known, would have argued against making a deal with Rockefeller. But he dismissed their concerns. "By going to see him in New York and working out differences that were more illusory than real," he later wrote, "I was able to insure his support for the Republican ticket."

The Compact of Fifth Avenue, to be sure, had bought Rockefeller's acquiescence in Nixon's nomination, yet the vice president now faced other problems. Eisenhower's ire was calmed by a few tweaks to the defense plank, but conservatives were not so easily appeased. Texas Republicans withdrew their pledge to vote for Nixon at the convention, and other delegations began talking about a revolt. Their real hero was Goldwater, who could barely control his fury. "The man," he said of Nixon, "is a two-fisted, four-square liar."

Goldwater decided to allow conservative delegates to formally submit his name for the nomination. His followers hoped that he would mount a full-scale challenge, but he refused to go beyond a symbolic protest. "I had absolutely no interest," Goldwater later said. "In fact, if they'd gotten the 300 delegates I told them to get, I'd have thought of some other reason to get out of it."

Nixon moved quickly to put down the conservative uprising. His aides fanned out across Chicago the evening before the convention was scheduled to vote. "We collected every political IOU we held in the country that night," said one. Nixon met with delegates on what he called "virtually a round-the-clock basis." He shook hands and posed with every one of the 2,600 delegates and alternates who wanted a photo—and that was almost all of them.

Goldwater's name was submitted to the convention on July 27 by Arizona Governor Paul Fannin. Enthusiastic delegates paraded with signs bearing Goldwater's picture, but it was all for show. The senator popped up in the midst of the hoopla, striding to the podium to withdraw. He exhorted Republicans to "put our shoulders to the wheel of Dick Nixon and push him across the line." Yet he also hinted at a future campaign, a battle against Nelson Rockefeller's liberal forces. "Let's grow up, conservatives," Goldwater said. "If we want to take this party back—and I think we can some day—let's get to work." His daughter, Peggy, hugged him as he left the podium. "Daddy," she asked, "next time, will it be for real?" He promised it would.

Nixon's nomination was a formality after that. Louisiana insisted on voting for Goldwater, but everybody else got behind the vice president. The nominee convened a late-night meeting of Republican leaders to choose a running mate. Two possibilities emerged—Henry Cabot Lodge Jr., the patrician ambassador to the United Nations; and Thruston Morton, the genial chairman of the Republican National Committee. Gerald Ford, a Michigan congressman, touted Morton, but gradually realized that Nixon was leaning the other way. "Making up his mind and then pretending that his options were still open—that was a Nixon trait that I'd have occasion to witness again," Ford wrote sourly. Nixon believed that Lodge, a Massachusetts native who had lost his Senate seat to Jack Kennedy in 1952, might help him carry the Northeast.

All that remained was Nixon's acceptance speech on July 28. The evening began inauspiciously, with Rockefeller offhandedly introducing the nominee as "Richard *E.* Nixon," inexplicably mangling Richard Milhous Nixon's middle initial. But the vice president rebounded with a crisp, emphatic performance, considerably more effective than Kennedy's address in Los Angeles. The *New Republic*—no fan of his—conceded that Nixon's speech was "one of the most impressively effective fifty minutes we ever witnessed. He rang every bell."

Nixon mocked the Democratic convention: "They promised everything to everybody with one exception—they didn't promise to pay the bill." He took a hard line on defense: "America will not tolerate being pushed around by anybody." He reached out to liberals on the issue of civil rights: "Each of us should be doing his part to end the prejudice which 100 years after Lincoln, to our shame, still embarrasses us abroad and saps our strength at home." And he pledged to run the most energetic campaign in American history, personally visiting all 50 states by November.

The Republicans departed Chicago on the final Friday of July considerably more excited—and united—than they had been a week earlier. Victory was in the air. The first postconvention Gallup Poll would show Nixon with a six-point lead over Kennedy.

Eisenhower, full of good cheer, met the Republican ticketmates on July 30. "You boys are in charge," he told Nixon and Lodge. "It's your campaign, and I'll do just as little or just as much as you want me to." He expected the latter. Ike's Gallup approval rating was 63 percent, amazingly high for a president who had served nearly two full terms. Who wouldn't make extensive use of an incumbent so popular?

Eisenhower did have one suggestion, despite the hands-off policy he had enunciated a moment earlier. Nixon, he said, should refuse to debate Kennedy on television. Debates merely tested reaction time, not administrative skill. And the vice president already enjoyed a much higher profile than his Democratic opponent. Why give Kennedy free exposure?

Nixon chatted agreeably with his boss, but he had no intention of following his advice. The vice president vividly recalled the many slights—both real and imagined—that he had endured in the previous eight years, especially during those nervous months in 1956 when Ike had left him dangling before confirming his presence on the ticket. Nixon planned to run the 1960 campaign *his* way. He sent telegrams the next day to the heads of the three TV networks. Yes, he told them, he would be happy to debate Kennedy in the fall.

9

August: Beginning to Stir

Eric Sevareid belonged to the generation that had produced the two presidential nominees. The CBS commentator and syndicated columnist was virtually the same age as Richard Nixon—just 44 days older than the vice president—and was 4½ years senior to John Kennedy. Yet he felt no political attraction to either man.

"The 'managerial revolution' has come to politics," Sevareid suggested gloomily in an August column, "and Nixon and Kennedy are its first completely packaged products." He recalled the dramatic events of the thirties, the decade in which he and the candidates had reached adulthood. The birth of the New Deal, the rise of the labor movement, and the bloody denouement of the Spanish Civil War, he wrote, had inspired millions of young men and women to hope, to dream, to work, and sometimes to cry.

"I can't find in the record that Kennedy or Nixon ever did, thought, or felt these things," he went on. "They must have been across the campus on Fraternity Row, with the law and business school boys, wearing the proper clothes, thinking the proper thoughts, cultivating the proper people. I always sensed that they would end up running the big companies in town, but I'm damned if I ever thought one of them would end up running the country."

Sevareid wasn't alone in his discontent. Noted journalist Richard Rovere—a contemporary of the nominees at age 45—complained that Kennedy and Nixon were interchangeable. The two men, he wrote in *Harper's*, "tend more and more to borrow from one another's platforms and to assume one another's commitments." Agnes Meyer, an influential supporter of Adlai Stevenson, took a darker view. "Today, unless you are as scurrilous as Nixon," she said in mid-August, "you can succeed only by being as shrewd and organization-conscious as Kennedy." The peak of cynicism was ascended by 33-year-old Mort Sahl, billed as the hippest comedian in America. "It's all over but the doubting," Sahl laughed. "My considered opinion of Nixon versus Kennedy is that neither can win."

Some of these observations were justified. The two candidates *were* remarkably similar. Both were young, clean-cut, and self-restrained. Neither was a firebrand or a humorist or a raconteur. But it was simplistic to suggest that they were cut from the same cloth. Nixon had grown up in poverty, Kennedy in wealth. Nixon enjoyed a higher public profile and better health. Kennedy was more graceful and self-assured. Nixon leaned slightly to the right on the ideological spectrum, Kennedy a bit to the left.

Their campaign styles differed, too. The vice president was unable to delegate responsibility. "Nixon did everything but sweep out the plane," said his campaign director, Bob Finch. "He even insisted on sitting in the back of the plane and painstakingly writing his own speeches. We had people who were supposed to do that." Speaking to newspapermen was the one task that Nixon disdained. His aversion to reporters was deep and long-standing, and he relied upon his young aides, especially Bob Haldeman, to shield him from their irritating questions. He refused all interview requests from Theodore White, who was toiling on his epic tale of the 1960 campaign. White later admitted that whenever he covered Nixon, he felt less a reporter than "an observer who, for weeks, followed a personality with whom he was forbidden personal contact."

Kennedy's approach was looser, more detached. He kept his hands off the day-to-day mechanism of his campaign, allowing brother Bobby and brother-in-law Steve Smith to run the show. "We were organized in such a way that all the candidate had to do was show up," said Ted Sorensen. Reporters were given frequent access to Kennedy, who truly seemed to enjoy their company. White recalled sharing a long flight with the candidate and CBS's Blair Clark late one night. "Blair and I sat around with John F. Kennedy all the way from Montana back to the East Coast, just shooting the breeze," he said with wonderment.

Nixon and Kennedy first met in 1947 as freshmen members of the House of Representatives. They cemented their acquaintance that

April, when both were invited to a public meeting in McKeesport, Pennsylvania, to argue their respective cases for and against a labor bill pending in Congress. They walked to a diner after the debate, chatting about baseball. "It was hard to tell who had come from the wealthy family and who had worked his way up," said the McKeesport stockbroker who served as moderator that night. "Neither could be called a stuffed shirt."

They remained friendly through the years, despite their partisan differences. Kennedy surreptitiously passed Nixon a $1,000 contribution for the latter's Senate campaign in 1950. Nixon sent Kennedy a basket of fruit in 1955 to welcome him back to the Senate after one of his many hospital stays. The two rivals even shared polling data in the years leading up to the 1960 campaign.

Nixon appeared on the *Tonight Show* shortly after the Republican convention. "Are you friendly with Jack Kennedy?" asked Jack Paar. The audience—anticipating the worst—laughed nervously. But Nixon simply said that, yes, they were friends. He insisted that the approaching contest would not damage their goodwill. "I don't believe this campaign will be a personal campaign from the standpoint of personal animosity," he said. "I would hope not."

Kennedy lingered at his family's compound in Hyannis Port, Massachusetts, as August began. But Nixon—feeling the weight of his 50-state pledge—could not afford to tarry. The vice president took flight on August 2, hitting four states (Nevada, California, Hawaii, and Washington) in four days. He planned to spend much of August in hard-to-reach states (such as Alaska and Hawaii) and places where he had no hope of victory (the Democratic strongholds in the Deep South), freeing him to concentrate on key battlegrounds as the election neared.

Political strategists couldn't understand why Nixon would waste his time in the South. No Republican presidential candidate—not even a military hero like Eisenhower—had ever carried Georgia. No Republican had won Alabama, Mississippi, or South Carolina since the end of Reconstruction 83 years earlier. There seemed no reason to believe that Nixon, long an advocate of civil rights, could curry sufficient favor with white Southerners to buck this trend. But he announced plans to visit Greensboro, North Carolina, on August 17, and Atlanta and Birmingham nine days later.

All three cities responded with unanticipated enthusiasm. "It is time for the Republican candidates to quit conceding the South to the

Democrats without a battle," Nixon declared in Birmingham. The reception later that day in Atlanta was truly impressive, with 150,000 people jamming five and six deep on the sidewalks to cheer his motorcade. Ralph McGill, the editor and publisher of the *Atlanta Constitution*, called Nixon's visit "the biggest thing in Atlanta since the premiere of *Gone With the Wind*."

The vice president reiterated his support for civil rights in every speech—"you know my convictions on that issue"—yet he also trimmed his sails. He reminded audiences that he had lived in the South while attending Duke University Law School in the thirties, and he hinted at common ground with white Southerners who adamantly opposed federally mandated school integration. "Let us never forget that in American education, we always want to preserve freedom," Nixon said in Greensboro, "and one of the essences of freedom in this country is local and state control of the educational system."

The vice president had long assured fellow Republicans that black voters would be easier to attract—and more politically influential—than white Southerners. "Something is going to happen that will get more Negroes voting," he had insisted at a 1957 meeting with Republican congressional leaders. But he was beginning to have doubts, as proven by the rhetorical tightrope that he walked in Birmingham and Atlanta. "It was a curse in disguise," Richard Goodwin, then a Kennedy aide, wrote of the vice president's triumphant swing. "It persuaded Nixon that he might actually carry the South. To do so, however, he would have to mute his advocacy of civil rights."

The implications of this subtle adjustment would not become clear until November. The Southern trips seemed at the time to be an unmitigated success. Nixon had only one complaint, a fleeting one at that. He had injured his left knee in Greensboro, jamming it sharply into a car door. "The immediate pain soon passed," he recalled, "and I thought no more about it."

Kennedy could only watch with envy as Nixon crisscrossed the nation. The Democratic nominee was marooned in Washington, the prisoner of his running mate's ill-fated brainstorm. Lyndon Johnson had decided in early July—shortly after announcing his presidential candidacy—to reconvene the Senate on August 8. The majority leader envisioned the special session as a showcase for his legislative talents. If he were fortunate enough to return to Washington as his party's nominee, the resulting publicity would surely boost his presidential campaign.

Los Angeles, of course, had ruined those plans. But Johnson was determined to make the best of things. "We expect to have evening sessions," he told his unhappy colleagues when they arrived. "We expect to have Saturday sessions. We expect to convene early and to stay in session late."

Tourists flocked to the Senate chamber to watch three of the four national candidates in action, but they didn't see much. Kennedy sat in the back, quietly fuming as the days slipped away. Johnson struggled mightily to orchestrate the action from his desk in the front, though with little success. Nixon, who was technically the president of the Senate, occasionally appeared on the rostrum. But his only duty was to break tie votes, which usually left him free to campaign.

Stephen Young, an Ohio Democrat, tried to make an issue of Nixon's infrequent attendance. He announced that he had timed the vice president's appearances in the presiding officer's chair—just 2 hours, 55 minutes, and 40 seconds during the first week of the special session. Barry Goldwater shot back that Kennedy seemed to have missed several roll calls while on short campaign jaunts of his own. "Where is the distinguished senator from Massachusetts?" Goldwater asked. "I don't know. He might be on his yacht."

Everybody wanted to leave Washington. Labor Day—the traditional opening date for the fall presidential campaign—was drawing near. "The sooner we get out of here, the better it will be," said Mike Mansfield, the Democratic whip. Johnson, unable to get anybody to pass anything, waved the white flag after three weeks.

The main event was nearly at hand.

LEXICON: AUGUST 1960

Ban the Bomb

The peace movement was gathering steam. Twenty thousand protesters marched in London in April, brandishing signs that said "Ban the Bomb." Massive rallies followed in New York, San Francisco, and Los Angeles. Nikita Khrushchev, seeking to ride the wave, called on August 1 for a "broad and comprehensive discussion" of disarmament. He invited the heads of all 82 governments represented in the United Nations to join him at the UN's mid-September session in New York. It would be, he said grandly, the biggest summit conference ever.

Belka and Strelka

The Soviets launched a Vostok capsule on August 19. It carried two dogs, Belka ("Squirrel") and Strelka ("Arrow"), who circled the earth 17 times before their spacecraft floated down in Kazakhstan. They were the first creatures to orbit the globe and return safely. Veterinarians detected no ill effects from their daylong adventure. The importance of Belka and Strelka's flight was difficult to overstate. "We have crossed the threshold of manned spaceflight," crowed a Soviet space scientist.

Echo I

The satellite that soared from Cape Canaveral on August 12—*Echo I*—was the biggest object launched during the first three years of the space age. It inflated after reaching orbit, expanding into a silvery balloon as tall as a 10-story building. *Echo I* was designed for a simple task—reflecting radio waves from one end of America to the other—but its impact was far-reaching. NASA called it the forerunner of a new era, the first of a series of satellites that would eventually provide instantaneous communications around the globe.

Hall of Columns

Moscow's ornate Hall of Columns had been the site of several dramatic events, including the funerals of Vladimir Lenin and Joseph Stalin. It served as the venue for Francis Gary Powers's three-day trial, which began August 17 before a crowd of 2,000 Soviet dignitaries. Powers pleaded guilty to espionage—his court-appointed attorney said it would be futile to fight the charges—and received a 10-year sentence. But Khrushchev didn't intend to imprison him that long. "What use is he to us? We just have to feed him," the Soviet leader said privately. "Let a little time pass, and we'll release him."

Sovereign Capacity

Jimmie Davis declared on August 17 that his "sovereign capacity" as governor of Louisiana allowed him to take charge of New Orleans's school system. He immediately prohibited classroom integration. An appeals court ruled 10 days later that Davis's seizure was unconstitutional. It reinstated Labor Day as the deadline for desegregation.

Judge J. Skelly Wright, who had issued the original order, decided that a cooling-off period might ease tensions. He announced on August 30 that he would delay integration until November 14—but not one day further.

Space Needle

Seattle intended to stage a world's fair in 1962, and organizers hoped to build a distinctive structure on the fairgrounds. Eddie Carlson, the owner of a regional hotel chain, suggested a tower similar to one he had seen in West Germany. He made a rough sketch on a napkin. Architect Victor Steinbrueck added a tripod whose legs converged two-thirds of the way up the 520-foot main structure and then diverged to support an observation deck and restaurant. He drew this clean, futuristic design in August 1960. Foundation work for the Space Needle would begin eight months later.

***

It was difficult to imagine the superpowers having any interest in Laos. The Southeast Asian country was sleepy, mountainous, and lacking in national spirit. Its residents belonged to 42 separate tribes that had been jumbled together by mapmakers at a 1954 conference in Geneva. *Time* quoted an anonymous U.S. military officer who scoffed at the very idea of a Cold War confrontation there. The Laotian people were apathetic, he said, and the roads were often impassable. "It would be like fighting the French and Indian War all over again," he moaned.

Yet the United States was deeply entangled in Laotian politics. John Foster Dulles had proclaimed in 1954 that America would never allow Laos to fall into communist hands, a declaration that triggered $300 million of military and economic aid in the following six years. "The Southeast Asian peninsula is a target for Communist China, and Laos is the first point of entry," explained Admiral Harry Felt, the U.S. commander-in-chief in the Pacific. This was the famed domino theory. If one Asian country fell to the communists, went the thinking, its neighbors were sure to follow.

It was difficult to keep track of the players in Laos. Prime ministers came and went with great frequency. Some were friendly to the United States, while others were neutral. The 29,000-man Laotian army battled sporadically with the communist Pathet Lao, but neither side made much headway.

The situation became even more confusing in the early morning hours of August 9. Kong Le, a 26-year-old captain of paratroopers, staged a coup in the capital city of Vientiane. His goal, he said, was to drive foreign agents and advisers out of Laos. He accused the Americans and Soviets of exploiting his country's civil war for their own selfish purposes. "Lao must stop killing Lao," he said. "I have fought for many years and have killed many men, but I have never seen a foreigner die."

Kong Le's rationale seemed too pat to the State Department and the CIA, which feared that he might be a Soviet agent himself. Reporter Tillman Durdin voiced their concerns in the *New York Times*. "This week's coup in Vientiane," he wrote, "may be what the communists have been looking for." But President Eisenhower came closer to the truth at his August 17 press conference. "Well," he began, "Laos is a very confused situation." And it would remain so, causing the administration to temporarily suspend military aid in October. "The situation is so confused," said General Williston Palmer, the director of military assistance, "that we have not been sure who is responsible for anything."

Conditions weren't much better in the adjacent domino. U.S. aid had been flowing to South Vietnam for a decade, ever since Harry Truman's 1950 decision to help France maintain its grip on its Indochinese colonies. The French were driven out by Ho Chi Minh in 1954—despite having received $3 billion in American assistance—and the anti-communist burden rested thereafter on the United States.

Eisenhower refused to send troops to Vietnam, but he had no qualms about shipping an endless stream of military equipment to Ngo Dinh Diem's army. Vietnam had been partitioned by the same Geneva conference that invented Laos. Ho's communists were confined to the northern half of the country, Diem's rightists to the south. The two sides were supposed to reunite after a plebiscite in 1956, but Diem scuttled the agreement, contending that the election would not be "absolutely free."

Civil war had raged ever since. Communist guerrillas, known as the Vietcong, took the offensive. They mounted their biggest attack to date in February 1960, storming a South Vietnamese regimental headquarters. Thirty-four of Diem's soldiers were killed, the bloodiest toll in the war so far. Political assassinations were also on the rise, with 50 to 75 South Vietnamese officials being slain by the Vietcong in a typical week.

These unhappy developments demoralized South Vietnam's citizens. It didn't help that Diem was a devout Catholic in an overwhelmingly Buddhist country, or that he was a distant figure who disdained the hallmarks of democracy. He made no apologies for censoring the press or using the secret police to harass his critics. "Security," he insisted, "must come before liberty."

Eisenhower was deluged with conflicting advice about America's future course in Southeast Asia. A House of Representatives subcommittee suggested in 1960 that the aid program for South Vietnam should be scaled back, but the State Department recommended an increase in military assistance. Few people on either side of the debate were happy with Diem, but there were no obvious alternatives.

John Foster Dulles had once been asked why the United States had tied its fortunes to a leader as flawed as Diem. His reply was simple: "Because we knew of no one better." The State Department's old warrior had been dead for 15 months, but his logic still held. His successors in Washington were desperately searching for a solution to their Vietnamese problem, but they had yet to come up with a better answer.

RISING STAR: GERALDYN COBB

Geraldyn Cobb was born in a time and place—1931 in Oklahoma—where girls were expected to be demure. But the energetic tomboy dreamed of flying airplanes. She first took the rudder at age 12, soloed at 16, and earned her commercial license at 18. She was determined to make her living as a pilot.

"The one little thing," Cobb said later, "was that no one would hire me." Her big break didn't come until 1953, an assignment to ferry planes to the Peruvian air force. Male pilots spurned the job—they could make better money in more comfortable conditions—so she was hired. Regular runs over the Andes Mountains proved she had the necessary skill and courage. She never lacked for work again.

Cobb secured the respect of her male peers in the late fifties, when she piloted a twin-engine Aero Commander to world records for altitude, distance, and speed. The National Pilots Association chose her as 1959's Pilot of the Year, and the Federation Aeronautique

Internationale presented her with its Gold Wings of Achievement, the first woman so honored.

If all of this had happened a generation earlier, Jerrie Cobb might have become a household name. But aviation was evolving in 1959. Children no longer dreamed of flying their own jets. They wanted to blast off from Cape Canaveral. Susan Kleinberg, a 10-year-old girl from California, eagerly wrote President Eisenhower that she hoped to be a space pioneer. "We are not taking little girls in the astronaut corps," Ike replied.

One expert wondered if this was the best policy. Randy Lovelace, the head of NASA's Life Sciences Committee, asked Cobb if she would be willing to undergo the same evaluation process as the Mercury astronauts. Technicians ran a battery of tests in February 1960. She was jabbed repeatedly with an electric needle; locked for 9 hours in an isolation chamber; peppered with 195 psychological questions; and strapped into MASTIF, the dizzying simulator the astronauts had come to hate.

Lovelace was astounded by the results. Cobb tolerated heat as well as the astronauts did, outlasted them in the isolation tank, and had a higher pain threshold. She was qualified, according to his report, to "live, observe, and do optimal work in the environment of space." Lovelace revealed his findings at the Space and Naval Medicine Congress in Stockholm on August 18, 1960. "We are already in a position," he declared, "to say that certain qualities of the female space pilot are preferable to those of her male colleague."

News stories from Stockholm hailed the new "astronette." *Time* predicted, "If all goes well, perhaps in late 1962, Jerrie Cobb will don a formless pressure suit, tuck her ponytail into a helmet, and hop atop a rocket for the long, lonely trip into space." Readers were left with the erroneous impression that NASA had hired its newest astronaut.

Cobb lobbied NASA's administrator, James Webb, to make her dream a reality. The space program, he replied, had no room for a female astronaut. So she turned to Congress. "There were women on the *Mayflower* and on the first wagon trains west, working alongside the men to forge new trails to new vistas," she testified before a House subcommittee in July 1962. NASA fired back with its most powerful weapon, John Glenn, the first American to orbit the earth. Glenn insisted that Lovelace's tests didn't prove anything. "My mother could probably pass the physical exam that they give preseason for the

Jerrie Cobb trains on the MASTIF simulator: "There were women on the *Mayflower* and on the first wagon trains west." (National Aeronautics and Space Administration)

Washington Redskins," he laughed, "but I doubt if she could play too many games for them."

"After that," Cobb wrote, "we didn't have a chance." She ground her teeth when the Soviets launched the first woman into space, Valentina Tereshkova, in June 1963. She retreated to Latin America two years later, transporting food and vaccines across the Amazon basin on behalf of several church groups. She was still there in 1983—when Sally Ride became the first American woman in outer space—and continued her humanitarian work into the 21st century.

But Jerrie Cobb never lost her fascination with the space program. Seventy-seven-year-old John Glenn was cleared for his second mission in 1998, and she found herself drawn to Cape Canaveral. "I was here for his first flight, and I'm back," she said. "I'm here to wish him Godspeed again. I only wish I could be going with him."

Yet Cobb was a realist. She knew her time had passed, even though she was a decade younger than Glenn. Her spirit, on the other hand, was as willing and eager as ever. "I would give my life to fly in space," she said. "I would have then. I would now."

***

Almost three decades had passed since the repeal of Prohibition—an idealistic experiment gone sadly awry—and alcohol had become more firmly entrenched in American society than ever. U.S. distillers produced 285 million gallons of spirits in 1960. It was the largest output of liquor in the nation's history, up 9.5 percent from the previous year. Consumption of beer also reached record levels.

Other forms of intoxication, however, did not share alcohol's popularity. Illegal drugs were spurned by upstanding adults and ignored by the younger generation. Only 169 people were arrested in 1960 for violating the federal law against possession of marijuana. Heroin and cocaine were used primarily by hardcore junkies in big cities, and their ranks seemed to be dwindling. The *Britannica Book of the Year* confidently noted a "general decrease in the incidence of addiction."

Yet it would be wrong to infer that Americans rejected all things pharmaceutical. They were exceptionally receptive to mood-altering drugs blessed with the government's seal of approval. The Hoffmann-La Roche chemical firm patented a powerful sedative, Librium, in 1959. Sales skyrocketed in 1960, and the company hastily set to work on Valium, a tranquilizer that was five times stronger. Psychiatrists hailed a drug of even greater potency—lysergic acid diethylamide—for its therapeutic benefits. Their only quibble was with its multisyllabic name, which was such a tongue-twister that they preferred its informal lab designation, LSD.

A *Time* reporter paid a visit in early 1960 to 2 Los Angeles psychiatrists who had used LSD as a "facilitating agent" in treating 110 patients. Arthur Chandler and Mortimer Hartman said the drug caused their clients to see "illusions" that helped to overcome inhibitions and sharpen mental focus. "Some patients," the doctors wrote, "describe it by saying that it is as though a 3-D tape were being run off in the visual field." Actor Cary Grant subsequently identified himself as one of their clients. LSD, he said, had shown him that he had "a tough inner core of strength."

This wonder drug, despite its sudden notoriety, was not new. LSD had been synthesized in 1938 by Albert Hofmann, a Swiss chemist. He inadvertently ingested the drug five years later and was stunned by the vivid hallucinations that resulted. His scientific curiosity led him to consume 250 micrograms of LSD three days later, this time yielding darker visions. "A demon had invaded me, had taken possession of my body, mind, and soul," he recalled. "I was seized by the dreadful fear of going insane."

What could possibly be done with such a volatile chemical? Sandoz Laboratories began sending samples to researchers in 1949. LSD, the company suggested, might be useful in the study of schizophrenia. Other adherents touted it as a cure for alcoholism, a weapon against mental illness, or a tool to enhance creativity.

UCLA professor Sidney Cohen launched a government-sponsored study in the late fifties to nail down the therapeutic values—if any— of LSD. His subjects included Henry Luce, the founder of *Time*; and his wife, Clare Boothe Luce, the playwright and politician. Clare kept diaries during her drug trips, combining incomprehensible notes ("capture green bug for future reference") with portentous aphorisms ("feel all true paths of glory lead but to the grave"). Her husband conducted an invisible symphony in their backyard.

Cohen augmented these personal observations with a survey of 65 researchers who had tested LSD on 25,000 subjects. He concluded in a 1960 report that the drug did indeed have value in psychotherapy. "No one was ever harmed" by the controlled use of LSD, he wrote.

These research projects exposed a growing number of Americans to hallucinogens. Ken Kesey, an aspiring novelist, volunteered for drug tests at California's Menlo Park Veterans Hospital in 1960. Poet Allen Ginsberg took LSD at the Mental Research Institute in Palo Alto, California. Both were attracted by the fee that participants received, but they evolved into passionate advocates. Philosopher Alan Watts voiced similar excitement in *This Is It*, a book published in December 1960. Watts described LSD as a harmless, yet extremely beneficial drug that had endowed him with "illuminated consciousness."

Timothy Leary seemed an unlikely candidate to join the ranks of these enthusiasts. Harvard University had appointed him as a lecturer in clinical psychology in 1959, and he did his best to fit the part. "With my horn-rimmed glasses," he wrote, "I looked like a caricature of a professor—except for the white tennis shoes, which I wore everywhere."

But Leary's life was not as serene as it appeared. His first wife had committed suicide in 1955, his second wife had opted for a divorce, and he had developed a severe drinking problem. Depression haunted him as he departed for a vacation in Cuernavaca, Mexico, in the summer of 1960. His 40th birthday loomed in October, and he saw no reason for hope. "I was a middle-aged man," he wrote, "involved in the middle-aged process of dying."

An anthropologist from the University of Mexico, Lothar Knauth, frequently visited Leary and the friends with whom he was sharing a villa in Cuernavaca. Knauth described the religious rites practiced by local Indians, including the ingestion of sacred mushrooms that were said to promote heightened consciousness. He brought a handful of black, moldy mushrooms to the villa on August 9. They smelled to Leary like "forest damp and crumbling logs and New England basement." He was certain they were poisonous. But Knauth ate one, and the others followed his lead. Leary finally took a bite. The mushrooms tasted even worse than they smelled. "Bitter, strong, filthy," he recalled. "I took a slug of Carta Blanca and jammed the rest in my mouth and washed them down."

Leary settled back, expecting the worst, but soon began to enjoy the experience. He felt as if he were floating across the room. Colors flashed kaleidoscopically before his eyes. "I gave way to delight," he wrote, "as mystics have for centuries when they peeked through the curtains and discovered that this world—so manifestly real—was actually a tiny stage set constructed by the mind." He quickly became convinced that psilocybin—the compound that gave the mushrooms their hallucinogenic punch—possessed great educational potential. "I learned more in the six or seven hours of this experience," he said, "than in all my years as a psychologist."

The eager convert was determined to spread the word. Leary established the Harvard Psychedelic Project in the fall of 1960—ostensibly to conduct academic research into hallucinatory drugs, though a few of his colleagues suspected he simply wanted an excuse to eat more mushrooms. The assumption wasn't far from the truth.

It was remarkably easy to obtain psilocybin in tablet form. Leary sent a request to Sandoz Laboratories, expecting a stringent application process to follow. But a box arrived in his office just before Thanksgiving. Inside were four bottles, each filled with tiny pills and imprinted with a warning label: "Not To Be Sold: For Research Investigation." The Harvard Psychedelic Project was suddenly and unexpectedly in business.

Leary began administering psilocybin to a wide range of subjects— more than 100 in the next four months. Poets Peter Orlovsky and Allen

Ginsberg, who participated in a notorious session on a Sunday night in November, tried to place a telephone call to Nikita Khrushchev while under the influence. "By Monday afternoon, the rumors were spreading around Harvard Yard," Leary wrote. "Beatniks. Orgies. Naked poets. Junkies. Homosexuality. Drug parties." The head of his department demanded to know what was going on. Leary laughed. "I'll send you the reports from the session as soon as they're typed," he said. "It was a good session. God would approve. We're learning a lot."

His plans were much bigger than that. Leary sat in his kitchen with Ginsberg, who was still excited about the "cosmic electronic networks" revealed by psilocybin. The two men agreed that everybody deserved the chance to "turn on" with hallucinogenic mushrooms, that America desperately needed what Leary called a "psychedelic revolution." They would be its apostles, and they believed they could convert the entire country.

"We'll turn on Arthur Schlesinger," Leary gleefully predicted. "And then—we'll turn on John F. Kennedy."

QUOTATIONS: AUGUST 1960

"We gradually got used to the presence of spies in the sky, as you adjust to everything in life. It simply came to resemble somewhat the life of lizards in a glass terrarium, where anyone who wanted to, could peer in."

> —Nikita Khrushchev's son, Sergei, reacting to Corona,
> the first American spy satellite. Its launch on August 18
> was top secret, but the Soviets soon learned of its presence.
> CIA officials privately bragged that Corona's photos were so
> precise that they could isolate individual players in a soccer game.

"I appeal to Mr. Khrushchev as one father to another for the sake of my boy."

> —Oliver Powers, tearfully pleading for his son's freedom
> on August 13, four days before the start of his trial
> in Moscow. Khrushchev was not persuaded.

"I don't know. I just turned on the switches."

> —Francis Gary Powers, responding to a Soviet prosecutor
> who asked how the U-2's camera system worked.

"Encouraged by the success of their efforts thus far, Negro South-erners can be expected to increase their economic and moral pressures for equal treatment by business and government."

> —*The Southern Regional Council, predicting in an*
> *August 6 report that the drive for racial equality*
> *would accelerate in the years to come. Blacks had*
> *scored a major victory two weeks earlier, when the*
> *Greensboro Woolworth's finally caved in and*
> *integrated its lunch counter.*

"I do not want another Little Rock."

> —*Robert Ainsworth, the president of the Louisiana State*
> *Senate, urging his colleagues to prevent Governor Jimmie*
> *Davis from seizing control of the New Orleans school*
> *system. Ainsworth warned that "disorder or even bloodshed"*
> *would result, similar to the chaotic situation in Little*
> *Rock in 1957. The Senate hooted down his objections.*

* * *

It is axiomatic that a political candidate must transform negatives into positives—turn lemons into lemonade—to maximize his odds of victory. So Jack Kennedy emphasized his youthfulness as he darted on short campaign trips in August, briefly escaping the somnolent session of Congress. Richard Nixon might chide him for inexperience and immaturity, but Kennedy preferred to spin his tale a happier way. He promised to bring vigor and vitality to the White House.

"What shall we do in this country?" he asked at a rally in Portland, Maine. "What shall we do around the world to reverse the trend of history, to take those actions here in this country and throughout the globe that shall make people feel that, in the year of 1961, the American giant began to stir again, the great American boiler began to fire up again, this country began to move ahead again?"

It was an effective line, yet Kennedy was wary of pushing the youth-and-vigor angle too far. He could not afford to alienate the millions of middle-aged and elderly voters who remained fond of Franklin Roosevelt and Harry Truman. So he began to reach out to old-line Democrats, stressing that he and his advisers were not "a collection of angry young men."

The living icons of the Democratic Party—Adlai Stevenson, Eleanor Roosevelt, and Truman—had deep reservations about the nominee.

They brooded about his age, doubted his liberalism, and scorned his father. Kennedy considered it essential to win their favor. He took personal control of what he called his "fence-mending chores."

Stevenson was the easiest to convince. He was coy in public—"I would look on any office with great respect"—but privately harbored an ambition to be secretary of state. He traveled to Hyannis Port on July 31. "There followed five hours in the bosom—or the shark's teeth—of the Kennedy family ashore and afloat," Stevenson wrote to a friend. "Even the Black Prince and wife were there." The latter was a pointed reference to Bobby Kennedy, whose relationship with Stevenson had never been comfortable. But the older man camouflaged his distaste. He volunteered to campaign for Jack Kennedy and to prepare a detailed report about foreign policy.

Eleanor Roosevelt posed a greater challenge. She held no political office—nor desired any—yet remained influential, the embodiment of the New Deal and American liberalism. Kennedy dreaded their August 14 meeting at her estate in Hyde Park, New York. "She hated my father," he insisted privately, "and she can't stand it that his children turned out so much better than hers." The first part, at least, was accurate. The former first lady still resented Old Joe's abandonment of Great Britain in World War II.

Her disdain extended to the son. Kennedy had dodged the most controversial issue to face the Senate during the fifties, the matter of Joseph McCarthy, the red-baiting senator from Wisconsin. Liberals had demanded that McCarthy be censured, but many of Kennedy's constituents were opposed. "Hell," he told a friend, "half my voters in Massachusetts look on McCarthy as a hero." The roll call in December 1954 coincided with one of Kennedy's hospital stays, providing an easy escape for the future author of *Profiles in Courage.* His failure to vote on the censure resolution earned Roosevelt's contempt. The presidency, she told reporters in 1958, should not go to "someone who understands what courage is and admires it, but has not quite the independence to have it."

Kennedy anticipated a scolding at best, a flat refusal of support at worst. He was certain that Roosevelt would make demands, perhaps insisting that her great friend, Stevenson, be named secretary of state. But none of these scenarios occurred. "I liked him better than I ever had before," Roosevelt wrote after their amiable conversation. "I think I am not mistaken in feeling that he would make a good president if elected." Kennedy was elated by Roosevelt's unexpected willingness to help his cause. "The senator came out of there like a boy who has just made a good confession," aide David Powers recalled. "It was a great load off his mind."

That left the plainspoken Truman. Cynics suggested that the former president's opposition was religious in nature. The crusty Baptist, they said, could never abide a Catholic in the White House. "It's not the pope I'm afraid of," Truman shot back. "It's the pop." He, too, would not forgive Joe Kennedy for abandoning America's truest ally in its darkest hour.

Yet there was more to it than that. Only a month had passed since Truman's suggestion that Kennedy should withdraw from the race, and his opinion of the nominee had not improved since the convention. Truman unhappily laid out the options in a letter he wrote (but never sent) to Dean Acheson, who had been his secretary of state. "You and I are stuck with the necessity of taking the worst of two evils or none at all," he contended. "So I'm taking the immature Democrat as the best of the two. Nixon is impossible."

Several high-profile Democrats urged Truman to bestow his blessings on Kennedy. The ex-president grumbled but finally consented. A meeting was arranged for August 20 at the Truman Library in Independence, Missouri. "Come right on in here, young man," Truman said. "I want to talk to you." He pulled Kennedy inside, where they spoke for 40 minutes. The subsequent endorsement was anything but hearty. "The convention nominated this man," Truman snappishly told reporters, "and I am going to support him. And what are you going to do about it?" But he agreed to campaign for Kennedy, and he lived up to his word, maintaining an active schedule throughout the fall.

Nixon was having similar problems with his party's old guard—or, more specifically, its oldest general. "Damn it," President Eisenhower growled at his aides that summer, "don't you fellows forget that I'm going to be around for quite some time yet." He had no intention of playing a supporting role to his vice president, or of modifying his policies to help his understudy's campaign. Nixon dropped hints that a tax cut might energize the economy, not to mention his chances of defeating Kennedy. Ike turned him down. Nixon, for his part, made no effort to involve his boss in the planning process. "Dick never asked me how I thought the campaign should be run," the president said with pained surprise.

Nixon intended to portray himself as a man of independent spirit, a seasoned veteran of global diplomacy. He boasted about having met 35 presidents, 9 prime ministers, 2 emperors, and the shah of Iran. His campaign slogan was "It's Experience That Counts."

The press corps repeatedly asked Eisenhower to describe the true extent of Nixon's experience. What programs had the vice president initiated? What key decisions had he made? Ike conceded that his second-in-command had been helpful—"Mr. Nixon has taken a full part in every principal discussion"—but he bridled at the suggestion that any of his underlings might be calling the shots.

Charles Mohr, a reporter for *Time,* dared to bring up the subject again at Eisenhower's August 24 press conference. "We understand that the power of decision is entirely yours, Mr. President," he said gingerly. "I just wondered if you could give us an example of a major idea of [Nixon's] that you had adopted in that role, as the decider and final. . . ."

Eisenhower, obviously irritated, cut Mohr off. "If you give me a week," he said, "I might think of one. I don't remember."

It was a devastating putdown—14 simple words that punctured Nixon's claims of leadership ability and unparalleled experience. Eisenhower returned to the Oval Office and immediately called the vice president to apologize, while pundits speculated about his eruption. Perhaps Ike was angry at the implication that he had lost control of his administration, or maybe he had simply lost another skirmish in his ongoing war with the English language.

Eisenhower's zinger confirmed the vice president's decision to chart his own course. "That burned Nixon up," Barry Goldwater remembered, "and he said he'd win his election without Ike's help." But there was a more immediate concern. Nixon's injury—the knee he had bumped in Greensboro—was getting worse, finally forcing him to submit to tests at Walter Reed Army Medical Center.

Walter Tkach, the assistant White House physician, called on August 29 with the results. "We want you to come out to the hospital right away," he said.

Nixon replied that he had no time.

"You had better get out to the hospital," the doctor retorted, "or you will be campaigning on one leg." Nixon's knee was infected with hemolytic staphylococcus aureus. The only remedy was massive doses of antibiotics, supplemented with bed rest. Tkach informed him that he would be confined to Walter Reed for two weeks.

"God sometimes makes us lie down so that we will look up more," a 12-year-old girl from Baltimore wrote Nixon. But he took no solace from her letter or the thousands of get well cards piling up in his hospital room. Congress had finally wrapped up its special session, and Kennedy was on the loose. Nixon—he of the 50-state pledge—needed to be out among the voters, too.

The vice president chafed at the inactivity. His knee pain was "bad enough," he told everybody who visited him, but "the mental suffering was infinitely worse." It was the most frustrating moment of his campaign—and one of the bleakest of his entire career.

10

September: Substance and Appearance

Richard's Nixon's postconvention lead over John Kennedy—6 percentage points as of mid-August—vanished by the beginning of September. A new Gallup Poll found them locked in a dead heat. Kennedy had picked up three points in half a month, while Nixon had lost three. Each was now supported by 47 percent of the electorate.

The vice president's campaign—so smooth and ebullient a month earlier—was encountering economic turbulence. The U.S. Labor Department reported in early September that the unemployment rate had risen again, its third straight monthly increase. The Dow Jones Industrial Average was heading in the opposite direction, plummeting to its lowest level in 19 months. Economic experts, who had greeted 1960 with high expectations, were baffled. "I've never seen a year when our forecasts and actual production were so out of line," grumbled Joseph Block, the chairman of Inland Steel Company.

These recessionary portents posed a danger to Nixon, the candidate of the party in power, but there was little he could do. He remained in Walter Reed as the month began, fussing and fuming while antibiotics waged war against the staph infection in his knee. Kennedy happily filled the media void, promising reporters that he would not "mention [Nixon], unless I could praise him, until he got out of the hospital." He paused playfully. "And," he smiled, "I have not mentioned him."

The doctors finally set Nixon free on the evening of September 9, urging him to take it easy for a few days. There was no chance of that. The vice president—gaunt, haggard, and favoring his knee—set out on a 14-state, 9,000-mile swing. He raced from Maryland to Indiana to

Texas to California to the Pacific Northwest and back to the Midwest in the first three days, desperately seeking to make up for lost time.

The momentum clearly belonged to Kennedy, who had formally launched his fall campaign in Detroit on Labor Day. He was engulfed by thousands of supporters at the Detroit airport, an image of mass adulation that was prominently displayed on the front pages of newspapers from coast to coast. "My God, I can't believe that crowd," Kennedy excitedly told Jerry Bruno, his advance man in Detroit. "How did you do it?"

Bruno didn't tell his candidate that the airport greeting had been accidental. A rickety fence had collapsed, allowing Kennedy's supporters to push forward. "It looked so good on film and in the press that, from then on, we made sure that crowds surged over Kennedy," Bruno recalled. "I'd have two men holding a rope by an airport or along a motorcade. Then, at the right time, they'd just drop the rope."

Kennedy's speeches were still erratic in quality—eloquent and compelling on some occasions, rushed and high-pitched at other times. But he struck the right notes more often than not, lashing the "ruthless, godless" communist system, raising the specter of an alleged missile gap, and always promising to infuse the White House with vigor.

Yet Kennedy, like Nixon, had areas of vulnerability. The voters knew nothing of his numerous extramarital affairs, but the leaders of both parties were well aware of his penchant for womanizing. "Much too much talk about Jack's girls," Adlai Stevenson wrote to a friend after dining with well-connected Democratic politicians in early August. The same rumors reached Republicans. Bob Finch recalled hearing "the usual business about some promiscuity," but he made no use of the stories. Thomas Dewey advised the rest of Nixon's staff to follow Finch's example. "That's the one thing you can't discuss in a campaign," the former New York governor said. "It will boomerang on anyone who tries."

That was precisely Nixon's attitude toward Kennedy's other perceived weakness: his religion. Newspaper columnists focused on the negative aspects of the Catholic issue, predicting it would doom the Democratic nominee. But the vice president found it difficult to imagine that Northern states such as New York, Pennsylvania, and Illinois would turn against Kennedy because he was Catholic. "I believed that Kennedy's religion would hurt him in states he could afford to lose anyway," Nixon wrote, "and that it would help him in states he needed to win." He feared that public attacks would inspire Catholic voters from both parties to flock to Kennedy in record numbers.

Hence his decision in mid-August to avoid the religious issue completely. Finch sent a confidential memo to Nixon's top aides, imposing a strict gag order. They were not to accept support from anti-Catholic groups, distribute anti-Catholic literature, or make personal comments or jokes about Kennedy's religion. The memo included a direct statement from Nixon. "Religion will be in this campaign to the extent that the candidates of either side talk about it," he wrote. "I shall never talk about it, and we'll start right now."

Norman Vincent Peale, to Nixon's misfortune, was not among the memo's recipients. The charismatic Protestant clergyman was one of the nation's most influential media figures, reaching an estimated 30 million Americans through his radio program, newspaper column, and best-selling books such as *The Power of Positive Thinking.* Peale, who was politically conservative, had known the vice president for years and planned to vote for him.

But Peale had other motivations, too. He journeyed to Washington on September 7 to join 150 Protestant clergy and laymen in founding an organization whose innocuous name, the National Conference of Citizens for Religious Freedom, masked a strong anti-Catholic bias. Peale served as the group's spokesman. He publicly questioned whether Kennedy or any Catholic president could resist the pope's ultimatums—and he had no doubt that such demands would be forthcoming. "Our American culture is at stake," Peale said. "I don't say it won't survive, but it won't be what it was."

The religious controversy, seemingly dormant since the beginning of summer, was suddenly back in the headlines. Kennedy blasted Peale for having "loosed the floodgates of religious bigotry." The Greater Houston Ministerial Association had previously invited the Democratic nominee to deliver a speech on the Catholic issue, but he had been hesitant to accept. He now agreed to appear in Texas the following Monday.

Nixon and his team were no happier about the dramatic turn of events. Finch bemoaned Peale's "terribly unfortunate" statement, which "undid what we thought we had pretty well structured." Nixon attempted to minimize the damage. "I have no doubt whatever about Senator Kennedy's loyalty to his country," he said on *Meet the Press* on September 11, "and about the fact that if he were elected president, he would put the Constitution of the United States above any other consideration."

But it was Kennedy, not Nixon, whom the nation was waiting to hear. The senator was unusually subdued, almost grim, when he walked into the ballroom of Houston's Rice Hotel on the evening of September 12. He wore a black suit and black tie. A *Time* reporter ventured that he looked "something like a parson himself."

Kennedy spoke matter-of-factly—and more slowly than usual—to the assembled Protestant ministers. "I am not the Catholic candidate for president," he told them. "I am the Democratic Party's candidate for president who happens also to be a Catholic. I do not speak for my church on public matters, and the church does not speak for me." He reminded the ministers that religious prejudice could cut both ways. "Today I may be the victim," he warned, "but tomorrow it may be you."

It was, all in all, an impressive performance. Ted Sorensen insisted years later that Kennedy's address was "the best speech of his campaign and one of the most important in his life." Several members of the audience were equally laudatory. "Martin Luther himself would have welcomed Senator Kennedy and cheered him," said the Reverend George Reck, a Lutheran minister. But a few could not shake their suspicions, including W.A. Criswell, the pastor of the nation's largest Baptist congregation. "Senator Kennedy is either a poor Catholic," Criswell snapped, "or he is stringing the people along."

Kennedy's address was televised live throughout Texas, and the tape would eventually be broadcast in 39 states—10 times in New York alone. Nixon, who had always fared well with Catholic voters, worried that the heavy airplay would pull Republican Catholics into the Democratic camp. Kennedy had concerns of his own. He now doubted that the religious issue could be put to bed before the November election. "It seems difficult," he complained, "to ever give some people the assurance they need that I'm as interested in religious liberty as they are."

LEXICON: SEPTEMBER 1960

Organization of Petroleum Exporting Countries

American, British, and Dutch corporations—known as the Seven Sisters—controlled most of the Middle East's oil supply. They implemented price cuts in 1960, thereby slashing the royalties they paid to Middle Eastern nations. Iran, Iraq, Kuwait, Saudi Arabia, and Latin America's top producer, Venezuela, retaliated on September 14 by creating the Organization of Petroleum Exporting Countries (OPEC). They pledged to break the Seven Sisters' stranglehold on oil prices. The premier of Iraq, Abdul Kassem, vowed that OPEC would be "a thorn in the eyes of those who deviate from the right path."

Prince Edward County

A new school year began in September for white children—but not blacks—in Prince Edward County, 65 miles southwest of Richmond, Virginia. Federal courts had ordered Prince Edward to integrate its 21 schools in 1959, but the board of education opted to suspend operations. Fourteen hundred white students attended the county's new system of private schools. The county's 1,700 black students were excluded. Fifty blacks were sent to Northern schools by the American Friends Society Committee, a Quaker organization. The rest simply went without an education.

Shaler Triangle

The Panama Canal Zone, a 10-mile strip bisected by the famous canal, was America's smallest territory. A 1903 treaty gave the United States perpetual control of the zone, though a growing number of Panamanians resented the American presence. President Eisenhower, seeking to improve relations, announced on September 17 that Panama's flag would henceforth fly alongside the U.S. flag in Shaler Triangle, a plaza in the Canal Zone. Panama's leading newspaper hailed Ike's move as "a first step toward a more cordial entente," yet stressed it was nothing more than that—a first step.

Sharon Statement

A hundred college students and young adults met on September 9 in Sharon, Connecticut, to create Young Americans for Freedom, a national conservative organization. They issued a declaration of principles, the Sharon Statement, two days later. "In this time of moral and political crisis," it began, "it is the responsibility of the youth of

America to affirm certain eternal truths." Government, according to the Sharon Statement, had only three functions—"the preservation of internal order, the provision of national defense, and the administration of justice"—and no responsibility for social activism.

The Flintstones

ABC launched television's first prime-time cartoon series on September 30. *The Flintstones* featured a Stone Age couple, Fred and Wilma Flintstone; and their neighbors, Barney and Betty Rubble. They lived in caves and wore animal skins but otherwise enjoyed modern conveniences—albeit with a prehistoric twist, such as foot-powered cars. *The Flintstones* punctuated TV's transition from longer, live shows to shorter, taped programs. The cartoon debuted just 8 months after CBS canceled the weekly version of *Playhouse 90*, a heralded series of 90-minute teleplays.

Travels with Charley

John Steinbeck, the author of such classics as *The Grapes of Wrath* and *Of Mice and Men,* had suffered a stroke in December 1959 and still felt enveloped by a "feeling of gray desolation." His self-prescribed remedy was to leave his Long Island home shortly after Labor Day 1960, and drive across "this monster of a land," accompanied only by his poodle, Charley. The resulting book, *Travels with Charley*, would be published in 1962. Critics praised it as Steinbeck's best work in years—a sweetly nostalgic narrative spiced with trenchant commentary about present-day America.

*** *

A year had elapsed since the arrival of Nikita Khrushchev's massive TU-114 at Andrews Air Force Base on September 15, 1959. Memories of the first secretary's visit to the United States had already assumed a surrealistic quality. The friendly welcome from President Eisenhower, the whirlwind trip from coast to coast, the Spirit of Camp David—all were difficult to imagine in the post-U-2 world.

Khrushchev was on his way to America again, though not as a welcome guest. He was heading to New York for the fall session of the United Nations General Assembly. The Soviet leader left the TU-114 in its hangar this time, traveling instead on the *Baltika*, a 429-foot passenger liner. "Father very much wanted to cross the ocean on a ship, just like the first settlers in America, whose adventures he had read about," son Sergei wrote. Khrushchev avoided seasickness during the nine-day Atlantic voyage, but several members of his party were not as fortunate, much to his amusement.

The *Baltika* eased toward Pier 73 on the cold, wet morning of September 19. A boat chartered by the International Longshoremen's Association steamed alongside, festooned with signs of a decidedly unfriendly nature. "Roses Are Red, Violets Are Blue," read one. "Stalin Dropped Dead, How About You?" Khrushchev appeared to take the negativity in stride, smiling as he walked off the ship on a red carpet hastily rolled out by his aides.

American officials were displeased with his arrival, though there was nothing they could do. UN delegates were guaranteed unobstructed passage to New York. But that didn't give Khrushchev free rein. Eisenhower sent word that his Soviet counterpart was to be confined to Manhattan, as were Fidel Castro and the leaders of Albania and Hungary. "More than this," he wrote, "I felt the United States was not required to do." Khrushchev lodged a formal protest with the State Department, which blandly insisted the restrictions were for his own security.

The American press speculated freely about the motivation for this unusual visit. Perhaps Khrushchev intended to embarrass Eisenhower by launching the first cosmonaut into orbit during the UN session. Or maybe he hoped to make peace with the president in a face-to-face meeting. (Not that Ike would have gone along. "I could not have had less interest," he said.) Or possibly he wanted to size up Eisenhower's prospective successors. (The nominees were wary of appearing too friendly. Kennedy said he would meet Khrushchev only if Nixon went with him. Nixon expressed doubt that either man would need to make room in his schedule.)

None of these hypotheses mattered to Stephen Kennedy, the police commissioner of New York. It was his task to protect Khrushchev, Castro, and the other high-profile leaders who were streaming into the city. The commissioner set up a cot in his office, canceled all leaves, and put his 24,000 officers on a 60-hour-a-week schedule. Two hundred policemen were assigned to Khrushchev alone, forming a ring around the Soviet UN mission on Park Avenue whenever he was there.

It was hectic duty. Protesters—many of them refugees from Eastern Europe—stood outside the mission at all hours. They held banners emblazoned "Khrushchev is a Murderer" and "Khrushchev, Go Home," and they chanted "butcher," "murderer," and similar epithets. The crowd occasionally sang "God Bless America." The first secretary listened from the mission's iron-railed balcony, 20 feet above the street. "Let them sing," he yelled to the reporters below. "We also sing the 'Internationale,' and we sing it well." He proceeded to belt out a few bars of the communist anthem.

Khrushchev, despite the travel restrictions, was not often at the mission. He seemed to be everywhere in Manhattan—meeting other world leaders, holding press conferences, trading gibes with everyday Americans. "He played up to the crowd and luxuriated in its attention," wrote author Saul Bellow, "behaving like a comic artist in a show written and directed by himself." He spoke without restraint on any subject. President Eisenhower? "A liar," Khrushchev spat back. Dag Hammarskjold, the UN's secretary-general? "A fool." Chiang Kai-shek's Taiwanese government, which still represented China in the UN? "A corpse we have to cast right out of here, straight to hell."

The first secretary even appeared on a television talk show, *Open End*, as if he were a garden-variety presidential candidate. He was amiable at first but grew tired of host David Susskind's badgering questions. "I'm old enough to be your father," Khrushchev said sternly, "and young man, it's unworthy of you to speak to me like this. I do not permit an attitude like that toward myself." Susskind was intrigued by his guest's mixture of charm and belligerence. "The guy is one part Santa Claus," he said after the show, "one part doctrinaire, one part demeaning uncle."

But Khrushchev wasn't the only larger-than-life character in town. Castro had touched down at Idlewild International Airport on September 18, the day before the Soviet ship docked. The Cuban delegation intended to occupy 20 suites at the Shelburne Hotel on Lexington Avenue, but the owners demanded payment in advance. Castro refused. "We'll sleep in the UN garden or in Central Park," he sputtered. A better idea eventually dawned. He led his delegation to the dowdy Hotel Theresa, billed as the "Waldorf-Astoria of Harlem."

Castro received a steady stream of visitors in Harlem—poets Langston Hughes and Allen Ginsberg; controversial sociologist C. Wright Mills; black activist Malcolm X; and, of course, Khrushchev. The first secretary swept up Castro in a bear hug. A lively conversation ensued, and the two men agreed on the desirability of forging closer ties, though Khrushchev hedged on military assistance. "Castro is like a young horse that hasn't been broken," he told his aides as they returned to the Soviet mission. "He needs some training, but he's very spirited, so we will have to be careful."

This political theater—entertaining though it may have been—obscured the ostensible reason for the unprecedented gathering of world leaders. Khrushchev had proposed in August that the UN engage in a wide-ranging discussion of disarmament. Neither he nor his counterparts followed through. The General Assembly resembled a speaking society, not a chamber for negotiations. Each prime minister, president, and king took his turn at the podium—a ceaseless parade that dominated the agenda. Castro's name was called on September 26. He promised his audience that he would "endeavor to be brief," then prattled on for 4½ hours, the longest speech in UN history. He returned to Cuba two days later on a Soviet airliner. His own plane had been seized by U.S. authorities as payment for outstanding Cuban debts.

Khrushchev stuck around. He disrupted Harold Macmillan's speech on September 29, expressing indignation after the British prime minister lamented the failure of the Paris summit. "You sent your planes over our territory," the first secretary shouted. "You are guilty of aggression." He engaged in a finger-shaking argument with a Spanish representative a few days later. And, in the enduring image of the UN session, he reacted furiously after a delegate from the Philippines suggested that Eastern Europe had been "swallowed up by the Soviet Union." Khrushchev yanked off his shoe, brandished it at the Filipino, and then banged it repeatedly on his desk.

The Soviet leader was clearly under stress. His critics in the Kremlin were gaining power, the Chinese were becoming a major irritant, the stalemate in Berlin was still unresolved, and his country's grain harvest was falling well below expectations. But Eisenhower expressed no sympathy. He was tired of Khrushchev's antics and the resulting escalation of international tensions. If only the Constitution had given him dictatorial powers, the president joked to his aides, he could "launch an attack on Russia while Khrushchev is in New York."

The hypothetical opportunity soon vanished. Khrushchev climbed aboard the TU-114 on the evening of October 13—there would be no ocean voyage home—and flew 10 hours and 25 minutes to Moscow. The Presidium greeted him at the airport, as did Llewellyn Thompson, the American ambassador.

"Did you enjoy your trip?" Thompson asked politely.

"Certainly, certainly, certainly," Khrushchev boomed with a broad grin, shaking the ambassador's hand briskly. Then his smile faded. "But it wasn't the same at all," he said. "Not like last time."

Nikita Khrushchev is the center of attention at the United Nations: "It wasn't the same at all. Not like last time." (Warren Leffler/Library of Congress)

RISING STAR: LAMAR HUNT

Lamar Hunt may have been a mild-mannered, soft-spoken boy, but he never shied away from competition. His nickname, "Games," confirmed his affinity for sports of all kinds. He could have attended any college he wished—his father, oil baron H. L. Hunt, was the richest man in the world—yet he chose Southern Methodist University because it was the alma mater of his favorite athlete.

"My big motivation for going to SMU was that Doak Walker went there," Lamar said. "When I was a teenager and played football—not very well—I envisioned that I was a Doak Walker." He went out for the team at SMU, though he never rose above third string. His teammates, with a fine sense of affectionate irony, called him "Poor Boy."

Hunt earned his geology degree in 1956 but had no desire to join the family oil business. He believed he was destined for the sports world. He approached the National Football League about securing a new franchise for Dallas, only to be rejected. He tried to purchase an existing team, the Chicago Cardinals, but was rebuffed. "I wanted to buy an NFL team real bad," he said.

An alternative flashed into his mind one night in 1959. He flew to Houston the next day to share his idea with Bud Adams, another football-crazy oil heir. "I'm thinking about starting a new league," Hunt said. "Would you be interested in joining me?" Adams didn't hesitate. "Hell, yeah," he replied. Six other franchises signed up, and Hunt formally announced the creation of the American Football League (AFL) in August 1959, aiming to take the field the following year.

The NFL fought him every step of the way. The older league abruptly granted Dallas a team. Its Cowboys would compete with Hunt's Texans. "They want this league to fold," said Joe Foss, the AFL's new commissioner. "Well, Lamar won't quit, and we're not going to fold."

Opening day arrived at last on September 9, 1960, when the Denver Broncos defeated the Boston Patriots, 13–10, in the AFL's first game. Hunt's Texans debuted the next day. The new league played a surprisingly exciting brand of football—long on offense, short on defense—but had difficulty attracting fans. The eight AFL teams lost $4 million in 1960. The red ink ran particularly deep in Dallas.

"Your son, with this new league, has lost $1 million," a horrified friend told H.L. Hunt as the first season ended.

"At that rate," the old man replied, "he can only go another 100 years."

He actually lasted just two more seasons in Dallas before calling off the bloody battle with the Cowboys. "We had to do something," Lamar said. "Not only for ourselves, but for the good of the league." He moved the Texans to Kansas City in 1963. The newly renamed Chiefs prospered.

Hunt branched out to other professional sports. He started a tennis tour, co-founded two soccer leagues, and invested in basketball's Chicago Bulls. But football remained his first love. He was the AFL's driving force, its quiet dynamo. The NFL finally wearied of the costly competition and sent out peace feelers in 1966. It was Hunt who represented the AFL in secret talks that led to a merger. And it was Hunt who named the new AFL-NFL championship game. He dubbed it the Super Bowl, taking his cue from a popular toy, the Wham-O Super Ball.

H.L. Hunt died in 1974, and two of his sons, Bunker and Herbert, assumed control of the family's business interests. They moved to corner the world's supply of silver, amassing several billion dollars before the market collapsed in March 1980. They remained supremely confident—detractors called them arrogant—even though bankruptcy loomed. Bunker insisted that his losses didn't bother him. "People who know how much they're worth," he sniffed, "usually aren't worth that much."

Lamar was Bunker's polar opposite—humble, likable, a regular guy despite his immense wealth. "He has got to be the most popular person I ever heard of in Kansas City," marveled Buzz Kemble, a fellow SMU benchwarmer and lifelong friend. Hunt was inducted into the halls of fame of three sports—tennis, soccer, and football—before his death in 2006.

"All through our school years, everybody knew Lamar as my younger brother," Herbert Hunt once said. "Now that he's involved in the sports world, every time I meet somebody, they say, 'Oh, you're Lamar's brother.'" He and Bunker, both hard-driving oil men, never comprehended—or matched—the fame and popularity of their sports-loving sibling.

* * *

Ansel Adams predated the nascent environmental movement. America's premier landscape photographer, renowned for his stark, clear images of the West, had been active since the twenties in efforts to preserve California's Sierra Nevada wilderness. His work had drawn the scorn of certain photographers—Walker Evans and Dorothea Lange among them—who preferred to focus on poverty and other human tribulations. Adams waved them off. "I think there is more social significance in a rock or a tree," he said, "than there is in a bread line."

Fellow believers had long encouraged Adams to collect his photographs in a single volume, a testament to his love of the outdoors. He finally acceded in May 1960, teaming with author Nancy Newhall to produce *This is the American Earth,* an oversized, full-color book that posed a challenge to its readers. "This, as citizens, we all inherit," wrote Newhall. "This is ours, to love and live upon, and use wisely down all the generations of the future." William Douglas, a Supreme Court justice avidly interested in environmental issues, applauded Adams and Newhall for making "one of the great statements in the history of conservation."

But their work—powerful though it was—could not match the emotional punch of a manuscript being crafted that fall by an unassuming author in a Washington, D.C., suburb. Rachel Carson was a marine biologist who had written two books about the world's oceans. *The Sea Around Us* spent 86 weeks on the best-seller list in 1951 and 1952, freeing Carson from her day job with the U.S. Fish and Wildlife Service, allowing her to write about the subjects that most interested her.

A powerful chemical with a complex name—dichlorodiphenyltrichloroethane—was her current topic. Municipal officials touted DDT as a miraculous pesticide that killed mosquitoes without endangering humans or wildlife. A dubious Carson had begun to investigate calamities possibly linked to DDT—birds dying, bees and grasshoppers vanishing. But her work was repeatedly sidetracked by health problems—a duodenal ulcer; pneumonia; sinusitis; and worst of all, the discovery of two cysts in her left breast. Surgeons performed a radical mastectomy in the spring of 1960. The recurrence of her cancer would be confirmed a few months later, forcing her to undergo radiation treatments.

Yet she forged ahead with her manuscript, which carried the working title of *Man Against the Earth*. Carson had amassed a wealth of anecdotal evidence and scientific studies by September, removing any doubt in her mind that DDT was a menace to all living creatures. "This pollution is for the most part irrecoverable," she warned. "The chain of evil it initiates not only in the world that must support life, but in living tissues, is for the most part irreversible."

Carson made her case with scientific precision, but her editors were more impressed with the haunting quality of her prose. Her first chapter described a hypothetical paradise endangered by DDT. "There was a strange stillness," Carson wrote. "The birds, for example— where had they gone? Many people spoke of them, puzzled and disturbed. The feeding stations in the backyards were deserted. The few birds seen anywhere were moribund; they trembled violently and could not fly. It was a spring without voices."

Carson's agent, Marie Rodell, was greatly moved by this vignette, believing it dramatized DDT's capacity for destruction more effectively than any case study or scientific formula possibly could. She urged her client to scrap the title of *Man Against the Earth* and replace it with *Silent Spring*, a suggestion that Carson accepted in November.

Several intense months of work—and radiation treatments—lay ahead. Carson would finally submit a full manuscript to her publisher in 1961, and another year would pass before *Silent Spring* arrived in bookstores. It became an instant sensation, spurring creation of a federal panel to investigate pesticide abuse. *Booklist* named it the most influential book of the year.

Carson was typically modest about her success. "Now I can believe I have at least helped a little," she said. But she had done much more than that. *Silent Spring* inspired a popular movement that demanded an end to the use of DDT. The author was hopeful of victory, though she did not expect to live to see it. "Now, when there is the opportunity to do so much," she wrote, "my body falters, and I know there is little time left." The U.S. Environmental Protection Agency banned DDT in 1972, long after cancer and heart problems had taken Rachel Carson's life. She died in 1964—in the spring—at the age of 56.

QUOTATIONS: SEPTEMBER 1960

"There is only one possible word to describe his purposes and his actions. That word is treason."
> —*Robert Welch, vice president of a Massachusetts candy company, lambasting President Eisenhower. Welch had founded a right-wing political group, the John Birch Society, two years earlier. It claimed 18,000 members in 34 states by 1960, and was beginning to attract the attention of the national press.*

"The hell you can."
> —*Barry Goldwater, dismissing Welch's assertion that he could prove that Eisenhower, Harry Truman, and Eleanor Roosevelt were communists.*

"You have the ability of putting complicated technical ideas into words everyone can understand. Those of us who have spent a number of years in Washington too often lack the ability to express ourselves in this way."
> —*Richard Nixon, urging Ronald Reagan to become more involved in politics. The vice president had maintained a correspondence with the actor since the late fifties. Reagan, a registered Democrat, told Nixon that he considered John Kennedy's proposals to be "a frightening call to arms." Nixon replied that he appreciated Reagan's support and admired his skill as a public speaker.*

"It would have been better if they had cut off my arm or leg, or took out my eye. I could have got by with one arm. Or no arms. But the thing they took, it's priceless."
> —*John Hurt, a black resident of Prince Edward County, Virginia, looking back on his life in 2004. Hurt had finished first grade in 1959, but would not start second grade until 1964, when the Supreme Court finally compelled the county to reopen its public schools. He eventually dropped out, ashamed of attending classes with children a half-decade younger.*

"Impeachment of American presidents has been urged for far less than this."
> —*Daniel Flood, a congressman from Pennsylvania, complaining about President Eisenhower's decision to fly Panama's flag in the Canal Zone.*

***

It took a lengthy series of negotiations—15 meetings in all—but the Kennedy and Nixon teams and the television networks finally cobbled together a framework for the upcoming presidential debates.

ABC, CBS, and NBC—seeking maximum exposure for their display of altruism—proposed eight telecasts. Kennedy preferred five, Nixon three. They agreed on four. Each program would be an hour long, beamed simultaneously on all three networks. The candidates would bracket each show with opening and closing statements, fielding questions from a panel of reporters during the intervening 40 minutes. The telecasts, in effect, would not be debates at all, but joint appearances.

Most pundits believed that Nixon would outperform Kennedy. They expected him to build on his two previous triumphs: the Checkers speech and the kitchen debate against Khrushchev. Nixon shared their confidence. He had grown to consider himself an expert on the subject of television, and he disdained advice from broadcasting consultants. "They put too much emphasis on how a man is going to look or sound," he said, "instead of bringing out his basic character and his beliefs." His television adviser, Ted Rogers, could not get Nixon's team to take his recommendations seriously. "They thought," Rogers said, "that I was a pain in the ass."

Kennedy was receptive to outside suggestions. He made an unpub-licized stop at Chicago's Midway Airport in mid-September to meet CBS's Don Hewitt, who would direct the initial debate. Kennedy bom-barded Hewitt with questions. Where would the candidates stand? How long would they be allowed to speak? Could they interrupt each other? "He wanted to know everything," Hewitt said. "Nixon I never saw until he arrived that night in the studio."

The first debate was slated for Monday, September 26, at WBBM-TV, the CBS affiliate in Chicago. The two men prepared in ways that re-flected their divergent styles. Nixon sequestered himself for 5 hours that afternoon, silently working his way through more than 100 ques-tions prepared by his staff. Kennedy engaged in a lengthy game of rhe-torical pepper with three aides who carted around the "Nixopedia," a binder that catalogued the Republican nominee's public comments.

Nixon arrived first at WBBM, cracking his still-tender knee on the edge of the car door as he alighted. A waiting reporter saw the vice president's face go "white and pasty," adding to the toll exacted by his recent hospital stay. "He looked," said Hewitt, "like death warmed over." Nixon appeared to be at least 10 pounds underweight. His com-plexion was sallow, and he was running a slight fever. His shirt collar was noticeably loose.

"I was standing there talking to him," Hewitt went on, "and all of a sudden, I noticed out of the corner of my eye that Jack Kennedy [had] arrived. And it was awesome. Here was this guy running for president of the United States who looked like a matinee idol." Ken-nedy, who had been in California much of the previous week, sported a deep tan. He was trim and smartly dressed.

Hewitt offered both men the services of CBS's top makeup art-ist, Frances Arvold. Kennedy declined. He intended to have a light coat applied in secret by a member of his staff. "Nixon, who needed makeup, also said no," said Hewitt. "I'm convinced [it was] because he didn't want history to record that he was made up and Kennedy wasn't." Nixon, like his opponent, opted for a surreptitious touch-up. An aide, Everett Hart, ineptly dusted him with Lazy Shave, a drug-store pancake makeup.

The effect was unfortunate. Hewitt settled into his chair in the con-trol room a few minutes before the telecast. Cameramen were begin-ning to zoom in on the candidates, who had just taken the stage. The director, glancing at his monitor, was stunned by the disparity. "Ken-nedy looked great," he said. "Nixon looked terrible." Hewitt urgently summoned Ted Rogers and the president of CBS, Frank Stanton. They gazed at Nixon's waxy image on the screen. Stanton finally broke the silence. "Are you satisfied," he asked, "with the way your candidate looks?" Rogers said he was. Stanton motioned Hewitt out to the hallway. "It's none of our business," he told the director. "That's the way they want it."

The studio went live at 8:30. The first presidential debate in the nation's 184-year history began with Kennedy's opening statement. He predictably contended that the United States needed a fresh infusion of leadership. "I am not satisfied as an American with the progress that we're making," he said. Nixon was surprisingly congenial when his turn came. "I subscribe completely to the spirit that Senator Kennedy has expressed tonight, the spirit that the United States should move ahead," he said mildly. "Where, then, do we disagree?" He suggested that their biggest dispute was over the Eisenhower administration's record, which he defended at length. But he pulled his punch. "Good as this record is," he said, "may I emphasize it isn't enough?"

Nixon maintained this agreeable tone for the rest of the hour. He had made his mark as an aggressive, slashing campaigner, condemned by Walter Lippmann for being a "ruthless partisan." Attack had been a logical strategy in his campaigns for the House and Senate, when he had run as a challenger, an outsider. But he was a quasi-incumbent now, the front man for the current administration. "So he was on the defense to that extent," said Bob Finch, "and Kennedy could bring the attack to him, and did."

Yet there was an element of calculation behind Nixon's bland demeanor. "Erase the assassin image," his running mate, Henry Cabot Lodge, had urged him in a pre-debate phone call. Attorney General William Rogers, one of his closest friends, had encouraged him to come off as "the good guy." So the vice president charted a pleasant, reasonable course through the historic telecast. "I know Senator Kennedy feels as deeply about these problems as I do," he said at one point, "but our disagreement is not about the goals for America, but only about the means to reach those goals."

Political insiders were initially impressed with this new Nixon. Columnist Joe Alsop, an unabashed Kennedy supporter, had journeyed to Chicago for the debate. "Nixon," he wrote unhappily, "seemed to do very well to those of us who watched him in person." Barry Goldwater and Gerald Ford, traveling to their own campaign events that evening, listened to the debate on radio. Both men—loyal

Republicans—believed that Nixon had won. Lyndon Johnson, the staunchest of Democrats, came to the same conclusion after catching the radio broadcast. Even Frank Stanton, who was in the control room, gave the vice president the edge. "Dick Nixon in that debate, I thought," he said, "was on top of his subject a little better than Jack Kennedy was."

But the TV audience reacted differently. Nixon's blandness—his willingness to praise his opponent and treat him as an equal—had elevated Kennedy's stature. Nixon's sickly appearance—his pale complexion and sheen of perspiration—had enhanced Kennedy's image of youth and vigor. "Millions more voters now knew Kennedy," crowed Ted Sorensen, "and knew him favorably."

The vice president received his first inkling of disaster immediately after the telecast. His secretary, Rose Mary Woods, told him that his mother had called. A concerned Hannah Nixon wanted to know if her son was feeling all right. Other callers were more pungent. "The first order of the day," a friend snapped at press secretary Herb Klein, "is to fire the makeup man." Nixon's doctor, Malcolm Todd, offered a simple explanation. "You looked weak and pale and tired tonight on TV," he told his patient, "because, in fact, you *are* weak and pale and tired."

Henry Cabot Lodge sounded a note of doom after watching Nixon. "That son of a bitch," he blurted, "just lost us the election." But the actual trend was less dramatic. A mid-September Gallup Poll, conducted prior to the debate, had found Kennedy leading Nixon by a single percentage point. Subsequent surveys would show the gap widening by a few points, though the vice president remained in striking distance.

Yet there was no doubt that Kennedy had benefited tremendously. He had become an instant television star. His crowds swelled. Reporters began to notice "jumpers" in the back rows at his speeches and motorcades—young women who sprang up and down to get a better view of the handsome Democrat.

Nixon, too, had gained exposure, though not in a totally flattering way. His crowds also grew larger after the debate. Aides began to notice another change, a new flexibility. The Republican candidate abandoned his belief that "basic character and beliefs" were the essential tools for success on TV. "I had concentrated too much on substance," he conceded, "and not enough on appearance." He went on a reverse diet to fill out his frame, drinking four milkshakes a day.

Six weeks (and three debates) remained before Americans would choose Eisenhower's successor. But that single hour on September 26 had changed the rules for 1960's presidential election—and all elections to come. "That night," *New York Times* columnist Russell Baker wrote 30 years later, "image replaced the printed word as the natural language of politics."

Newspaper reporters were displeased by this transition, and so—surprisingly—were a pair of influential broadcasters. Edward Murrow, the famous CBS anchorman, dismissed the debate as "a puny contribution—capsulized, homogenized, perhaps dangerous in its future implications." Murrow disliked Nixon, but felt the vice president was being treated unfairly. "There has been considerable comment upon the obvious fact that Mr. Nixon perspired," he said. "It so happens that some people sweat mightily under those lights, and others don't. It is no proof of either nervousness or uncertainty."

The debate's director shared Murrow's concerns. Don Hewitt recalled leaving WBBM's studios with an uneasy feeling, "That's how you pick Miss America—who is the most attractive? That's not the way to pick a president," he remembered thinking. The disillusionment would linger for the rest of his life, as television became the dominant variable in the nation's political calculus. "That night was a great night for Jack Kennedy," said Hewitt, "and the worst night that ever happened in American politics."

11

October: A Suitcase of Votes

Fidel Castro kept pressing Dwight Eisenhower's buttons. The Cuban leader expropriated $700 million of American-owned property in August, literally ripped up the U.S.-Cuba mutual defense pact in September—"by the sovereign will of the Cuban people, this treaty is annulled"—and nationalized 382 sugar mills, factories, stores, railways, and banks in mid-October.

An exasperated Eisenhower struck back on October 19, imposing an embargo on almost all American exports to Cuba. Critics warned that a trade ban would push the Castro regime into a closer relationship with the Soviet Union. "Too bad," replied Frederick Mueller, Eisenhower's commerce secretary. "After all, we've been the ones who've been pushed around lately."

The CIA was encountering difficulties with its own scheme for retaliation. "Castro was consolidating his position," Richard Bissell said, "and our original plan was way behind its timetable." The agency's brain trust decided to upgrade Operation Pluto. It abandoned the initial concept of infiltrating a few dozen guerrillas into Cuba, now opting to assemble a well-equipped invasion force of several hundred men.

Operation Pluto, despite its top-secret classification, began to spring leaks in October. John Patterson, the Democratic governor of Alabama, was told about the upcoming attack by a National Guard officer who was training anti-Castro pilots. Patterson hustled to New York to pass the news to his party's presidential candidate. "I made him promise that he wouldn't breathe a word," he said of his meeting with John Kennedy, "and I told him what was going on." A Guatemalan newspaper was more explicit, running a detailed story about the CIA's preparations on October 30.

The agency had better luck maintaining the secrecy of its parallel plan to assassinate Castro. A former FBI agent, Robert Maheu, was recruited as the CIA's go-between with the Mafia. "They asked if I'd help 'dispose' of Castro," he recalled. Maheu made the necessary arrangements with Johnny Rosselli, who managed the Chicago syndicate's West Coast operations. Bissell was confident that Rosselli and his men could take care of business without implicating the agency. "There was very little chance," he said, "that anything the syndicate would try to do would be traced back."

Bissell believed the CIA was finally on the right track, but its anti-Castro plots were unfolding much too slowly for Richard Nixon. "What in the world," the vice president snapped, "are they doing that takes months?" He had hoped for an October invasion, believing it would boost his chances of winning the election. His only remaining recourse was to apply rhetorical pressure. "The United States has the power—and Mr. Castro knows this—to throw him out of office any day that we would choose," Nixon blustered to a Detroit audience.

Allen Dulles, the CIA director, had briefed Kennedy about the world situation in late July. Dulles left no record of what they discussed, and historians have been unable to determine whether Operation Pluto was on their agenda. But Kennedy's public pronouncements in the ensuing months were every bit as dire and belligerent as Nixon's. "Today," he repeatedly warned, "the Iron Curtain is ninety miles off the coast of the United States."

Cuba was the hottest topic when the two men met on October 7 at NBC's Washington affiliate for their second debate. Nixon wore makeup this time. His aides made sure that the air conditioning was cranked, reducing the likelihood of perspiration. A livid Robert Kennedy walked into the frosty studio. "What are they trying to do," he asked, "freeze my brother to death?" The thermostat was turned back up.

The debate's very first question dealt with Castro. Nixon asserted that the people of Cuba "are going to be supported and that they will attain their freedom." He accused Kennedy of "defeatist talk" for criticizing the Eisenhower administration's Cuban policy. Kennedy did not relent. "Today, Cuba is lost for freedom," he said. "I hope some day it will rise, but I don't think it will rise if we continue the same policies toward Cuba that we did in recent years."

The candidates also clashed on the status of Quemoy and Matsu—two soon-to-be-forgotten islands off the coast of China—and on the general direction of the country. CBS's Paul Niven, one of four journalists posing questions, asked Kennedy why he lambasted Nixon for the nation's alleged deterioration, yet never mentioned his boss.

"Now," Niven asked, "isn't Mr. Eisenhower, and not Mr. Nixon, responsible for any such decline?"

Kennedy knew that nothing could be gained by attacking the popular president. "In hundreds of speeches," aide Richard Goodwin later wrote, "in continual assaults on the Republican Party, on the Republican record, and on the Republican candidate, the name of Eisenhower was omitted." But the Democrat was now forced to confront the matter directly.

"Well, I understood that this was the Eisenhower-Nixon administration, according to all the Republican propaganda that I've read," he said to Niven. "Mr. Nixon has been part of that administration. He's had experience in it." It was a major concession by Kennedy, who had previously belittled the vice president's role. "I'm glad to hear tonight that he does suggest that I have had some experience," Nixon said in rebuttal.

The second debate went considerably better than the first for Nixon, though Kennedy also did well. The race remained tight. A mid-October Gallup Poll showed Kennedy in the lead by 3 percentage points, 49 percent to 46 percent, with 5 percent of the voters undecided. Election was less than a month away.

The final two debates followed in rapid succession. The October 13 telecast originated from opposite ends of the country, with Kennedy in New York and Nixon in Los Angeles. Identical sets were constructed in both studios, though the temperatures differed. Kennedy's thermostat was set at 72 degrees, Nixon's at 58. The picture from New York was transmitted to Los Angeles, blended with the latter signal, and then broadcast. Nixon seemed to benefit from the split-screen arrangement. Most pundits gave him the edge for the night.

The candidates reunited on October 21 in New York for the last debate, with Cuba again the prime topic. The Kennedy campaign had issued a press release recommending American assistance to "democratic anti-Castro forces in exile and in Cuba itself, who offer eventual hope of overthrowing Castro." This dramatic proposal was splashed on the front page of the *New York Times* on the morning of the debate. "Kennedy Asks Aid for Cuban Rebels to Defeat Castro," declared the headline.

Nixon was astounded. He was unaware of Governor Patterson's warning, but he knew that Dulles had briefed Kennedy about foreign affairs, presumably including Operation Pluto. The Democrat now seemed to be exploiting this information in a desperate grab for votes. "For the first and only time in the campaign, I got mad at Kennedy—personally," Nixon wrote. "I thought that Kennedy, with full knowledge of the facts, was jeopardizing the security of a United States foreign policy operation." Kennedy later denied any knowledge of the CIA's invasion plans. Goodwin and Ted Sorensen were said to have issued the proposal without his authorization. "If I win this thing, I won it," Kennedy reprimanded them. "But if I lose it, you guys lost it."

Nixon—the harshest of anti-Castro hawks—responded in a peculiar way to Kennedy's press release. The vice president decided that he "had no choice but to take a completely opposite stand" on Cuba, in order to protect what remained of Operation Pluto's cloak of secrecy. So he blasted Kennedy during the debate for "the most shockingly reckless proposal ever made by a presidential candidate." Nixon warned that an invasion of Cuba—an invasion he privately supported—"would be an open invitation for Mr. Khrushchev to come into Latin America."

Even the Nixon-haters in the press corps were impressed by his moderate stand. *New York Post* columnist Murray Kempton applauded him for showing greater restraint than his opponent. "I really don't know what further demagoguery is possible from Kennedy on this subject," Kempton added, "short of announcing that, if elected, he will send Bobby and Teddy and Eunice to Oriente Province to clean Castro out." Nixon, for his part, would later call his Cuban deception "the most uncomfortable and ironic duty" that he had ever performed. He was convinced that it had cost him votes.

And so the debates came to a close. The television ratings were astoundingly large. Nine of every 10 families with a TV set had watched at least one of the broadcasts. A quarter had seen all four. Voter turnout on November 8 would hit 64 percent, the highest rate since women's suffrage had greatly expanded the electorate in 1920. It seemed likely that television deserved some of the credit. "The debates so stimulated interest in the election and in the issues," said Frank Stanton, the president of CBS, "that more voters cast ballots for the presidency than ever before."

But would the televised debates decide the *outcome* of the election? Political analyst Samuel Lubell conceded that Kennedy had benefited, yet his surveys found no evidence of a seismic shift in support. Lubell cited two interviews that typified the nation's mood. A Jacksonville housewife, expressing admiration for both candidates, couldn't make up her mind. "Well, now, let me see," she said. "Who did I listen to last?" A New York salesman spoke for voters who disliked both choices. "They don't answer each other directly," he complained. "Each says the other is wrong, but they don't give us any proof of what they say."

Lubell concluded that television was one of several variables that would determine whether Kennedy or Nixon moved into the White House. It would not be the sole factor. "My own judgment," he said, "is that the debates did not bring any basic change in the voting pattern of the nation."

Yet it could not be denied that Kennedy had seized the lead around the time of the first debate—and still held it. A Gallup Poll released on October 26, five days after the final telecast, showed him four percentage points ahead of Nixon. The Democrats were buoyant. Their candidate had performed well and now stood on the threshold of victory, perhaps by a substantial margin. Kennedy himself, according to Murray Kempton, acted "as though the campaign were over, and there remained the thanking of the troops." A Kennedy staffer offered to bet Theodore White that Nixon wouldn't carry six states.

George Gallup had been down that road. He still had nightmares about 1948, when he had mistakenly predicted a lopsided victory for Thomas Dewey. The reams of data generated by Gallup's computers foreshadowed a close election, no matter what the current trends might be. "Unless this situation changes markedly between now and November 8," he told reporters, "no poll has any scientific basis for making a prediction."

LEXICON: OCTOBER 1960

Declaration of New Realism

Artists were in an experimental mood in 1960—incorporating everyday objects in their works, copying images from advertisements, and staging live performances known as "happenings." *Time* bemoaned the "bewildering jumble of horrors" they produced, but critic Lawrence Alloway hailed their "mass popular art," a phrase later reduced to "pop art." Painter Yves Klein and several colleagues issued the Declaration of New Realism on October 27, seeking both to defend this new movement and to give it direction. Their goal, the artists announced, was to develop "new perceptive approaches to reality."

Expansion

The framework of Major League Baseball had not changed since 1901, with 16 teams split equally between the American and National Leagues. But the specter of a potential competitor, the Continental League, stirred interest in expansion. The National League added two franchises on October 17, and the American League followed suit nine days later. (The Continental League would never play a game.) Other sports also caught expansion fever in 1960. The National Football League granted teams to Dallas and Minnesota, and the National Basketball Association moved into Chicago and Los Angeles.

Maz

Baseball's World Series was deadlocked after six games—three wins for the Pittsburgh Pirates, three for the New York Yankees. The Pirates took the lead in the final game on October 13, but the Yankees tied the score in the ninth inning. The momentum belonged to New York, the winner of 8 of the previous 13 World Series. "Those damn Yankees are going to do it again," Pittsburgh second baseman Bill Mazeroski muttered to himself. But Maz turned the tide in the bottom of the ninth, belting a dramatic home run to bring the Pirates their first championship since 1925.

Republic of South Africa

Prime Minister Hendrik Verwoerd proposed that the Union of South Africa be converted into a free-standing republic, no longer pledging allegiance to Great Britain. It was the only way, he said, to prevent foreign interference with his policy of apartheid. An October 5 referendum was surprisingly close, yet Verwoerd's republic was approved by 75,000 votes. Historian Robert Harvey called the election a milestone for white South Africans. "They had," he wrote, "at last created their isolated, racist nirvana."

Reunification

Capitalist West Germany had never been more prosperous, but communist East Germany was struggling. Roughly 4,000 refugees per week escaped from East to West in 1960. British diplomats heard whispers that the Soviets planned to stop the outflow by sealing the border, perhaps by building a wall. It was dismissed as a ludicrous rumor. West German officials were optimistic that the trend was actually running in their favor, that East and West would merge one day. Konrad Adenauer, the West German chancellor, called reunification "the supreme objective of German policy."

Speed Mail

"Here and now, our American postal system moves into the future," bragged Postmaster General Arthur Summerfield, as the nation's first mechanized post office whirred into action on October 20. Machines in the Providence, Rhode Island, facility took over much of the mail sorting previously done by hand. The Post Office Department launched a second innovation—speed mail—12 days later. Facsimile machines instantly transmitted letters between Chicago and Washington, another step toward Summerfield's goal of one-day delivery throughout the United States.

***

The Kennedy-Nixon race wasn't the only political marathon approaching the finish line. Americans would also elect 27 governors, 34 senators, and 437 members of the House of Representatives on November 8. Nearly all of the contenders were men, though more women were on the ballot than ever before. Three female candidates were running for the Senate, 26 for the House, and more than 100 for state legislatures and statewide offices.

The press corps was fascinated by a high-profile contest in Maine, where both parties had nominated women, an unprecedented development in a Senate election. Margaret Chase Smith, the tart-tongued Republican incumbent, faced personable Lucia Cormier, a Democratic state legislator. Smith was baffled by all the fuss. "I consider that women are people," she said, "and that the record they make is a matter of ability and desire." The *New York Times* covered the Smith-Cormier race with a condescending slant. "So far," it reported, "there has been no political hair-pulling."

Smith would score an easy victory, no surprise in a state as Republican as Maine. She would be joined by a second female senator, Maurine Neuberger of Oregon, a Democrat who had previously served in the state legislature. Her husband, Oregon's incumbent senator, had died in March, and she ran to replace him. The election of two women to the Senate on the same day was another American first. What the country needed next, in Neuberger's opinion, was a female president. "Women," she said, "are nicer than men, mostly."

These gains—small though they were—reflected the increasing strength of women in American society. Men had comprised a majority of the electorate since the 18th century, but the pool of eligible female voters outnumbered the corresponding group of men in 1960. The assistant chairwoman of the Republican Party, Clare Williams, welcomed the shift. "Women," she crowed, "now hold the balance of power." They also wielded more financial clout than ever before, despite the lingering myth that all women of that era were homemakers. Thirty-eight percent of adult females belonged to the labor force in 1960, up from 34 percent in 1950 and 28 percent in 1940.

Yet it was still a man's world, and many women were unhappy. A March edition of *Newsweek* investigated the boredom and stagnation that afflicted thousands upon thousands of young wives. "She is dissatisfied with a lot that women of other lands can only dream of," the magazine reported. "Her discontent is deep, pervasive, and impervious to the superficial remedies which are offered at every hand." *Redbook* offered a $500 prize in September for the best essay on "Why Young Mothers Feel Trapped." It triggered an unexpectedly large response: 24,000 entries.

Good Housekeeping tapped into this vein of unhappiness with a September article of its own, "I Say: Women Are People, Too." It noted "a strange stirring, a dissatisfied groping, a yearning" by American women, a sense that there must be more to life than raising children and maintaining a clean, comfortable home. The magazine urged its readers to overcome their malaise by taking charge of their lives. "She can't live through her husband and children," it said of the typical housewife. "They are separate selves. She has to find her own fulfillment first."

The author of the *Good Housekeeping* article was Betty Friedan, a 39-year-old freelance writer from the suburbs of New York. Friedan had graduated summa cum laude from Smith College in 1942, intent on pursuing a career as a psychologist, but her dream proved elusive. She settled for being a married mother of three, eking out what time she could to write for women's magazines. "I felt so guilty, somehow," she said later, "that I hadn't done the big things everybody expected me to do with my brilliant Smith education."

Friedan was asked to assemble a booklet for her college class's 15th reunion in 1957. She sent out a questionnaire, expecting to be inundated with cheerful stories about successful careers and young families. Many of her classmates, however, responded with tales of depression and frustration. It was Freidan's first clue that thousands of women—perhaps millions—shared her dissatisfaction.

The Smith questionnaire inspired her to undertake a detailed examination of what she called "the problem that has no name," interviewing hundreds of women in New York, Chicago, and Boston. The *Good Housekeeping* piece sprang from this research, though Friedan's aspirations were grander than that. She had started a book manuscript by October 1960, juggling it with her responsibilities as a wife and mother. "I chauffeured, and did the PTA and buffet dinners," she recalled, "and hid, like secret drinking in the morning, the book I was writing when my suburban neighbors came for coffee."

Her publisher had low expectations—paying Friedan a meager advance of $3,000—and the author suffered occasional doubts, too. The writing went slowly. The book, entitled *The Feminine Mystique*, would only be half-done by early 1961 and wouldn't be published until 1963. It expanded upon the *Good Housekeeping* article, making the case that women were defined solely by their relationship to men—"wife, sex object, mother, housewife"—but also possessed the power to redefine and improve their lives.

"I did not set out consciously to start a revolution," Friedan said toward the end of her life. Yet start one she did. *The Feminine Mystique* struck a chord with women across America, eventually selling more than 3 million copies. It became the handbook for a feminist movement that lay below the surface in 1960 but would soon sweep the nation. Betty Friedan—the reluctant revolutionary—inspired women to demand equality in the workplace and other aspects of life. "You have nothing to lose," she exhorted her new followers, "but your vacuum cleaners."

RISING STAR: CASSIUS CLAY

It all began with a brand-new Schwinn bicycle. A gangly 12-year-old boy left a bazaar at Louisville's Columbia Auditorium in 1954, only to discover that his cherished bike had been stolen. He raced back into the building, angrily telling a police officer that he intended to beat the tar out of the thief.

The officer, Joe Martin, listened patiently. He couldn't imagine the boy thrashing anybody. "Well," he asked, "do you know how to fight?"

"No," said Cassius Clay, "but I'd fight anyway."

It might be helpful, Martin suggested, if Clay first learned how to box. He pointed the boy to the nearby Columbia Gym, which Martin ran in his spare time. Clay's bike would never be recovered, but the young man found a new passion. "All he ever wanted to do," said Jimmy Ellis, a friend and workout partner, "was run and train and spar."

Clay developed into a surprisingly good boxer, mixing lightning-fast punches with blinding footwork. He won 100 of 108 amateur bouts, culminating in two national Golden Gloves championships. Martin encouraged his protégé to take the next step, the 1960 Summer Olympics in Rome. "If you win," he said, "you'll be as good as the tenth-ranked pro. It can open the door to fame and wealth."

It went as Martin predicted. Clay, just 18 years old, defeated a seasoned Polish boxer on September 5 to win the gold medal in the light-heavyweight division. The brightest star in Rome was Wilma Rudolph, a sprinter who earned three gold medals in track, the first American woman to do so in a single Olympics. But the humble Rudolph shunned the spotlight, unlike the loquacious Clay. "I can still see him strutting around the Olympic Village with his gold medal on," she said later. "He slept with it. He went to the cafeteria with it. He never took it off. No one else cherished it the way he did."

And nobody had plans as grandiose as his. "That was my last amateur fight," he told reporters. "I'm turning pro." He set his sights on becoming the heavyweight champion of the world.

Boxers must serve lengthy apprenticeships before fighting for a title. Clay launched his professional career on October 29, 1960, in Louisville against a run-of-the-mill opponent, Tunney Hunsaker, the police chief of Fayetteville, West Virginia. "He kept me away from him," Hunsaker said years later, "but I nailed him." It was partly true. Hunsaker did land a few solid punches, but the Olympic hero was too fast on his feet. Clay won easily.

That first bout was far from impressive. Several fans booed the lack of action. Nor did it bring Clay instant riches. His purse was just

$2,000. But it did set him on the road toward the heavyweight title. He won 19 straight fights, finally earning a bout with the reigning champion, Sonny Liston, in February 1964. Only 3 of the 46 sportswriters covering the fight in Miami picked Clay to win, but win he did. "I am the king!" he shouted after Liston threw in the towel. "I am the greatest! I shook up the world! I am the greatest thing that ever lived!"

The white establishment did not take kindly to the new champ's braggadocio. Nor was it happy about his involvement with the Nation of Islam (commonly known as the Black Muslims), his decision to change his name to Muhammad Ali, and his unwillingness to serve in the army during the Vietnam War. "Man," he said famously, "I ain't got no quarrel with them Vietcong." He was stripped of his heavyweight title after refusing military induction in 1967.

Ali presented a defiant face to white America—"I was determined to be one nigger that the white man didn't get"—but his image softened with time. The reconciliation process began in 1971. Ali and heavyweight champion Joe Frazier captured the public's imagination in March with the first of three classic slugfests. (Ali lost the first but won both rematches.) And the Supreme Court granted him a religious exemption from army service in June, upholding his initial stand against the war. He regained the heavyweight title three years later, reigning until 1979.

The insolent, controversial upstart had evolved into a more sympathetic character by then. Ali's popularity expanded further during his retirement, especially after doctors diagnosed him with Parkinson's disease in 1984. Sportswriter William Nack noted this once-unthinkable phenomenon a decade later. "Today, navigating the sweet land of liberty and religious freedom, he is as loved and embraced as he was once scorned and despised," Nack wrote. "Now they gather round him in airports. Now they wave to him from passing cars."

***

The presidential campaign devolved into chaos by the tail end of October. The candidates were tightly scheduled, but their days always seemed hectic and disorderly. Nixon, determined to fulfill his 50-state pledge, flitted around the country. Kennedy, unburdened with geographic requirements, moved at an equally frantic pace, touching down in 27 states in a single week.

"In the middle of the day," Kennedy joked, "I look down at the schedule, and there's five minutes allotted for the candidate to eat and rest." Everybody laughed, but it was close to the truth. The Democratic nominee found it more and more difficult to start his day before sunrise. His aide, Dave Powers, would ask, "What do you suppose Nixon's doing while you're lying there?"

Tempers ran short on both sides. Kennedy had heard too much about his opponent's prowess as a public speaker. "Mr. Nixon may be very experienced in kitchen debates," he barked, "but so are a great many other married men I know." Nixon had grown weary of his adversary's promises to get the country moving again. "All of this yakking about America with no sense of purpose," he snapped, "all of this talk about America being second-rate—I'm tired of it."

Inconsequential issues bloomed in the superheated political environment. Harry Truman rebuked potential Nixon voters in San Antonio—"you ought to go to hell"—and the candidates were dragged into the resulting controversy. "When a man is president of the United States, or a former president," Nixon said piously, "he has an obligation not to lose his temper in public." Kennedy was more practical, admitting that he lacked the power to control Truman's choice of words. "Perhaps Mrs. Truman can," he said, "but I don't think I can."

The tightness of the race spawned allegations that both camps had resorted to questionable tactics. Nixon aide John Ehrlichman charged that a San Francisco rally had been "thoroughly sabotaged by John Kennedy's merry men," who supposedly cut the microphone and lighting cables while Nixon was in mid-speech. Ehrlichman provided no evidence. Thieves reportedly ransacked the files of Kennedy's endocrinologist, and attempted to break into the office of his personal physician. Historian Robert Dallek speculated that Nixon's operatives were seeking documentation of Kennedy's health problems. He offered no proof.

The moment of truth was nearly at hand—election day was just a couple of weeks away—and the outcome remained uncertain. Both candidates faced serious impediments to victory.

Nixon worried incessantly about the economy, which seemed to be locked in a downward spiral. Unemployment reached 6.1 percent in October—the worst rate in two years—while the Dow Jones Industrial Average fell to a nine-year low. The National Association of Business Economists concluded on October 20 that America had entered a recession, which came as no surprise to Nixon's campaign director, Bob Finch. "I personally think the unemployment factor, which ran strongly against us in that last month in the industrial states," said

Finch, "was a greater factor than anything else, up to and including the debates."

Kennedy's biggest problem remained the religious issue. The National Association of Evangelicals—a group of 38 fundamentalist denominations with 10 million members—charged that the Vatican's "declared opposition to American institutions is well-known and has been fully documented." The association urged its 28,000 ministers to deliver sermons against the Catholic Church on October 30, Reformation Sunday.

Anti-Catholic literature flooded into susceptible communities, inspiring a sense of déjà vu in Raymond De Paulo, who had worked on Kennedy's primary campaign in West Virginia. "It's the same old stories amplified," he said, "printed on better paper, given wider circulation, published in hardback books instead of paperbacks." Much of this material was distributed anonymously, though a few groups stood behind their allegations, including an organization with an interminable name, Protestants and Other Americans United for Separation of Church and State. It issued ominous warnings about the "Vatican-inspired colossal political machine whose announced purpose is to control the world."

These slurs seemed to be having an impact, especially in the Protestant South. Analyst Samuel Lubell asked a retired railroad engineer in Georgia why he supported Nixon. The man was tight-lipped. "I'm against Kennedy," he said, "but I'm not going to explain why. You might be a Catholic." Yet Kennedy's religion was also proving to be an asset in the seven states where Catholics cast at least 30 percent of the vote. "If only Nixon were a Catholic," a Long Island engineer said wistfully to Lubell. "He's the better man on foreign policy. But I'm Catholic, and it's not right that all men shouldn't have an equal chance to be president."

Civil rights was another issue on which the candidates treaded carefully. Both men advocated racial equality, though Nixon had been more vociferous over the years. He had earned the support of black leaders such as baseball great Jackie Robinson and the Reverend Martin Luther King Sr., whose son had coordinated the Montgomery bus boycott. Kennedy demonstrated no real passion on the subject of race relations. "It was a cold intellectual issue and political issue with him," suggested James Forman, a black activist.

Martin Luther King Jr. had met both candidates. He considered Nixon to be "magnetic" and apparently forthright, yet he wondered whether the vice president was truly committed to black-white equality. "If Richard Nixon is not sincere," King said, "he is the most dangerous man in America." Kennedy seemed no better. King concluded that the Democratic nominee lacked a "depthed understanding" of civil rights. Further doubts were raised by the bonds between the two men and the white South. Kennedy was counting on the electoral votes of several Southern states, while Nixon had been bedazzled by Atlanta's boisterous reception in August.

The younger King soon received an opportunity to put the candidates to the test. He was arrested while leading a sit-in at Rich's department store in Atlanta on October 19, and was sent to jail for the first time in his life. He refused bail. "I'll stay in jail a year or 10 years," he said, "if it takes that long to desegregate Rich's."

That wasn't what Mayor William Hartsfield wanted to hear. Hartsfield was no racial liberal, but he understood that segregation was bad for business. He had declared earlier in the year that Atlanta was "too busy to hate," and he now set out to prove the point. The mayor asked

Martin Luther King is put behind bars for the first time in his life: "I'll stay in jail a year or 10 years, if it takes that long to desegregate Rich's." (Marion Trikosko/Library of Congress)

black leaders to postpone their protest for 30 days, allowing him to hammer out a compromise with Atlanta merchants. He secured the release of King and 50 other blacks from jail.

Hartsfield believed he had defused the situation, only to be surprised by an unanticipated twist. King had been ticketed a few months earlier for using an Alabama driver's license after moving to Georgia. He had been given a suspended sentence. A DeKalb County judge now ruled that the arrest at Rich's constituted a parole violation. He ordered King to serve four months of hard labor in Georgia's state prison. King's wife, Coretta, was certain that her husband was going to be lynched.

It was only natural, given King's prominence, that this turn of events would become an issue in the presidential campaign. The candidates groped for a safe course of action—a way to express sympathy for the black leader's plight without alienating white voters, especially those in the South.

A pair of Democratic aides, Harris Wofford and Louis Martin, urged a bold response. They suggested that Kennedy make a telephone call to Coretta King. It would be merely a symbolic gesture, they conceded, but it might have political value. They had no luck in selling their idea until Wofford reached Kennedy's brother-in-law, Sargent Shriver, in Chicago.

"It's not too late," Shriver said enthusiastically. "Jack doesn't leave O'Hare for another forty minutes. I'm going to get it to him. Give me her number, and get me out of jail if I'm arrested for speeding."

Kennedy had no objections. "Can you get her on the phone?" he asked. The subsequent conversation took less than three minutes. "All he did," said Shriver, "was to express his sympathy and interest—as a citizen and as a political leader—over the plight of the King family, and then he hung up." Coretta King mentioned the call to a reporter shortly thereafter, and the word leaked out.

Robert Kennedy was beside himself. "Do you know that this election may be razor-close," he said heatedly to Wofford and Martin, "and you have probably lost it for us?" But he eventually fell in line with his brother, even placing his own call to the judge who had sent King to prison, seeking to arrange bail.

Nixon moved cautiously. His press secretary, Herb Klein, suggested that he intervene in King's case, but the vice president said it would "look like pandering." Jackie Robinson urged him to at least make a phone call, but Nixon declined. "He thinks calling Martin would be grandstanding," Robinson said unhappily. Nixon did ask Attorney General William Rogers if the federal government could secure King's release, but President Eisenhower refused to authorize action. "Had this recommendation been adopted," Nixon wrote, "the whole incident might have resulted in a plus rather than a minus as far as I was concerned."

It was Kennedy who reaped the rewards. The white press said little about his role—the *New York Times* buried the story of his phone call on page 22—but black newspapers were lavish with their praise. They were even happier when King was released on $2,000 bond after Bobby's conversation with the judge.

King received a hero's welcome on October 27 at Ebenezer Baptist Church in Atlanta, where his father revealed a stunning political conversion. Yes, Daddy King said, he had been supporting Nixon, and yes, he was opposed to having a Catholic president. But those considerations were no longer relevant. "I've got a suitcase of votes," he declared, "and I'm going to take them to Mr. Kennedy and dump them in his lap."

Kennedy was grateful for the support—and the likelihood of picking up thousands of black votes—though he shook his head at the elder King's anti-Catholic bias. "That was a hell of an intolerant statement, wasn't it? Imagine Martin Luther King having a father like that," Kennedy said to his aides. Then he grinned. "Well," he said, "we all have our fathers, don't we?"

QUOTATIONS: OCTOBER 1960

"That will mean the end of the occupation regime in West Berlin."
>   —*Nikita Khrushchev, renewing his threat to sign a peace treaty*
>   *with East Germany. The Soviet leader had been low-key on the*
>   *Berlin issue since 1959, but he resumed a belligerent course on*
>   *October 7. An East German treaty, he insisted, would require*
>   *the United States, Great Britain, and France to withdraw*
>   *their troops from West Berlin.*

"For color! Against line and drawing!"
>   —*Yves Klein, declaring war on traditional art. Klein painted a*
>   *series of monochromatic panels—all ultramarine blue—in the*

late fifties. He moved on to anthropometry in 1960. "My models were my brushes," he said. "I made them smear themselves with color and imprint themselves on a canvas." Klein often produced these artworks in front of live audiences, an early example of performance art.

"It is a strange assumption that art should be understood."
—*Philip Guston, an abstract expressionist, defending the avant-garde direction of modern art. Guston's paintings were dominated by bold squares, broad strokes, and splashes of color.*

"I'll never make the mistake of being 70 again."
—*Casey Stengel, speaking to reporters after being fired as manager of the New York Yankees on October 18. Stengel had won 10 American League pennants in 12 years, but the Yankees wanted to make way for a younger manager, 41-year-old Ralph Houk.*

"The contestants' faces were grim. Mr. Van Doren sat in one of the first-row seats, his eyes moist with tears."
—New York Times reporter *Jack Roth, describing the October 17 arraignment of Charles Van Doren and 13 other quiz-show contestants on charges of perjury. Van Doren would finally plead guilty in 1962, receiving a suspended sentence.*

* * *

The future held no excitement for an 18-year-old boy in Liverpool, a dreary British port city on the Irish Sea. He considered enrolling in a teacher training college, though without enthusiasm. "I didn't want to go back to school or college," Paul McCartney said, "but there wasn't much alternative."

That changed with a telephone call from Allan Williams, a Liverpool nightclub owner who served as an agent for local musical groups. Williams knew of a club in Hamburg, West Germany, that was seeking a British act. McCartney and his friends had enjoyed some success playing gigs around Liverpool the past three years. Would they be willing to go to Hamburg? They agreed without hesitation—and with more than a little relief. "That meant I definitely didn't need to go back to school," McCartney said. "There was now something else to do."

Their band had gone through several members—and names—since McCartney's July 1957 encounter with John Lennon, a student at a different Liverpool high school. Lennon had started his own group, the Quarry Men, earlier that year. McCartney attended a performance at a church festival, and introduced himself afterward. He demonstrated his own skills—banging out a Jerry Lee Lewis tune at the piano, ripping out an Eddie Cochran hit on a guitar. Lennon was impressed, though he waffled for a few days before inviting McCartney to join the band. "I'd been kingpin up to then," Lennon later said. "Now, I thought, 'If I take him on, what will happen?'"

Lennon's schoolmates, the original Quarry Men, gradually drifted away. McCartney recruited a friend, George Harrison, as a guitarist, and Stuart Sutcliffe signed on as the bass player. The four young rockers—now known as the Silver Beatles—played concerts in England and Scotland on a hit-or-miss basis, picking up a drummer whenever they landed a club date.

Stardom was not their goal. They were having fun—and, in the process, delaying the onset of adulthood. It would have been absurd to imagine achieving the fame and fortune enjoyed by their favorite singer, the man whom McCartney called "our greatest idol," Elvis Presley.

Presley had quickly reestablished himself as king of the music world after resuming civilian life in March. Three of his singles shot to Number One on the *Billboard* chart within 10 months of his military discharge. "Stuck on You," "It's Now or Never," and "Are You Lonesome Tonight" spent a total of 15 weeks in the top spot in 1960. The first two were certified platinum, signifying sales of more than 1 million records. The latter went multiplatinum, surpassing 2 million units.

Yet something had changed—in Lennon's mind, at least. "Up until Elvis joined the army, I thought it was beautiful music," he said. But he was not as impressed with the king's new tunes. They didn't have the same drive, the same edginess. "He played *some* good stuff after the army," Lennon conceded, "but it was never quite the same."

Lennon and McCartney had discovered a second hero in the late fifties—Buddy Holly, a rising star who died in a fiery airplane crash in Iowa in 1959—and it was he who became their role model. Holly wrote the songs that he performed, something that virtually no one in the music industry did. Elvis *never* wrote his own material. "John and I started to write because of Buddy Holly," McCartney recalled.

"It was like, 'Wow! He writes *and* is a musician.'" Holly's backup band had been known as the Crickets. The Quarry Men became the Silver Beatles in entomological tribute.

The group's biggest concern after receiving Allan Williams's call was the same as always—finding a drummer. McCartney recruited Pete Best, who passed a brief audition. The five young Englishmen set off for Germany on August 16, sporting a newly shortened name, now just the Beatles. They were booked into the Indra, a club where they were expected to play four-and-a-half to six hours a night, seven nights a week.

It turned out to be just what they needed. "We got better and got more confidence," said Lennon. "We couldn't help it with all the experience playing all night long. It was handy, them being foreign. We had to try even harder, put our heart and soul into it, to get ourselves over." The Beatles had been accustomed to one-hour sets in Liverpool, but they had to greatly expand their repertoire—adding their own songs, current hits, rock standards, anything else they could pick up—to fill the endless void in Hamburg.

They developed a following at the Indra, and moved on October 4 to a bigger club, the Kaiserkeller, where they alternated on stage with a second British band. The drummer for the other group, Rory Storm and the Hurricanes, watched the Beatles with a wary eye, often interjecting snide comments or demanding that they play his favorite songs. "I didn't like the look of Rory's drummer myself," said George Harrison. "He looked the nasty one, with his little gray streak of hair." The drummer, Richard Starkey, had adopted the name of Ringo Starr.

The Beatles came into their own on the Kaiserkeller's large stage. "We really got a lot of material down, a lot of material we would never have learned if we hadn't gone there," Harrison said. "It was one great rehearsal, and it really got the group going." They were improving day by day—they were certain of it—and began to think of music as more than a diversion. It might possibly become a career.

Theirs was a dream that was shared by a rising generation of musicians.

Berry Gordy worked on the Lincoln-Mercury assembly line in Detroit but desperately wanted to become a songwriter and producer. He secured an $800 loan to launch Tamla Records in 1959, then changed the name of his fledgling label to Motown a year later. "They thought the Wright Brothers had a stupid idea," he said of his plunge into the recording business. "So I say, 'Bring on stupid ideas.'" A song he produced for the Miracles, "Way Over There," hit the *Billboard* chart in the summer of 1960. "I had gone national," Gordy recalled. "Motown had now entered the music scene."

Aretha Franklin's father was a Baptist minister who ran a traveling revival show. She joined the tour in 1955 at the age of 13, singing gospel hymns, though she hoped to branch into rhythm and blues. Her big break, an audition with Columbia Records, came in the winter of 1960. "This is the best voice I've heard in twenty years," raved Columbia's talent scout, John Hammond, who signed her to a six-year deal. Franklin began work on her first album in August 1960 and released her first R&B hit, "Today I Sing the Blues," in October. "I was just happy to be recording, glad to be singing some of my songs," she said. "I didn't care about the money or any of that."

Seventeen-year-old Jimmy Hendrix was already considered one of the Seattle area's most promising guitarists, having played with such locally popular groups as the Velvetones, the Rocking Kings, and Thomas and the Tom Cats. But he was also deeply unhappy. Hendrix—later to shorten his first name to Jimi—had dropped out of high school and couldn't find work. He and a friend, James Williams, spent the last night of 1960 together, with nothing better to do than sing Dean Martin's latest hit, "Memories Are Made of This," over and over. Hendrix vaguely considered joining the army in the year to come.

The Beatles had been similarly aimless a few months earlier, but their success in Hamburg had given them direction. The Kaiserkeller was booming. The club's owner sweetened their contract on October 15, extending it through the end of the year. A prominent Hamburg nightclub, the Top Ten, soon came across with an even better offer, one that was impossible to resist. "Naturally," McCartney said, "the manager of the Kaiserkeller didn't like it."

His anger would bring their German adventure to an abrupt end. The manager informed local authorities that the 17-year-old Harrison was an underage worker, leading to his deportation on November 21. The others were deported a few days later. They always claimed that the Kaiserkeller's owner pulled strings to get them tossed out of West Germany.

Their only option—admittedly an unhappy one—was to return to the old grind. They secured a date at Litherland Town Hall on December 27, just another appearance at another Liverpool venue. But this show would be different. The Hamburg experience had changed the

Beatles. Their skills had grown, their repertoire had expanded, and their confidence had blossomed. Their fans responded eagerly. "The kids went mad," Best recalled.

John Lennon always dated the emergence of the Beatles—the evolution of their distinctive style and sound—to that final Tuesday night of 1960. The future suddenly seemed limitless. "It was that evening," Lennon said, "that we really came out of our shell and let go. We stood there being cheered for the first time."

12

November: The Help of a Few Close Friends

John Kennedy had chosen Lyndon Johnson as his running mate for the simplest of reasons. "Kennedy knew from his own polls that he had to have Johnson to even make a showing in some of the Southern states—and particularly carrying Texas," said George Smathers, the junior senator from Florida. "He could not carry Texas unless Johnson was on the ticket, and he had to have Texas."

The prospects, however, did not seem particularly bright as October faded into November. Johnson remained popular in his home state—he had received 85 percent of the vote in his last Senate election—but the Democratic campaign was burdened with the twin controversies of religion and race. Richard Nixon appeared likely to carry at least four Southern states, and he had pulled within striking distance in Texas. "Lyndon knew he had a selling job to do," said his wife, Lady Bird. "He never tried harder in his life to do a selling job."

Johnson campaigned feverishly throughout the South. He even took to the rails, boarding a 13-car train for an old-style whistle-stop tour from Virginia to New Orleans in mid-October. The vice presidential candidate billed himself as "the grandson of a Confederate soldier," imploring white Southerners to stick with the party that had dominated their region since Reconstruction. He sought to defuse the Catholic issue by talking about Kennedy's brother, Joe Jr., who had flown to his death in World War II with a Protestant copilot from Fort Worth, Texas. "When those boys went out to die so that you could live," Johnson said, "nobody asked them what church they went to."

He encountered resistance everywhere. Mississippi Governor Ross Barnett charged that the Democratic platform's endorsement of civil rights was "so horrible, so obnoxious, and so contrary to our form of government, I don't see how the people of the South can accept it." Barnett's state and neighboring Alabama were offering their citizens a chance to vote for "none of the above," putting slates of unpledged electors alongside Kennedy and Nixon on the presidential ballot. Several prominent Southern Democrats—South Carolina Senator Strom Thurmond among them—were rumored to be surreptitious Nixon supporters. Thurmond said only that he intended to vote his conscience, "even if this does not suit the party bosses of the national Democratic Party."

The intensity of this opposition was driven home on November 4, when Lyndon and Lady Bird Johnson arrived for a campaign event at the Adolphus Hotel in Dallas. Hundreds of right-wing protesters swarmed around them—shouting, spitting and waving large signs. It took the Johnsons half an hour to push 75 feet through the angry crowd. A policeman tried to intervene, but the senator ordered him to back off. "If the time has come when I can't walk through the lobby of a hotel in Dallas with my lady without a police escort," he said, "I want to know it." It had already dawned on Johnson that photos of the incident might galvanize enough sympathy to help him carry Texas. "If he could have thought this up, he would have thought it up," said aide Bill Moyers. "But the moment it happened, he knew."

Nixon's running mate wasn't nearly as active. Henry Cabot Lodge had a well-deserved reputation for laziness, dating back to the 1952 loss of his Senate seat to the energetic Jack Kennedy. Lodge was also prone to making snap judgments and intemperate statements. "There should be a Negro in the Cabinet," he told a Harlem audience in mid-October. "It is part of our program, and it is offered as a pledge." Nixon, who had never made such a commitment, immediately issued a statement that "race or religion would not be a factor" in his presidential appointments. But polls began to detect a decline in Southern support for the Nixon-Lodge ticket. "Whoever recommended that Harlem speech," groused a Southern Republican leader, "should be thrown out of an airplane at 25,000 feet."

Lodge was correct in one respect. Black voters were likely to affect the outcome on November 8. Harry Truman had carried California, Illinois, and Ohio by a combined margin of just 58,600 votes in 1948, the last presidential election to be tightly contested. Black support for the Democratic ticket had been the decisive factor in all three states—and

John Kennedy and Lyndon Johnson team up in the final days
of the campaign: "Lyndon knew he had a selling job to do.
He never tried harder in his life to do a selling job." (Lyndon
Baines Johnson Library and Museum, photo by Frank Muto)

those states, in turn, had been responsible for Truman's victory over
Thomas Dewey.

Kennedy was anticipating a similar scenario. Blacks had favored
Democratic candidates since Franklin Roosevelt's administration. The
party's most recent nominee, Adlai Stevenson, received 61 percent of
the black vote in 1956. Kennedy's response to Martin Luther King Jr.'s
recent incarceration had inspired hopes that he might do even better.

The Democratic campaign pressed its advantage. Kennedy's team
culled positive comments from black newspapers, publishing them
in a pamphlet entitled *"No Comment" Nixon Versus a Candidate With a
Heart, Senator Kennedy: The Case of Martin Luther King.* The pamphlet,
which was printed on light blue paper, was known within the Kennedy campaign as the Blue Bomb. Two million copies were distributed

at black churches on November 6, two days before the election. The Blue Bomb perfectly suited Kennedy's purposes, arousing black support without drawing the attention of white voters.

Yet Nixon also carried a powerful weapon in his holster. President Eisenhower remained extremely popular. His latest Gallup Poll approval rating—58 percent—eclipsed the corresponding figures for both presidential candidates. Ike had confined himself to two dozen "nonpolitical" speeches between Labor Day and late October, but he was eager to take off the gloves. He summoned his vice president to the White House on October 31 to plot strategy.

The lunch began well. Eisenhower said magnanimously that he would merely be a soldier in this final battle. Nixon was now the commander, and he, Eisenhower, awaited his orders. Len Hall, the chairman of the Republican campaign, had already worked out an intensive schedule of appearances. He happily pulled it from his briefcase.

Nixon interrupted. He thanked Eisenhower for his support, but suggested that a more limited itinerary would be appropriate. Hall was baffled. The president barely contained his anger as the meeting wrapped up.

"Goddammit," Ike snapped after Nixon departed, "he looks like a loser to me." He hunched his shoulders and bent his head in a passable imitation of the vice president. "When I had an officer like that in World War II," Eisenhower told Hall, "I relieved him."

Nixon's decision—so clearly contrary to his own best interests—confounded Republican strategists. A partial explanation leaked out in 1966, though the full story wasn't published until 1978. Nixon wrote in his memoirs that Mamie Eisenhower had called Pat Nixon the night before the fateful meeting, expressing concern that an intense schedule would strain her husband's heart. The White House doctor, Howard Snyder, phoned the vice president the next morning. "Please," Snyder said, "either talk him out of it, or just don't let him do it—for the sake of his health." Eisenhower was unaware of these calls. "His pride prevented him from saying anything," Nixon wrote, "but I knew that he was puzzled and frustrated by my conduct."

Yet Ike's schedule was still busy enough, taking him to Philadelphia, New York City, Cleveland, Pittsburgh, and other cities in the waning days of the campaign. The crowds were enormous, and the president was in fighting form. He mocked Kennedy as a "young genius" and "a player who knocks the team all season and then wants to become coach." He recited a litany of statistics—9 million homes built during his administration, a 75 percent increase in college enrollment, a 45 percent gain in gross national product. "In glib political oratory," Eisenhower said, "we have heard this progress called 'standing still.' If the great things [we] have done are 'standing still,' then I say America needs more of it."

Kennedy publicly scoffed at the president's intervention. "While we meet tonight," he sarcastically told a San Francisco audience on November 2, "the rescue squad has been completing its job in New York." Eisenhower, Nixon, and Nelson Rockefeller had drawn large crowds at four New York rallies earlier in the day. "We are not choosing a team," Kennedy said dismissively. "We are not choosing a triumvirate." But he was privately concerned that Eisenhower was turning the tide. "With every word he utters, I can feel the votes leaving me," Kennedy told an old navy friend, Red Fay, that night. "It's like standing on a mound of sand with the tide running out. If the election were held tomorrow, I'd win easily. But six days from now, it's up for grabs."

Pollsters noted the same trend. The Gallup Poll, which had recently shown Kennedy with a comfortable lead of six percentage points, now cut it to a single point. The competing Roper Poll reported that Nixon had actually moved ahead of Kennedy for the first time since early September. The candidates and their surrogates raced from coast to coast in the days that remained, desperately striving to tilt the numbers in their favor. Nixon flew to Alaska (the final installment of his 50-state pledge) on November 6, zipped east to Detroit to host a nationwide telethon on election eve, and jetted home to Los Angeles, arriving at 4 A.M. on election day. Kennedy scurried in the opposite direction—from California to Chicago to New England, with several intermediate stops. He closed with a nationally televised address from Boston's historic Faneuil Hall.

"Well, it's all over," Kennedy said after the final broadcast. "I wish I had spent forty-eight hours more in California." He was convinced that he had dallied too long in friendly locales such as Chicago and New York, when he should have been campaigning in the nation's second-largest state, where the race was exceptionally tight. Nixon had regrets, too. Bob Finch had urged him to abandon the Alaska flight, deriding it as an unwise use of last-minute resources. Nixon eventually came to agree. "But having made the pledge," he later wrote, "I was stubborn and determined to carry it through."

It was out of their hands now. Nearly 69 million Americans would go to the polls the following day to decide their fate. Both men settled in to await the returns—Kennedy at his family's compound in Hyannis Port, Nixon at the Ambassador Hotel in Los Angeles. Nothing more could be done.

LEXICON: NOVEMBER 1960

Harvest of Shame

Famed newscaster Edward Murrow concluded his 25-year CBS career on November 25 with a hard-hitting TV documentary about the plight of migrant workers. *Harvest of Shame* followed poor whites, blacks, and Hispanics as they made their way from Florida to New York, picking crops for subsistence wages. Murrow urged federal action to improve the living conditions of these itinerant laborers. "The people you have seen have the strength to harvest your fruits and vegetables," he told his audience. "They do not have the strength to influence legislation. Maybe we do."

Off-Track Betting

The mayor of New York City, Robert Wagner, envisioned a new source of government revenue. Betting on horse races was legal only at racetracks, but Wagner proposed that it also be allowed at outside parlors. "I can see no moral difference," he said. The mayor submitted his plan to New York's state legislature on November 15, predicting that off-track betting (OTB) would generate an annual windfall of $200 million for city and state coffers. A decade of legislative wrangling would ensue before New York opened its first OTB parlor in April 1971.

PDP-1

The typical computer in 1960 was an enormous mainframe whose vital statistics were expressed in tons and cubic feet. But Digital Equipment Corporation unveiled a dramatically different concept in November. The PDP-1 had four components—a data processor, keyboard, paper-tape reader, and video terminal. It was, in essence, the first minicomputer. Potential customers were baffled. The PDP-1 defied the popular image of a computer, a key reason why relatively few units were sold. Yet DEC kept refining its prototype, finally hitting it big with the PDP-8 in 1965.

Presidential Commission on National Goals

America was in an introspective mood in 1960. Journalists, intellectuals, and political candidates talked endlessly about the country's objectives and sense of purpose. Dwight Eisenhower tapped into this mood in February, creating a 10-member Presidential Commission on National Goals. It issued its report on November 27, urging Americans to meet the challenges of the sixties with "extraordinary personal responsibility, sustained effort, and sacrifice." The panel endorsed the pursuit of universal disarmament, the desegregation of public schools, and the doubling of education funding within 10 years.

Radio Soaps

Soap operas were a staple of every radio network's schedule in the thirties and forties. Millions of listeners followed the ongoing stories of their favorite heroes and heroines, with deep-voiced announcers providing the narration and organ music punctuating the drama. Most of these programs shifted to television in the fifties, leaving CBS as the only network still broadcasting radio soaps. It finally surrendered on November 25. The oldest of the seven shows canceled by CBS was *Ma Perkins,* which had been produced five days a week since August 1933: more than 7,000 episodes in all.

Speed Dialing

Morris, Illinois, a quiet town 60 miles southwest of Chicago, seemed an unlikely place to find the next generation of communications equipment. But Bell Telephone picked Morris as the site for a $25 million test project. It equipped the city with an ultramodern phone system, which was dedicated on November 17. Telephones no longer rang. They beeped. Customers could use two-digit codes for frequently called numbers—an innovation known as speed dialing—and could transfer calls from phone to phone. Bell officials predicted that these services eventually would be available everywhere.

***

Nikita Khrushchev watched the American presidential campaign with a mixture of amusement and nervousness. The perpetual motion of the candidates perplexed him. Their constant flitting from state to state seemed an absurd waste of energy. "The battle between the Democrats and Republicans," Khrushchev laughed, "is like a circus wrestling match." Yet he held a great stake in the outcome. He had despised Nixon ever since the kitchen debate. The wealthy Kennedy, he suspected, would merely be a tool of Wall Street. "I wish Nixon would win because I'd know how to cope with him," the first secretary told Llewellyn Thompson. "Kennedy is an unknown quantity."

That, of course, was beyond his control. Of more immediate concern was Khrushchev's desire to repair—or at least conceal—the expanding rift between the Soviet Union and China. He summoned Communist Party officials from 81 nations to a conference at the Kremlin. The meeting—billed as a communist summit—began on November 11 and dragged through the rest of the month.

It did not go well, at least not at first. Khrushchev and Deng Xiaoping argued violently in the closed-door sessions. The Soviet leader blasted Mao Zedong as a "megalomaniac warmonger." The Chinese delegate accused Khrushchev of being soft on capitalism. It took weeks of negotiations to reach a middle ground. The Chinese halfheartedly endorsed Khrushchev's doctrine of peaceful coexistence with the United States and its allies, while the Soviets reluctantly agreed to join Mao in encouraging Third World revolutions. But the conference's 20,000-word manifesto did not fool communist insiders. "It was a temporary armistice," said Mao's interpreter, Yan Mingfu. "In the long run, events were already out of control."

The same could be said of Southeast Asia. Ngo Dinh Diem, the austere president of South Vietnam, continued to enjoy strong American support, both financially (three-quarters of a billion dollars in the past two years alone) and physically (685 U.S. military advisers). Yet he was becoming increasingly unpopular with his own people.

South Vietnamese paratroopers staged a coup at 3 A.M. on November 11. They were led by Colonel Vuong Van Dong, who fumed about the government's failure to subdue the communist Vietcong. Dong's forces seized control of Saigon's radio stations and declared victory by 8 A.M., announcing that Diem had been ousted because of his failure "to accomplish the task of reconstruction and safeguarding of the country."

There was one small problem. The rebels had not yet captured their prey. They had not even cut the telephone lines to Diem's palace or blocked the roads into Saigon. The president called for reinforcements, and loyal troops streamed into the capital city. Dong and his aides fled to Cambodia, then on to exile in France. Diem—whom the rebels had accused of "totalitarian, authoritarian, and nepotistic" tendencies—tightened the screws even further after the abortive coup. His secret police rounded up politicians and intellectuals, accusing them of participating in the uprising.

North Vietnam's communist leaders hoped to capitalize on this chaos, employing a strategy devised two months earlier at a party congress in Hanoi. Le Duan, who was second-in-command to Ho Chi Minh, proposed a "long and arduous struggle" to overthrow Diem. Everybody applauded the goal, but no one—not even Le Duan—wished to commit the North Vietnamese army to a lengthy war in a neighboring country. The congress opted to establish a separate organization to foment a South Vietnamese revolution.

The National Liberation Front was founded on December 20, less than six weeks after Diem had stamped out the brief revolt by his paratroopers. Sixty delegates—most of them communists—met at a secret conference in a forested region of South Vietnam, close to the Cambodian border. The NLF pledged to defeat the "U.S. imperialists" who had sided with "Diem and his clique." The group selected a Saigon lawyer, Nguyen Huu Thom, as its chairman, but he was merely a figurehead. The real orders would come from Hanoi.

The situation was even more turbulent in Laos, which shared a border with both Vietnams. President Eisenhower willingly funneled aid to pro-American forces, hoping to prevent the communist Pathet Lao from taking control. But he refused to commit U.S. soldiers to the impassable jungles and rugged mountains of Laos. "I came into office because of Korea," he told an aide. "I'm not going to fight another Korea. This place is even worse than Korea."

Kong Le's August coup had not brought clarity. Several factions were still trying to maneuver Laos in one ideological direction or another. Kong Le claimed to be neutral but subsequently formed an alliance with the Pathet Lao. Phoumi Nosavan, a former defense minister, advocated closer ties with the United States. The country's prime minister, Souvanna Phouma, struggled to walk a tightrope between these competing interests, finally fleeing the country in frustration on December 9. The whole thing was too confusing for outsiders to comprehend.

Troops loyal to Kong Le and Phoumi battled for control of the capital city of Vientiane in mid-December. The pro-American side prevailed after three days of fighting. Much of the city was in shambles. Kong Le retreated north, resupplied by a Soviet airlift as he moved.

Laos was beginning to seem like a replay of Korea, with the United States and Soviet Union escalating a local conflict into a Cold War standoff. Eisenhower convened his foreign-policy and military advisers on December 31. The president was no longer circumspect about Laos. If Khrushchev wanted to push, he contended, perhaps the United States needed to shove back. "We cannot let Laos fall to the communists," Eisenhower said urgently, "even if we have to fight—with our allies or without them."

RISING STAR: BERTRAND GOLDBERG

Bertrand Goldberg was always a nonconformist.

The Chicago native moved to Berlin in 1932, not the best year for a Jew to take up residence in Germany. The famed Bauhaus School of Design had accepted him as a student. Nothing—not even political turmoil—could deter him from enrolling. Goldberg was especially eager to meet legendary architect Ludwig Mies van der Rohe, who doubled as the school's director.

Their association was brief, yet influential. "I got from Mies an enormous amount of understanding that I would not easily have gotten from anyone else," Goldberg said. But their relationship was truncated by Adolf Hitler's ascension to power in January 1933. Goldberg ran afoul of German sensibilities by making a prank telephone call to his landlady. He impersonated a Nazi official, accusing her of harboring suspicious characters. She threatened to turn him in. "I took whatever the next train out of Berlin was," he recalled. Nazi pressure forced the Bauhaus to close a few weeks later.

Yet Goldberg had glimpsed his future. He would become an architect like his hero, though he would not emulate Mies's cold, disciplined style. He branched into the field of prefabrication, designing two-bedroom houses that sold for $2,900, ready-made bathrooms that could be installed within a few hours, even a prefab ice cream parlor. He also worked extensively with plywood, using it to make everything from boxcars to high-end furniture.

It seemed a strange career for an architect who had been educated at Harvard and the Bauhaus. Why waste time creating such trivialities as the Stanfab bathroom and molded plywood chairs? Goldberg waved off the question. It was precisely *because* of his training that he designed mundane objects, not skyscrapers. "The architect is meant in [the Bauhaus] tradition," he said, "to be capable of and interested in the design of everything that has to do with living."

That didn't mean he was opposed to large-scale projects. William McFetridge, the president of a national janitorial union, approached Goldberg with an unusual proposal in 1959. The flood to the suburbs was at high tide; cities were being drained of population. Yet McFetridge had millions of dollars in pension funds to invest, and he wanted to construct affordable housing in downtown Chicago. Who better than an iconoclastic architect to tackle such a counterintuitive project?

Most skyscrapers of that era were rectilinear structures of steel and glass, a style pioneered by Mies. Goldberg had no intention of copying his mentor. "I was revolting against a century of static space," he said, "against the straight line, against the idea of a man made in the image of a machine."

He designed Marina City, a pair of 60-story concrete cylinders that would become the world's tallest residential buildings. Box-shaped rooms, in Goldberg's opinion, were "psychological slums." His apartments would be pie-shaped, fanning out from 8-foot entry walls to 21-foot balconies. Marina City's distinctive appearance struck many critics as shockingly futuristic. The circular towers were compared to corncobs or flower petals on a stem.

Goldberg, McFetridge, and civic officials gathered on November 22, 1960, for a groundbreaking ceremony alongside the Chicago River. "We were scared to death," Goldberg recalled, "that people would be inhibited from occupying it because of its unusual room shapes, that people basically are afraid of what is new." Their concern was unnecessary. Marina City was fully leased by the completion of construction in 1964: an early sign that residents could indeed be lured back to the city. Goldberg's corncobs became an internationally recognized landmark, hailed by the *Washington Post* as "a symbol of both the Windy City itself and of a certain spirit of urban optimism in general."

The project raised Goldberg's profile dramatically. Clients across the country hired him to design hospitals, housing complexes, even a university campus. His small office, which had 10 employees prior to Marina City, swelled to a workforce of 150, with branches in Boston and Phoenix. "That was too much," he said three decades later. He downsized prior to his death in 1997, focusing on a variety of Chicago projects.

Goldberg left an eclectic mixture of work—from the grandiosity of Marina City to the mundanity of public housing. "Critics have frequently said they don't know where to place me in the mainstream," he acknowledged. "Am I a sort of variation—the Goldberg variation, if you please?" But he saw no inconsistency. What mattered was the usefulness of his creations. "I am satisfied," he said, "that I have served my society and my time."

* * *

J. Skelly Wright was a mild-mannered, soft-spoken federal judge, yet his patience was not infinite. He had issued a desegregation order six months earlier, requiring the admission of black first graders to white schools in New Orleans. State and local officials responded with inflammatory rhetoric and blatant defiance, so Wright shifted the compliance deadline from Labor Day to November 14, hoping that tempers might cool. But he had no intention of granting another extension.

The uproar in New Orleans had not surprised him. Wright was a native son who had earned his undergraduate and law degrees locally at Loyola University. He had not questioned segregation as a young man. "Blacks were something apart," he admitted. "The injustice was lost on me basically. I took it like everybody else took it." He began to change his opinion while serving in the coast guard during World War II. "The Negro went to war like the white person did," Wright said. "He fought like the white person. We saw this, those of us who were in the service. We saw this."

The desegregation order had turned his life upside down. Old friends and professional acquaintances snubbed him. The judge lunched alone each day at a private club and went directly home after work, taking care to walk as far from the curb as possible. A fellow pedestrian had recently tried to shove him into traffic. Wright and his wife frequently received crank calls and threatening letters. He was hanged in effigy near the state capitol building in Baton Rouge. A swastika was painted on the back of the effigy, a hammer and sickle on the front. An accompanying sign said "J. Wrong."

Opposition to Wright's order was spearheaded by Jimmie Davis, who had been inaugurated as Louisiana's governor in May. The amiable Davis had served a previous term as governor from 1944 to 1948, yet he was primarily known as a singer. He claimed to have written "You Are My Sunshine"—an assertion disputed by music historians—and would be voted into the Country Music Hall of Fame in 1972.

Davis promised his white constituents that his administration would "use every means we can" to prevent mixing of the races. "No one," he asserted, "is interested in segregation more than I am." The governor had attempted to seize control of the New Orleans school system in August, only to be rebuffed by the federal courts. He now tried again, submitting a package of 29 bills on November 8. State legislators approved them all—abolishing the school board in New Orleans, denying free textbooks to integrated schools, and granting Davis the power to close any school confronted with a desegregation order.

Judge Wright countered on November 10, striking down the new laws. Davis resubmitted the bills to the legislature three days later. He added a twist by proclaiming November 14 to be a statewide holiday. All schools were to remain closed. Telegrams were sent to principals across the state, warning them that "penalties are provided for any violations." Wright issued a restraining order a few hours later.

James Redmond watched this game of judicial ping-pong with a rising sense of concern. The Missouri native had served as an administrator in Chicago's school system before becoming the school superintendent of New Orleans in 1953. His integration plan was limited in scope, providing for the enrollment of four black girls in two white schools. Federal marshals had already arrived to protect the children. Redmond, however, had no idea if the white community would react with violence. Nor did he know if Governor Davis would intervene at the last minute. He was certain of only one thing: tough times lay ahead.

The superintendent sat in his office, discussing the volatile situation with the parents of Ruby Bridges, one of the four black pioneers. He asked, "Do you believe in praying, Mrs. Bridges?"

"Yes," she replied.

"I'm going to be here now," Redmond said, "but you may not see me any more, because they're going to pretty near hate me as much as they're going to hate you. All I can ask is to pray—and pray for me also."

The first court-ordered integration of public schools in the Deep South occurred the next morning. Two cars arrived at William Frantz Elementary School shortly after 9:00, awaited by a crowd of protesters. Marshals escorted six-year-old Ruby into the building, as white adults shouted angrily at her and her parents. "I thought it was Mardi Gras," she said years later. "I had no idea it was all about me." Three other girls—Gail Etienne, Tessie Prevost, and Leona Tate—endured similar experiences a few blocks away at McDonogh Number 19 Elementary School.

The protesters were boisterous. They booed, yelled, and sang "glory, glory, segregation" to the tune of "The Battle Hymn of the Republic." One man outside McDonogh repeatedly shouted, "Kill them niggers." But there was no violence, much to Redmond's relief.

Outraged white parents had no intention of participating in this brave new world of integrated education. Most kept their children at home on November 14. Others arrived during the day to pull their kids out of class. Fewer than 50 of Frantz's 575 pupils remained for the closing bell that Monday. Thirty of McDonogh's 460 students stayed until dismissal.

Those small numbers dwindled in subsequent days, evolving into a full-scale boycott throughout the city. More than 2,000 white students were absent from New Orleans's high schools by Wednesday, even though the court order did not apply to their buildings. Hundreds of unruly teens congregated at City Hall, chanting, "Two, four, six, eight, we don't want to integrate." Some threw rocks at a black painter on a scaffold. Others tried to tip over a car driven by a black man. Police finally resorted to fire hoses to disperse the crowd. "I never remember anything like this in New Orleans before," said Joseph Giarrusso, the city's police chief.

Hecklers, most of them female, showed up each morning at the two integrated schools. "You wanna be white, we'll make you white," one screamed at Ruby Bridges. "We're gonna throw acid in your face!" The women—who became known as the "cheerleaders"—saved their harshest invective for parents of the few white children still attending school. They shrieked at a Catholic priest who accompanied one such family, calling him a "bastard," a "communist," and a "nigger-lover." Gail Etienne, one of the black girls at McDonogh, had nightmares about running the daily gauntlet. "If these people could get at me," she remembered thinking, "they would kill me."

Author John Steinbeck, nearing the end of his counterclockwise circuit of America, arrived in New Orleans at the height of this fury. He stood outside Frantz one morning to watch the marshals escort Ruby Bridges—"the whites of her eyes showed like those of a frightened fawn"—past the long line of cheerleaders. "Now I heard the words, bestial and filthy and degenerate," he wrote in *Travels with Charley.* "In a long and unprotected life, I have seen and heard the vomitings of demoniac humans before. Why, then, did these screams fill me with a shocked and sickened sorrow?"

A few whites eventually condemned these verbal excesses. A newspaper advertisement signed by 105 "Business and Professional People of Greater New Orleans" demanded "an immediate end to threats, defamation, and resistance to those who administer our law." But the ad didn't appear until December 14, one month after integration. Several white parents also reconsidered their positions. Twenty-three white children were attending Frantz by the first week of December, up from a low point of two. But the vast majority of whites were unrepentant. Leander Perez, a local political boss and former district attorney, exhorted them to hold fast against integration. "Are you going to wait until Congolese rape your daughters?" Perez asked. "Are you going to let these burrheads into your schools? Do something about it now!"

Dwight Eisenhower simmered as he watched the widespread defiance of federal authority. He placed a call to Harold Tyler Jr., the assistant attorney general who was overseeing the New Orleans case. Ike asked if the marshals had the situation under control. Tyler replied that they did. The president said he was weary of seeing the law broken and children endangered. He was not averse to using additional force to bring the white South into line. "If we have to mobilize the troops, we'll do it," he told Tyler. "Little Rock was a tragedy, and I hoped they learned their lesson. But if they need to learn it again, we'll deal with it."

QUOTATIONS: NOVEMBER 1960

"We used to own our slaves. Now we just rent them."
—*An unidentified farmer, speaking on CBS's* Harvest of Shame *about America's growing reliance on migrant workers.*

"Our enduring aim is to build a nation and help build a world in which every human being shall be free to develop his capacities to the fullest."
—*The Presidential Commission on National Goals, proclaiming its belief in racial equality. The commission's report, issued on November 27, anticipated several emerging issues of the sixties, including the battle for civil rights and the war on poverty.*

"Instead of printing checks for a company, which the employee has to deposit, why not print deposit slips?"

> *—Seth Clark Beise, president of the Bank of America, outlining the*
> *plan for an innovative service known as "direct deposit."*
> *Employees of his bank were no longer to receive paychecks. Their*
> *salaries would be transferred electronically into their accounts.*

"Without too much imagination, we can see the Presidential Sweepstakes becoming the main event, combining the excitement of a national lottery with the thrill of a coronation."

> *—Joseph Tussman, author of* Obligation and the Body Politic,
> *envisioning the deterioration of the American political system.*
> *Tussman, a University of California philosophy professor, predicted*
> *that presidential campaigns would sink "deeper into the morass of*
> *public relations" unless voters became better informed about*
> *issues and more demanding of quality.*

"What you really need on election night is a damned good adding machine."

> *—William McAndrew, NBC's vice president of news, downplaying*
> *the value of high-powered computers in compiling election returns.*
> *All three networks invested in computers anyway, with NBC*
> *installing an RCA 501 mainframe for its November 8 coverage.*

*** *

Election day dawned fair in Boston, though a bit cooler than normal for early November. The Weather Bureau predicted a high temperature in the upper forties. The Democratic nominee and his wife arrived shortly after 8:30 at their polling place, the West End branch of the Boston Public Library.

"Your names?" asked Evelyn Hiltz, one of the poll watchers.

"John F. Kennedy, 122 Bowdoin Street," replied the candidate, who was surrounded by reporters and photographers. Jacqueline Kennedy, eight months pregnant, signed in after him. She and her husband were directed to two of the six voting booths. They made their choices in less than a minute, said their goodbyes, and headed to the airport to catch a 60-mile flight to the family compound on Cape Cod.

Robert Kennedy's house in Hyannis Port had been converted into a command post for the evening ahead, complete with 30 telephones and 4 teletypes. Campaign workers occupied every available space, even the children's bedrooms. Several staffers were already making calls—getting the early word on voter turnout—by the time the candidate arrived. The phone bill for the next 24 hours would top $10,000.

Richard Nixon and his wife voted at 7:35 A.M. (10:35, Eastern time) in Whittier, California. The booths for their precinct were set up in the playroom of Roger and Mary McNey's house. The Nixons climbed into separate cars after casting their ballots. Pat took their daughters, 14-year-old Tricia and 12-year-old Julie, to Beverly Hills to get their hair done. The vice president spoke briefly with Herbert Klein, his press secretary, before driving off. "I'm going to try to get away from you and the damn press," Nixon said. "I want to be away from everything today, understand?"

Nixon left with military aide Don Hughes, Secret Service agent Jack Sherwood, and John DiBetta, a driver from the Los Angeles Police Department. They intended to wander aimlessly down the Pacific Coast Highway for an hour or so. But it was a pleasant morning—with the temperature climbing into the sixties—and they eventually found themselves at the Mexican border, 125 miles south of Whittier. Hughes mentioned that he had never been to Tijuana, so Nixon suggested they cross over for lunch. The four men chose the Old Heidelberg, a restaurant that served Mexican food despite its incongruous name. The mayor of Tijuana, learning of Nixon's unexpected visit, hustled over to welcome the foreign dignitary.

The vice president and his companions recrossed the border in early afternoon, stopping at the Spanish mission of San Juan Capistrano, where Nixon conducted an impromptu tour. They walked past the windows of a Catholic grade school on the mission grounds. One of the nuns, who recognized the Republican candidate, flashed a V-for-victory sign. DiBetta wheeled Nixon back to Los Angeles around 5:00, just as the first returns began trickling in from the Eastern time zone.

The early numbers did not bode well for the Republicans. Kennedy quickly took Connecticut by a larger margin than Nixon's team had anticipated. The Carolinas fell into the Democratic column, too, though the races were fairly close in both states. The polls soon closed in the major urban centers of the East. Massachusetts's 16 electoral votes, to no one's surprise, went to Kennedy in a landslide. The contests in New York (45 electoral votes), Pennsylvania (32), and New Jersey (16) were considerably more competitive, yet all three states were leaning toward Kennedy.

The television networks had added a new dimension to their election coverage, using computers for the first time. Technicians typed in a stream of raw data from precincts across the nation. The mainframes matched the new numbers against the returns from previous elections, periodically spitting out projections. CBS's IBM 7090 computer declared at 9:00 (all subsequent times are Eastern unless otherwise indicated) that Kennedy would finish with 52 percent of the popular vote. NBC's RCA 501 soon chimed in with its own projection. Kennedy, it said, would take 401 electoral votes, far more than the 269 needed to win. "We are pretty confident now of a Kennedy victory," CBS's Eric Sevareid announced at 9:45. "All of the computing machines are now saying Kennedy."

It was all a bit surprising. The public-opinion surveys conducted just before election day—both Gallup and Roper—had predicted a cliffhanger. Len Hall, the chairman of Nixon's campaign, sourly watched state after state fall to the Democrats. "I think we should put all of those electronic computers in the junk pile so far as election returns are concerned," he snapped at a reporter. "This one is going down to the wire—a squeaker, a real close election."

Hall had reason for optimism. NBC's computer had already projected Kennedy as the winner of Ohio's 25 electoral votes, but the returns from that state were going Nixon's way, and his lead widened all evening. Kennedy watched the news from Ohio with great unhappiness. "This was one [state] that he looked for and counted on and expected," said aide John Seigenthaler. Kennedy had campaigned extensively in Ohio, apparently for naught. He rolled back his sleeve and held up his right hand, which was scratched and inflamed from months of handshaking. "Ohio did that to me," he said. "They did it there."

Ohio was the beginning of Nixon's comeback. He carried five Southern states, all but Oklahoma by close margins. It was a respectable showing in a region that had been solidly Democratic just 15 years earlier. The Republican states of the Midwest and West also began dropping into his column after 10:00, slowly boosting his total.

The biggest prize in the Midwest was Illinois, with 27 electoral votes. The city of Chicago, controlled by Mayor Richard Daley's political machine, was overwhelmingly Democratic, but the outlying counties of downstate Illinois were just as rabidly Republican. Kennedy placed a call to Daley, seeking reassurance. "With a little bit of luck and the help of a few close friends," Daley told him, "you're going to carry Illinois." Kennedy's early statewide lead, however, dwindled steadily as more votes were counted. The same erosion was occurring in Texas. "I aim to carry Texas for this ticket. We are not going to lose Texas," Lyndon Johnson had promised. But his confidence was being sorely tested. Nixon was doing unexpectedly well in the state's traditionally Democratic counties.

Kennedy had been running ahead in the popular vote all evening— NBC showed him 1.7 million votes in front of Nixon at midnight—but his margin was shrinking. It narrowed to 1.5 million by 1:00, and fell below 1 million votes by 3:30 A.M. Media outlets began to rethink their early projections. The *New York Times* had set an explicit headline in type—"Kennedy Elected President"—but it replated the front page at 2:00. "Kennedy Apparently Elected," said the new banner. Turner Catledge, the paper's managing editor, was afraid of making a mistake that would live in black and white for the rest of his career. He would remember the 1960 election as "one of the most nerve-racking nights of my life."

Separate counts by all three networks put Kennedy in the vicinity of 260 electoral votes by 3:00—breathtakingly close to the magic number of 269, yet not good enough. Democratic hopes momentarily soared when the Nixons appeared in the Ambassador Hotel's ballroom at 3:17 A.M. (12:17, Pacific). The vice president wore a fixed smile. His wife was crying. "If the present trend continues," Nixon told his supporters, "Senator Kennedy will be the next president of the United States." But he did not formally concede.

"Why don't you give up?" a Kennedy aide said angrily to the television set in Hyannis Port.

"Why should he?" the Democratic candidate said. "I wouldn't, in his place." Kennedy soon went to bed, as did Nixon.

The situation had clarified by the time they awakened. Kennedy rose at 9:00. Ted Sorensen, the first aide to see him, congratulated him on his victory. Kennedy had taken California's 32 electoral votes overnight, Sorensen said, cementing a comfortable win. (He was incorrect. Nixon would carry California by the razor-thin margin of 35,000 popular votes out of 6.5 million cast.) Texas and Illinois had proved to be decisive. Kennedy won Texas by 46,000 votes. His lead in Illinois was even smaller—8,800 votes—but it was sufficient to carry the state and secure the presidency. Nixon's aides unhappily agreed. They told their man that Kennedy had locked up more than 300 electoral votes.

Nixon's formal concession came at 12:45 P.M. on November 9. "I know you will have the united support of all Americans," he wired his opponent, "as you lead the nation in the cause of peace and freedom in the next four years." Kennedy drove to the Hyannis Armory, where 300 correspondents and a battery of television cameras awaited. The president-elect seemed solemn and tired. He displayed no evidence of jubilation during his short speech. "Now my wife and I prepare for a new administration," he said, "and a new baby."

It had been an uncomfortably close call. Kennedy finished with 34.2 million popular votes, 49.7 percent of the national total. Nixon, at 49.5 percent, was 118,600 votes behind. The margin was wider in the Electoral College—Kennedy 303, Nixon 220, unpledged electors 14— though it was not an overwhelming victory by any means. A switch of 11,874 popular votes in Hawaii, Illinois, Missouri, Nevada, and New Mexico would have transferred those five states—and the presidency itself—from Kennedy to Nixon. If that had occurred, Len Hall told Nixon, "we would have been the heroes, and they would have been the bums."

Some Republicans believed they still had a chance. Thruston Morton, the party's national chairman, dispatched telegrams to Republican officials in 11 states, directing them to investigate allegations of voting fraud or irregularities. Illinois and Texas received the most attention. Republicans claimed that Chicago's returns had been grossly inflated. A precinct that contained fewer than 50 registered voters had reportedly cast 79 votes for Kennedy, with a single voter dropping 6 ballots into the box. Democratic-controlled election boards in Texas had allegedly invalidated thousands of ballots cast for Nixon. Richard Daley reacted angrily to the charges. "This is a Republican conspiracy," the Chicago mayor said, "to deny the presidency to the man who was elected by the people."

Nixon faced a difficult choice. Some of the allegations appeared to have merit, yet they would be difficult to prove. It would take months to conduct a recount in Illinois, and there was always the danger that fraud committed by downstate Republicans might also be uncovered. Texas lacked any provisions for a recount. The vice president also had to consider the ramifications of a formal challenge. If he succeeding in overturning Kennedy's election, the nation would be badly polarized the next four years. If a recount failed to change the outcome, his image would be sullied. "Charges of 'sore loser' would follow me through history," he wrote, "and remove any possibility of a further political career."

Nixon decided that his best option was the high road. He told Morton to call off the investigation. "I could think of no worse example for nations abroad, who for the first time were trying to put free electoral procedures into effect, than that of the United States wrangling over the results of our presidential election," he wrote with more than a trace of sanctimony. Nixon signaled his acquiescence on November 14 by agreeing to meet Kennedy in Florida. Their parley was cordial, yet uneventful. "I asked him how he took Ohio, but he didn't tell me," the president-elect joked with reporters afterward. "He's saving it for 1964."

Analysts would sift through 1960's election returns for years to come, seeking to identify the magic ingredient in Kennedy's narrowly successful recipe. Nixon considered it a worthless pursuit. "To ascribe defeat or victory to a single factor in such a close contest," he said, "is, at best, guesswork and oversimplification."

The televised debates had helped Kennedy, to be sure, and they would emerge in political mythology as the decisive reason for his victory. But contemporary surveys did not support such a conclusion. Kennedy had led the Gallup Poll by one percentage point prior to the first debate. He won the election by virtually the same margin, a fraction of a point.

Democratic efforts to cultivate black voters were considerably more important. A postelection survey found that 68 percent of blacks cast votes for Kennedy, a sufficiently large bulge to tip the balance in Illinois, Michigan, and New Jersey. The religious issue also broke in Kennedy's favor, as Nixon had feared from the beginning. Eleven Southern and Western states (with 110 electoral votes) rejected Kennedy because of his Catholicism, according to a Massachusetts Institute of Technology computer analysis, but 5 Eastern and Midwestern states and New Mexico (with 132 electoral votes) switched his way for the same reason. The result was a net gain of 22 votes in the Electoral College.

Robert Finch considered the economy to be the key factor in his boss's defeat, "up to and including the debates." A total of 4.3 million Americans were unemployed as of election day, the highest figure for any November since the Depression. "Conceding the worst on everything else," Finch said, "we still would have won if 400,000 people had not become unemployed during the last thirty days of the campaign."

Two prominent politicians played key roles, too. The Democrats took Texas and five other Southern states—victories that Mississippi Senator James Eastland attributed solely to Lyndon Johnson. "I don't think that Kennedy [by himself] would have carried any Southern state," Eastland said. "And I think Kennedy would have been defeated if Johnson had not been on the ticket." Nixon's reluctance to make greater use of Dwight Eisenhower also helped the Democrats. The president had almost turned the tide during that final frantic week of campaigning. "I shall never cease to wonder whether a more extensive program of political speaking on my part might have had a favorable effect on the outcome," Ike wrote in his memoirs.

The candidates were too exhausted to contemplate these various factors in any great detail. They both retreated to Florida—the vice president to Key Biscayne, the president-elect to Palm Beach. Nixon, in Herb Klein's opinion, was "more unresponsive than at any time I had known him." Kennedy hoped to regain his strength before assembling his Cabinet. He dashed up to Washington to celebrate Thanksgiving with his wife, whose delivery date was a week away, and flew back to Florida that evening.

A call from Georgetown University Hospital awaited him upon his arrival. Mrs. Kennedy had been whisked to the hospital at 10:00 and had given birth at 12:22 A.M. Kennedy rushed back to Washington by 4 A.M. to visit his wife and meet his six-pound, two-ounce son.

A crowd of well-wishers greeted the haggard president-elect when he returned to his Georgetown home just before dawn on November 25. Reporters asked the baby's name. Kennedy, illuminated by the flashing lights of police cars, was momentarily at a loss. "Why, it's John F. Kennedy Jr., I think she decided," he stumbled, but then his habitual air of self-assurance returned. "It *has* been decided. Yes— John F. Kennedy Jr."

13

December: The Can-Do Society

Robert Gilruth, the director of NASA's Space Task Group, felt like the manager of a second-place baseball team that always came close, yet never broke through to win its league.

Project Mercury was slowly rounding into form—Gilruth had great confidence in his technicians and astronauts—but the Soviet Union seemed to have an unassailable lead in the space race. Belka and Strelka's August mission obviously foreshadowed a manned flight, perhaps before the end of 1960. "I would say that you could wake up any morning and find a Russian in space," Gilruth told reporters on December 1. "I'm frankly surprised that they haven't done it before now."

His prediction appeared to have come true earlier that day, when the Soviets launched a Vostok capsule big enough to carry a cosmonaut. Radio Moscow, however, soon announced that the passengers were not humans but canines named Pchelka ("Little Bee") and Mushka ("Little Fly"). The dogs completed 17 orbits—the same number as Belka and Strelka—before suddenly disappearing from tracking screens. Vostok's retro rockets had misfired, pushing the capsule into what Radio Moscow called "a non-calculated trajectory." It disintegrated while reentering the atmosphere.

The Soviets resolved to try again, but their December 22 launch was ill-fated. The upper-stage booster engine failed, which caused the capsule to separate prematurely from its rocket. The two dogs on board—Damka ("Little Lady") and Krasavka ("Little Beauty")—landed far off course in the frigid wilderness of Siberia. They were found, still alive, two days later.

December's twin failures shook the confidence of Sergei Korolev, the chief designer of the Soviet space program. Yet he continued to push his cosmonauts as if their historic mission were imminent. They ran several miles a day, lifted weights, made dozens of parachute jumps, and practiced endlessly in simulators. Korolev would soon be selecting the cosmonaut to make the first flight, and he watched the 20 trainees closely. He gradually winnowed the field to 6 candidates.

Gherman Titov—an air force pilot, accomplished gymnast, and student of classical literature—seemed the ideal man to lead the Soviet Union into space. Titov was polished, well-rounded, and supremely confident. But Korolev had grown fond of Yuri Gagarin, a farmer and smelter who had found his way into the military and become a jet pilot. "I like this boy," the chief designer told a colleague. "He is so communicative and gentle." Korolev was especially impressed with Gagarin's performance in the pressure chamber, an apparatus that most trainees hated. He asked the cosmonaut what had passed through his mind as the pressure intensified. "I have been thinking about the future," Gagarin replied mystically.

The American space program had its own dreams of future success, yet it continued to suffer disheartening setbacks. The November 8 launch of an empty Mercury capsule was billed as a key step toward manned spaceflight. But the capsule failed to separate from its booster, and both components plummeted into the Atlantic Ocean. NASA scheduled another attempt for November 21. The seven astronauts arrived to watch. The Redstone rocket ignited, rose a few inches, and suddenly lost power, settling back on its pad. The capsule's parachutes popped out and flapped in the breeze. NASA officials feared that a gust of wind might inflate a parachute, topple the fully fueled rocket, and trigger an explosion. They detained the astronauts in Cape Canaveral's blockhouse for several hours as a precaution.

The space agency sought to minimize its embarrassment. Wernher von Braun, the German engineer in charge of American rocket development, dismissed the latest debacle as "a little mishap." An electrical plug had disengaged 21 milliseconds behind schedule, cutting power to the engine. The problem, von Braun said, could easily be corrected. It would not prevent the United States from sending an astronaut into space in 1961.

His optimism was finally borne out by NASA's successful launch of a Mercury capsule on December 19. The unmanned spacecraft soared to an altitude of 135 miles before splashing into the Atlantic 244 miles downrange, precisely as planned. The astronauts, who were again on hand, expressed satisfaction. The Mercury capsule, said Scott Carpenter, needed "no changes, none at all."

NASA's brain trust was already allowing its imagination to wander beyond Project Mercury. President Eisenhower had given his approval in late July for Apollo, a series of lunar flights that would follow Mercury's sequence of orbital missions. Design work on the three-man Apollo capsule had begun by December. The agency's timetable called for an astronaut to set foot on the moon by 1971.

Eisenhower allowed NASA to proceed with its planning, even though he failed to see any real point to Apollo. Landing on the moon, he scoffed, would be "a multibillion-dollar project of no immediate value." A panel of scientists arrived at the White House in December to argue the opposite viewpoint. One participant suggested that Eisenhower was in the position of Queen Isabella, who had supposedly pawned her jewels to finance Christopher Columbus's voyages to the New World. Ike brusquely replied that he was "not about to hock [the country's] jewels" just so a man could walk on the moon.

Apollo—a major expansion of the space program—would require an infusion of new astronauts, and NASA was already scouting possible recruits. Among the top prospects was 30-year-old Neil Armstrong, who made his first flight in the rocket-powered X-15 on November 30, soaring over the Mojave Desert at 1,155 miles per hour. Armstrong was fully committed to the X-15—he hoped to be designated its chief pilot—but he knew that alternate possibilities lay ahead. "There was this other project, [the] Apollo program," he recalled. "It wasn't clear to me which of those paths [would be best]." He wouldn't be asked to decide until 1962.

NASA's current roster of seven astronauts had a more immediate concern: Who among them would enter history as the first American in outer space? Two frontrunners had emerged by the end of 1960. Thirty-nine-year-old John Glenn—an energetic, straitlaced marine pilot—was the oldest member of the astronaut corps. His chief competitor was Alan Shepard, a navy commander who was prone to broad mood swings—icy one day, fun loving the next. Glenn showed remarkable skill in dealing with reporters, while Shepard scorned the press. Most journalists, naturally enough, expected their favorite to be selected. Glenn agreed with the consensus. "I thought I had a good shot at being named for the first flight," he said.

Glenn, however, had an unfortunate tendency to impose his moral standards on others. He took several of his colleagues to task at a December meeting, accusing them of extramarital affairs. "I was mad," he recalled, "and I read the riot act, saying that we had worked too hard to get into this program and that it meant too much to the country to see it jeopardized by anyone who couldn't keep his pants zipped." His criticism struck too close to home for his uninhibited rival. "Why is this even coming up?" Shepard snapped at Glenn. "Doesn't everyone have the right to do what they want to do?"

Glenn was unconcerned. "I had made my point," he wrote, "and I didn't think being an astronaut was a popularity contest." He would be disabused of that notion later in the month, when Gilruth called the seven men together. "I know all of you want to go first," he told them. "What I want you to do is vote on which one should be first if you couldn't go yourself. List your choices in order." Glenn knew he was doomed. His straight-arrow personality had alienated a few of his colleagues in recent months, and his latest diatribe had only made matters worse.

NASA undoubtedly took other factors into account, but the astronauts believed their informal election sealed the decision. Gilruth waited until the final night of the Eisenhower era—January 19, 1961—before convening a closed-door meeting to reveal the hierarchy. Shepard would make the first suborbital flight, a 15-minute ballistic trajectory from Cape Canaveral to a target zone in the Atlantic. Glenn would be his backup. "It was a very poignant moment," Shepard said, "because they all came over, shook my hand, and pretty soon I was the only guy left in the room."

Glenn played the role of good loser, but he was furious. He sent a letter to Gilruth, protesting the use of a straw vote. "I might have been penalized," he wrote to the director, "for what I thought was the good of the program." But NASA refused to reconsider. It intended to launch a man into space sometime in 1961—the date had not yet been chosen—and that man would be Alan Shepard.

LEXICON: DECEMBER 1960

Algerian Referendum

Charles de Gaulle decided it was time to settle the question of Algeria once and for all. The French president visited the colony in mid-

December. Moslems cheered him. Many European settlers, anticipating an imminent French withdrawal, reacted violently. "De Gaulle to the gallows," some of them shouted. The old general was not dissuaded. He scheduled an Algerian referendum for January 8, 1961, certain in his mind that the Moslem majority would choose independence. "The Algeria of tomorrow," he predicted during a December 20 television address, "will be Algerian."

Anti-Colonialism

The colonial powers were in full retreat by the end of 1960—not only in Algeria, but everywhere. The United Nations confirmed the trend with a December 14 resolution calling for "a speedy and unconditional end to colonialism." Harvard professor Rupert Emerson contended in his new book, *From Empire to Nation*, that imperialism was doomed. It had "scattered the revolutionary seeds of Western civilization" throughout Africa and Asia, he wrote, and had ironically given birth to a spirit of anti-colonialism that "worked to make [imperialism's] continuance impossible."

Cinderella Bowl

The Philadelphia Eagles and Green Bay Packers were terrible in 1958, winning just three National Football League games between them. They improved dramatically by 1960, squaring off on December 26 for the NFL championship. Sportswriters dubbed the game the Cinderella Bowl. The Eagles hung on to win, 17–13, but the Packers' second-year coach, Vince Lombardi, believed his team's future was bright. "Perhaps you didn't realize that you could have won this game," he told his players. "But I think there's no doubt in your minds now. And that's why you will win it all next year."

Dimona

Four nations possessed nuclear weapons in 1960—the United States, Soviet Union, Great Britain, and France. The *London Daily Express* reported on December 16 that Israel might soon join their ranks. American U-2 overflights had spotted a nuclear reactor being built near the town of Dimona. Israel's ambassador to Washington dismissed the reports as "just newspaper stories." But Premier David Ben-Gurion admitted the facility's existence on December 21. He denied, however, that it would be making weapons. The reactor, he said, was "designed exclusively for peaceful purposes."

La Brigada

The Eisenhower administration reviewed the status of Operation Pluto at a December 8 meeting. The CIA's plans called for 600 to 750 exile soldiers—collectively known as La Brigada—to hit the beaches of Cuba sometime in 1961. They were being trained at a secret base in Guatemala. Colonel Edward Lansdale, an expert in guerrilla warfare, offered a dissenting viewpoint. He told the CIA's brass he was "extremely doubtful" that their scheme would trigger a revolt against Fidel Castro. An invasion so small, Lansdale said, was bound to fail. Yet the preparations continued.

Zaire

Joseph Mobutu had promised to step aside by the end of 1960 after seizing control of the Congo in mid-September. He surprised everybody by living up to his word, restoring Joseph Kasavubu to authority. Yet he did not deal as kindly with Patrice Lumumba, whom he considered a traitor. Mobutu's troops captured the prime minister, tortured him, and turned him over to Katangan forces, who executed him on January 17, 1961. Mobutu would resurface in 1965 after mounting another coup. He gave the Congo (including the restored province of Katanga) the new name of Zaire and stayed in power until 1997.

***

John Kennedy wasn't the president, not quite yet.

Three checkpoints remained on the lengthy, tortuous road to the White House. It was assumed that Kennedy would pass all three, but the formalities had to be observed. His victory would not be official until the Electoral College's 537 members cast ballots in their respective state capitals on December 19. Congress would tabulate the electoral votes on January 6, certifying Kennedy as the next president. His journey to the nation's highest office would conclude two weeks later—January 20, 1961—with inaugural festivities on the east portico of the U.S. Capitol.

Richard Nixon had conceded defeat, but various hardcore elements were unreconciled to Kennedy's triumph. They made two last-ditch efforts in December—one political, the other homicidal—to prevent him from taking the oath of office.

The disaffected citizens of two Southern states had spurned both Kennedy and Nixon on November 8, voting instead for 14 unpledged electors. The 6 from Alabama announced on December 10 that they preferred a Democratic president "who sympathizes with our peculiar problems in the South." They met with their 8 Mississippi colleagues two days later, and all 14 agreed to cast electoral votes for Harry Byrd, a dour septuagenarian who had represented Virginia in the Senate since 1933. Byrd was adamantly opposed to integration. He was willing to do almost anything—even shutting down his state's schools—to prevent racial mixing in classrooms. "If Virginia surrenders," he warned, "if Virginia's line is broken, the rest of the South will go down, too."

Mississippi Governor Ross Barnett sent letters to other Southern electors, urging them to join the nascent Byrd movement. If Barnett could attract 35 defectors, Kennedy would fall short of a majority in the Electoral College, and the task of choosing the next president would pass to the House of Representatives, where anything might happen.

Conservative Southerners regretted the Democratic landslide in Chicago and surrounding Cook County, which had given Kennedy a cushion in the Electoral College. "I think if the votes in Illinois had been counted correctly," Barnett said, "we would have needed only four more [defecting electors] to have thrown the election into the House of Representatives, and I believe that we could have gotten them probably from Arkansas." But Illinois was firmly in Kennedy's column, and Barnett managed to lure only a single Oklahoma elector to his cause. The final count was Kennedy 303, Nixon 219, Byrd 15.

Richard Pavlick, who was 73 years old, disliked Kennedy as intensely as Barnett did, but he had no patience for arcane political maneuvers. The retired postal clerk from New Hampshire preferred straightforward action. He rigged his 1950 Buick with blasting caps and seven sticks of dynamite—and set out for Florida to kill the president-elect. "The Kennedy money bought him the White House," he said later. "I wanted to teach the United States that the presidency is not for sale."

Pavlick waited outside of Kennedy's Palm Beach home on the morning of December 11. He intended to ram the senator's limousine, flip a switch, and explode the dynamite. But the would-be assassin changed his mind when three-year-old Caroline appeared in the doorway to say goodbye to her father. Local police, who had been alerted by the

Secret Service, captured him four days later, before he had an opportunity to try again. "In a way, I'm glad it's turned out the way it has," Pavlick said. "But I don't like the publicity."

Kennedy seemed undisturbed by the schemes against his career and his life. He was immersed in preparations for the transfer of power, especially when Dwight Eisenhower invited him to the White House on December 6. "Good morning, Mr. President," Kennedy said as he jogged up the steps and extended his hand. The U.S. Marine Band struck up "Stars and Stripes Forever." Eisenhower led his guest inside, where they talked alone for an hour and 45 minutes.

They hit it off surprisingly well. The two men had been privately caustic—Eisenhower deriding the president-elect as callow and naive, Kennedy dismissing the incumbent as lazy and ineffectual. But they warmed to each other. Ike wrote in his diary that his successor's attitude "was that of a serious, earnest seeker for information." Kennedy told his brother that Eisenhower exhibited "a surprising force." The presidential transition from Harry Truman to Eisenhower in 1953 had been acrimonious. Eisenhower and Kennedy pledged to do better, agreeing to cooperate fully during the month and a half to come.

Most of Kennedy's time was devoted to filling hundreds of key positions in his administration. Eager Democratic office seekers swamped him with resumés. "Jesus Christ, this one wants that, that one wants this," he complained in the car one afternoon. "Goddamn it, you can't satisfy any of these people. I don't know what I'm going to do about it all." His father, sitting in the front seat, was unsympathetic. "Jack," Old Joe reminded him, "if you don't want the job, you don't have to take it. They're still counting votes up in Cook County."

The most prominent position at Kennedy's disposal was secretary of state. Pundits assumed that he would choose the party's elder statesman, Adlai Stevenson, but there was no chance of that. "Jack used to talk about him frequently—what a pain in the ass he was," Bobby Kennedy recalled. Stevenson's vacillation at the Democratic convention had earned the scorn of the president-to-be, dooming any possibility of a high-profile appointment.

Kennedy preferred J. William Fulbright, an ex-president of the University of Arkansas who had served in the Senate since 1945, but the opposition was fierce. Dean Acheson, himself a former secretary of state, ridiculed Fulbright as a "dilettante." Other Democrats questioned his lack of commitment to civil rights. "We can't have a secretary of state from Little Rock," said one. Kennedy reluctantly backed off. "The Africans and our own blacks will raise a terrible howl if I appoint him," the president-elect said privately, "even though he's probably the best man for the job."

There was a brief boom for David Bruce, who had served as ambassador to France and West Germany. But the 62-year-old Bruce was too stodgy for Kennedy's taste. Harry Truman's last secretary of defense, Robert Lovett, was even older—he had recently turned 65—yet he possessed the vitality that Bruce lacked. Kennedy offered him the job one December afternoon as the two men chatted by the fireplace. Lovett recoiled. "No, sir, I can't," he said. "My bearings are burnt out."

Few options remained. "It finally had come down to where everybody else had been eliminated," said Bobby Kennedy, "and Rusk was left." Dean Rusk was the cautious, soft-spoken son of a Georgia cotton farmer. He had been an assistant secretary of state during the Truman administration and now served as president of the Rockefeller Foundation. Acheson recommended him highly—"I thought he had been strong and loyal and good in every way"—and Lovett seconded the endorsement.

Kennedy met Rusk on December 8—finding him acceptable, though a bit bland—and formally offered the appointment the next day. "Kennedy never explained why he chose me," Rusk wrote, "and I never asked." There was only one hitch. The secretary-designate was required to fill out an FBI questionnaire, which asked if any of his relatives had ever attempted to overthrow the government of the United States. Rusk answered affirmatively and supplied their names. Nervous FBI agents eventually learned that both of his grandfathers had fought with the Confederate army.

Stevenson, meanwhile, had to content himself with a consolation prize—becoming the ambassador to the United Nations. His initial impulse was to reject the offer.

"What are you going to do instead?" asked his aide, Newton Minow.

"I'm going to continue as we are—speeches, articles," Stevenson replied.

Minow didn't see the point. "You'll be on page forty-six in the *New York Times*," he said, "with three lines of space." Stevenson eventually accepted the post, though not happily. "Of course, I expected to be secretary," he confided to a friend in 1964. "It was a great blow."

The other Cabinet members were chosen more easily. Lovett made a surprising suggestion for secretary of defense—44-year-old Robert McNamara, who had just become president of Ford Motor Company

Robert McNamara is the surprise choice to be
secretary of defense: "The can-do man in the
can-do society." (U.S. Department of Defense,
photo by Master Sgt. Frank Hall, U.S. Army)

on November 9. Kennedy was dazzled by McNamara's intelligence,
intensity, and self-confidence—author David Halberstam would label
him "the can-do man in the can-do society"—and the auto executive's
appointment was announced on December 13. The lesser Cabinet
posts were filled in workmanlike fashion, with the names of new secretaries being released on a daily basis.

The one exception was the position of attorney general. The president-elect offered the job to Abraham Ribicoff, the governor of Connecticut, who turned it down, preferring to become the secretary of
health, education, and welfare. No one was happier with Ribicoff's
decision than Joseph Kennedy. The best choice for attorney general,
Old Joe insisted, was right under their noses. It was none other than
his son Bobby.

Jack wasn't convinced. He asked his personal lawyer, Clark Clifford, to travel to New York to reason with his father. Bobby was just 35, Clifford reminded Joe, and he had never tried a case in a courtroom. A less prominent job—perhaps serving as McNamara's deputy at the Pentagon—might be preferable. "Give him the chance to grow," Clifford said. "He will be outstanding."

"Thank you very much, Clark," Joe replied. "I am so glad to have heard your views. I do want to leave you with one thought, however—one firm thought. Bobby is going to be attorney general." And so he was. Jack bowed to his father's will, though he sought to downplay his brother's appointment. "Well," he said, "I think I'll open the front door of the Georgetown house some morning about 2 A.M., look up and down the street, and if there's no one there, I'll whisper, 'It's Bobby.'"

Kennedy's Cabinet, with an average age of 47, would be the youngest of the 20th century. He relied heavily on career politicians and academicians to staff his administration, despite initial promises to cast a wider net. Approximately one-third of the top-rank appointments went to men who had attended Kennedy's alma mater. The new agriculture secretary, Orville Freeman, was one of the exceptions. Reporters asked him why he was selected. "I'm not really sure," Freeman said, "but I think it has something to do with the fact that Harvard doesn't have a school of agriculture."

Older Democrats watched the flurry of appointments with misgivings. Sam Rayburn, the 78-year-old speaker of the House, listened skeptically as Lyndon Johnson described the team that would explore the New Frontier. They were the smartest people available, Johnson said excitedly, the cream of the crop from the nation's greatest corporations (McNamara), foundations (Rusk), and universities (all of the Harvard appointees).

But it was those very qualities—their youth, their academic orientation, their lack of political experience—that dismayed Rayburn. "Well, Lyndon, you may be right," he said wearily, "and they may be every bit as intelligent as you say. But I'd feel a whole lot better about them if just one of them had run for sheriff once."

RISING STAR: BOB DYLAN

There was nothing exceptional about Robert Zimmerman's teenage years, nothing that foreshadowed greatness. The defining characteristics of his life—the small-town upbringing, the early love of music, the urgent need to perform—were common enough in the late fifties. Thousands of young Americans with similar backgrounds dreamed of becoming stars in the new world of rock and roll.

Zimmerman grew up in Hibbing, Minnesota, an unattractive community on the lip of one of the world's largest open-pit iron mines. Winters were long and cold, and the sense of isolation was tangible. The nearest big city—barely worthy of the title with a population of 106,000—was Duluth, 80 miles to the southeast.

Bob would always have ambivalent feelings about his hometown. "There is a great spiritual quality throughout the Midwest," he said. "Very subtle, very strong, and this is where I grew up." But he bridled at the intense pressure to conform. "The teachers in school taught me everything was fine," he once told a reporter. "That was the accepted thing to think. It was in all the books. But it ain't fine, man."

Music offered a way out. Zimmerman took up the guitar and began playing in local bands. His singing voice was nothing special—thin, nasal, sometimes raspy—but he showed remarkable facility as a lyricist. His hero was Buddy Holly, the prototypical singer-songwriter who had also impressed John Lennon and Paul McCartney. Bob, then a high school senior, caught Holly's show at the Duluth Armory on January 31, 1959, just three days before the young star died in a plane crash.

The footloose life of a musician wasn't what Zimmerman's parents desired for their son, so they sent him to the University of Minnesota. "Don't keep writing poetry, please don't," his mother said. "Go to school and do something constructive. Get a degree." But his heart wasn't in it. A university counselor recalled that Zimmerman was "hard to know, kept very odd hours, and moped a lot." He carried a notebook in which he wrote songs, and he skipped classes to perform in coffeehouses.

It was in Minneapolis that he became fixated on Woody Guthrie, the Oklahoma-born folk musician. Zimmerman patterned his life after his new role model. "He gave us all the dust-bowl Okie-hobo routine," fellow singer Jackie Washington remembered. He completed the transformation by changing his name to Bob Dylan, supposedly in tribute to famed poet Dylan Thomas. Bob denied any link. "I just chose that name," he said, "and it stuck."

His restlessness increased in his sophomore year. He caught a Greyhound bus home in December 1960, telling his parents that he wanted to pursue a music career. They were surprisingly supportive. "We couldn't see it," his father recalled, "but we felt he was entitled to the chance." They agreed to give him a year. If it didn't work out, he would return to school.

His destination was the city where most of America's major recording companies were located, and where Guthrie was hospitalized with a nervous-system disorder. "I'm leaving for New York," Dylan excitedly told a friend. "I'm going to see Woody." He hitchhiked to Chicago before Christmas, wandering east by late January 1961. He had little to say when he visited his idol. "Bobby sort of hung back in the shadows, just watching everything, just listening," said Jack Elliott, a noted folk musician.

Dylan was not as shy when it came to promoting his own music. He soon attracted a following in New York's coffeehouses. His songs were unusual for that era, dealing with weighty subjects such as war, poverty, and racial injustice—"seeking out the explosive areas of life," as he put it. John Hammond, the same scout who had discovered Aretha Franklin, signed Dylan to a contract with Columbia Records in October 1961. He would not be returning to the University of Minnesota.

Dylan achieved superstardom by the mid-sixties. A contemporary review in the *New York Times* noted his "small and homely" voice, but hailed his skill as a guitarist, and praised him for writing lyrics that sparkled "with the light of an inspired poet." He remained a musical icon into the 21st century. Every conceivable accolade came his way—16 platinum albums, induction into the Rock and Roll Hall of Fame, even a Pulitzer Prize.

Dylan, however, applied a much simpler measure to his career. It was enough that he had moved beyond Hibbing and enjoyed a creative life. "A man is a success," he always said, "if he gets up in the morning and goes to bed at night, and in between does what he wants to do."

* * *

Bruce Boynton was hungry. The 21-year-old law student had boarded a Trailways bus in Washington, D.C., earlier in the evening, setting off on an 800-mile journey to Alabama. The last-minute rush to the bus station had left him no time for supper. He decided to grab a sandwich and a cup of tea in Richmond, the first scheduled stop.

It was an unfortunate plan. The lunchroom in Richmond's terminal was segregated, and Boynton was black. A policeman arrested him on a charge of misdemeanor trespassing. Most black Southerners would have avoided conflict by paying the $10 fine, but Boynton was young and idealistic. He appealed his conviction to Virginia's highest court—which predictably ruled against him—and then to the U.S. Supreme Court.

It took two years to navigate the judicial maze from his 1958 arrest to the final verdict, yet the outcome justified Boynton's persistence. The Supreme Court ruled in his favor on December 5, 1960. "Interstate passengers have to eat," wrote Justice Hugo Black, and they had a right to expect service "rendered without discrimination." The court's decision applied to all vehicles and facilities operated by any transportation carrier—bus line, railroad, or airline—that traveled across state borders. Interracial groups of civil rights protesters, known as "freedom riders," would put this new desegregation order to the test in the coming year.

The Boynton case fit the stereotype held by most Northerners, who believed that racial discrimination was solely a Southern problem. It was a natural assumption, given that America's black population had been concentrated below the Mason-Dixon Line for more than two centuries. The 1950 census had counted 10.3 million nonwhites (the era's catchall term for minorities) in the Southern states, compared to just 5.4 million in the rest of the country. But the northward migration of blacks, which had begun with a trickle in 1910, flowed at a rapid pace during the fifties. The census of April 1960 found that 44 percent of all nonwhites now lived outside the South. It seemed possible that a 50-50 equilibrium might be achieved in the decade ahead.

Northern whites often reacted with self-conscious ambivalence when dealing with blacks. The Chicago suburb of Park Forest had admitted its first black residents in late December 1959—Charles and Doris Wilson and their three children—but only after a careful screening. The Wilsons were interviewed by a seven-member committee that inquired if they had stable employment (Charles was a professor at DePaul University) or belonged to any political pressure groups (they didn't). Yet a substantial percentage of Park Forest's residents were still displeased. "They may not be happy about a Negro living in Park Forest," admitted Robert Dinerstein, the village's president. "But given the facts, they respect [the Wilson family's] rights under the law."

Such consideration was lacking in other Northern communities. Six hundred white residents jammed a town board meeting in Deerfield, another Chicago suburb, to protest a plan that would have allowed blacks to move into a housing development being built in 1960. "In essence," said Harold Lewis, an investment broker who led the opposition, "they are trying to force integration down the throats of the people of Deerfield, and we are resentful." Both sides threatened to go to court. "I urge you to try to get along peaceably," U.S. District Court Judge Joseph Sam Perry told them. "Forget the emotionalism, and try to work this out like cultured, refined, civilized people." It was easier said than done.

Blacks throughout the North felt a mounting sense of frustration. Newspapers carried numerous stories about Southern integration orders and civil rights protests but ignored Northern racial disparities. A prominent white journalist, Harry Ashmore, predicted that this imbalance would shortly disappear. "The not-yet-fully recognized fact is that the race problem is no longer the exclusive or even the primary property of the South," he wrote in *The Other Side of Jordan,* a book published in late 1960. Adam Clayton Powell, a fiery black congressman from Harlem, agreed that the entire nation would soon pay the price for racial discrimination. "The Negro leader," said Powell, "makes no distinction any longer between the North and the South."

A harbinger of this contentious future could be seen in New Rochelle, New York, a city of 76,000 people situated two miles north of the Bronx. Eighty-six percent of New Rochelle's residents were white. School administrators had drawn boundary lines with care, funneling almost all of the community's black children to Lincoln Elementary, a school attended by just 29 white students. The city's other schools were virtually all white.

Pauline Flippin had been complaining about this inequality since the late forties. She went door to door in minority neighborhoods, year after year, seeking to raise awareness among her fellow black parents. Her efforts finally bore fruit on September 21, 1960, when she and 22 other blacks staged a sit-down strike outside of a white elementary school. Police dispersed the protesters. The parents of 11 black children filed a lawsuit four weeks later, accusing New Rochelle of operating a segregated school system.

Similar legal action had been initiated against dozens of school districts in the South but never in the North. Local officials expressed confusion when the case came before a federal judge on December 13. "All children in New Rochelle—Negro and white—are treated alike," insisted Julius Weiss, the school system's lawyer. But the parents' attorney, Paul Zuber, proved that Lincoln's boundaries had been expanded as more and more blacks moved into New Rochelle. Judge

Irving Kaufman issued a desegregation order the following month, stressing that no community was exempt from *Brown v. Board of Education*. "Compliance with the Supreme Court's edict," he said, "was not to be less forthright in the North than in the South. No double standard was to be tolerated."

The battle for civil rights, up to this point, had merely been a picture in the newspaper or an image on the television screen for most white Northerners. But it had now become—all of a sudden—a full-blown local issue. Harry Ashmore had seen the change coming. "We are all, white and black alike," he wrote, "in for a nervous time."

QUOTATIONS: DECEMBER 1960

"I don't believe we should conserve moose for the sake of future moose."
> —*Alaska Senator Ernest Gruening, decrying the creation of the Arctic National Wildlife Range. The 8.9-million-acre reservation in northern Alaska, established by Interior Secretary Fred Seaton on December 7, extended federal protection to 200 species of mammals, birds, and fish.*

"Lombardi. Lombardi raises hell."
> —*Paul Hornung, a halfback with the Green Bay Packers, offering his explanation for the football team's rapid improvement. The Packers posted only one victory in 1958, the year before Vince Lombardi arrived as coach. They won 8 of their 12 games in 1960.*

"I am convinced that the consequence would be immediate civil war, degenerating into tribal conflicts fought in the most uninhibited manner."
> —*Dag Hammarskjold, secretary-general of the United Nations, rejecting demands on December 14 that the UN withdraw its troops from the Congo. The Soviet Union remained highly critical of the UN's intervention.*

"Now is the time for all who fear seasickness to take to the lifeboats. The rest of you must cling to the mast."
> —*Charles de Gaulle, warning the French Cabinet that the approaching referendum on Algerian self-determination would trigger intense controversy.*

"This unique good fortune has isolated America, I think rather dangerously, from the common experience of the rest of mankind, all the great peoples of which have, without exception, known the bitter taste of defeat and humiliation."

> —*Historian C. Vann Woodward, disputing the value of America's unbeaten record in foreign wars. His new book,* The Burden of Southern History, *warned the South—and the entire nation—against believing "that we are somehow immune from the forces of history."*

"Nuts."

> —*James Hagerty, President Eisenhower's press secretary, responding on New Year's Eve to a Cuban allegation that an American invasion was imminent.*

***

Julie Nixon, like most 12-year-olds, craved certainty and stability. Washington had always been her home. It was where her friends lived, where she attended school. But her father's defeat raised the unwanted specter of change. Julie began bombarding him with questions the day after the election. "What are we going to do?" she asked. "Where are we going to live? What kind of job are you going to be able to get? Where are we going to school?"

Dick Nixon didn't have any answers, at least not right away. Failure was a new experience for him. Success had not always come easily, but he had invariably attained it. He had risen in 14 years from political neophyte to congressman to senator to vice president to presidential nominee, winning every election along the way. Nixon had envisioned moving his family into the White House in January. He was confronted instead with the first setback of his career, the first necessity to adjust his future course.

Unemployment was not a concern. The vice president fielded job offers from three foundations, four universities, and numerous corporations and law firms. Thomas Dewey, who had lost two presidential elections, urged him to take several months before deciding what to do next. It was sound advice, but Nixon felt pressure—from without and within—to tie up his loose ends before leaving office. He wanted to be able to answer his daughter's questions.

Political considerations, of course, were central to his calculations. Nixon would turn 48 in January—still young enough to make another run at the White House. What he needed was a job that would keep him in the public spotlight and preserve his base of power. President Eisenhower predicted that Nixon would remain influential. "The vice president," Ike announced on December 1, "will be the head of the Republican Party for the next four years, and he will have my support."

Other prominent Republicans were dubious. Nelson Rockefeller, who had been an irritant to Nixon all year, was foremost among the skeptics. "I don't think, frankly, between elections when a party loses the presidency, that the party has an actual head," Rocky said. He confided to intimates that he had made a mistake in 1960. He should have run, he said, and he was convinced that he could have beaten Kennedy. It was taken for granted that he would be a candidate the next time. William Brinton, who had founded the short-lived Draft Rockefeller Committee in June, expressed confidence that his hero's brand of liberal Republicanism would be victorious in 1964. "Rockefeller," he said, "can win in just those areas that Nixon lost—the big cities."

That was precisely what Barry Goldwater did not want to hear. The Arizona senator also had a strong following in the Republican Party—his defiant speech at the Chicago convention had thrilled the conservative bloc—and he too was considered a likely presidential contender. "I want to figure in 1964, not necessarily as the top candidate," he said, "but I don't want Rockefeller in that spot." Goldwater believed that Nixon had lost because he was insufficiently conservative. Rockefeller, to his mind, would be even worse. "We cannot win," Goldwater insisted, "as a dime-store copy of the opposition's platform." Nor did he consider Nixon to be the party's titular head. If the vice president wished to exert leadership in the future, Goldwater told reporters on December 1, he would have to be elected to another public office.

Nixon's wife, Pat, wanted to return to California; and the more Dick thought about it, the more sensible the move seemed. He still had a political base in his native state—only 10 years had passed since his landslide Senate victory—and future opportunities were bound to turn up. A Christmas Day story in the *New York Times* even suggested that he might run for governor in two years against Pat Brown, the gregarious incumbent who was considered a bit of a bumbler.

But Nixon quietly passed the word that 1962 would be too soon for a political comeback. He intended to write his memoirs, practice law in Los Angeles, and campaign for Republican candidates across the country. There appeared to be no reason to pursue the governor-ship. "A loss to Brown," *Time* noted in mid-December, "would surely be the end of the Nixon road. Is the gain worth the big risk?" The magazine answered in the negative. If Kennedy remained popular in 1964, it would be more logical for Nixon to step aside and watch Goldwater and Rockefeller battle for an essentially worthless Republican nomination. "Then," *Time* concluded, "1968 would be Nixon's."

His first priority was to restore his reputation. Critics within the Republican Party were already sniping that Nixon had blown an unblowable election. Eisenhower remained popular, the country was at peace, the economy had grown prodigiously in the previous eight years, the Democrats nominated a Catholic—and still the Republicans had lost. Goldwater and Rockefeller—and their ardent followers—placed the blame directly on Nixon.

Yet the opposite case could also be made, and it would be the key to Nixon's renaissance. Significant factors had been aligned against him in 1960. Forty-seven percent of Americans professed themselves to be Democrats, but only 30 percent were Republicans, according to the Gallup Poll. The economy spiraled into a recession. The vice president had been required to defend the administration's record, leaving Kennedy free to go on the attack. And yet Nixon had fought the good fight, losing by just two-tenths of a percentage point.

William Miller, the chairman of the Republican Congressional Campaign Committee, was as conservative as any member of the House of Representatives. He was inclined to support Goldwater for president in 1964, but he scoffed at the reporters who were writing Nixon's political obituary. "Any man who, at forty-seven, comes within [118,600] votes of winning the presidency—for a party that is greatly outnumbered—has to be reckoned with," Miller said as the year drew to a close. "It's far too early to bury Dick Nixon."

14

Epilogue: Passing the Torch

It had been a tumultuous, occasionally unpleasant year for Nikita Khrushchev. The Soviet leader had seemed weak, impetuous, and foolish at varying stages of the U-2 crisis; and his odyssey to the United Nations had accomplished virtually nothing. His critics, as a result, accumulated considerable strength in 1960. The Chinese now flouted his authority, and his political opponents in the Kremlin had grown more numerous.

Yet Khrushchev insisted on putting a positive spin on the negative situation, inviting 2,000 guests to St. George's Hall in Moscow to celebrate New Year's Eve. The clock struck midnight, and the first secretary proposed a toast. "No matter how good the old year has been," he declared, "the new year will be better still!" He expressed hope for improved relations with the United States in 1961—"with the coming of a new president, a fresh wind will blow"—and he concluded with an expansive pledge. "For peaceful coexistence among nations," he said in a strong voice. "For peaceful coexistence among all peoples."

Khrushchev would soon make a symbolic gesture of amity, releasing the two Americans who had survived the RB-47 crash. Yet he was unable to resist his combative impulses. The tenuous links between the United States and Cuba finally disintegrated on January 2. Fidel Castro demanded that the American embassy in Havana reduce its staff by 90 percent, and President Eisenhower responded by breaking off diplomatic relations. "This message from Castro," Ike huffed, "was the last straw." Khrushchev couldn't refrain from stirring the pot. "Alarming news is coming from Cuba at present," he said, "news that the most aggressive American monopolists are preparing a direct attack on Cuba."

The Soviet leader further belied his New Year's toast with a bellicose speech on January 6. He expressed support for "wars of national liberation"—a category in which he placed Castro's revolution and the Algerian imbroglio—and he hinted that similar conflicts would be desirable in other parts of the world. "The communists," Khrushchev said, "support just wars of this kind wholeheartedly and without reservations."

The speech was a logical extension of November's communist summit, where the Soviets had reached a temporary compromise with the more belligerent Chinese. Eisenhower saw no reason for worry. Khrushchev often spoke harshly, Ike told his aides, but the Soviets rarely converted their chief's words into action. President-elect Kennedy, however, was convinced that the address marked a harsh departure in Soviet foreign policy. He instructed his advisers to "read, mark, learn, and inwardly digest it."

The outgoing administration was more concerned about the past than the future. Eisenhower could not shake his regrets about the U-2. If only Francis Gary Powers had completed his flight to Norway, Ike thought, then the Spirit of Camp David might have reached full bloom. "I had longed to give the United States and the world a lasting peace," the president said unhappily. "I was able only to contribute to a stalemate." Powers would be released from a Soviet prison in February 1962, but the damage caused by his flight would haunt the world for years. "I often dream about the U-2," Ike's secretary of defense, Thomas Gates, said in 1967. "One of the big problems of my Washington life was the U-2."

The Soviets also felt remorse. Anastas Mikoyan, then the deputy premier, later accused Khrushchev of engaging in "inexcusable hysterics" during the U-2 crisis. "He was guilty of delaying the onset of detente for fifteen years," Mikoyan said. Khrushchev traced his own political demise to that fateful May Day. "Things were going well until one thing happened," he told a visiting American doctor in 1969. "From the time Gary Powers was shot down, I was no longer in full control." His enemies in the Kremlin, Khrushchev said, would not allow peaceful gestures toward the United States after that.

The next four years were a period of gradual decline, punctuated by Khrushchev's attempt to install missiles in Cuba, which Kennedy rebuffed in October 1962. China, growing more powerful and intransigent, realized the first secretary's worst fears by exploding a nuclear bomb on October 16, 1964. Khrushchev had always responded to such challenges with bluster and defiance, yet he was speechless on this occasion. Presidium hard-liners had removed him from office 48 hours earlier, leaving him with a pension, an apartment, and a small house in the country. Khrushchev was relegated to the status of non-person—ignored by the Soviet government, visited by few foreigners—a belated victim of the chaotic events of May 1960.

***

The Constitution says little about the vice president. One of the job's few responsibilities is to oversee the tabulation of votes cast by the Electoral College. That put Richard Nixon in a curious position, requiring him to serve as presiding officer for the January 6, 1961, ceremony that certified his defeat by Jack Kennedy.

Two boxes of inlaid wood were carried into the chamber of the House of Representatives. Ballots from the 50 states were removed in alphabetical order, beginning with Alabama, which cast six electoral votes for Harry Byrd and five for Kennedy. "The gentleman from Virginia is now in the lead," said Nixon, grinning at the old senator seated below.

The roll call proceeded smoothly until it reached Hawaii, which had submitted conflicting sets of electoral votes. Nixon had initially been declared the winner in the nation's newest state, but a recount gave Kennedy a slight edge. The vice president proposed that Hawaii be awarded to his opponent, and it was. Votes from the remaining states were tabulated without a hitch.

Nixon gave a short speech after the roll call was completed. "In our campaigns, no matter how hard-fought they may be, no matter how close the election may turn out to be," he said, "those who lose accept the verdict and support those who win." It was his "very great honor," the vice president said, to formally declare Kennedy the victor. Congressmen and senators from both parties gave him a standing ovation as he departed.

The ceremony in the House chamber lasted just 47 minutes, yet it carried symbolic importance. It was the final act of the 1960 presidential campaign—the longest, busiest, costliest campaign that Americans had ever seen. Franklin Roosevelt's fireside chats and Harry Truman's whistle-stops now seemed to be quaint relics of a distant age. Future campaigns would emulate the frenzied motion, slick commercials, and copious spending of 1960. Nixon had visited all 50 states, and Kennedy had reached 46—an unprecedented pace. The two nominees had spent $14 million on television commercials alone—an unequaled sum. "You had two relatively young men with enormous drive," said Robert Finch, "and it was quite a show." Politics would never be the same.

Future candidates, even those who weren't ideologically compatible, naturally preferred the winner as a role model. Kennedy had defied the Democratic bosses, trusting his fate to the primaries. It was no coincidence that the bosses of both parties began to lose power during the sixties, or that the primaries soon became the only route to a presidential nomination. Kennedy had built a powerful organization that was loyal only to him, not his party. Other politicians—both Democrats and Republicans—followed his lead. Larry O'Brien ran into Barry Goldwater during the Arizona senator's 1964 presidential campaign. "We had a chat that I remember quite well," O'Brien said, "because Barry wanted to let me know he had followed the Kennedy campaign procedure throughout."

The 1960 election—close though it was—removed one barrier to the White House. Kennedy became the first Catholic to be elected president. Norman Vincent Peale had assumed that a majority of Americans shared his fear of the Vatican, but he discovered differently. Several newspapers dropped Peale's column because of his intolerance, and his influence began to wane. "I ruined myself," Peale admitted to a friend. Never again would a Catholic candidate be forced to answer questions about his religious beliefs. Other barriers, however, still remained. A 1963 Gallup Poll found that only 58 percent of men and 51 percent of women would support a "well-qualified" female presidential candidate. The concept of a black president was so outlandish that no pollster even posed the question.

The campaign of 1960 also changed the way that presidential candidates—and presidents themselves—were covered by the media. The debates had revealed the raw power of visual images, elevating television to a dominant role from that point onward. Kennedy decided to break with tradition in 1961, allowing his press conferences to be televised live. "This is the right thing," he told his press secretary, Pierre Salinger. "We should be able to go around the newspapers if that becomes necessary." Print reporters complained that they were being demoted to minor roles in a sideshow. Kennedy paid them no heed.

Theodore White also had an unexpected impact on political reporting. White doubted that his new book, *The Making of the President 1960*, would be widely read, but it soared to the top of the best-seller list in 1961, eventually selling 4 million copies. Readers, it turned out, were fascinated by his inside scoop on the presidential candidates. Newspapers took notice. They no longer confined themselves to covering speeches and election returns, but began copying White's observational style. They reported on candidates' off-the-record comments, secret deals, even what they ate for breakfast. "Which I think I invented as a method of reporting, and which I now sincerely regret," White wearily told a colleague in 1972. "If you write about this, say that I sincerely regret it."

Kennedy had insisted from the start that 1960 would usher in "a new generation of leadership," and he was proven correct. The men he defeated for the Democratic nomination faded from the scene, at least temporarily. Hubert Humphrey and Stuart Symington returned to the Senate. Adlai Stevenson drifted off to the anonymity of the UN. Lyndon Johnson settled into the somnolence of the vice presidency.

Prominent among the new powers in the Democratic Party were Kennedy's brothers. "Fervent admirers of the Kennedys," the *Saturday Evening Post* had noted in 1957, "confidently look forward to the day when Jack will be in the White House, Bobby will serve in the Cabinet as attorney general, and Teddy will be the senator from Massachusetts." It all came to pass. "Whatever he wants, I'm going to see he gets it," Joe Kennedy said of his youngest son, and the patriarch was true to his word. Ted was elected to Jack's old Senate seat in 1962, just 8 months after turning 30.

The Republicans braced themselves for ideological warfare in the years ahead, with Nelson Rockefeller leading the forces of the left and Goldwater battling for the right. Nixon lacked solid ties to either side, though he expected to seek the presidency again. "Once you get used to the fast track," he admitted, "it's hard to be entirely happy slowing down."

But Nixon would run as a different type of candidate. The vice president was publicly magnanimous, yet privately considered himself a victim. "We won," he told friends after the election, "but they stole it from us." He had always been an uninhibited campaigner—never shy about slashing at Democrats—but he added an element of ruthlessness after 1960. He behaved henceforth as if the outcome of any election were in doubt—even when he held a sizable lead in the polls—and he never took his eye off the Kennedys. "Something bad is going to come of this," he warned after Bobby announced for president in 1968. He was equally concerned that Ted might challenge him in 1972. "I guess the Kennedy crowd is just laying in the bushes," he told an aide, "waiting to make their move."

The ghosts of 1960 would haunt Nixon for the rest of his career—indeed, the rest of his life. "From this point on, I had the wisdom and wariness of someone who had been burned by the power of the Kennedys and their money and by the license they were given by the media," he wrote in his memoirs. "I vowed that I would never again enter an election at a disadvantage by being vulnerable to them—or anyone—on the level of political tactics."

***

Time was running short for Dwight Eisenhower. He stood at a White House window in mid-January, watching workmen erect the reviewing stand for Kennedy's inaugural parade. "It's like being in the death cell," Ike said, "and watching them put up the scaffold."

He wasn't ready to leave, not quite yet. A pair of important matters required his attention in the few days that remained.

Eisenhower, despite his army background, had done his best to restrain the Pentagon's budget during the past eight years. "Unjustified military spending," he once wrote, "is nothing more than a distorted use of the nation's resources." But he worried that the recent escalation of U.S.-Soviet tensions might inspire Kennedy to dramatically increase funding for the armed forces. Eisenhower resolved to include a final warning in his farewell address on January 17.

It would come to be considered the greatest speech of his career—certainly the most prescient. Eisenhower noted that the armaments industry had grown tremendously since World War II, constantly lobbying for more and more money from the federal government. It was the president's duty, he contended, to reject those requests when they were nonessential. "In the councils of government," Eisenhower said, "we must guard against the acquisition of unwarranted influence, whether sought or unsought, by the military-industrial complex. The potential for the disastrous rise of misplaced power exists and will persist." It was an admonition that would be routinely ignored during the decades to come.

Ike's other piece of unfinished business was a final meeting with the president-elect. Eisenhower and Kennedy reconvened on January 19, the day before the inauguration. Their December get-together had been a simple man-to-man conversation, but key members of the outgoing and incoming Cabinets were invited to this second session.

Eisenhower surprised Kennedy's team by stressing the importance of Southeast Asia. "The loss of Laos," he predicted, "would be the loss of the 'cork in the bottle,' and the beginning of the loss of most of the Far East." This was more extreme than anything Eisenhower had expressed publicly and was starkly at odds with his refusal to commit American troops to the region. Ike's new urgency had an impact on the president-elect. "The way Eisenhower discussed the issue that day," wrote Clark Clifford, one of the aides who accompanied Kennedy, "made an important, and unfortunate, contribution to the development of American policy toward Indochina."

Cuba was another major topic. Eisenhower had decided earlier in the month that Operation Pluto should either be implemented by March 1961 or abandoned. He favored the former course. "When we turn over responsibility on the twentieth," he told his aides, "our successors should continue to improve and intensify the training, and undertake planning when the Cubans are themselves properly organized." He now framed the options for Kennedy. The United States should find a prominent Cuban refugee to head a government-in-exile, Ike suggested, and then should act quickly to remove Castro. "We cannot let the present government there go on," he said. Nobody disagreed.

It was a gloomy meeting, perhaps reflecting Eisenhower's lingering doubts about Kennedy's ability to do the job. The elderly president had grown to like his successor—and even respect him in some ways—but he still could not envision the young man standing up to Khrushchev or running the country effectively. He doubted that the president-elect truly understood what awaited him.

Eisenhower made one last attempt to enlighten Kennedy about the power that would soon be his, to provide a demonstration of the unadulterated authority wielded by the nation's commander-in-chief. Ike pushed a button. "Send a chopper," he barked into an intercom. A helicopter landed six minutes later on the lawn outside the Oval Office. The president-to-be was suitably impressed.

***

There was a palpable sense of excitement on the eve of the inauguration. "Suddenly, the campus mood seemed to shift," recalled Todd

Gitlin, then a Harvard sophomore, later an author and sociologist. "Without question, a major reason was that the end of the Eisenhower era was looming. Whatever doubts attached to John F. Kennedy, one could anticipate a thaw, a sense of the possible."

The expectations were excessive. Kennedy was no radical, not even a social reformer. He was a pragmatic politician, a self-described "Northern Democrat with some sense of restraint." Dean Rusk, himself a cautious man, recognized similar traits in his new boss. "Sobered by the narrowness of his victory," Rusk said of Kennedy, "he selected carefully the issues over which to battle." Historian William O'Neill would render a harsher judgment a decade later. "Kennedy had promised new leadership and new departures," O'Neill wrote, "yet his ideas were commonplace."

It should not have been a surprise. None of 1960's candidates—not Kennedy, Nixon, or any of the others—had pursued the presidency to advance an ideology or save the world. Their motives were uncomplicated. They were politicians, and the White House was the ultimate prize in their chosen field. They all sought the personal validation of victory.

Kennedy now faced the challenge of governing a nation that was becoming more sophisticated, yet also more acrimonious; a country that was growing more diverse, yet also more self-centered. The president-elect had reached political maturity during the prosperous and stable fifties, a period very different from the turbulent decade that was beginning to unfold. He was unprepared for the political, racial, and societal tumult that lay ahead.

The desire for freedom had never been stronger in the United States or around the world. The latest case in point was Algeria, where Moslems voted overwhelmingly for independence on January 8. Reactionary elements of the French army vented their frustration in April 1961 by staging a second uprising, but Charles de Gaulle persevered. Algeria joined the ranks of free nations in 1962—full of hope, yet plagued with instability. It was an unfortunately common condition. African countries would suffer more than 70 coups during the remaining 40 years of the 20th century.

America's civil rights movement was driven by similar impulses. The genie released by the Greensboro Four could not be pushed back into its bottle. Blacks protested racial inequality in growing numbers—and with greater vehemence—as the sixties progressed. Federal courts supported their cause, directing a stream of desegregation orders to

Southern and Northern communities alike. Whites often resisted. The four black girls who integrated the schools of New Orleans endured abuse for years. White classmates spat on them and called them names, but all four graduated from high school in 1972.

The Deep South suffered a new shock just 10 days before Kennedy's inauguration. A federal judge ordered the admission of two black applicants to the University of Georgia on January 10, the first breach of the region's lily-white system of higher education. More than 1,000 angry whites gathered outside the dorm room of one of the black students, Charlayne Hunter. "One, two, three, four," the mob chanted, "we don't want no nigger whore."

A university dean, William Tate, charged into the crowd, ordered the protesters to disperse, and somehow succeeded. Twenty local policemen backed him up, though state troopers refused to get involved. Tate received more than 600 letters from Georgia citizens in the days that followed. Most, to his surprise, were positive. Many acknowledged the inevitability of desegregation. "All of us would probably like to take a ten- or twenty-year vacation somewhere while it's all being worked out," wrote an Atlanta man. "But it looks like we've used up all of our vacation time."

Gender inequality—still accepted as society's natural order—soon met a similar fate. Betty Friedan finally completed *The Feminine Mystique,* which became a surprise best-seller in 1963 and galvanized feminists across the country. "I'm an author," she said. "I'm not an organization person." But the times demanded that she become one. Friedan helped to found the National Organization for Women (NOW) in 1966, serving as the group's first president. She was the obvious choice to write NOW's statement of purpose, which pledged "to take the actions needed to bring women into the mainstream."

The feminist movement—augmented by another by-product of 1960, Enovid—would reshape American society. Women were suddenly free to blossom beyond their traditional roles as wives and mothers. Seventy percent of white American women had husbands in 1960, the highest concentration of married females at any point of the 20th century. The figure dropped below 60 percent by 1998. The share of women in the workforce, on the other hand, climbed steadily from 38 percent in 1960 to 60 percent in 1997.

Enovid provided the impetus for a sexual revolution, which was not what its devoutly Catholic cocreator, John Rock, had intended. Rock collaborated on the birth control pill to prevent overpopulation. He was initially troubled by the promiscuity that Enovid enabled, though he made peace with the changing world before his death in 1984. "Pre-marital sex," he said, "doesn't hurt most level-headed young people if they act responsibly about it."

Pleasure and self-expression were elevated to new levels of impor-tance after 1960. Sexually explicit books and magazines became more readily available because of the *Lady Chatterley* decision. Hugh Hefner's *Playboy,* with a monthly circulation of roughly 1 million copies at the start of the sixties, surpassed 6 million before the end of the seven-ties. Recreational use of illegal drugs became common, due in part to proselytizing by Timothy Leary and LSD researchers. Authorities ar-rested only 169 people for violating the federal law against marijuana possession in 1960, but the total soared beyond 50,000 by 1966. Ex-perimentation with LSD, mescaline, and peyote rose at similarly rapid rates. Rock music—with the Beatles and Bob Dylan in the vanguard—reflected this societal chaos by growing more intense, more controver-sial, and more political.

The result was a perfect atmosphere for radicalism, a hothouse for extreme viewpoints of all kinds. Alan Haber had envisioned such a scenario in January 1960, when he had quietly assumed control of Stu-dents for a Democratic Society (SDS). "The challenge ahead," he said, "is to appraise and evolve radical alternatives to the inadequate so-ciety of today." SDS was destined to emerge as a powerful force by the mid-sixties—the dominant voice of the left—under the guidance of Haber and Tom Hayden. Its conservative counterpart, Young Ameri-cans for Freedom, also gained influence at a quick pace, helping to secure the Republican presidential nomination for Goldwater in 1964.

The undercurrents of these disparate movements and trends had been exposed in 1960, revealing the potential for turmoil in a seem-ingly placid country. John Kennedy expressed confidence that he could channel this raw energy in a positive direction. "I ask you to join us in all the tomorrows yet to come," he had urged the audience at his final campaign appearance in Boston, "in building America, moving Amer-ica, picking this country of ours up, and sending it into the Sixties." It would be a difficult task, but he was eager to get started.

***

Snow began falling on Washington shortly after noon on January 19—and it didn't stop. Traffic became immobilized within a few hours. More than 10,000 cars were stuck on unplowed streets or abandoned in snowdrifts. Thirty members of Eisenhower's staff were unable to get home. Many spent the final night of the outgoing administration in a shelter in the White House basement.

Troops from nearby military bases were bused into Washington to help local authorities dig out. Three thousand men, using 700 plows and trucks, worked overnight to clear the roads of 8 inches of snow. They managed to reopen the city's thoroughfares by morning.

Frigid air poured in behind the storm. The temperature on inauguration day hovered around 20 degrees, and a northerly wind of 18 miles per hour made it seem even colder. The 50,000 people attending the ceremony on the Capitol's east portico bundled up as best they could. A *New York Times* reporter noted that many of the assembled dignitaries sported incongruous wardrobes of "top hats and polar gear."

The formal event finally began at 12:20 P.M., a bit behind schedule. Richard Cardinal Cushing, the Catholic archbishop of Boston, stepped forward to give the invocation. Blue smoke suddenly began to rise from the lectern. "Here's where I steal the show," the archbishop remembered thinking. "If that smoke indicates a bomb, and if the bomb explodes while I'm praying, I'm going to land over on the Washington Monument." The problem was more prosaic—a short in an electrical system—and was easily solved.

Yet it seemed as if a curse hovered over the ceremony, what with the blizzard, the chilly temperatures, and the small fire. The hex intensified when elderly poet Robert Frost rose to present a poem composed for the occasion. "A golden age of poetry and power," he had written, "of which this noonday's the beginning hour." Frost stumbled over the first stanza, temporarily blinded by sunlight reflecting off the snow and the Capitol's marble steps. He eventually abandoned the new poem—"I can't see in this light"—and recited one of his older works from memory.

All of this, however, was prelude. The key attraction was the new president's inaugural address. He had been jotting down ideas for weeks. Aides, prominent Democrats, and other influential figures had deluged him with suggestions. Kennedy had entrusted Ted Sorensen with the task of hammering out a first draft, with only two stipulations attached. The speech should be short, Kennedy told Sorensen, and it should focus on foreign affairs.

The address was shaped and reshaped during the final week. Columnist Walter Lippmann suggested that references to the Soviet Union as an "enemy" be changed to "adversary." Adviser John Kenneth

Galbraith proposed a new ending. Aide Harris Wofford objected to the lack of domestic content. "There's an equal rights struggle here at home, too," he said. "You have to say something about it. You have to." Kennedy incorporated each of these ideas, though Wofford remained unhappy that only a single sentence was altered to acknowledge the issue of civil rights.

The result was a speech of uncommon eloquence. Historian David Greenberg, offering his assessment in 2009, ranked it as the fifth-best inaugural address of all time, lauding it as "the last expression of a now-eclipsed strain of Churchillian oratory" and a "brilliant articulation of a liberal internationalism." Kennedy's address would be remembered primarily for a rhetorical device known as chiasmus, a deliberate inversion of words. "Let us never negotiate out of fear," he said, "but let us never fear to negotiate." And then at the very end: "Ask not what your country can do for you. Ask what you can do for your country."

John and Jackie Kennedy at an inaugural ball: "Let the word go forth, from this time and place, to friend and foe alike, that the torch has been passed to a new generation of Americans." (John F. Kennedy Presidential Library and Museum)

The familiar themes were there. The first reference to youth came just seven sentences from the beginning. "Let the word go forth," Kennedy said, "from this time and place, to friend and foe alike, that the torch has been passed to a new generation of Americans." Hard-edged Cold War rhetoric was prominent. "In the long history of the world, only a few generations have been granted the role of defending freedom in its hour of maximum danger," the new president said. "I do not shrink from this responsibility. I welcome it." The speech was of a high literary quality—terse, emphatic, occasionally lyrical—and it was widely applauded. A reporter asked John Steinbeck why he was so enthusiastic. "Syntax, my lad," the author responded. "It has been restored to the highest place in the republic."

The festivities continued all afternoon and evening. The inaugural parade lasted until 6:15, long past sundown. There were five inaugural balls that night. Democrats—reduced to political impotence during the Eisenhower years—enthusiastically celebrated their return to power.

But two men—destined to become the presidents who succeeded Kennedy—saw no reason for jubilation. Lyndon Johnson bade farewell to the Senate that day, leaving the chamber he had ruled with absolute authority since 1955. "It was an emotion-charged moment," said his wife. "Then we walked out of the Senate, and into the new job." Lady Bird's husband quickly came to hate the obscurity and powerlessness of the vice presidency. "In the end, it is nothing," he said years later. "I detested every minute of it."

Johnson's predecessor in the nation's second-highest office, Richard Nixon, was without a government job for the first time since 1946. He attended a luncheon for Dwight and Mamie Eisenhower after Kennedy's inauguration, his last official function before returning to Los Angeles. The move would not go as smoothly as hoped. "The pressures to run for governor," Nixon said, "began almost from the day I arrived back in California." He finally consented to make the race—against his better instincts—and lost to Pat Brown. ABC summarized the conventional wisdom in the title of a November 1962 documentary, *The Political Obituary of Richard Nixon*.

Kennedy's assassination would elevate Johnson from semi-anonymity to the White House in November 1963. He would win a presidential term in his own right in 1964. Six years of hard work and considerable luck would reinvigorate Nixon's career and secure him the presidency in 1968. But all of this—the immediate tribulations and subsequent comebacks—could not be foreseen by either man on the evening of January 20, 1961.

Nixon, though no longer the vice president, still had the use of his government car and chauffeur until midnight. He decided to take one last drive to the Capitol. He walked past the entrance to the Senate, through the rotunda, and onto a balcony that overlooked the snowbound city. He stood there for five minutes, gazing at the Washington Monument in the distance. "As I turned to go inside," Nixon recalled, "I suddenly stopped short, struck by the thought that this was not the end—that someday I would be back here." He returned to the car with a new sense of purpose.

***

John Glenn had arrived earlier that day at his suburban Washington home—just five miles west of the Capitol—after driving up from the astronauts' training center at Langley Air Force Base. He and his passenger, Loudon Wainwright, an editor at *Life*, had planned to listen to Kennedy's inaugural address during their three-hour trip from southeastern Virginia. But the radio kept fading in and out.

Glenn was in a terrible mood. "His usual friendliness and good spirits were completely missing," Wainwright recalled. "He seemed very tense and preoccupied, and as he drove—as the astronauts all did, with a skill somehow beyond ordinary drivers—his face was taut and unsmiling." Glenn frequently slammed the steering wheel with his hands. Wainwright was surprised that something as insignificant as poor audio reception made him so angry.

The radio, of course, had nothing to do with his frustration. Glenn and his colleagues had been informed the previous evening that Alan Shepard would fly the first Mercury mission. Wainwright was unaware of it—NASA wouldn't announce the decision until May 2—but Glenn's hopes of becoming the first man in outer space had been dashed forever.

His anger would become irrelevant within 12 weeks. Sergei Korolev selected Yuri Gagarin as the first Vostok cosmonaut on April 8. Gagarin soared into space four days later at 9:07 A.M., Moscow time, winning the immortality reserved for the initial pioneer. Korolev and his flight controllers waited anxiously to hear if the cosmonaut had survived the intense g-forces of liftoff and the sudden transition to weightlessness. They needn't have worried. "Flight is proceeding normally," Gagarin calmly radioed back. "I feel well." But Nikita Khrushchev was not reassured. "Is he alive? Is he alive?" the first secretary kept shouting over the phone to Korolev.

Gagarin was most definitely alive. He completed a single orbit in an hour and 48 minutes, glided toward the Soviet Union, and ejected through Vostok's hatch. He parachuted to earth near the village of Smelovka, where a peasant woman and her daughter witnessed the landing. They gazed nervously at Gagarin's orange flight suit and white pressure helmet. "Have you come from outer space?" the woman asked hesitantly. Gagarin beamed. "Yes," he replied happily. "Would you believe it? I certainly have."

America's plans seemed unimpressive by comparison. Shepard finally rocketed skyward on May 5, though his mission lasted just 15 minutes. He plunked into the Atlantic Ocean 302 miles from Cape Canaveral and was swiftly retrieved by a marine helicopter. The nation rejoiced, but everyone knew the Soviets had accomplished the greater feat. Gagarin had achieved a maximum speed of 17,000 miles per hour, while Shepard had peaked at 4,500. And the cosmonaut had traveled 80 times farther than the astronaut. "We are going to make a substantially larger effort in space," Kennedy pledged later that day.

The president went to Capitol Hill on May 25 to lay out the specifics. Eisenhower had seen little value in large-scale space projects, but Kennedy was of a different mind. "I believe this nation should commit itself to achieving the goal, before this decade is out, of landing a man on the moon and returning him safely to earth," he told Congress. "No single space project in this period will be more impressive to mankind or more important for the long-range exploration of space. And none will be so difficult or expensive to accomplish."

The astronauts were thrilled by their sudden promotion to the front lines of the Cold War. Shepard, speaking in 1998, recalled his astonishment at Kennedy's bold proclamation. "After fifteen minutes of space time?" Shepard said. "Now, you don't think he was excited? You don't think he was a space cadet? Absolutely, absolutely!" But even the astronauts had their doubts about the president's deadline. America had yet to orbit the earth, and it was supposed to land a man on the moon by 1969? "There was also a little bit of a gulp in there, because he put a time cap on the deal," Shepard admitted. "I don't think that any of us thought that we would be able to make it."

Kennedy knew the risks, but he was determined to win the space race. It was, for him, more a matter of pride than of science. "The news will be worse before it is better," he admitted after Gagarin's flight, "and it will be some time before we catch up." He was right. Another cosmonaut, Gherman Titov, orbited the earth 17 times in August, covering 435,000 miles during his 25-hour mission. "The Americans don't launch any [orbiting capsules]," laughed Khrushchev. "They hop up and fall down in the ocean."

It wasn't until February 1962—10 months after Gagarin—that an astronaut finally circled the globe. John Glenn, so angry about missing his rendezvous with destiny the previous year, was given the new assignment. He completed three orbits, permanently eclipsing Shepard in the history of the U.S. space program. President Kennedy acclaimed him as "the kind of American of whom we are most proud," and declared that the country had finally embarked on the "new ocean" of space. "I believe the United States must sail on it," he said, "and be in a position second to none."

The race was on.

***

Jack Kennedy had schemed and toiled since 1956 to escape Congress, but he wasted little time in coming back. The president visited the chamber of the House of Representatives on January 30 to deliver his first State of the Union address. "It is a pleasure to return from whence I came," he told the assembled senators and congressmen. "You are among my oldest friends in Washington—and this House is my oldest home. It was here, more than fourteen years ago, that I first took the oath of federal office."

Yet it was not to be a pleasant homecoming. Kennedy almost immediately sounded an alarm. "No man entering upon this office, regardless of his party, regardless of his previous service in Washington, could fail to be staggered upon learning—even in this brief ten-day period—the harsh enormity of the trials through which we must pass in the next four years," he said. "Each day the crises multiply. Each day their solution grows more difficult." He suggested that the outcome was uncertain. "While hoping and working for the best," he said, "we should prepare ourselves now for the worst."

A headline in the next day's *New York Times*—"Eisenhower's View of Conditions Was Brighter Than Kennedy's"—understated the contrast. The new president's pessimism was difficult to comprehend. He had not inherited any imminent crises. He had privately learned, in fact, that America's defenses were stronger than he had previously believed. Robert McNamara, the new defense secretary, told Kennedy that the United States possessed more than 100 intermediate and intercontinental ballistic missiles and 1,700 intercontinental bombers. The corresponding figures for the Soviet Union were 50 and 150. The missile gap, McNamara said flatly, was a "myth."

Kennedy had harped on America's alleged deficiency in firepower since 1958. It had been an effective issue against the Republicans, yet its inaccuracy was now exposed. Columnist Joseph Alsop later asked Kennedy what would have happened if the missile gap had been disproved during the 1960 campaign. What if Eisenhower had released U-2 or satellite photos of Soviet bases prior to the election? "Sometimes I wonder about that," Kennedy replied, "and when I let myself do so, I lose most of my night's sleep."

Eisenhower's warning about the military-industrial complex—issued just two weeks earlier—had made no impact on the new president. His administration would boost defense spending by $6 billion in 1961, surpassing Ike's final Pentagon budget by 14 percent. Kennedy seemed intent on demonstrating America's military resolve. "Before my term has ended," he told Congress, "we shall have to test anew whether a nation organized and governed such as ours can endure."

The obvious site for the first test was Cuba. The CIA's special projects—clever though they seemed—had come to nothing. The Mafia had been unable to recruit a volunteer to assassinate Fidel Castro. Potential gunmen were dissuaded by their poor odds of survival. A box of poisoned cigars was delivered to Cuba in early 1961, but there was no evidence that Castro ever received it.

That left Operation Pluto. The Joint Chiefs of Staff conceded that the proposed invasion might work if sufficient force were applied. "This plan has a fair chance of ultimate success," said a secret JCS report on February 3, "and even if it does not achieve immediately the full results desired, could contribute to the eventual overthrow of the Castro regime."

It failed on all counts. The brigade of 1,400 exiles landed on Cuba's southern coast at the Bay of Pigs on April 17. Castro's army repulsed the invaders with surprising ease. A total of 114 exiles were killed in action, and almost 1,200 were captured. There was no popular uprising against Castro.

Kennedy summoned Richard Nixon to the Oval Office after the dimensions of the fiasco became clear. "What would you do now?" the president asked. Nixon was predictably belligerent. "I would find a proper legal cover," he said, "and I would go in." But Kennedy drew the line at involving American troops. He grew philosophical about the defeat as time passed. "Thank God the Bay of Pigs happened when it did," he said. "Otherwise, we'd be in Laos by now—and that would be a hundred times worse."

The Pentagon did attempt to involve the United States in Laos in the spring of 1961, proposing that a division of marines be landed north of Vientiane. "We can get them in, all right," admitted General Lyman Lemnitzer, the chairman of the Joint Chiefs of Staff. "It's getting them out that worries me." Kennedy adopted a cautious approach, contenting himself with endorsing the creation of a neutral Laotian government.

Yet the president's prudence in Laos did not foreshadow a softening of his hard-line stance toward the Cold War. Kennedy and Khrushchev held a contentious summit meeting in June 1961, with the Soviet leader renewing his threat to conclude a treaty with East Germany. James Reston, the *New York Times* columnist, spoke to Kennedy after his final session with Khrushchev in Vienna. "Worst thing in my life. He savaged me," Kennedy muttered. Reston thought the president was in a state of shock. Even Arthur Schlesinger Jr., a Kennedy aide and partisan, admitted that his boss was "tense and tired" after the summit.

Relations between the superpowers worsened in the weeks following Vienna. Kennedy told a national television audience on July 25 that Germany—and specifically West Berlin—had now become "the great testing place of Western courage and will." The Soviets responded on August 13 by stringing barbed wire between the two halves of Berlin, then constructing a permanent wall. The Pentagon volleyed back on August 25, ordering 76,500 reservists to active duty, the first installment of a plan to add 250,000 men to the armed forces.

The Cold War had somehow spiraled out of control within a matter of months, and it was about to get worse. "Now we have a problem in making our power credible," Kennedy told Reston in Vienna, "and Vietnam is the place." He further stressed its importance during his July 25 address. "We face a challenge in Berlin," he said, "but there is also a challenge in Southeast Asia, where the borders are less guarded, the enemy harder to find, and the dangers of communism less apparent to those who have so little."

The president dispatched General Maxwell Taylor to South Vietnam on October 11, ordering him to find "ways in which we can, perhaps, better assist the government of Vietnam in meeting this threat to their independence." The commitment of troops—a step that Eisenhower had resisted—now seemed inevitable. Two U.S. army helicopter companies arrived in Saigon on December 11, representing America's first direct military support for Ngo Dinh Diem's regime.

More than 3,000 U.S. servicemen would be stationed in Vietnam by the first anniversary of Kennedy's inauguration, with additional thousands on their way. Robert Kennedy pledged in early 1962 that his brother's administration would stand by Diem "until we win." But *New York Times* correspondent Homer Bigart advised caution. "The United States," he wrote in February of that year, "seems inextricably committed to a long, inconclusive war."

It was a nervous time. The New Frontier—which had begun so boldly on that cold, snowy day in Washington—suffered through a difficult first year, as even its most fervent supporters conceded. "It was tougher than people think," Bobby Kennedy later admitted. "It wasn't just the Bay of Pigs; '61 was often a very mean year because of Berlin, what to do about Berlin, and the fact that the Russians thought they could kick [President Kennedy] around." Nobody talked about the Spirit of Camp David anymore. Peace seemed a very distant hope indeed.

* * *

Dwight Eisenhower had been looking forward to retirement since the mid-fifties. A series of arduous assignments had consumed his time and energy for nearly two decades—commander-in-chief of Allied forces in North Africa and Europe, military governor of Germany, army chief of staff, president of Columbia University, supreme commander of NATO, president of the United States. He was, quite simply, exhausted.

A fellow World War II general dropped by the White House a few days before the Eisenhowers moved out. Omar Bradley, who had resigned from active duty in 1953, promised the president that the years ahead would be among his most enjoyable.

"Omar," Eisenhower asked eagerly, "what's it like to be in private life?"

"It's great," Bradley replied. "You still have decisions to make, but you don't have to make them yesterday."

That was precisely what Eisenhower wanted to hear. He had made enough executive decisions to last a lifetime. All he wanted now was the peace and quiet of his 192-acre farm near Gettysburg, Pennsylvania, 85 miles north of the White House.

Ike and Mamie departed Washington as soon as decently possible on January 20. They hit the road in their 1955 Chrysler Imperial at 3:30 that afternoon, while Kennedy's inaugural parade was still wending its way up Pennsylvania Avenue. "We were free," Eisenhower wrote of that sublime moment, "as only private citizens in a democratic nation can be free."

The ex-president happily reclaimed the informality that had vanished from his life eight years earlier. He asked his intimates to call him Ike, not Mr. President. "No longer," he wrote, "do I propose to be excluded from the privileges that other friends enjoy." But some adjustments to civilian life were not as easily made. Eisenhower tried to contact his son that first evening in Gettysburg, only to be confounded by the telephone. He hadn't dialed a call himself since 1941. "Come show me how you work this goddamned thing," he barked at a Secret Service agent.

The old general did not disappear completely from public view. He occasionally resurfaced with a speech or interview during the eight years of life that remained. But he was no longer at the center of current events. The federal government was now controlled by a new generation—by younger men and women who considered Dwight Eisenhower little more than a voice from the past, a relic of American history.

The first assessments of his presidency were unflattering. Seventy-five prominent historians—surveyed in 1962 by Harvard professor Arthur Schlesinger Sr.—banished Eisenhower to the bottom third of their rankings. He finished 22nd out of 31 former presidents, slotted behind such relative nonentities as Rutherford Hayes, William Howard Taft, Benjamin Harrison, and Chester Arthur. Eisenhower, according to conventional wisdom, had been an unintelligent, unimaginative, and uninvolved president—a captive of events, not a shaper of destinies.

But scholars began to reappraise his record in the seventies, and many liked what they saw. Ike's steady hand and calm demeanor contrasted favorably with the frenetic administrations of his successors, especially Lyndon Johnson and Richard Nixon. His insistence on a balanced budget had great appeal in an era of skyrocketing inflation. His refusal to commit troops to Vietnam seemed unusually wise. "General Eisenhower's intellectual stature has been unduly and unfairly disparaged by caustic academic and journalistic critics," concluded Adam Ulam, a noted Harvard historian.

Several of Ulam's colleagues published similar evaluations, with Fred Greenstein's 1982 book, *The Hidden-Hand Presidency*, wielding the greatest influence. The *New Republic*, which rarely commented favorably about Republicans of any stripe, was instantly converted. "By his painstaking analysis," the magazine wrote, "Greenstein should convince even the most unrelenting critic of Eisenhower's that the man had greater skills as chief executive than have been recognized." Ike's stock rose steadily in the rankings issued periodically by academicians and news organizations. A 2009 C-SPAN survey of 65 historians placed him in the highest quintile—8th out of 42 presidents.

John Kennedy had once dismissed the Eisenhower administration as "the years the locusts have eaten," a lengthy siesta that dulled America's competitive spirit and endangered its security. But several of Kennedy's prominent supporters eventually experienced a change of heart.

Theodore White had tilted heavily toward Kennedy in his book about the 1960 election—*Time* gibed that "there is no question whose campaign button adorned his lapel"—but the author's initial disdain for Eisenhower melted as the years passed. White confessed in 1978 that he had grown to consider Ike's foreign policy superb—"a matchless record of clean decisions"—and his leadership skills remarkable. "I cannot now deny my recognition that Eisenhower's years in Washington, from 1954 through 1960, were the most pleasant of our time," White admitted. "Once [Joseph] McCarthy had been eliminated, a placid quality probably never to be seen again slowly settled over Washington."

Richard Goodwin composed dozens of speeches for Kennedy in 1960, always emphasizing the need to "get this country moving again," an unsubtle condemnation of Eisenhower's alleged impotence. But he, too, changed his mind after the heartbreak and chaos of the sixties and seventies. "Only much later," Goodwin wrote in 1988, "after years of turbulence and rivers of blood, did I come to understand how much I had underestimated Eisenhower." He was especially impressed by the former general's commitment to peace, the quality that had attracted such enormous crowds in so many foreign lands. "He was infused by an essential goodwill toward his companions of the earth. They knew it. And they loved him for it," Goodwin concluded. "There were worse things than inaction. Much worse."

Eisenhower's final year as president had not been a happy one— not with the crash of the U-2, the collapse of the Paris summit, the demise of his plans for personal diplomacy, and the repudiation of his anointed successor. Nixon's defeat may have been the hardest blow of all. "I felt as though I had been hit in the solar plexus with a ball bat," Eisenhower wrote after the 1960 election. It momentarily seemed that his eight years of work had been for naught.

But time brought perspective. The nation's next three presidents—Kennedy, Johnson, and Nixon—became national figures in their own right during the 1960 campaign. They would rule from 1961 to 1974, elevating America to rhetorical peaks and plunging it to the depths of despair. They demanded removal of Soviet missiles from Cuba, declared war on poverty, sent men to the moon, and established relations with China; yet they also dispatched hundreds of thousands of troops to Vietnam, alienated millions of young people, and set the wheels of Watergate into motion. The Eisenhower years looked stable—and comfortably appealing—by comparison.

Ike shook off any self-doubt long before his death in 1969. He was undeniably proud of his presidential record, especially of his success in steering a moderate course in foreign affairs. Hard-liners on both sides—Soviets and Americans—had repeatedly tried to escalate the Cold War, but he had blocked them. Doomsayers had predicted the imminence of World War III, but it had not erupted on his watch.

"The United States never lost a soldier or a foot of ground in my administration. We kept the peace," Eisenhower once said, satisfaction ringing through every word. "People ask how it happened. By God, it didn't just happen, I'll tell you that."

Notes

1. PROLOGUE: THE SPIRIT OF CAMP DAVID

Page	Paragraph(s) Ending	Sources
1	"become enjoyable"	Ambrose, *Eisenhower: The President*, 534–537; Eisenhower, *Waging Peace*, 415; *New York Times* (August 26, 1959).
2	"have believed it"	*New York Times* (August 27, 1959); Ambrose, *Eisenhower: The President*, 540–541.
2	"the enormous crowd"	Ambrose, *Eisenhower: The President*, 541.
3	"he snapped"	Brzezinski, *Red Moon Rising*, 170; Halberstam, *The Fifties*, 701.
3	"on Eisenhower's job"	Kennedy, *The Strategy of Peace*, 69.
3	"as puppet master"	Brzezinski, *Red Moon Rising*, 275–276; O'Neill, *Coming Apart*, 5–7; Greenstein, *The Hidden-Hand Presidency*, passim.
3	"just confuse them"	Greenstein, *The Hidden-Hand Presidency*, 67; O'Neill, *Coming Apart*, 6.
4	"hope, I hope"	*Time* (January 18, 1960).
4	"to use it"	Eisenhower, *Waging Peace*, 486–487; *Time* (December 7, 1959); Ambrose, *Eisenhower: The President*, 551–552.

5	"within two months"	Oakley, *God's Country*, 355–356, 366.
5	"political maneuvering"	Nixon, *RN*, 203; Beschloss, *The Crisis Years*, 52.
5	"me, gentlemen, why"	Gunther, *Inside Europe Today*, 316–317; Beschloss, *The Crisis Years*, 34.
6	"in distant Stavropol"	Gunther, *Inside Europe Today*, 318–319; Crankshaw, *Khrushchev*, 249–252; Ulam, *Expansion and Coexistence*, 604.
6	"to be secured"	Gunther, *Inside Europe Today*, 52; Khrushchev, *Nikita Khrushchev and the Creation of a Superpower*, 428.
7	"of West Berlin"	Large, *Berlin*, 438–439; Perret, *Eisenhower*, 573.
7	"you are lost"	Graebner, *An Uncertain Tradition*, 291–303; Mosley, *Dulles*, 395.
7	"John Foster Dulles"	Crankshaw, *Khrushchev*, 234; Mosley, *Dulles*, 445–448; Perret, *Eisenhower*, 575–576.
7	"on August 3"	Perret, *Eisenhower*, 575–576; *Time* (January 4, 1960); Manchester, *The Glory and the Dream*, 854; Hughes, *The Ordeal of Power*, 286.
8	"Eisenhower that don't"	Manchester, *The Glory and the Dream*, 858; Oakley, *God's Country*, 386–387; Taubman, *Khrushchev*, 433.
8	"to Moscow himself"	Eisenhower, *Waging Peace*, 444; Taubman, *Khrushchev*, 438; Ambrose, *Eisenhower: The President*, 542–543; Perret, *Eisenhower*, 579; Manchester, *The Glory and the Dream*, 858.
9	"first U.S. installment"	Taubman, *Khrushchev*, 416–418; Ambrose, *Nixon: The Education of a Politician*, 519.
9	"the Soviet leader"	Ambrose, *Nixon: The Education of a Politician*, 520.
9	"face in rebuttal"	Ambrose, *Nixon: The Education of a Politician*, 523–524; Eisenhower, *The President is Calling*, 329; Manchester, *The Glory and the Dream*, 855–857.

10	"the U.S. presidency"	Wicker, *One of Us*, 220–221; Ambrose, *Nixon: The Education of a Politician*, 529.
10	"few extra dollars"	Sevareid, *Candidates 1960*, 74; White, *Breach of Faith*, 60.
11	"to his durability"	Barber, *The Presidential Character*, 135; Strober and Strober, *The Nixon Presidency*, 32.
11	"as Tricky Dick"	Mitchell, *Tricky Dick and the Pink Lady*, 44, 233; Gellman, *The Contender*, 221–241.
11	"come this quickly"	Matthews, *Kennedy and Nixon*, 79.
12	"the Democratic Party"	Sevareid, *Candidates 1960*, 88; Martin, *Adlai Stevenson of Illinois*, 692–693.
12	"Alsop in 1958"	Mazo and Hess, *Nixon*, 220; Sevareid, *Candidates 1960*, 69–71; Wicker, *One of Us*, 24.
12	"the United States"	O'Neill, *Coming Apart*, 20; Parmet, *Richard Nixon and His America*, 261; Roberts, *The Washington Post*, 326–327; White, *Breach of Faith*, 64.
13	"chance in 1960"	Wicker, *One of Us*, 214–215; Ambrose, *Nixon: The Education of a Politician*, 492–493, 503; Finch oral history.
13	"on the governorship"	Collier and Horowitz, *The Rockefellers*, 199; O'Neill, *Coming Apart*, 19.
14	"with the electorate"	Sevareid, *Candidates 1960*, 27–28; Smith, *Thomas E. Dewey and His Times*, 624; Kramer and Roberts, *I Never Wanted to Be Vice President of Anything*, 201–203.
14	"through to California"	Collier and Horowitz, *The Rockefellers*, 339; *New York Times* (December 24, 1959); Persico, *The Imperial Rockefeller*, 39; Finch oral history.
14	"of Democrats"	*Time* (November 30, 1959, December 14, 1959, and December 28, 1959).
14	"Nixon being president"	Collier and Horowitz, *The Rockefellers*, 339.

15	"hit the market"	*Time* (December 21, 1959); Roper Center for Public Opinion Research website.
15	"were tagging along"	*Time* (December 7, 1959, and December 14, 1959); Hughes, *The Ordeal of Power,* 292–293; *New York Times* (December 4, 1959).
15	"Vatican official smiled"	*New York Times* (December 5, 1959); *Time* (December 14, 1959).
15	"of the route"	*Time* (December 14, 1959, and December 21, 1959); *New York Times* (December 7, 1959).
16	"of the parade"	*New York Times* (December 10, 1959); Eisenhower, *Waging Peace,* 499–500; Manchester, *The Glory and the Dream,* 859–860.
16	"blessing to all"	*Time* (December 21, 1959); *New York Times* (December 12, 1959).
17	"to get out"	*New York Times* (December 8, 1959); Lash, *Eleanor: The Years Alone,* 283–284; *Time* (December 21, 1959); McKeever, *Adlai Stevenson,* 426.
17	"least to yourself"	*Time* (November 24, 1958); Humphrey, *The Education of a Public Man,* 142.
17	"isn't a candidate"	*Time* (December 14, 1959, and December 21, 1959).
18	"get the nomination"	Strober and Strober, *The Kennedy Presidency,* 5.
18	"a false step"	O'Brien, *No Final Victories,* 31; Schlesinger, *A Thousand Days,* 115; Parmet, *JFK,* 355; Rusk, *As I Saw It,* 293; Halberstam, *The Best and the Brightest,* 96.
19	"third term"	Sevareid, *Candidates 1960,* 187–188; Whalen, *The Founding Father,* 288, 300, 347.
19	"sank my boat"	Sevareid, *Candidates 1960,* 189–194; Sorensen, *Kennedy,* 19.

19	"a better opportunity"	Sevareid, *Candidates 1960*, 195; Alsop oral history; Whalen, *The Founding Father*, 396–399; O'Neill, *Man of the House*, 87.
20	"by 70,000 votes"	Whalen, *The Founding Father*, 419; Matthews, *Kennedy and Nixon*, 77–78; Sorensen, *Kennedy*, 75; Sevareid, *Candidates 1960*, 201–203.
20	"Kennedy years later"	Sorensen, *Kennedy*, 86; Humphrey oral history.
20	"of the nomination"	Matthews, *Kennedy and Nixon*, 111; Bailey oral history.
21	"Kennedy's daughter"	Brauer, *John F. Kennedy and the Second Reconstruction*, 20; O'Donnell and Powers, *Johnny, We Hardly Knew Ye*, 129; Sorensen, *Kennedy*, 100; *Time* (February 15, 1960).
21	"made to happen"	Dallek, *An Unfinished Life*, 199–210; Sorensen, *Counselor*, 151–152; Matthews, *Kennedy and Nixon*, 115.
22	"win, win, win"	*Time* (February 15, 1960); Sorensen, *Kennedy*, 116–117; Newfield, *Robert Kennedy*, 42.
22	"Henry Cabot Lodge"	Halberstam, *The Fifties*, 717; Bourne, *Fidel*, 55, 64.
22	"next two years"	Bourne, *Fidel*, 64–66, 111; Ulam, *Expansion and Coexistence*, 646–647.
23	"are entirely free"	*New York Times* (January 2, 1959); Manchester, *The Glory and the Dream*, 861.
23	"Castro's next targets"	*New York Times* (January 3, 1959); Bourne, *Fidel*, 168; *Time* (January 4, 1960).
23	"fall into another"	Bourne, *Fidel*, 157, 185; Bissell oral history.
23	"for self-government"	De Witte, *The Assassination of Lumumba*, xvii; *Time* (December 21, 1959).
24	"end of 1959"	White, *Theodore H. White at Large*, 217; Gunther, *Inside Europe Today*,

		98–103; Williams, *The Last Great Frenchman*, 400; Lustick, *Unsettled States, Disputed Lands*, 240.
24	"its own borders"	Edgerton, *The Troubled Heart of Africa*, 182–183; *Time* (November 30, 1959, and January 4, 1960).
24	"communism in Africa"	*Duke Law Journal* (December 2006); *New York Times* (January 3, 1960).
25	"five or six years"	Gates oral history.
25	"to our prestige"	Lewis, *Appointment on the Moon*, 54–55; Boorstin, *The Americans: The Democratic Experience*, 591; Glenn, *John Glenn*, 175.
26	"moon, he scoffed"	Lewis, *Appointment on the Moon*, 56; Oakley, *God's Country*, 346; Brown, *The Faces of Power*, 117.
26	"was badly shaken"	Lewis, *Appointment on the Moon*, 58; Brown, *The Faces of Power*, 123; Schefter, *The Race*, 100; *Time* (January 4, 1960).
27	"along for awhile"	Schefter, *The Race*, 50–55; Glenn, *John Glenn*, 184; Schirra oral history.
27	"damn thing yet"	Schefter, *The Race*, 70–73; Glenn, *John Glenn*, 197; Schirra oral history.
27	"must be brave"	Cadbury, *Space Race*, 199.
28	"was nothing else"	*New York Times* (February 28, 1960); Cadbury, *Space Race*, 141–142, 147–148; Schefter, *The Race*, 70–73.
28	"the people's side"	Smith, *The Tiger in the Senate*, 401–402; *New York Times* (December 23, 1959); *Time* (January 4, 1960).
28	"their own destiny"	Solberg, *Hubert Humphrey*, 203; *New York Times* (December 31, 1959); *Time* (January 11, 1960).
28	"support of him"	Sorensen, *Kennedy*, 99.
29	"surely coming soon"	*Time* (December 28, 1959); Collier and Horowitz, *The Rockefellers*, 339; Kramer and Roberts, *I Never Wanted to Be Vice President of Anything*, 222–223.

29	"definite and final"	Finch oral history; *Time* (December 28, 1959); Kramer and Roberts, *I Never Wanted to Be Vice President of Anything*, 222–223; *New York Times* (December 27, 1959).
30	"shoulders and smiled"	*New York Times* (December 27, 1959); Finch oral history.
30	"feel this way"	Ambrose, *Eisenhower: The President*, 552–553; *Time* (December 28, 1959).
30	"April 27, 1960"	Eisenhower, *Waging Peace*, 508–509; Taubman, *Khrushchev*, 415–416.
31	"a straight face"	Eisenhower, *Waging Peace*, 510–512; *New York Times* (December 23, 1959).
31	"international tensions"	Eisenhower, *Waging Peace*, 512–513; *Time* (December 28, 1959).
32	"could be solved"	*New York Times* (December 31, 1959); Beschloss, *The Crisis Years*, 52; Taubman, *Khrushchev*, 449.
32	"very good year"	Beschloss, *The Crisis Years*, 21; *Time* (January 4, 1960).

2. JANUARY: AROUND THE NEXT CORNER

Page	Paragraph(s) Ending	Sources
33	"and the election"	Sorensen, *Kennedy*, 122–123; *Time* (January 11, 1960).
34	"should be going"	Crespi and Mendelsohn, *Polls, Television, and the New Politics*, 56–57; Bartlett oral history; *New Republic* (July 23, 2007).
34	"from reading"	Gillon, *Politics and Vision*, 131–132; Hersh, The *Dark Side of Camelot*, 33.
34	"since Reconstruction"	Carty, *A Catholic in the White House?* 29; Thomas, *The Pursuit of the White House*, 119.
34	"would disagree"	*Time* (February 15, 1960); *New York Times* (January 3, 1960).
35	"see the humor"	Sorensen, *Counselor*, 180; Sorensen, *Kennedy*, 119.

35   "the previous June"   *Time* (February 15, 1960); Burns,
                                   Edward Kennedy and the Camelot
                                   Legacy, 65.

35   "here on in"   Bradlee, *Conversations With Kennedy,*
                                   143; Whalen, *The Founding Father,*
                                   421, 457; Newfield, *Robert*
                                   Kennedy, 28.

36   "heated arguments"   O'Neill, *Man of the House,* 83; *Ameri-*
                                   can Spectator (October 1993); Guth-
                                   man and Shulman, *Robert Kennedy*
                                   in His Own Words, xiv–xv.

36   "sweep the table"   Lawrence oral history; Sorensen,
                                   Kennedy, 128.

36   "lay ahead"   Solberg, *Hubert Humphrey,* 201–202;
                                   White, *The Making of the President*
                                   1960, 87.

37   "enter the race"   *Time* (December 14, 1959, January
                                   25, 1960, and February 1, 1960).

37   "would not come"   McKeever, *Adlai Stevenson,* 428–431.

38   "than almost anybody"   *Presidential Studies Quarterly* (De-
                                   cember 2003); *Time* (January 25,
                                   1960).

38   "didn't start it"   *New York Times* (January 14, 1960);
                                   Jackson, *Big Beat Heat,* 244; *Time*
                                   (December 7, 1959).

38   "student movement"   Sale, *SDS,* 15–17, 24–29; Unger, *The*
                                   Movement, 51–52.

39   "out of contracts"   Freedman, *Prime Time,* 33–37, 55–58;
                                   Time (August 3, 1962); *Planning*
                                   (January 1996).

39   "the pictures public"   Taubman, *Khrushchev,* 443–444;
                                   Mosley, *Dulles,* 366–368; Halbers-
                                   tam, *The Fifties,* 618–619; Ambrose,
                                   Eisenhower: The President, 563; Per-
                                   ret, *Eisenhower,* 581.

39   "the East River"   Collier and Horowitz, *The Rockefel-*
                                   lers, 222, 408; Darton, *Divided We*
                                   Stand, 71–74, 78; *New York Times*
                                   (January 27, 1960).

40	"campaigning candidate"	*New York Times* (January 10, 1960); *Time* (January 18, 1960).
40	"he said incongruously"	*Time* (January 25, 1960); Ambrose, *Nixon: The Education of a Politician*, 569.
41	"John Ehrlichman"	White, *Breach of Faith*, 81–83; *New York Times* (October 11, 1995).
41	"the ethnic appeals"	Ambrose, *Nixon: The Education of a Politician*, 541; White, *Breach of Faith*, 83; Finch oral history.
41	"in attendance"	*New York Times* (January 28, 1960); *Time* (February 8, 1960).
41	"is a damned liar"	*New York Times* (January 9, 1960).
42	"to an aide"	Ambrose, *Nixon: The Education of a Politician*, 387–398.
42	"economic stagnation"	Ambrose, *Nixon: The Education of a Politician*, 485, 535; *Time* (January 25, 1960).
43	"again was negative"	*New York Times* (January 14, 1960); Perret, *Eisenhower*, 596–597; Eisenhower, *Waging Peace*, 591; Ambrose, *Nixon: The Education of a Politician*, 540.
43	"the next corner"	*New York Times* (February 4, 1960).
44	"Protestant parents"	Marley, *Pat Robertson*, 3–8; *Business Week* (June 23, 1986); Donovan, *Pat Robertson*, 10.
44	"seek worldly success"	*Virginia Quarterly Review* (Spring 2008); Marley, *Pat Robertson*, 1.
44	"I never expected"	Donovan, *Pat Robertson*, 30, 39; *Virginia Quarterly Review* (Spring 2008).
44	"very first day"	*Virginia Quarterly Review* (Spring 2008); Marley, *Pat Robertson*, 20–23; Donovan, *Pat Robertson*, 50–52.
45	"Regent University"	*Virginia Quarterly Review* (Spring 2008); Marley, *Pat Robertson*, 22–26; Donovan, *Pat Robertson*, 64, 100–102, 119–120; *Fortune* (June 10, 2002).

45	"George H. W. Bush"	Donovan, *Pat Robertson*, 181–182; *Virginia Quarterly Review* (Spring 2008).
45	"you are poor"	*Time* (May 12, 1997); *Virginia Quarterly Review* (Spring 2008).
45	"California desert"	Schefter, *The Race*, 83; *New York Times* (January 24, 1960).
46	"higher, he said"	*New York Times* (May 28, 1960, and August 13, 1960).
47	"fly the vehicle"	*Time* (December 14, 1959); Schefter, *The Race*, 96–102; Schirra oral history.
47	"through the air"	Schefter, *The Race*, 102; Wainwright, *The Great American Magazine*, 268; Voas oral history.
47	"going crazy"	Carpenter oral history.
48	"was a gut-buster"	Glenn, *John Glenn*, 216–217; Glenn oral history.
48	"heavy as mercury"	Khrushchev, *Nikita Khrushchev and the Creation of a Superpower*, 432; Cadbury, *Space Race*, 204–205.
48	"deal of trouble"	*Time* (February 1, 1960); *New York Times* (January 23, 1960).
49	"Soviets would improve"	*New York Times* (January 8, 1960); American Presidency Project website; *Time* (January 18, 1960).
49	"issue of *Esquire*"	Hayes, *Smiling Through the Apocalypse*, xvii–xviii.
49	"many times over"	Ambrose, *Eisenhower: The President*, 567–568.
49	"of personal diplomacy"	*New York Times* (January 10, 1960).
49	"of any wrongdoing"	*New York Times* (April 30, 1960); Jackson, *Big Beat Heat*, 183–187, 287.
50	"the very end"	*New York Times* (December 18, 1959, and February 21, 1960); *Time* (December 28, 1959).
50	"and French territories"	*Time* (December 28, 1959, and February 22, 1960); Edgerton, *The Troubled Heart of Africa*, 183–184; *New York Times* (January 21, 1960, and February 21, 1960).

50	"waning since 1958"	Gunther, *Inside Europe Today*, 98–99, 115; Lustick, *Unsettled States, Disputed Lands*, 240.
51	"matter the cost"	*Time* (February 8, 1960); Gunther, *Inside Europe Today*, 72–73, 97–98.
51	"from machine guns"	Gunther, *Inside Europe Today*, 102–103; *New York Times* (January 23, 1960); Lustick, *Unsettled States, Disputed Lands*, 278–280; *Time* (February 1, 1960).
51	"of France itself"	*Time* (February 8, 1960).
51	"chief of state"	Williams, *The Last Great Frenchman*, 402; Gunther, *Inside Europe Today*, 79–80.
52	"a second uprising"	Gunther, *Inside Europe Today*, 79–80; *Time* (February 8, 1960, and February 15, 1960).

3. FEBRUARY: STRIDING TOWARD FREEDOM

Page	Paragraph(s) Ending	Sources
53	"following afternoon"	Ashmore, *Hearts and Minds*, 321; Wolff, *Lunch at the Five and Ten*, 16.
54	"away black customers"	Wolff, *Lunch at the Five and Ten*, 76–77.
54	"She walked away"	*History Today* (February 2000); Wolff, *Lunch at the Five and Ten*, 11–13; Halberstam, *The Children*, 92–94.
55	"else to them"	Ashmore, *Hearts and Minds*, 321; Wolff, *Lunch at the Five and Ten*, 15–16.
55	"page 22"	Wolff, *Lunch at the Five and Ten*, 31–39; *New York Times* (February 3, 1960).
55	"the other schools"	Branch, *Parting the Waters*, 275; *Journal of African American History* (March 2003); *New York Times* (February 10, 1960).

56	"We Shall Overcome"	*Time* (March 21, 1960, and March 28, 1960); Branch, *Parting the Waters,* 278–280, 310.
56	"had to stand"	Manchester, *The Glory and the Dream,* 848–849; *Time* (February 22, 1960).
56	"the wrong approach"	*Time* (March 28, 1960); Wolff, *Lunch at the Five and Ten,* 63–66, 120.
57	"in the country"	Wolff, *Lunch at the Five and Ten,* 115.
57	"the older persons"	Farmer oral history.
57	"struggle for freedom"	Branch, *Parting the Waters,* 272–276.
58	"sign of distress"	*New York Times* (February 24, 1960); Baseball Reference website; *Time* (April 28, 1958).
58	"years to come"	Van Dulken, *Inventing the 20th Century,* 110; Campbell-Kelly and Aspray, *Computer,* 130–131, 212–213; *Technology Review* (January 2000).
58	"and Los Angeles"	*Maclean's* (March 20, 2006); Halberstam, *The Fifties,* 571–573; Brady, *Hefner,* 160–164; *Chicago* (July 2009).
59	"regulating machines"	*New York Times* (July 17, 1960).
59	"changed that forever"	Miller, *Athens to Athens,* 153–155; *New York Times* (February 19, 1960); *Time* (February 8, 1960, and February 29, 1960).
59	"federal bureaucracy"	Fox, *The American Conservation Movement,* 299–301; *New York Times* (February 24, 1960); American Presidency Project website.
59	"was flat-out crazy"	Schoultz, *That Infernal Little Cuban Republic,* 113; Paterson, *Contesting Castro,* 241.
60	"were endangered"	*Time* (December 7, 1959, and January 25, 1960); Bourne, *Fidel,* 195–196.
60	"grudgingly agreed"	*Time* (February 8, 1960); Ambrose, *Eisenhower: The President,* 556.
60	"trip to Havana"	Khrushchev, *Nikita Khrushchev and the Creation of a Superpower,* 406–407; *New York Times* (February 5, 1960).

61	"a few months"	*Time* (February 15, 1960, and February 22, 1960); Ulam, *Expansion and Coexistence*, 649; Bourne, *Fidel*, 199–202.
62	"in the Caribbean"	Bourne, *Fidel*, 199; *New York Times* (February 21, 1960); *Time* (April 4, 1960); Schoultz, *That Infernal Little Cuban Republic*, 114.
62	"was law school"	*CPA Journal* (August 2003); *Newsweek* (April 15, 2005); Newhart, *I Shouldn't Even Be Doing This*, 34–35.
63	"fire to it"	Newhart, *I Shouldn't Even Be Doing This*, 40–49; *People* (May 9, 1983).
63	"that rarefied slot"	Newhart, *I Shouldn't Even Be Doing This*, 54, 70–74; *People* (May 9, 1983); *National Review* (July 19, 2005).
63	"still Number One"	Newhart, *I Shouldn't Even Be Doing This*, 73–76, 143; *New York Times* (July 11, 1960).
64	"to all concerned"	*New York Times* (October 22, 1961); Newhart, *I Shouldn't Even Be Doing This*, 229–230; *Time* (June 6, 1960); *CPA Journal* (August 2003).
64	"months to come"	*Time* (February 1, 1960); *New York Times* (February 17, 1960).
64	"Let's get started"	Goodwin, *Remembering America*, 76.
65	"short of money"	*New York Times* (February 14, 1960); Carty, *A Catholic in the White House?* 85; Smith, *The Tiger in the Senate*, 402–404; Peirce, *The Pacific States of America*, 207–208.
65	"liberals ever since"	*Time* (February 1, 1960); Goodwin, *Remembering America*, 82; Solberg, *Hubert Humphrey*, 125.
65	"can't help it"	Berman, *Hubert*, 32; Sevareid, *Candidates 1960*, 148–149.
66	"in the Kremlin"	Humphrey, *The Education of a Public Man*, 143–148; Taubman, *Khrushchev*, 406–407; Sevareid, *Candidates 1960*, 145.

66	"from you, either"	Schlesinger, *Journals 1952–2000*, 63; Marshall oral history; Galbraith, *A Life in Our Times*, 357.
66	"never had it"	Sevareid, *Candidates 1960*, 205; Vare, *The American Idea*, 137–139; Schlesinger, *Journals 1952–2000*, 58.
67	"time is now"	Dallek, *An Unfinished Life*, 249; Thomas, *Advice From the Presidents*, 31.
67	"had been arrested"	*Duke Law Journal* (December 2006).
67	"power of television"	*New York Times* (February 12, 1960); *Time* (February 22, 1960).
67	"$200,000 a year"	*Time* (February 22, 1960, and March 21, 1960); *New York Times* (March 8, 1960)
68	"on February 29"	Brady, *Hefner*, 160.
68	"watched devotedly"	Gates, *Air Time*, 56; *Time* (August 13, 1951); U.S. Census Bureau, *Historical Statistics of the United States: Colonial Times to 1970*, 796.
68	"makes you smile"	White, *In Search of History*, 429.
69	"of John Kennedy"	Eisinger, *The Evolution of Presidential Polling*, 117.
69	"corporations as well"	Eisinger, *The Evolution of Presidential Polling*, 77–78; Boorstin, *The Americans: The Democratic Experience*, 154–156.
69	"pollster on retainer"	Wilson, *Character Above All*, 52; Thomas, *Advice From the Presidents*, 175–176; Eisinger, *The Evolution of Presidential Polling*, 113; *New York Times* (February 21, 1960).
69	"Evelyn Lincoln"	Sorensen, *Kennedy*, 106–107; Vidal, *United States*, 817.
70	"making the exchanges"	Goldwater oral history; Sorensen, *Kennedy*, 107.
70	"deal with Atheneum"	Hoffmann, *Theodore H. White and Journalism as Illusion*, 108; White, *Theodore H. White at Large*, 264.

71	"it frightens me"	Crouse, *The Boys on the Bus*, 35; Hoffmann, *Theodore H. White and Journalism as Illusion*, 113–115.

4. MARCH: THE WIND OF CHANGE

Page	**Paragraph(s) Ending**	**Sources**
73	"known as Velcro"	*New York Times* (December 18, 1960); *Popular Mechanics* (June 1960); *Time* (February 8, 1960, September 19, 1960, and November 7, 1960); Van Dulken, *Inventing the 20th Century*, 134, 144.
74	"two generations back"	U.S. Census Bureau, *Historical Statistics of the United States: Colonial Times to 1970*, 957–958; *New York Times* (February 14, 1960).
74	"the open market"	Ellis, *Joe Wilson and the Creation of Xerox*, 230; Boorstin, *The Americans: The Democratic Experience*, 400–401.
74	"electrophotography"	*Weekly Standard* (September 20, 2004); *Smithsonian* (August 2004); Van Dulken, *Inventing the 20th Century*, 96; Boorstin, *The Americans: The Democratic Experience*, 400–401.
75	"six years alone"	Ellis, *Joe Wilson and the Creation of Xerox*, 46–47; Boorstin, *The Americans: The Democratic Experience*, 400–401.
75	"first word completely"	*Business Week* (July 10, 2006); *Smithsonian* (August 2004); Ellis, *Joe Wilson and the Creation of Xerox*, 86–88, 114–116.
76	"on its investment"	Ellis, *Joe Wilson and the Creation of Xerox*, 192–195, 214, 230–233; *Smithsonian* (August 2004).
76	"life, Wilson said"	Ellis, *Joe Wilson and the Creation of Xerox*, 233–236; *Smithsonian* (August

		2004); *Weekly Standard* (September 20, 2004).
77	"nonstick frying pan"	Haig, *Brand Failures*, 87; Jeffrey, *Machines In Our Hearts*, 96–105; Bromberg, *The Laser in America*, 10, 87–91.
77	"gliding on ice"	*Newsweek* (March 11, 1985); Van Dulken, *Inventing the 20th Century*, 102.
78	"expect no less"	Van Dulken, *Inventing the 20th Century*, 102; *Cook's Illustrated* (May/June 2005); *Invention & Technology* (Summer 2000); *Newsweek* (March 11, 1985).
78	"his bill passed"	*Time* (February 28, 1960, and March 14, 1960); Dallek, *Lone Star Rising*, 563; Fite, *Richard B. Russell Jr.*, 346–348; Miller, *Lyndon*, 228–229; Nichols, *A Matter of Justice*, 253.
78	"communist tendencies"	O'Reilly, *Hoover and the Un-Americans*, 198; Cunningham, *There's Something Happening Here*, 28–29.
79	"believe I saw"	*New York Times* (February 23, 1960, and March 2, 1960); *Time* (February 29, 1960, and March 14, 1960).
79	"the best-seller list"	Ladenson, *Dirt For Art's Sake*, 131–144, 152–155; *Economist* (November 4, 2000); *New York Times* (March 26, 1960).
79	"anti-Castro battalion"	Ambrose, *Eisenhower: The President*, 557; Wyden, *Bay of Pigs*, 20–25; Jones, *The Bay of Pigs*, 19.
79	"charts in April"	*New York Times* (March 4, 1960); Keogh, *Elvis Presley*, 121; Nash, *The Colonel*, 177–178, 186.
80	"was foreordained"	O'Brien, *No Final Victories*, 62–64; *Time* (March 21, 1960).
80	"on their ballots"	*Chicago Tribune* (April 28, 1991); *New York Times* (March 10, 1960); *Time* (March 21, 1960).

80	"roared with laughter"	*New York Times* (March 13, 1960, and March 17, 1960); *Time* (March 28, 1960).
81	"Democratic conventions"	*Time* (March 21, 1960); Thomas, *The Pursuit of the White House*, 130–131.
81	"have some fun"	*New York Times* (March 13, 1960); *Time* (March 21, 1960).
81	"facts of life"	Solberg, *Hubert Humphrey*, 205; Humphrey, *The Education of a Public Man*, 151; *Time* (February 22, 1960).
82	"accepting or forgetting"	Humphrey, *The Education of a Public Man*, 56–57, 152–153; *Time* (February 22, 1960).
82	"be true now"	*Time* (March 7, 1960, and March 28, 1960).
83	"wise or foolish"	Bonazzi, *Man in the Mirror*, 4–7, 22; *Texas Monthly* (August 2004).
83	"way resembled me"	*Time* (March 28, 1960); Oakley, *God's Country*, 382–383; *Texas Monthly* (August 2004); Bonazzi, *Man in the Mirror*, 29, 37–38.
83	"a white man"	Griffin, *Black Like Me*, 14–15, 74, 101–103; *Texas Monthly* (August 2004).
84	"remain, he said"	Bonazzi, *Man in the Mirror*, 113, 130–134; *Time* (March 28, 1960); Griffin, *Black Like Me*, 124, 158.
84	"of our society"	Bonazzi, *Man in the Mirror*, 172; *Texas Monthly* (August 2004).
84	"of everything"	Bonazzi, *Man in the Mirror*, xii, 144–145, 168; *Newsweek* (September 22, 1980); *Texas Monthly* (August 2004).
85	"federal authority"	Cray, *Chief Justice*, 292, 337; Perret, *Eisenhower*, 552.
85	"and good order"	Nichols, *A Matter of Justice*, 250–252; Perret, *Eisenhower*, 546–548.
86	"civil rights movement"	*Time* (March 28, 1960); *New York Times* (March 16, 1960); Branch, *Parting the Waters*, 283; Moore and

		Burton, *Toward the Meeting of the Waters,* 341; Lau, *Democracy Rising,* 217; *National Journal* (January 20, 2007).
86	"their Bibles, too"	*New York Times* (March 16, 1960).
86	"add to them"	*New York Times* (March 27, 1960); *Time* (February 15, 1960, and April 11, 1960); Harvey, *The Fall of Apartheid,* 50; Gunther, *Inside Europe Today,* 225–227; Sampson, *Mandela,* 127.
86	"in total membership"	*Economist* (September 14, 1985).
87	"Verwoerd 1960"	Sampson, *Mandela,* 129–131; *Time* (April 4, 1960, and April 11, 1960); Harvey, *The Fall of Apartheid,* 61–62.
87	"blown itself out"	Sampson, *Mandela,* 124, 131–137; *Economist* (September 14, 1985).
87	"be made illegal"	*Time* (May 2, 1960).
88	"allowed to register"	Carter, *Turning Point,* 23–25.
88	"on March 5"	*Time* (March 14, 1960).
88	"Latin American trip"	Ambrose, *Eisenhower: The President,* 558.
88	*"Chatterley's Lover"*	Ladenson, *Dirt For Art's Sake,* 154; *Economist* (November 4, 2000).
88	"happy about it"	*New York Times* (March 26, 1960); Ladenson, *Dirt for Art's Sake,* 154–155.
89	"presidential contender"	Sorensen, *Kennedy,* 128; *Time* (April 4, 1960); Sevareid, *Candidates 1960,* 273.
89	"a large margin"	Goodwin, *Remembering America,* 78; Sevareid, *Candidates 1960,* 247–269.
89	"entrance in January"	White, *The Making of the President 1960,* 39; *Time* (April 4, 1960); *New York Times* (March 25, 1960).
89	"achieve his goal"	White, *The Making of the President 1960,* 126–127; Clifford, *Counsel to the President,* 316.
90	"to the bathroom"	Sevareid, *Candidates 1960,* 217–219; Martin, *Adlai Stevenson and the*

		World, 454; Halberstam, *The Best and the Brightest*, 23.
90	"He demands them"	Martin, *Adlai Stevenson of Illinois*, 450–457, 603, 759; McKeever, *Adlai Stevenson*, 416–417; Halberstam, *The Best and the Brightest*, 27.
90	"presidential material"	Doyle oral history; Martin, *Adlai Stevenson and the World*, 483–484; Lash, *Eleanor: The Years Alone*, 279–283.
90	"shut the door"	Martin, *Adlai Stevenson and the World*, 491; McKeever, *Adlai Stevenson*, 438–439.
91	"he despised"	Caro, *Master of the Senate*, 111; Sevareid, *Candidates 1960*, 298, 319.
91	"out of them"	Caro, *The Path to Power*, 363; Fite, *Richard B. Russell Jr.*, 301–302; Sevareid, *Candidates 1960*, 296–297; Miller, *Lyndon*, 175; Robertson oral history.
91	"aide, Jack Valenti"	Dallek, *Lone Star Rising*, 484–486; *Time* (April 25, 1960); Valenti oral history.
91	"him busy enough"	Reedy, *Lyndon B. Johnson*, 127–128; White, *The Making of the President 1960*, 43.
92	"Absolutely nothing"	Edwards oral history.

5. APRIL: PAPER TIGERS

Page	Paragraph(s) Ending	Sources
93	"and her maid"	*Time* (April 11, 1960).
94	"urban development"	Thomas, *The United States of Suburbia*, 47–48; Goldman, *The Tragedy of Lyndon Johnson*, 15–17; U.S. Census Bureau website; White, *The Making of the President 1960*, 216–217.
94	"a black majority"	Caplow, Hicks, and Wattenberg, *The First Measured Century*, 16–17;

		White, *The Making of the President 1960*, 231.
94	"below 15 percent"	Caplow, Hicks, and Wattenberg, *The First Measured Century*, 26–27; U.S. Census Bureau, *Historical Statistics of the United States: Colonial Times to 1970*, 457.
94	"326 every hour"	U.S. Census Bureau, *Historical Statistics of the United States: Colonial Times to 1970*, 8; *Time* (June 27, 1960).
94	"had ever happened"	*New York Times* (June 21, 1960); Jackson, *Crabgrass Frontier*, 377; White, *Theodore H. White at Large*, 290–291; Caplow, Hicks, and Wattenberg, *The First Measured Century*, 96–97.
95	"pedal and brake"	*Time* (June 20, 1960).
95	"at 8 percent"	U.S. Census Bureau website.
95	"been 23 percent"	Boorstin, *The Americans: The Democratic Experience*, 357; Bernard and Rice, *Sunbelt Cities*, 12; U.S. Census Bureau, *Historical Statistics of the United States: Colonial Times to 1970*, 89.
96	"the rise again"	Bartley, *The New South*, 145–146.
96	"could not disagree"	*New York Times* (April 22, 1960); *Time* (April 25, 1960); Shoumatoff, *The Capital of Hope*, 35–36.
96	"project was completed"	Anderson and Roskrow, *The Channel Tunnel Story*, 3; *Time* (January 4, 1960); *New York Times* (April 21, 1960).
97	"began in 1960"	Pelkonen and Albrecht, *Eero Saarinen*, 223–226; Roman, *Eero Saarinen*, 128; Ashmore, *Britannica Book of the Year 1961*, 613.
97	"face disintegration"	*New York Times* (April 1, 1960); Mullen, *The Rise of Cable Programming in the United States*, 51–52; *Time* (April 25, 1960).

97	"Control District"	*Los Angeles Times* (July 19, 1998); *Forbes* (September 15, 1977); Krier and Ursin, *Pollution and Policy,* 137–138; *New York Times* (April 10, 1960).
97	"the Weather Bureau"	Lewis, *Appointment on the Moon,* 319; *New York Times* (April 3, 1960, and April 11, 1960).
98	"presidential campaigns"	Sorensen, *Kennedy,* 135; Burns, *Edward Kennedy and the Camelot Legacy,* 66; *Time* (April 4, 1960).
99	"JFK 9, HHH 1"	White, *In Search of History,* 463; Bradlee, *Conversations With Kennedy,* 17.
99	"I felt sick"	*Time* (April 18, 1960); Runyon, Verdini, and Runyon, *Source Book of American Presidential Campaign and Election Statistics,* 15; O'Brien, *No Final Victories,* 65.
99	"all of them"	Dallek, *An Unfinished Life,* 251; Goodwin, *Remembering America,* 83.
100	"the state capital"	Humphrey oral history; Humphrey, *The Education of a Public Man,* 156; White, *The Making of the President 1960,* 95; Solberg, *Hubert Humphrey,* 208.
100	"presidential nomination"	Bradlee, *Conversations With Kennedy,* 26; Parmet, *JFK,* 40; *Time* (April 25, 1960).
100	"you can convert"	Sorensen, *Kennedy,* 139; *Time* (March 28, 1960); Goodwin, *Remembering America,* 84.
101	"said darkly"	De Paulo oral history; *Historian* (March 2001).
101	"I was baptized"	*Historian* (March 2001); Salinger, *With Kennedy,* 35; Burns, *Edward Kennedy and the Camelot Legacy,* 66–67; Goodwin, *Remembering America,* 87.
102	"in West Virginia"	*Time* (April 25, 1960).

102	"all the momentum"	Sorensen, *Kennedy,* 141; Donaldson, *The First Modern Campaign,* 52; *Time* (May 2, 1960).
102	"office, he said"	Hersh, *The Dark Side of Camelot,* 97; Humphrey, *The Education of a Public Man,* 157.
103	"play as well"	*New York Times* (September 24, 2001); *Newsweek* (December 31, 2001).
103	"does no good"	*New York Times* (December 6, 1959, and September 24, 2001).
103	"story skyscraper"	*New York Times* (March 6, 1960, and June 19, 2005); *Stern, My First 79 Years,* 140; Schickel, *The World of Carnegie Hall,* 412.
104	"the wrecking ball"	Stern, *My First 79 Years,* 143–153; *New York Times* (March 15, 1960, April 17, 1960, and April 28, 1960).
104	"to that degree"	*New York Times* (May 24, 1960, and September 28, 1960); Stern, *My First 79 Years,* 154–155.
104	"after Carnegie Hall"	*New York Times* (September 24, 2001); Stern, *My First 79 Years,* 157.
105	"meeting, he said"	*New York Times* (September 28, 1959); *Time* (April 25, 1960).
105	"ruin [my] effectiveness"	Beschloss, *Mayday,* 226–229, 239; Ambrose, *Eisenhower: The President,* 568–569.
106	"the Soviet Union"	Beschloss, *Mayday,* 147, 239; Khrushchev, *Memoirs of Nikita Khrushchev,* 236.
106	"in the relationship"	Taubman, *Khrushchev,* 454; *Time* (February 22, 1960, and May 2, 1960); Tusa, *The Last Division,* 193–195; Ulam, *Expansion and Coexistence,* 619.
106	"a nuclear power"	*China Journal* (January 2006); Salisbury, *The New Emperors,* 157; Beschloss, *The Crisis Years,* 42–43; Crankshaw, *Khrushchev,* 268.

106	"but expendable"	Taubman, *Khrushchev*, 391–395; Beschloss, *The Crisis Years*, 42–43; MacMillan, *Nixon and Mao*, 88–89.
107	"system for themselves"	Ulam, *Expansion and Coexistence*, 630–631; Crankshaw, *Khrushchev*, 275; *New York Times* (April 23, 1960); *Time* (May 2, 1960).
107	"and tyrannical"	Beschloss, *The Crisis Years*, 42; Jones and Kevill, *China and the Soviet Union*, 17; Taubman, *Khrushchev*, 470–471; Ulam, *The Rivals*, 312; Short, *Mao*, 504.
108	"The Frigid Friends"	Middleton, *The Duel of the Giants*, 44–45; Ulam, *Expansion and Coexistence*, 638; Jones and Kevill, *China and the Soviet Union*, 21; *Time* (August 29, 1960).
108	"over the cabin"	*Time* (June 6, 1960); Walter, *Space Age*, 87–88.
108	"of all articles"	Wainwright, *The Great American Magazine*, 270–272.
108	"its key provisions"	McPherson oral history.
109	"rendered ineffective"	Fite, *Richard B. Russell Jr.*, 374; *Time* (April 18, 1960).
109	"budget in balance"	American Presidency Project website; Wicker, *One of Us*, 246; Nixon, *Six Crises*, 309–310.
109	"month before election"	*New York Times* (April 10, 1960); Ambrose, *Nixon: The Education of a Politician*, 544.
110	"than Wall Street"	Parmet, *Richard Nixon and His America*, 60–62.
110	"merchandising dynamo"	Goldberg, *Barry Goldwater*, 27, 39, 54, 138–142; *Time* (May 2, 1960); Vidal, *United States*, 829.
110	"use nuclear weapons"	Goldwater oral history; *Time* (May 2, 1960); Goldberg, *Barry Goldwater*, 141–142.
111	"the right track"	Tillett, *Inside Politics: The National Conventions*, 17; Rusher, *The Rise of*

		the Right, 87–88; Goldberg, *Barry Goldwater*, 142–143; Andrew, *The Other Side of the Sixties*, 27–28, 46–47; Goldwater oral history.
111	"by its hero"	Wicker, *One of Us*, 221; *Time* (April 18, 1960).
112	"the presidential ring"	Collier and Horowitz, *The Rockefellers*, 332; Abramson, *Spanning the Century*, 565; Smith, *Thomas E. Dewey and His Times*, 624; *New York Times* (April 23, 1960).
112	"political history"	*Time* (April 11, 1960).

6. MAY: SPOILING FOR A FIGHT

Page	Paragraph(s) Ending	Sources
113	"for April 25"	Taubman, *Khrushchev*, 445; Perret, *Eisenhower*, 582–583.
113	"a salami sandwich"	Manchester, *The Glory and the Dream*, 867–875; *Time* (May 16, 1960); Halberstam, *The Fifties*, 707.
114	"at 6:26 A.M."	*Time* (May 16, 1960); Beschloss, *Mayday*, 17; Halberstam, *The Fifties*, 709–710.
114	"an evasive maneuver"	Manchester, *The Glory and the Dream*, 867–875; Halberstam, *The Fifties*, 706–710; Beschloss, *Mayday*, 26–28; Khrushchev, *Nikita Khrushchev and the Creation of a Superpower*, 374.
114	"take him away"	Beschloss, *Mayday*, 26–28; Khrushchev, *Nikita Khrushchev and the Creation of a Superpower*, 376.
115	"an investigation"	Beschloss, *Mayday*, 42; Ambrose, *Eisenhower: The President*, 571–574; Khrushchev, *Nikita Khrushchev and the Creation of a Superpower*, 380; O'Neill, *Coming Apart*, 16–17.

115	"labeled Most Urgent"	Taubman, *Khrushchev*, 456–457; Beschloss, *Mayday*, 53–54.
115	"take better pictures"	Taubman, *Khrushchev*, 456–457; Ambrose, *Eisenhower: The President*, 574; Beschloss, *Mayday*, 58–61; Halberstam, *The Fifties*, 711.
116	"another Pearl Harbor"	Beschloss, *Mayday*, 58–61, 259; Eisenhower, *Waging Peace*, 553; Oakley, *God's Country*, 388–390; *New York Times* (May 12, 1960).
116	"lead to war"	Taubman, *Khrushchev*, 459; *Time* (May 23, 1960); Ambrose, *Eisenhower: The President*, 575–576.
117	"happen in Paris"	Taubman, *Khrushchev*, 460; Khrushchev, *Nikita Khrushchev and the Creation of a Superpower*, 388–389; Ambrose, *Eisenhower: The President*, 577; Perret, *Eisenhower*, 583–584; Beschloss, *Mayday*, 281.
117	"toward fond guests"	Taubman, *Khrushchev*, 462–464; *Time* (May 23, 1960); Ambrose, *Eisenhower: The President*, 577.
117	"hands are clean"	Halberstam, *The Fifties*, 712; Taubman, *Khrushchev*, 463–464; Ambrose, *Eisenhower: The President*, 577–579.
118	"are with you"	*Time* (May 23, 1960); Eisenhower, *Waging Peace*, 555–556; Taubman, *Khrushchev*, 463–464; Hughes, *The Ordeal of Power*, 305.
118	"such planes down"	*New York Times* (May 19, 1960); *Time* (May 30, 1960); Gunther, *Inside Europe Today*, 297; Beschloss, *Mayday*, 300.
119	"in a decade"	*Time* (May 30, 1960); Khrushchev, *Nikita Khrushchev and the Creation of a Superpower*, 391; Ambrose, *Nixon: The Education of a Politician*, 549; Gunther, *Inside Europe Today*, 303.
119	"of his presidency"	Ambrose, *Eisenhower: The President*, 580.

119	"in bomb shelters"	Kramer and Roberts, *I Never Wanted to Be Vice President of Anything*, 219; *Time* (February 29, 1960); Collier and Horowitz, *The Rockefellers*, 343–344.
120	"can hit back"	Bascomb, *Hunting Eichmann*, 69–70, 90–99, 225–227; *Time* (June 6, 1960); *New York Times* (December 18, 1960).
120	"222 million barrels"	Lewis, *Divided Highways*, 127–128; Ashmore, *Britannica Book of the Year 1961*, 606; White, *Breach of Faith*, 44; U.S. Census Bureau, *Historical Statistics of the United States: Colonial Times to 1970*, 596–597.
120	"next half-hour"	*New York Times* (May 4, 1960, and May 5, 1960); Branch, *Parting the Waters*, 303; Beschloss, *Mayday*, 45–47.
121	"of its copper"	*New York Times* (May 4, 1960); *Time* (May 30, 1960, and June 6, 1960); Reader, *Africa*, 651.
121	"84 days"	Beach, *Salt and Steel*, 262; Beach, *Around the World Submerged*, 46; *New York Times* (May 11, 1960, and December 2, 2002).
121	"Larry O'Brien"	Symington oral history; *New York Times* (May 5, 1960); O'Brien, *No Final Victories*, 77.
122	"ate it up"	O'Donnell and Powers, *Johnny, We Hardly Knew Ye*, 165; O'Brien, *No Final Victories*, 72–73.
122	"the slander"	*Time* (May 9, 1960); Donaldson, *The First Modern Campaign*, 56–57.
122	"on the Bible"	Sorensen, *Kennedy*, 143–145; White, *In Search of History*, 466.
122	"less than $100,000"	O'Neill, *Man of the House*, 77; O'Brien, *No Final Victories*, 68–69, 74; Hersh, *The Dark Side of Camelot*, 90; O'Brien oral history.

123	"signs were up"	*Time* (May 9, 1960); Hersh, *The Dark Side of Camelot*, 99.
123	"55 counties"	Sorensen, *Kennedy*, 146; Bradlee, *Conversations With Kennedy*, 27–28; Runyon, Verdini, and Runyon, *Source Book of American Presidential Campaign and Election Statistics*, 15.
123	"by the Kennedys"	Strober and Strober, *The Kennedy Presidency*, 3; Humphrey, *The Education of a Public Man*, 159; Schlesinger, *A Thousand Days*, 26–27; *National Journal* (August 13, 2000).
124	"Democratic nomination"	*Time* (May 23, 1960, and May 30, 1960); *New York Times* (May 18, 1960, and May 21, 1960); O'Brien, *No Final Victories*, 77; Smith, *The Tiger in the Senate*, 405.
124	"had ever seen"	Halberstam, *The Children*, 145–147; Powledge, *We Shall Overcome*, 164; Olson, *Freedom's Daughters*, 152–153.
125	"am I doing"	Halberstam, *The Children*, 5–6; Hampton and Fayer, *Voices of Freedom*, 55–59; *History Today* (February 2000).
125	*"Nashville Tennessean"*	Olson, *Freedom's Daughters*, 157; *New York Times* (April 20, 1960); Branch, *Parting the Waters*, 295.
125	"for racial equality"	Branch, *Parting the Waters*, 297; Powledge, *Free at Last?* 262; Halberstam, *The Children*, 268–269.
126	"her sentence"	Powledge, *We Shall Overcome*, 169–173; Halberstam, *The Children*, 8–9; *Washington Post* (January 15, 2006).
126	"I really do"	Halberstam, *The Children*, 629–635; Powledge, *Free at Last?* 646.
126	"million by 1970"	U.S. Census Bureau, *Historical Statistics of the United States: Colonial Times to 1970*, 10, 368; *Time* (January 4, 1960).

127	"we dared hope"	Goodman, *Growing Up Absurd*, x, 11–13, 80, 239–241; *New York Times* (October 30, 1960); *New Republic* (August 31, 1998).
127	"were arrested"	Unger, *The Movement*, 45–46; Goodman, *The Committee*, 430–431; Manchester, *The Glory and the Dream*, 849; *New York Times* (May 14, 1960); *San Francisco Chronicle* (June 9, 2002).
128	"journalistic, in nature"	Goodman, *The Committee*, 433; Sale, *SDS*, 22–28; Ashmore, *Hearts and Minds*, 389; Hayden, *Rebel*, 30–32.
128	"was shot down"	Beach, *Around the World Submerged*, 281–282.
129	"as backdrops"	*Washington Post* (May 31, 1992); *Bulletin of the Atomic Scientists* (May 2003); *New York Times* (November 12, 2006).
129	"day in 1960"	*Time* (January 18, 1960); Boorstin, *The Americans: The Democratic Experience*, 269; Jackson, *Crabgrass Frontier*, 167.
129	"without a search"	*Time* (June 6, 1960); Bascomb, *Hunting Eichmann*, 279–280; Malkin and Stein, *Eichmann In My Hands*, 244.
130	"the U-2's cockpit"	*Time* (May 30, 1960); Roper Center for Public Opinion Research website.
130	"the original quote"	Beschloss, *The Crisis Years*, 22–23; *New York Times* (May 22, 1960).
130	"still be defeated"	*New York Times* (June 20, 1960); Beschloss, *The Crisis Years*, 22–23; Martin, *Adlai Stevenson and the World*, 499; Dallek, *Lone Star Rising*, 570.
131	"in the bag"	Ambrose, *Nixon: The Education of a Politician*, 549; Mazo and Hess, *Nixon*, 221.

| 131 | "until the convention" | *New York Times* (May 24, 1960, and May 26, 1960); Kramer and Roberts, *I Never Wanted to Be Vice President of Anything*, 227. |
| 131 | "lot more interesting" | *New York Times* (May 26, 1960); *Time* (June 6, 1960). |

7. JUNE: OFF AGAIN, ON AGAIN

Page	**Paragraph(s) Ending**	**Sources**
133	"be the nominee"	*Time* (June 6, 1960); McPherson oral history; Humphrey oral history.
134	"in his hair"	*New York Times* (June 3, 1960, and June 20, 1960); *Time* (June 13, 1960); *National Party Conventions*, 228; Dallek, *Lone Star Rising*, 570.
134	"pretentious upstart"	Dallek, *Lone Star Rising*, 565; Smathers oral history; Valenti oral history.
135	"a hundred years"	*National Party Conventions*, 228; Edwards oral history; Hodges oral history.
135	"Southern bastards"	Carty, *A Catholic in the White House?* 143; *Time* (June 13, 1960, and June 27, 1960); Schlesinger, *Journals 1952–2000*, 66.
135	"to sit down"	Sorensen, *Kennedy*, 22; Gillon, *Politics and Vision*, 132–133; Brauer, *John F. Kennedy and the Second Reconstruction*, 33.
136	"Daddy, he said"	Martin, *Adlai Stevenson and the World*, 507–509; Schlesinger, *A Thousand Days*, 24–26; Bartlett oral history.
136	"Eleanor, won't it"	*New York Times* (June 13, 1960); Lash, *Eleanor: The Years Alone*, 286–289.
136	"he was interested"	Martin, *Adlai Stevenson and the World*, 459–460, 517–521.

137   "newspapers   *Sports Illustrated* (June 13, 1994); *Time*
        everywhere"   (May 2, 1960, and June 27, 1960);
                                  Sampson, *The Eternal Summer*,
                                  126–127; O'Connor, *Arnie & Jack*,
                                  64–74.

137   "trips as president"   *Time* (January 25, 1960, June 13,
                                  1960, and June 27, 1960); Schaller,
                                  Altered States, 137–145; LaFeber, *The
                                  Clash*, 319–320; Eisenhower, *Waging
                                  Peace*, 563.

137   "ever being successes"   *New York Times* (June 17, 1998);
                                  Finler, *Hitchcock in Hollywood*,
                                  129–134; *Time* (June 27, 1960).

138   "three months hence"   *New York Times* (May 10, 1960,
                                  May 22, 1960, and June 5, 1960);
                                  Baker, *The Second Battle of New
                                  Orleans*, 332.

138   "100 greatest films"   Lally, *Wilder Times*, 297–299; *Time*
                                  (June 27, 1960); *New York Times*
                                  (June 17, 1998).

138   "slide into obscurity"   *New York Times* (June 20, 1960, and
                                  June 21, 1960); Remnick, *King of the
                                  World*, 6–8.

138   "16,000 every second"   U.S. Census Bureau, *Historical
                                  Statistics of the United States: Colonial
                                  Times to 1970*, 690; Caplow, Hicks,
                                  and Wattenberg, *The First Measured
                                  Century*, 144–145; *Time* (April 11,
                                  1960).

139   "the needle stuck"   Halberstam, *The Fifties*, 504–505;
                                  Kluger, *Ashes to Ashes*, 191; *Time*
                                  (April 11, 1960).

139   "conclusion   Kluger, *Ashes to Ashes*, 191–195,
        as Auerbach"   203–204; *Time* (December 14, 1959);
                                  National Center for Health Statis-
                                  tics, *Health, United States, 2009*, 190.

140   "for this practice"   *Time* (April 11, 1960); *New York
                                  Times* (June 7, 1960); *CA: A Bulletin
                                  of Cancer Progress* (January/Febru-
                                  ary 1961).

140	"dangers of cholesterol"	Fine, *The Great Drug Deception,* 15; *Time* (December 26, 1960, and January 13, 1961).
141	"take another nap"	*Time* (November 7, 1960).
141	"substantially true"	Time (January 2, 1961); Wallace and Gruber, *Creative People at Work,* 228, 237, 241–242.
141	"success in 1944"	Wasson, *Nobel Prize Winners,* 1147; *Boston Globe* (April 18, 1994).
142	"of an ounce"	*New York Times* (April 26, 1951, and July 10, 1960); *Chemistry and Industry* (July 10, 2000); Benfey and Morris, *Robert Burns Woodward,* 254; *Time* (July 18, 1960, and January 2, 1961).
142	"for the future"	*New York Times* (July 3, 1960, and July 10, 1960); *Time* (January 2, 1961).
142	"with chlorophyll"	Wasson, *Nobel Prize Winners,* 1148; *New York Times* (October 22, 1965).
142	"with much humor"	Wallace and Gruber, *Creative People at Work,* 230, 241–242; *Washington Post* (July 12, 1979).
143	"I was greedy"	Halberstam, *The Fifties,* 643–645, 649; Kisseloff, *The Box,* 466–467, 484.
143	"his resignation"	Halberstam, *The Fifties,* 651–652, 658, 662–663; Oakley, *God's Country,* 410; Goodwin, *Remembering America,* 54–57; *New Yorker* (July 28, 2008).
144	"drag into autumn"	*New York Times* (March 24, 1960, July 29, 1960, and July 15, 2007); Stone and Yohn, *Prime Time and Misdemeanors,* 286–290.
144	"soon followed suit"	White, *The Making of the President 1960,* 281; Kraus, *The Great Debates,* 57–60; Donaldson, *The First Modern Campaign,* 113; *New York Times* (June 28, 1960).
145	"do with RN"	*New York Times* (June 4, 1960); Ehrlichman, *Witness to Power,*

		20–22; Ambrose, *Nixon: The Education of a Politician*, 539.
145	"to, he said"	Kramer and Roberts, *I Never Wanted to Be Vice President of Anything*, 227–228; *New York Times* (June 9, 1960); Parmet, *Richard Nixon and His America*, 386.
145	"1964 or 1968"	Eisenhower, *Waging Peace*, 592–593; Ambrose, *Nixon: The Education of a Politician*, 540; Ambrose, *Eisenhower: The President*, 595.
146	"right with us"	*Time* (June 27, 1960); Kramer and Roberts, *I Never Wanted to Be Vice President of Anything*, 231; White, *The Making of the President 1960*, 186–187; *New York Times* (July 7, 1960).
146	"to shut up"	Nixon, *Six Crises*, 313; *Time* (June 20, 1960); Ambrose, *Nixon: The Education of a Politician*, 536.
146	"remained blank"	*New York Times* (July 27, 1960); *Time* (July 11, 1960).
146	"into the capsule"	Cadbury, *Space Race*, 205–209; Schefter, *The Race*, 105–106.
147	"in New Orleans"	Baker, *The Second Battle of New Orleans*, 332.
147	"delay integration"	Bartley, *The New South*, 249.
147	"sit-ins continued"	Wolff, *Lunch at the Five and Ten*, 179; Oakley, *God's Country*, 405.
147	"trip was canceled"	Manchester, *The Glory and the Dream*, 875–876.
148	"not regain it"	*Time* (April 18, 1960); Allyn, *Make Love, Not War*, 43.
148	"a UCLA dean"	Kinsey, Pomeroy, and Martin, *Sexual Behavior in the Human Male*, 549–557; *Time* (August 15, 1960).
148	"$3 million to come"	*Playboy* (December 1999); Freedman, *The Essential Feminist Reader*, 214; Van Dulken, *Inventing the 20th Century*, 138; McLaughlin, *The*

		Pill, John Rock, and the Church, 97–98, 106; *Time* (March 31, 2003).
149	"confused them again"	Halberstam, *The Fifties*, 599–602; Van Dulken, *Inventing the 20th Century*, 138; McLaughlin, *The Pill, John Rock, and the Church*, 27.
149	"not induce infertility"	Halberstam, *The Fifties*, 603–604; McLaughlin, *The Pill, John Rock, and the Church*, 131; *Time* (April 11, 1960).
149	"insurmountable obstacle"	Asbell, *The Pill*, 159–160; *Time* (April 11, 1960).
149	"pharmaceutical contraceptive"	McLaughlin, *The Pill, John Rock, and the Church*, 139; Asbell, *The Pill*, 163–164.
150	"to become rich"	McLaughlin, *The Pill, John Rock, and the Church*, 143; Asbell, *The Pill*, 166–167.
150	"2.3 million by 1963"	McLaughlin, *The Pill, John Rock, and the Church*, 141–142; *New York Times* (May 10, 1960, and August 4, 1960); Manchester, *The Glory and the Dream*, 849–850; *Time* (March 31, 2003); Halberstam, *The Fifties*, 605.
151	"a successful career"	Ethics and Medicine (Summer 2008); U.S. Census Bureau, *Historical Statistics of the United States: Colonial Times to 1970*, 49; Caplow, Hicks, and Wattenberg, *The First Measured Century*, 84–85; McLaughlin, *The Pill, John Rock, and the Church*, 207.

8. JULY: THE NEW FRONTIER

Page	Paragraph(s) Ending	Sources
153	"13½ years"	McCullough, *Truman*, 973; Sorensen, *Kennedy*, 151–152.
154	"to be won"	Parmet, *JFK*, 17; Jamieson, *Packaging the Presidency*, 141.

154	"the free world"	*Time* (July 18, 1960); Dallek, *Lone Star Rising*, 570–572; Miller, *Lyndon*, 242–243.
154	"a small dispensary"	Parmet, *JFK*, 17–18; *New York Times* (July 5, 1960); Edwards oral history; Dallek, *Lone Star Rising*, 572; Sorensen, *Kennedy*, 39–41.
154	"life, I find"	Ashmore oral history; Witcover, *Crapshoot*, 147; Sorensen, *Kennedy*, 13, 165.
155	"attend, too"	O'Brien oral history; Sorensen, *Kennedy*, 156–157.
155	"landslide, he said"	Valenti oral history; *New York Times* (July 13, 1960); Dallek, *Lone Star Rising*, 573–574; Sorensen, *Kennedy*, 156–157.
157	"as he could"	McKeever, *Adlai Stevenson*, 452, 457–458; Martin, *Adlai Stevenson and the World*, 522–526; Lash, *Eleanor: The Years Alone*, 295; *New York Times* (July 14, 1960); Schlesinger, *Journals 1952–2000*, 72–73.
157	"of Illinois"	Parmet, *JFK*, 10–11; McKeever, *Adlai Stevenson*, 462–463.
157	"ignited the frenzy"	Martin, *Adlai Stevenson and the World*, 527; *National Journal* (August 13, 2000); Bradlee, *Conversations With Kennedy*, 31; Dilworth oral history; McKeever, *Adlai Stevenson*, 462–463.
158	"nomination was his"	*National Party Conventions*, 228; Sorensen, *Kennedy*, 161–162.
158	"ease his burden"	Miller, *Lyndon*, 253; Witcover, *Crapshoot*, 150–152; Schlesinger, *A Thousand Days*, 40–41; Thomas, *The Pursuit of the White House*, 169–170; *National Party Conventions*, 228; Gillon, *Politics and Vision*, 133.
159	"Ted Sorensen"	O'Donnell and Powers, *Johnny, We Hardly Knew Ye*, 190–193; O'Brien

		oral history; Miller, *Lyndon,* 254–255.
159	"it won't be"	Schlesinger, *A Thousand Days,* 48–49, 54; Dallek, *Lone Star Rising,* 578–581; Guthman and Shulman, *Robert Kennedy in His Own Words,* 20; Miller, *Lyndon,* 254–255; Salinger, *With Kennedy,* 46.
160	"definitely defeat him"	White, *The Making of the President 1960,* 177; *Time* (July 25, 1960); Schlesinger, *A Thousand Days,* 59–61; Sorensen, *Kennedy,* 167; Matthews, *Kennedy and Nixon,* 135.
160	"to health protection"	*New York Times* (June 29, 1960, and December 7, 1980); *Journal of Public Policy and Marketing* (Fall 2004); *Washington Post* (May 10, 1984); *Pediatrics* (September 1961).
160	"until August 24"	*Time* (August 1, 1960); *Investor's Business Daily* (February 6, 2004); Leslie, *Francis Chichester,* 150–156; Chichester, *Alone Across the Atlantic,* 180.
161	"to target. Perfect"	Sapolsky, *Polaris System Development,* 3–4; Baar and Howard, *Polaris,* 237; *New York Times* (July 21, 1960).
161	"of the day"	Ambrose, *Eisenhower: The President,* 584–585; Beschloss, *Mayday,* 321–322; Eisenhower, *Waging Peace,* 568–571; Khrushchev, *Nikita Khrushchev and the Creation of a Superpower,* 393–394.
161	"31st birthday"	*Time* (June 6, 1960, and August 15, 1960); Beschloss, *Mayday,* 328; *New York Times* (July 19, 1960).
162	"book ever written"	*New York Times* (July 6, 1960, and July 10, 1960); *Time* (September 5, 1960); *Washington Post* (April 7, 2004); Brosnan, *The Long Season,* vii; ESPN website.

162	"land, he boasted"	Alexander, *Holding the Line,* 256; Schoultz, *That Infernal Little Cuban Republic,* 118; *New York Times* (June 30, 1960); *Time* (July 11, 1960).
162	"to nationalization"	Higgins, *The Perfect Failure,* 53; *New York Times* (July 7, 1960); Bourne, *Fidel,* 205–206; Schoultz, *That Infernal Little Cuban Republic,* 124–125.
163	"for missile bases"	Ulam, *Expansion and Coexistence,* 649–650; *New York Times* (July 10, 1960); Eisenhower, *Waging Peace,* 536–537.
163	"Bissell conceded"	Higgins, *The Perfect Failure,* 61–62; Mosley, *Dulles,* 465–466; Bissell oral history.
163	"talking about it"	Ambrose, *Eisenhower: The President,* 584; Jones, *The Bay of Pigs,* 20.
164	"work went on"	Wyden, *Bay of Pigs,* 33–34, 40–44; Jones, *The Bay of Pigs,* 29.
164	"had Idabel say"	Shields, *Mockingbird,* 39, 59; *New Yorker* (May 29, 2006).
165	"Overseas Airways"	Shields, *Mockingbird,* 16–17, 25–26, 100–101, 109–112; Plimpton, *Truman Capote,* 243; *New Yorker* (May 29, 2006).
165	"a polished book"	*New York Times* (July 13, 1960); *Time* (August 1, 1960); Shields, *Mockingbird,* 114, 126–128; *New Yorker* (May 29, 2006); *New Republic* (August 28, 2006).
165	"the following year"	Shields, *Mockingbird,* 14; *New York Times* (July 13, 1960); *New Yorker* (May 29, 2006).
166	"of south Alabama"	Shields, *Mockingbird,* 202, 240–241, 263; *New Republic* (August 28, 2006).
166	"Hell, no"	Shields, *Mockingbird,* 3, 186; *New Republic* (August 28, 2006); *New York Times* (January 30, 2006).
166	"into a wastebasket"	Edgerton, *The Troubled Heart of Africa,* 182–183; *New York Times*

		(June 25, 1960); *Time* (June 27, 1960, and July 4, 1960).
167	"to the other"	De Witte, *The Assassination of Lumumba*, 1–3; Zeilig, *Patrice Lumumba*, 96–100; *Time* (July 11, 1960).
167	"by July 10"	Edgerton, *The Troubled Heart of Africa*, 185–186; *New York Times* (July 7, 1960); Time (July 18, 1960).
167	"as his protectors"	*New York Times* (July 9, 1960, and July 10, 1960); *Time* (July 11, 1960, and July 18, 1960); De Witte, *The Assassination of Lumumba*, 7–8; Zeilig, *Patrice Lumumba*, 89–90, 105–106; Gunther, *Inside Europe Today*, 116.
168	"no U.S. aid"	De Witte, *The Assassination of Lumumba*, 7–8; Walton, *The Remnants of Power*, 70–72; *Time* (July 25, 1960, and August 8, 1960); Edgerton, *The Troubled Heart of Africa*, 191; Ambrose, *Eisenhower: The President*, 586–587; Mosley, *Dulles*, 461.
168	"and prime objective"	Zeilig, *Patrice Lumumba*, 116; Reader, *Africa*, 659; Edgerton, *The Troubled Heart of Africa*, 193; U.S. Senate Select Committee to Study Governmental Operations, *Alleged Assassination Plots Involving Foreign Leaders*, 13–15; *Newsweek* (December 1, 1975).
169	"in the Congo"	Bissell oral history; Ewald, *Eisenhower the President*, 276; U.S. Senate Select Committee to Study Governmental Operations, *Alleged Assassination Plots Involving Foreign Leaders*, 13.
169	"tossed it in"	Ewald, *Eisenhower the President*, 253; U.S. Senate Select Committee to Study Governmental Operations, *Alleged Assassination Plots Involving Foreign Leaders*, 19; Edgerton,

		The Troubled Heart of Africa, 194; Eisenhower, *Waging Peace*, 575; *Time* (September 26, 1960); *Newsweek* (December 1, 1975).
169	"save the environment"	*Time* (September 26, 1960).
170	"in 1970"	ESPN website; Burke and Fornatale, *Change Up*, 56.
170	"missile program"	Baar and Howard, *Polaris*, 231–232; *Time* (August 1, 1960).
170	"in the lead"	Leslie, *Francis Chichester*, 155.
170	"up their business"	Collier and Horowitz, *The Rockefellers*, 342–343; White, *The Making of the President 1960*, 196–198.
171	"of Fifth Avenue"	Finch oral history; Kramer and Roberts, *I Never Wanted to Be Vice President of Anything*, 232–233; Ambrose, *Nixon: The Education of a Politician*, 551–552; Parmet, *Richard Nixon and His America*, 388–389.
171	"the Republican ticket"	White, *The Making of the President 1960*, 198; American Presidency Project website; Kramer and Roberts, *I Never Wanted to Be Vice President of Anything*, 233–234; Ambrose, *Eisenhower: The President*, 597; Nixon, *Six Crises*, 316.
172	"four-square liar"	Ambrose, *Nixon: The Education of a Politician*, 552–553; Goldberg, *Barry Goldwater*, 145.
172	"all of them"	Goldwater oral history; Goldberg, *Barry Goldwater*, 145; Nixon, *Six Crises*, 316; White, *Theodore H. White at Large*, 301–302.
172	"promised it would"	*New York Times* (July 28, 1960); Time (August 8, 1960); Andrew, *The Other Side of the Sixties*, 51; Goldberg, *Barry Goldwater*, 145.
173	"carry the Northeast"	*New York Times* (July 28, 1960); Ambrose, *Nixon: The Education of a Politician*, 546, 553–554; Donaldson,

		The First Modern Campaign, 90–91; Lodge, *As It Was*, 211; Lodge, *The Storm Has Many Eyes*, 183.
173	"states by November"	Collier and Horowitz, *The Rockefellers*, 343; Ambrose, *Nixon: The Education of a Politician*, 554–555; White, *The Making of the President 1960*, 263.
174	"in the fall"	Runyon, Verdini, and Runyon, *Source Book of American Presidential Campaign and Election Statistics*, 275–276; Perret, *Eisenhower*, 597; Roper Center for Public Opinion Research website; Ambrose, *Nixon: The Education of a Politician*, 558–559.

9. AUGUST: BEGINNING TO STIR

Page	Paragraph(s) Ending	Sources
175	"running the country"	Ambrose, *Nixon: The Education of a Politician*, 584; Schlesinger, *A Thousand Days*, 64–65.
176	"neither can win"	Oakley, *God's Country*, 416; Parmet, *Richard Nixon and His America*, 361; *Time* (August 15, 1960).
176	"to the left"	*Time* (October 3, 1960); Ambrose, *Nixon: The Education of a Politician*, 584–587.
176	"with wonderment"	Jamieson, *Packaging the Presidency*, 151–153; Finch oral history; Wicker, *One of Us*, 245; *Presidential Studies Quarterly* (Summer 1999); Crouse, *The Boys on the Bus*, 35.
177	"would hope not"	Matthews, *Kennedy and Nixon*, 51–52, 137; Nixon, *RN*, 75; Mitchell, *Tricky Dick and the Pink Lady*, 248; Sorensen, *Kennedy*, 55; Strober and Strober, *The Kennedy Presidency*, 30.

177	"nine days later"	Ambrose, *Nixon: The Education of a Politician,* 560; *Time* (August 15, 1960); Mazo and Hess, *Nixon,* 229; Thomas, *The Pursuit of the White House, passim; New York Times* (August 13, 1960).
178	"educational system"	*Time* (August 29, 1960, and September 5, 1960); *New York Times* (August 27, 1960); White, *Theodore H. White at Large,* 304; Ambrose, *Nixon: The Education of a Politician,* 560; Donaldson, *The First Modern Campaign,* 106.
178	"more about it"	Ambrose, *Nixon: The Education of a Politician,* 435; Goodwin, *Remembering America,* 106–107; *Time* (September 12, 1960); Nixon, *RN,* 218.
179	"in session late"	Miller, *Lyndon,* 229–230; *Time* (August 15, 1960); U.S. Congress, *Congressional Record* (86th Congress, 2nd Session), 15928.
179	"nearly at hand"	Scott oral history; Miller, *Lyndon,* 230–231; *Time* (August 22, 1960, and August 29, 1960); Dallek, *Lone Star Rising,* 584; *New York Times* (September 2, 1960).
179	"conference ever"	Gunther, *Inside Europe Today,* 218; Oakley, *God's Country,* 371; *Time* (May 30, 1960, and August 15, 1960); *New York Times* (August 2, 1960).
180	"Soviet space scientist"	Schefter, *The Race,* 106–107; *New York Times* (August 21, 1960, and August 22, 1960); Cadbury, *Space Race,* 210–211; *Time* (August 29, 1960).
180	"around the globe"	*New York Times* (August 13, 1960); *Time* (August 22, 1960); Lewis, *Appointment on the Moon,* 298.

180	"we'll release him"	*New York Times* (August 17, 1960, August 18, 1960, and August 20, 1960); Beschloss, *Mayday*, 328; Khrushchev, *Nikita Khrushchev and the Creation of a Superpower*, 426.
181	"one day further"	Baker, *The Second Battle of New Orleans*, 350, 360–362; *New York Times* (August 18, 1960, and August 28, 1960).
181	"eight months later"	*Seattle Times* (April 4, 1990); *Seattle Post-Intelligencer* (April 5, 1990); Morgan, *Century 21*, 136–137; Ochsner, *Shaping Seattle Architecture*, 258–260, 278.
181	"sure to follow"	Halberstam, *The Best and the Brightest*, 87–88; Stevenson, *The End of Nowhere*, 9, 88–89; *Time* (June 6, 1960, and January 13, 1961); Walton, *Cold War and Counterrevolution*, 12–18.
182	"a foreigner die"	Stevenson, *The End of Nowhere*, 89–95; Adams and McCoy, *Laos*, 152–155.
182	"for anything"	*New York Times* (August 14, 1960, and August 18, 1960); *Time* (October 10, 1960).
182	"absolutely free"	Karnow, *Vietnam*, 55, 192, 220–221, 229–232, 234–239; Jones, *Death of a Generation*, 14; Perret, *Eisenhower*, 595.
183	"come before liberty"	Halberstam, *Ho*, 108–109; *Time* (March 7, 1960, and July 11, 1960); Perret, *Eisenhower*, 596.
183	"a better answer"	Halberstam, *Ho*, 107; *New York Times* (March 14, 1960, and May 22, 1960); Perret, *Eisenhower*, 596; Karnow, *Vietnam*, 229–232.
183	"for work again"	Nolen, *Promised the Moon*, 25–30, 53, 64; *Oklahoma City Daily Oklahoman* (May 17, 1998).

184	"Ike replied"	*New York Times* (June 15, 1957); Nolen, *Promised the Moon*, 66–68; Kevles, *Almost Heaven*, 8.
184	"her male colleague"	*Toronto Globe and Mail* (October 12, 2002); Nolen, *Promised the Moon*, 1–4, 93–98; *Time* (August 29, 1960); *New York Times* (August 19, 1960).
185	"games for them"	Nolen, *Promised the Moon*, 101, 183–185; *Time* (August 29, 1960); Weitekamp, *Right Stuff, Wrong Sex*, 144–146, 150.
186	"I would now"	*People* (October 19, 1998); Kevles, *Almost Heaven*, 31–32; Nolen, *Promised the Moon*, 266; *New York Post* (October 26, 1998); *Toronto Globe and Mail* (October 12, 2002).
186	"incidence of addiction"	Ashmore, *Britannica Book of the Year 1961*, 118, 403, 470; Davenport-Hines, *The Pursuit of Oblivion*, 361; Caplow, Hicks, and Wattenberg, *The First Measured Century*, 146–147.
186	"lab designation, LSD"	Davenport-Hines, *The Pursuit of Oblivion*, 327; *Time* (March 7, 1960, and March 28, 1960).
187	"of going insane"	*Time* (March 28, 1960); *Los Angeles Times* (March 25, 1991); Davenport-Hines, *The Pursuit of Oblivion*, 328–329; *Washington Post* (April 30, 2008).
187	"LSD, he wrote"	Davenport-Hines, *The Pursuit of Oblivion*, 329; *Los Angeles Times* (March 25, 1991); *Hartford Courant* (November 16, 1997); *Washington Post* (October 22, 1997); *New York Times* (May 17, 1987).
187	"illuminated consciousness"	Davenport-Hines, *The Pursuit of Oblivion*, 330–333; *New Yorker* (June 26, 2006); *New York Times* (December 18, 1960).

188	"process of dying"	Greenfield, *Timothy Leary*, 105, 110–112; *Chicago Tribune* (July 2, 2006).
188	"as a psychologist"	Greenfield, *Timothy Leary*, 111–113; Oakley, *God's Country*, 403; Leary, *Flashbacks*, 31–33; *Los Angeles Times* (June 1, 1996); *New York Observer* (June 19, 2006).
188	"in business"	Greenfield, *Timothy Leary*, 116–117; *New Yorker* (June 26, 2006); Leary, *Flashbacks*, 42.
189	"John F. Kennedy"	Leary, *Flashbacks*, 71; Hayes, *Smiling Through the Apocalypse*, 591–599; Greenfield, *Timothy Leary*, 125–126.
189	"a soccer game"	Khrushchev, *Nikita Khrushchev and the Creation of a Superpower*, 400–401; Mosley, *Dulles*, 432–433; Brzezinski, *Red Moon Rising*, 270.
189	"was not persuaded"	*Time* (August 22, 1960).
189	"camera system worked"	*New York Times* (August 18, 1960); *Time* (August 29, 1960).
190	"its lunch counter"	*New York Times* (August 7, 1960); Chafe, *Civilities and Civil Rights*, 97–98; *Greensboro News and Record* (January 29, 2010).
190	"down his objections"	Baker, *The Second Battle of New Orleans*, 385–386.
190	"move ahead again"	*Time* (September 12, 1960).
191	"fence-mending chores"	Schlesinger, *A Thousand Days*, 32; Donaldson, *The First Modern Campaign*, 97; O'Donnell and Powers, *Johnny, We Hardly Knew Ye*, 201–202.
191	"about foreign policy"	*Time* (January 25, 1960); Parmet, *JFK*, 34–35; Martin, *Adlai Stevenson and the World*, 531.
191	"to have it"	Vidal, *United States*, 821; Sorensen, *Counselor*, 168; Sevareid, *Candidates 1960*, 204–205; Schlesinger, *A Thousand Days*, 12–13; Matthews, *Kennedy and Nixon*, 99.

192	"off his mind"	Lash, *Eleanor: The Years Alone,* 297–298; Martin, *Adlai Stevenson and the World,* 535–536.
192	"Nixon is impossible"	McCullough, *Truman,* 970; Whalen, *The Founding Father,* 449; Donaldson, *The First Modern Campaign,* 100.
192	"throughout the fall"	Clifford, *Counsel to the President,* 322; McCullough, *Truman,* 974; *Time* (August 29, 1960); Bray oral history; Stowe oral history.
192	"with pained surprise"	*Time* (August 22, 1960); Strober and Strober, *The Nixon Presidency,* 7; Ambrose, *Nixon: The Education of a Politician,* 558.
193	"I don't remember"	Beschloss, *The Crisis Years,* 23; Ambrose, *Eisenhower: The President,* 600; Wicker, *One of Us,* 224–226; Ambrose, *Nixon: The Education of a Politician,* 559.
193	"Medical Center"	Wicker, *One of Us,* 226; Ewald, *Eisenhower the President,* 310; Goldwater oral history.
194	"his entire career"	Ambrose, *Nixon: The Education of a Politician,* 563–564; Nixon, *Six Crises,* 326–327; *Time* (September 12, 1960).

10. SEPTEMBER: SUBSTANCE AND APPEARANCE

Page	Paragraph(s) Ending	Sources
195	"Inland Steel Company"	Runyon, Verdini, and Runyon, *Source Book of American Presidential Campaign and Election Statistics,* 275–276; U.S. Bureau of Labor Statistics website; *Time* (September 19, 1960, and October 3, 1960).
196	"for lost time"	Sorensen, *Kennedy,* 185; *New York Times* (September 10, 1960); *Time* (September 19, 1960, and Septem-

		ber 26, 1960); Ambrose, *Nixon: The Education of a Politician*, 567.
196	"drop the rope"	*New York Times* (September 6, 1960); Bruno, *The Advance Man*, 47.
196	"anyone who tries"	*Time* (September 19, 1960); Beschloss, *The Crisis Years*, 25; Galbraith, *A Life in Our Times*, 387; Martin, *Adlai Stevenson and the World*, 532; Finch oral history; Smith, *Thomas E. Dewey and His Times*, 625.
197	"start right now"	Nixon, *Six Crises*, 307–308; Donaldson, *The First Modern Campaign*, 157; Carty, *A Catholic in the White House?* 88–89.
197	"what it was"	George, *God's Salesman*, 101, 131, 201–206; Sorensen, *Kennedy*, 188–189; Carty, *A Catholic in the White House?* 60.
198	"other consideration"	Ambrose, *Nixon: The Education of a Politician*, 564–565; Sorensen, *Kennedy*, 189; Carty, *A Catholic in the White House?* 61; Finch oral history; Nixon, *Six Crises*, 328.
198	"may be you"	Sorensen, *Kennedy*, 190–191; *Time* (September 26, 1960); Parmet, *JFK*, 43.
198	"as they are"	Sorensen, *Kennedy*, 190, 193; *Time* (September 26, 1960); Jamieson, *Packaging the Presidency*, 133–135; Reinsch, *Getting Elected*, 131.
199	"the right path"	Rustow, *Oil and Turmoil*, 96, 108–109; Skeet, *OPEC*, 1, 20–22.
199	"without an education"	*New York Times* (September 18, 1960); *Washington Post* (September 19, 2007); Lassiter and Lewis, *The Moderates' Dilemma*, 134–138.
199	"a first step"	Avalon Project website; Clymer, *Drawing the Line at the Big Ditch*, 3–5; Major, *Prize Possession*,

331–333; *New York Times* (September 19, 1960).

200   "for social activism"   Andrew, *The Other Side of the Sixties*, 54–57; Rusher, *The Rise of the Right*, 89–91.

200   "minute teleplays"   *Time* (October 10, 1960); Kisseloff, *The Box*, 462; *New York Times* (January 5, 1960).

200   "present-day America"   Railsback and Meyer, *A John Steinbeck Encyclopedia*, 398–400; Steinbeck, *Travels with Charley*, 185; Parini, *John Steinbeck*, 428.

201   "to his amusement"   *New York Times* (September 16, 1960, and September 17, 1960); Khrushchev, *Nikita Khrushchev and the Creation of a Superpower*, 409.

201   "his own security"   *New York Times* (September 20, 1960); Taubman, *Khrushchev*, 474; *Time* (September 12, 1960); Eisenhower, *Waging Peace*, 578.

201   "in his schedule"   Taubman, *Khrushchev*, 472; *Time* (September 12, 1960); Eisenhower, *Waging Peace*, 577.

202   "communist anthem"   *Time* (September 26, 1960, and October 3, 1960).

202   "demeaning uncle"   Hayes, *Smiling Through the Apocalypse*, 273; *Time* (October 24, 1960); Taubman, *Khrushchev*, 478.

203   "to be careful"   *New York Times* (September 18, 1960, and September 19, 1960); Bourne, *Fidel*, 206–210; *Time* (October 3, 1960); Wyden, *Bay of Pigs*, 43.

203   "Cuban debts"   *New York Times* (September 27, 1960); Bourne, *Fidel*, 209–210; Schoultz, *That Infernal Little Cuban Republic*, 135–136; *Time* (October 10, 1960).

203   "on his desk"   Taubman, *Khrushchev*, 475; *New York Times* (October 13, 1960); Khru-

		shchev, *Nikita Khrushchev and the Creation of a Superpower*, 414–416.
203	"like last time"	Ulam, *Expansion and Coexistence*, 637; Ambrose, *Eisenhower: The President*, 590; Oakley, *God's Country*, 394; *New York Times* (October 15, 1960).
204	"him Poor Boy"	*Dallas Morning News* (December 14, 2006); *New York Times* (August 23, 1964); Hill, *H.L. and Lyda*, 242–243; Hurt, *Texas Rich*, 170.
205	"bad, he said"	*Dallas Morning News* (December 14, 2006); Hill, *H.L. and Lyda*, 55; Shapiro, *Bottom of the Ninth*, 119–121; *Kansas City Star* (December 14, 2006).
205	"going to fold"	Miller, *Going Long*, 3; *Texas Monthly* (February 2009); *New York Times* (August 15, 1959, October 20, 1959, and January 29, 1960).
205	"another 100 years"	*New York Times* (September 10, 1960); *Time* (January 2, 1961); *Texas Monthly* (February 2009); *Kansas City Star* (December 14, 2006).
205	"Wham-O Super Ball"	*Dallas Morning News* (October 18, 1992, and December 14, 2006); *Texas Monthly* (February 2009).
206	"worth that much"	Hurt, *Texas Rich*, 412–417.
206	"sports-loving sibling"	Felser, *The Birth of the New NFL*, 62–66; *Dallas Morning News* (December 14, 2006); Hurt, *Texas Rich*, 329.
206	"of conservation"	*Art in America* (January 2005); Alinder, *Ansel Adams*, 250–251, 281–284; *Boston Herald* (April 19, 2002); *Smithsonian* (February 2002); *New York Times* (May 15, 1960).
207	"radiation treatments"	Fox, *The American Conservation Movement*, 293–294; Lytle, *The Gentle Subversive*, 9–11, 81–83, 121–122,

		136–137; Carson, *Silent Spring*, xi–xii.
207	"spring without voices"	Lytle, *The Gentle Subversive*, 2; Carson, *Silent Spring*, 1–2, 6.
208	"age of 56"	Lytle, *The Gentle Subversive*, 6, 156; Freeman, *Always, Rachel*, 324; Fox, *The American Conservation Movement*, 292–293, 299; Carson, *Silent Spring*, xiii; *Booklist* (June 1, 2005).
208	"the national press"	Goldberg, *Barry Goldwater*, 137; Rusher, *The Rise of the Right*, 59–61.
208	"were communists"	Goldwater oral history.
208	"a public speaker"	Ambrose, *Nixon: The Education of a Politician*, 541–542; Cannon, *President Reagan*, 53.
209	"half-decade younger"	*Philadelphia Inquirer* (May 12, 2004); *Washington Post* (September 19, 2007).
209	"the Canal Zone"	*New York Times* (September 18, 1960).
209	"but joint appearances"	Reinsch, *Getting Elected*, 134; Sorensen, *Kennedy*, 196–197; Kraus, *The Great Debates*, 74–77.
210	"in the studio"	O'Neill, *Coming Apart*, 21–22; Kisseloff, *The Box*, 401; Nixon, *Six Crises*, 337; Hewitt oral history.
210	"smartly dressed"	Kraus, *The Great Debates*, 79–80; Nixon, *Six Crises*, 337; Sorensen, *Kennedy*, 198; Goodwin, *Remembering America*, 112; Ambrose, *Nixon: The Education of a Politician*, 571–572; Hewitt oral history.
211	"they want it"	Hewitt, *Tell Me a Story*, 68–70; Hewitt oral history; Reinsch, *Getting Elected*, 141.
211	"it isn't enough"	Ambrose, *Nixon: The Education of a Politician*, 572; Ewald, *Eisenhower the President*, 300; Museum of Broadcast Communications website.

211	"reach those goals"	White, *Breach of Faith*, 64; Finch oral history; Matthews, *Kennedy and Nixon*, 147, 152.
212	"Jack Kennedy was"	Alsop, *I've Seen the Best of It*, 430; Goldwater oral history; Strober and Strober, *The Kennedy Presidency*, 32; Matthews, *Kennedy and Nixon*, 153; Stanton oral history.
212	"pale and tired"	Sorensen, *Kennedy*, 201; Ambrose, *Nixon: The Education of a Politician*, 575; Wicker, *One of Us*, 228.
212	"handsome Democrat"	Ambrose, *Nixon: The Education of a Politician*, 575; Runyon, Verdini, and Runyon, *Source Book of American Presidential Campaign and Election Statistics*, 275–276; Matthews, *Kennedy and Nixon*, 157.
212	"milkshakes a day"	Nixon, *Six Crises*, 342; *Time* (October 10, 1960); Ambrose, *Nixon: The Education of a Politician*, 575; Nixon, *RN*, 219.
213	"in American politics"	Halberstam, *The Fifties*, 732; Persico, *Edward R. Murrow*, 460; Hewitt oral history.

11. OCTOBER: A SUITCASE OF VOTES

Page	Paragraph(s) Ending	Sources
215	"pushed around lately"	*Time* (August 15, 1960, September 12, 1960, October 24, 1960, and October 31, 1960); Bourne, *Fidel*, 214; *New York Times* (October 19, 1960).
216	"on October 30"	Mosley, *Dulles*, 465–466; Bissell oral history; Hersh, *The Dark Side of Camelot*, 175–177; Bourne, *Fidel*, 212.
216	"be traced back"	Wyden, *Bay of Pigs*, 40–44; Hersh, *The Dark Side of Camelot*, 163.

216   "the United States"   Ambrose, *Nixon: The Education of a Politician*, 550, 569–570; Wyden, *Bay of Pigs*, 68; *Presidential Studies Quarterly* (December 2003); Beschloss, *The Crisis Years*, 29–30.

216   "in recent years"   Ambrose, *Nixon: The Education of a Politician*, 577–578; Reinsch, *Getting Elected*, 145; Kraus, *The Great Debates*, 102–103; Commission on Presidential Debates website.

217   "said in rebuttal"   Matthews, *Kennedy and Nixon*, 158–160; Goodwin, *Remembering America*, 75; Ambrose, *Nixon: The Education of a Politician*, 578–579; Commission on Presidential Debates website.

217   "for the night"   Runyon, Verdini, and Runyon, *Source Book of American Presidential Campaign and Election Statistics*, 275–276; Kraus, *The Great Debates*, 107–112; Reinsch, *Getting Elected*, 146–147; Ambrose, *Nixon: The Education of a Politician*, 582.

218   "guys lost it"   Kraus, *The Great Debates*, 114; Wyden, *Bay of Pigs*, 65–67; *New York Times* (October 21, 1960); Ambrose, *Nixon: The Education of a Politician*, 591–592; Parmet, *JFK*, 48–49; Goodwin, *Remembering America*, 126.

218   "cost him votes"   Nixon, *RN*, 220–221; Nixon, *Six Crises*, 355; Wyden, *Bay of Pigs*, 67–68; Ambrose, *Nixon: The Education of a Politician*, 591–592; Hersh, *The Dark Side of Camelot*, 181.

219   "of the nation"   U.S. Census Bureau, *Historical Statistics of the United States: Colonial Times to 1970*, 1071–1072; Kraus, *The Great Debates*, 68, 153.

219   "a prediction"   Runyon, Verdini, and Runyon, *Source Book of American Presidential Campaign and Election Statistics*,

		275–276; *Time* (October 31, 1960); White, *The Making of the President 1960*, 320.
220	"approaches to reality"	*Time* (March 14, 1960, and June 20, 1960); Lobel, *Image Duplicator*, 5–6; Leslie, *Pop Art*, 39–41; Stich, *Yves Klein*, 203–205.
220	"and Los Angeles"	*New York Times* (October 18, 1960, October 27, 1960, and December 25, 1960); Shapiro, *Bottom of the Ninth*, 213–214.
220	"since 1925"	Reisler, *The Best Game Ever*, 209–215; Golenbock, *Dynasty*, 391–394; *Time* (October 24, 1960).
220	"racist nirvana"	Sampson, *Mandela*, 128, 138; *Time* (October 17, 1960); *New York Times* (October 8, 1960); Harvey, *The Fall of Apartheid*, 60–61.
221	"of German policy"	Balfour, *West Germany*, 186–188; Gunther, *Inside Europe Today*, 52; Tusa, *The Last Division*, 223; Alexander, *Adenauer and the New Germany*, 177.
221	"the United States"	*New York Times* (October 21, 1960, and November 2, 1960); *Time* (September 19, 1960).
221	"political hair-pulling"	*New York Times* (November 5, 1960, and November 8, 1960); *Time* (September 5, 1960); Wallace, *Politics of Conscience*, 150–151.
222	"than men, mostly"	*Los Angeles Times* (February 24, 2000); *Time* (March 21, 1960, and November 16, 1960).
222	"percent in 1940"	*New York Times* (January 5, 1960); U.S. Census Bureau, *Historical Statistics of the United States: Colonial Times to 1970*, 128; Hayden, *Building Suburbia*, 147.
222	"own fulfillment first"	Oakley, *God's Country*, 407; *Good Housekeeping* (September 1960); Horowitz, *Betty Friedan and the Making of the Feminine Mystique*, 194–195.

223	"her dissatisfaction"	Halberstam, *The Fifties,* 592–597; Friedan, *Life So Far,* 97, 101.
223	"came for coffee"	Horowitz, *Betty Friedan and the Making of The Feminine Mystique,* 169–170, 193; Friedan, *Life So Far,* 108–109.
223	"your vacuum cleaners"	Friedan, *Life So Far,* 122; Horowitz, *Betty Friedan and the Making of The Feminine Mystique,* 200, 221–223; Friedan, *The Feminine Mystique,* ix; *New York Times* (February 6, 2006).
224	"train and spar"	Remnick, *King of the World,* 91–93; *New York Times* (August 14, 1960); *Sports Illustrated* (January 13, 1992).
224	"way he did"	*Sports Illustrated* (January 13, 1992); Gipe, *The Great American Sports Book,* 527; New York Times (September 6, 1960).
224	"Clay won easily"	Maraniss, *Rome 1960,* 280–283; Ezra, *Muhammad Ali,* 12–13; Brunt, *Facing Ali,* 15–16.
225	"induction in 1967"	Ezra, *Muhammad Ali,* 13, 62; Remnick, *King of the World,* 125, 200, 213–214, 285–287.
225	"from passing cars"	Ezra, *Muhammad Ali,* 151–154, 161; *Sports Illustrated* (September 19, 1994).
226	"tired of it"	Sorensen, *Kennedy,* 179, 182–183; *Time* (November 7, 1960).
226	"offered no proof"	*Time* (October 24, 1960); Stowe oral history; Ambrose, *Nixon: The Education of a Politician,* 582; Ehrlichman, *Witness to Power,* 49; Vare, *The American Idea,* 138.
227	"including the debates"	U.S. Bureau of Labor Statistics website; Wicker, *One of Us,* 181; *Time* (October 31, 1960, and November 7, 1960); *New York Times* (October 21, 1960); Finch oral history.

227	"control the world"	Carty, *A Catholic in the White House?* 63–64; *Time* (October 31, 1960); De Paulo oral history; *Historian* (March 2001).
227	"to be president"	Carty, *A Catholic in the White House?* 122–123, 151–152; White, *The Making of the President 1960*, 241.
228	"reception in August"	Brauer, *John F. Kennedy and the Second Reconstruction*, 29, 41–42; Branch, *Parting the Waters*, 219, 343; Ashmore, *Hearts and Minds*, 364–365; White, *In Search of History*, 471.
229	"blacks from jail"	Branch, *Parting the Waters*, 351–352; Ambrose, *Nixon: The Education of a Politician*, 596–597; Ashmore, *Hearts and Minds*, 319–321; Bernard and Rice, *Sunbelt Cities*, 47.
229	"word leaked out"	Branch, *Parting the Waters*, 357–358; White, *The Making of the President 1960*, 322; Wofford, *Of Kennedys and Kings*, 18–19; Strober and Strober, *The Kennedy Presidency*, 35–36.
230	"I was concerned"	Wofford, *Of Kennedys and Kings*, 19–21; Guthman and Shulman, *Robert Kennedy in His Own Words*, 70; Matthews, *Kennedy and Nixon*, 172; Wicker, *One of Us*, 239–240; Nixon, *Six Crises*, 362–363.
230	"fathers, don't we"	Branch, *Parting the Waters*, 365–366; Brauer, *John F. Kennedy and the Second Reconstruction*, 47–50; Ambrose, *Nixon: The Education of a Politician*, 596–597; Sorensen, *Kennedy*, 33.
230	"from West Berlin"	*New York Times* (October 8, 1960).
231	"performance art"	Stich, *Yves Klein*, 80–81, 171–172; *New York Times* (December 11, 2005); *Historical Methods* (September 2002).
231	"splashes of color"	*New York Times* (April 3, 1960).

231	"Ralph Houk"	Reisler, *The Best Game Ever*, 244; *New York Times* (October 19, 1960); Golenbock, *Dynasty*, 400.
231	"suspended sentence"	*New York Times* (October 18, 1960, and January 18, 1962); Stone and Yohn, *Prime Time and Misdemeanors*, 296–299.
231	"else to do"	Davies, *The Beatles*, 116–117.
232	"a club date"	*New Yorker* (June 4, 2007); *Time* (June 8, 1998).
232	"quite the same"	Lennon, McCartney, Harrison, and Starr, *The Beatles Anthology*, 191–192; Billboard website.
233	"entomological tribute"	Lennon, McCartney, Harrison, and Starr, *The Beatles Anthology*, 22; *New Yorker* (October 16, 2000, and June 4, 2007).
233	"become a career"	Davies, *The Beatles*, 114–116, 121–127; Pritchard and Lysaght, *The Beatles*, 38–40, 51; *Maclean's* (December 1, 2008); Miles, *The Beatles: A Diary*, 28.
234	"the music scene"	Gordy, *To Be Loved*, 103, 130–138; *Chicago Sun-Times* (September 30, 2001).
234	"any of that"	Bego, *Aretha Franklin*, 19–21, 37–39, 44; *Billboard* (February 9, 2008).
234	"year to come"	Henderson, *'Scuse Me While I Kiss the Sky*, 52–54.
235	"the first time"	Miles, *The Beatles: A Diary*, 29; Pritchard and Lysaght, *The Beatles*, 49; Davies, *The Beatles*, 136–142.

12. NOVEMBER: THE HELP OF A FEW CLOSE FRIENDS

Page	**Paragraph(s) Ending**	**Sources**
237	"a selling job"	Smathers oral history; Johnson oral history.
238	"Democratic Party"	*Time* (October 24, 1960); Bass and DeVries, *The Transformation of South-*

		ern Politics, 194–196; *New York Times* (July 20, 1960); Cohodas, *Strom Thurmond and the Politics of Southern Change*, 313–314.
238	"happened, he knew"	Dallek, *Lone Star Rising*, 586–588; Miller, *Lyndon*, 270–271; Donaldson, *The First Modern Campaign*, 136–137.
238	"at 25,000 feet"	Ambrose, *Nixon: The Education of a Politician*, 580; Donaldson, *The First Modern Campaign*, 130–131.
240	"of white voters"	White, *The Making of the President 1960*, 233; Scammon and Wattenberg, *The Real Majority*, 369; Brauer, *John F. Kennedy and the Second Reconstruction*, 47–50; Matthews, *Kennedy and Nixon*, 173; Branch, *Parting the Waters*, 372–373.
240	"I relieved him"	Roper Center for Public Opinion Research website; Ewald, *Eisenhower the President*, 311; Mazo and Hess, *Nixon*, 239–241; Wicker, *One of Us*, 242–243.
240	"by my conduct"	Nixon, *RN*, 221–223; Ambrose, *Nixon: The Education of a Politician*, 600–601.
241	"more of it"	Oakley, *God's Country*, 420–421; *New York Times* (November 5, 1960); Nixon, *Six Crises*, 369; Ambrose, *Eisenhower: The President*, 602.
241	"up for grabs"	*New York Times* (November 3, 1960); Goodwin, *Remembering America*, 122–123; Matthews, *Kennedy and Nixon*, 175.
242	"could be done"	Runyon, Verdini, and Runyon, *Source Book of American Presidential Campaign and Election Statistics*, 275–276; Crespi and Mendelsohn, *Polls, Television, and the New Politics*, 80–81; Ambrose, *Nixon: The Education of a Politician*, 604; Reinsch,

		Getting Elected, 157–158; Sorensen, *Kennedy,* 210; O'Donnell and Powers, *Johnny, We Hardly Knew Ye,* 221; Nixon, *RN,* 218.
242	"Maybe we do"	Persico, *Edward R. Murrow,* 460; Kendrick, *Prime Time,* 453; *Time* (December 5, 1960).
242	"in April 1971"	*New York Times* (November 16, 1960, and April 9, 1971); Boorstin, *The Americans: The Democratic Experience,* 73.
242	"PDP-8 in 1965"	*Technology Review* (August 2005); *Computer Design* (January 1991); *Forbes* (July 7, 1997); *Security Distributing and Marketing* (January 2002).
243	"within 10 years"	Oakley, *God's Country,* 413; *New York Times* (November 28, 1960, and May 18, 1997); *Time* (December 5, 1960).
243	"episodes in all"	*New York Times* (August 11, 1960, and December 4, 1960); *Time* (August 29, 1960).
243	"available everywhere"	*New York Times* (November 18, 1960); *Time* (December 5, 1960).
244	"an unknown quantity"	Beschloss, *The Crisis Years,* 31; Taubman, *Khrushchev,* 485.
244	"out of control"	Jones and Kevill, *China and the Soviet Union,* 21–22; Beschloss, *The Crisis Years,* 43; Ulam, *Expansion and Coexistence,* 637–638; Gunther, *Inside Europe Today,* 335; Taubman, *Khrushchev,* 472.
245	"in the uprising"	Oakley, *God's Country,* 392–393; Rusk, *As I Saw It,* 430–431; Karnow, *Vietnam,* 252–253; *New York Times* (November 11, 1960, and November 12, 1960); *Time* (November 28, 1960).
245	"come from Hanoi"	Jones, *Death of a Generation,* 17–18; Duiker, *Ho Chi Minh,* 523–526;

		Ulam, *The Rivals*, 345; Karnow, *Vietnam*, 254–256.
245	"to comprehend"	Stevenson, *The End of Nowhere*, 124; Eisenhower, *Waging Peace*, 608–609; *New York Times* (December 10, 1960).
246	"or without them"	Stevenson, *The End of Nowhere*, 118–120; *Time* (January 6, 1961); Eisenhower, *Waging Peace*, 609–610.
246	"few weeks later"	*Washington Post* (October 11, 1997); Blake, *The Master Builders*, 221; Goldberg oral history.
247	"do with living"	Larson and Pridmore, *Chicago Architecture and Design*, 186; *Chicago Sun-Times* (October 10, 1997); *New York Times* (December 19, 1950); Goldberg oral history.
247	"on a stem"	Saliga, *The Sky's The Limit*, 189–190; Larson and Pridmore, *Chicago Architecture and Design*, 188–190; *Chicago Sun-Times* (September 29, 2003); *Chicago Tribune* (October 9, 1997).
247	"optimism in general"	*Chicago Tribune* (November 20, 2010); Goldberg oral history; *Washington Post* (October 11, 1997).
248	"and my time"	Goldberg oral history; *Chicago Tribune* (October 9, 1997).
248	"said J. Wrong"	*Harvard Law Review* (December 1988); *New York Times* (November 16, 1960, and August 8, 1988); Baker, *The Second Battle of New Orleans*, 94, 106, 360, 423; *Time* (December 5, 1960).
249	"few hours later"	Baker, *The Second Battle of New Orleans*, 315, 321–323, 332; *Time* (September 5, 1960); *New York Times* (November 9, 1960, November 11, 1960, and November 14, 1960).
249	"for me also"	*Chicago Tribune* (March 23, 1993); Baker, *The Second Battle of New Orleans*, 393.

250   "stayed until   *Time* (November 28, 1960); *People*
        dismissal"   (December 4, 1995); Baker, *The
                                Second Battle of New Orleans,* 401;
                                New York Times (November 15,
                                1960).

250   "would kill me"   *New York Times* (November 17,
                                1960); Baker, *The Second Battle of
                                New Orleans,* 411; *Time* (Decem-
                                ber 12, 1960).

251   "and sickened sorrow"   Steinbeck, *Travels with Charley,*
                                224–229

251   "deal with it"   Baker, *The Second Battle of New
                                Orleans,* 433–435; *Time* (December 12,
                                1960); Nichols, *A Matter of Justice,*
                                260.

251   "on migrant workers"   *Time* (December 5, 1960).

251   "war on poverty"   *New York Times* (November 28, 1960,
                                and October 7, 2000).

252   "into their accounts"   *Time* (December 5, 1960).

252   "demanding of quality"   Tussman, *Obligation and the Body
                                Politic,* 106–107; *San Francisco
                                Chronicle* (October 30, 2005); *Polity*
                                (October 1999).

252   "November 8 coverage"   *New York Times* (November 6, 1960).

253   "would top $10,000"   *New York Times* (November 8, 1960,
                                and November 9, 1960); White,
                                The Making of the President 1960, 4;
                                O'Brien, *No Final Victories,* 94–95;
                                Sorensen, *Kennedy,* 211; O'Donnell
                                and Powers, *Johnny, We Hardly
                                Knew Ye,* 222; Reinsch, *Getting
                                Elected,* 158.

253   "Eastern time zone"   *New York Times* (November 9, 1960);
                                Nixon, *Six Crises,* 376–379; Nixon,
                                RN, 223; Klein, *Making It Perfectly
                                Clear,* 51; Ambrose, *Nixon: The Edu-
                                cation of a Politician,* 604–606.

254   "real close election"   *Time* (November 16, 1960); Donald-
                                son, *The First Modern Campaign,*
                                144–147; White, *The Making of the*

		President 1960, 12–14; Nixon, *Six Crises*, 380.
254	"boosting his total"	Donaldson, *The First Modern Campaign*, 144–147; Seigenthaler oral history; White, *The Making of the President 1960*, 20–21.
255	"Democratic counties"	Bradlee, *Conversations With Kennedy*, 33; Valenti, *This Time, This Place*, 66.
255	"as did Nixon"	*New York Times* (November 10, 1960); Wicker, *One of Us*, 248–250; White, *The Making of the President 1960*, 23–24; Nixon, *RN*, 223; O'Brien, *No Final Victories*, 96.
256	"a new baby"	Sorensen, *Kennedy*, 212; Thomas, *The Pursuit of the White House*, 170–171; Nixon, *Six Crises*, 397; Reinsch, *Getting Elected*, 158–160; *New York Times* (November 10, 1960).
256	"by the people"	McGillivray, Scammon, and Cook, *America at the Polls, passim*; Nixon, *Six Crises*, 294; Peirce, *The People's President*, 105; Mazo and Hess, *Nixon*, 247–249; Hersh, *The Dark Side of Camelot*, 132.
257	"it for 1964"	Nixon, *RN*, 224; White, *Breach of Faith*, 71; Matthews, *Kennedy and Nixon*, 182–187.
257	"the Electoral College"	Nixon, *RN*, 221; Runyon, Verdini, and Runyon, *Source Book of American Presidential Campaign and Election Statistics*, 275–276; Scammon and Wattenberg, *The Real Majority*, 369; Brauer, *John F. Kennedy and the Second Reconstruction*, 58–59; Pool, Abelson, and Popkin, *Candidates, Issues, and Strategies*, 117–118.
258	"in his memoirs"	Finch oral history; U.S. Bureau of Labor Statistics website; Mazo and

| | | Hess, *Nixon*, 243; Eastland oral history; Oakley, *God's Country*, 422. |
| 258 | "John F. Kennedy Jr." | Matthews, *Kennedy and Nixon*, 183; Salinger, *With Kennedy*, 60; Parmet, *JFK*, 71–72; *Time* (December 5, 1960). |

13. DECEMBER: THE CAN-DO SOCIETY

Page	Paragraph(s) Ending	Sources
259	"two days later"	National Aeronautics and Space Administration website; *Time* (December 5, 1960, and December 12, 1960); *New York Times* (December 2, 1960, and December 3, 1960); Cadbury, *Space Race*, 224–225; Schefter, *The Race*, 121.
260	"replied mystically"	Schefter, *The Race*, 107–109; Cadbury, *Space Race*, 205, 225–228.
260	"as a precaution"	*New York Times* (November 9, 1960, and November 22, 1960); Glenn, *John Glenn*, 230–231; Cadbury, *Space Race*, 219.
261	"none at all"	*Time* (December 5, 1960); Schefter, *The Race*, 114–116; Lewis, *Appointment on the Moon*, 110–111; *New York Times* (December 20, 1960).
261	"on the moon"	Schefter, *The Race*, 103; Lewis, *Appointment on the Moon*, 160; Ambrose, *Eisenhower: The President*, 591; Boorstin, *The Americans: The Democratic Experience*, 592–593.
261	"decide until 1962"	Hansen, *First Man*, 155–159; Armstrong oral history.
262	"made matters worse"	Thompson, *Light This Candle*, xiii, 234; Glenn, *John Glenn*, 220–221, 232.
262	"be Alan Shepard"	Glenn, *John Glenn*, 233; Shepard oral history; Wainwright, *The Great American Magazine*, 272–273;

		Thompson, *Light This Candle,* ix–x, 234.
263	"will be Algerian"	*Time* (December 19, 1960, December 26, 1960, and January 2, 1961); Williams, *The Last Great Frenchman,* 403–404; *New York Times* (December 21, 1960); Maier and White, *The Thirteenth of May,* 379.
263	"continuance impossible"	*New York Times* (December 15, 1960); Emerson, *From Empire to Nation,* 20, 407.
263	"all next year"	Pro Football Reference website; *New York Times* (December 25, 1960, and December 27, 1960); Maraniss, *When Pride Still Mattered,* 260–265.
264	"for peaceful purposes"	*Time* (December 26, 1960); Cohen, *Israel and the Bomb,* 83–93; *Middle East Policy* (Summer 2006); *Washington Post* (February 19, 2006); *New York Times* (December 19, 1960).
264	"preparations continued"	Wyden, *Bay of Pigs,* 69, 72–73; Manchester, *The Glory and the Dream,* 863–867; Ambrose, *Eisenhower: The President,* 608.
264	"power until 1997"	Reader, *Africa,* 661; *Time* (December 12, 1960); Edgerton, *The Troubled Heart of Africa,* 195–196; De Witte, *The Assassination of Lumumba,* 97.
265	"go down, too"	*New York Times* (December 13, 1960, and December 20, 1960); Peirce, *The People's President,* 106–108; Thomas, *The Pursuit of the White House,* 206.
265	"Byrd 15"	Peirce, *The People's President,* 108; Barnett oral history; *New York Times* (December 20, 1960).
266	"like the publicity"	*New York Times* (December 17, 1960); *Time* (December 26, 1960); Schlesinger, *A Thousand Days,* 161–162; Sorensen, *Kennedy,* 238–239.

266	"half to come"	Reeves, *President Kennedy*, 21–23; Clifford, *Counsel to the President*, 341–342; Ambrose, *Eisenhower: The President*, 606–607; Schlesinger, *A Thousand Days*, 125.
266	"in Cook County"	Reeves, *President Kennedy*, 25; Matthews, *Kennedy and Nixon*, 187.
267	"for the job"	Guthman and Shulman, *Robert Kennedy in His Own Words*, 38–39; Isaacson and Thomas, *The Wise Men*, 591–592; *Time* (December 12, 1960); Steel, *Walter Lippmann and the American Century*, 523–524.
267	"Confederate army"	Schlesinger, *A Thousand Days*, 138; Halberstam, *The Best and the Brightest*, 31; Isaacson and Thomas, *The Wise Men*, 593–596; Guthman and Shulman, *Robert Kennedy in His Own Words*, 5; *Time* (December 19, 1960); Acheson oral history; Rusk, *As I Saw It*, 202–205.
267	"a great blow"	Martin, *Adlai Stevenson and the World*, 558–559, 563; Walton, *The Remnants of Power*, 19.
268	"a daily basis"	Isaacson and Thomas, *The Wise Men*, 596–597; Halberstam, *The Best and the Brightest*, 10, 215; *New York Times* (December 14, 1960).
269	"It's Bobby"	Guthman and Shulman, *Robert Kennedy in His Own Words*, 42; Clifford, *Counsel to the President*, 336–337; Schlesinger, *A Thousand Days*, 142.
269	"for sheriff once"	*New York Times* (December 18, 1960); Parmet, *JFK*, 66; Manchester, *Portrait of a President*, 73–74; Schlesinger, *A Thousand Days*, 144; Halberstam, *The Best and the Brightest*, 41.
270	"ain't fine, man"	*Playboy* (March 1978); Shelton, *No Direction Home*, 52.

270	"in coffeehouses"	Shelton, *No Direction Home*, 53, 65–66, 75; Sounes, *Down the Highway*, 42.
271	"return to school"	*Entertainment Weekly* (September 26, 1997); Shelton, *No Direction Home*, 75; *Playboy* (March 1978); Sounes, *Down the Highway*, 68.
271	"of Minnesota"	Shelton, *No Direction Home*, 75, 85–87, 100–102; Sounes, *Down the Highway*, 70; Heylin, *Bob Dylan*, 12–13; *Playboy* (March 1978); Rotolo, *A Freewheelin' Time*, 10; *Weekly Standard* (January 1, 2001).
271	"wants to do"	*New York Times* (April 13, 1963); Pulitzer Prizes website; *Los Angeles* (September 2005).
272	"the coming year"	*Time* (December 19, 1960); *New York Times* (December 6, 1960, and December 11, 1960); *Human Rights* (Summer 2007); *Washington Post* (January 20, 2009).
272	"the decade ahead"	U.S. Census Bureau, *Census of Population: 1950*, IV-3B:15; U.S. Census Bureau: *Census of Population: 1960*, I:158.
273	"said than done"	*Time* (December 7, 1959, and January 18, 1960); Wilson, *Crossing Learning Boundaries by Choice*, 167–176.
273	"and the South"	Ashmore, *Unseasonable Truths*, 399; Ashmore, *The Other Side of Jordan*, 13; *Time* (May 30, 1960).
274	"a nervous time"	U.S. Census Bureau, *Census of Population: 1960*, I-34:47; *New York Times* (September 22, 1960, October 21, 1960, January 25, 1961, and June 7, 1961); *White Plains Journal News* (August 12, 2002); Ashmore, *The Other Side of Jordan*, 153–155.
274	"birds, and fish"	*Anchorage Daily News* (November 20, 2005); *National Journal* (December 15, 1979).

274	"games in 1960"	*Time* (December 19, 1960).
274	"UN's intervention"	*New York Times* (December 15, 1960); *Time* (December 26, 1960).
274	"intense controversy"	*Time* (November 21, 1960, and December 19, 1960); *New York Times* (December 10, 1960).
275	"forces of history"	Woodward, *The Burden of Southern History,* 188–189.
275	"invasion was imminent"	*New York Times* (January 1, 1961); Walton, *The Remnants of Power,* 26–27.
275	"daughter's questions"	Ambrose, *Nixon: The Education of a Politician,* 608; *Time* (January 13, 1961); Nixon, *In the Arena,* 195.
276	"the big cities"	*New York Times* (December 2, 1960); *Time* (November 21, 1960, and December 12, 1960); Bradlee, *Conversations With Kennedy,* 121; Collier and Horowitz, *The Rockefellers,* 344.
276	"another public office"	*Time* (November 21, 1960); Goldberg, *Barry Goldwater,* 147; *New York Times* (December 2, 1960).
277	"would be Nixon's"	Ambrose, *Nixon: The Education of a Politician,* 608; *New York Times* (February 18, 1996); Witcover, *The Resurrection of Richard Nixon,* 26; *Time* (December 12, 1960, and January 13, 1961).
277	"bury Dick Nixon"	Parmet, *Richard Nixon and His America,* 358, 411–412; Wicker, *One of Us,* 251; Ambrose, *Nixon: The Education of a Politician,* 607; *Time* (November 21, 1960).

14. EPILOGUE: PASSING THE TORCH

Page	Paragraph(s) Ending	Sources
279	"among all peoples"	Beschloss, *The Crisis Years,* 46–47.
280	"inwardly digest it"	*Time* (February 3, 1961); Bourne, *Fidel,* 215–216; Eisenhower, *Waging*

		Peace, 613; Paterson, *Contesting Castro,* 258; Higgins, *The Perfect Failure,* 70–71; Brown, *The Faces of Power,* 163–164; Taubman, *Khrushchev,* 487.
280	"was the U-2"	Halberstam, *The Fifties,* 712; Beschloss, *Mayday,* 348–349; Gates oral history.
281	"of May 1960"	Taubman, *Khrushchev,* 446–447, 468; Beschloss, *Mayday,* 325, 384–386; Brzezinski, *Red Moon Rising,* 272.
281	"as he departed"	Peirce, *The People's President,* 17–19; *New York Times* (January 7, 1961).
282	"procedure throughout"	Oakley, *God's Country,* 421; Finch oral history; O'Brien oral history.
282	"posed the question"	George, *God's Salesman,* 192, 206–208; Carty, *A Catholic in the White House?* 62; Sherman, *No Place for a Woman,* 181–183.
283	"sincerely regret it"	Salinger, *With Kennedy,* 56–59; *Presidential Studies Quarterly* (Summer 1999); Crouse, *The Boys on the Bus,* 37.
283	"after turning 30"	Sorensen, *Kennedy,* 37; Bellow, *In Praise of Nepotism,* 448.
284	"of political tactics"	Ambrose, *Nixon: The Triumph of a Politician,* 121, 145; Wicker, *One of Us,* 256; White, *Breach of Faith,* 71; Barber, *The Presidential Character,* 163; Nixon, *RN,* 225–226.
284	"up the scaffold"	Oakley, *God's Country,* 424.
284	"decades to come"	Eisenhower, *Waging Peace,* 615; Manchester, *The Glory and the Dream,* 877; Ambrose, *Eisenhower: The President,* 612.
285	"toward Indochina"	Clifford, *Counsel to the President,* 342–343; Ambrose, *Eisenhower: The President,* 614–615; Rusk, *As I Saw It,* 428; Jones, *Death of a Generation,* 5–7.
285	"suitably impressed"	Ambrose, *Eisenhower: The President,* 609, 614–615; Eisenhower, *Waging Peace,* 617.

286	"were commonplace"	Gitlin, *The Sixties*, 81; Sorensen, *Kennedy*, 22; Rusk, *As I Saw It*, 293; O'Neill, *Coming Apart*, 23–24.
286	"the 20th century"	*New York Times* (January 9, 1961); Williams, *The Last Great Frenchman*, 404–405; Reader, *Africa*, 667.
287	"our vacation time"	Baker, *The Second Battle of New Orleans*, 478–481; *New York Times* (January 11, 1961); *Time* (January 20, 1961); *Journal of Blacks in Higher Education* (Summer 2006).
287	"percent in 1997"	Horowitz, *Betty Friedan and the Making of the Feminine Mystique*, 227; Caplow, Hicks, and Wattenberg, *The First Measured Century*, 82–83; U.S. Census Bureau website.
288	"and more political"	McLaughlin, *The Pill, John Rock, and the Church*, 36; *New York Times* (June 14, 1961); Encyclopedia of Chicago website; *New Yorker* (June 26, 2006).
288	"to get started"	Sale, *SDS*, 24–25; Ashmore, *Hearts and Minds*, 428–429; *Nation* (March 26, 1988); Sorensen, *Kennedy*, 210.
289	"by morning"	*Time* (January 27, 1961); Eisenhower, *Waging Peace*, 617.
289	"works from memory"	Reinsch, *Getting Elected*, 164–168; *New York Times* (January 21, 1961); Parmet, *JFK*, 4; Schlesinger, *A Thousand Days*, 3.
290	"of civil rights"	Sorensen, *Kennedy*, 240–243; Schlesinger, *A Thousand Days*, 163; Galbraith oral history; Reeves, *President Kennedy*, 39.
291	"in the republic"	*Wall Street Journal* (January 20, 2009); American Presidency Project website; *New York Times* (January 21, 1961); Kennedy, *Public Papers of President John F. Kennedy, 1961*, 2;

		Benson, *The True Adventures of John Steinbeck, Writer*, 892.
291	"minute of it"	Parmet, *JFK*, 7; Sorensen, *Kennedy*, 240; Johnson oral history; Dallek, *Flawed Giant*, 44.
292	"sense of purpose"	Ambrose, *Nixon: The Education of a Politician*, 608; Nixon, *RN*, 227–228, 237; White, *Breach of Faith*, 72.
292	"been dashed forever"	Wainwright, *The Great American Magazine*, 272–273; *New York Times* (May 3, 1961).
293	"I certainly have"	Bond, *Heroes in Space*, 12–13; *New York Times* (April 13, 1961); Cadbury, *Space Race*, 240–241.
293	"to accomplish"	*New York Times* (May 6, 1961); Glenn, *John Glenn*, 237; Cadbury, *Space Race*, 244–247; Boorstin, *The Americans: The Democratic Experience*, 594–596.
294	"race was on"	Shepard oral history; Glenn, *John Glenn*, 237; *New York Times* (August 8, 1961, and February 22, 1962).
294	"for the worst"	Kennedy, *Public Papers of President John F. Kennedy, 1961*, 19–27; Brown, *The Faces of Power*, 159.
295	"my night's sleep"	*New York Times* (January 31, 1961); Walton, *Cold War and Counterrevolution*, 6–7; Oakley, *God's Country*, 356; *Presidential Studies Quarterly* (December 2003); Brown, *The Faces of Power*, 160–161; Alsop, *I've Seen the Best of It*, 415.
295	"ever received it"	Kennedy, *Public Papers of President John F. Kennedy, 1961*, 19–22, 658–659; Hersh, *The Dark Side of Camelot*, 165–167; U.S. Senate Select Committee to Study Governmental Operations, *Alleged Assassination Plots Involving Foreign Leaders*, 73.

296	"hundred times worse"	Wyden, *Bay of Pigs*, 87–90, 294–295; Hersh, *The Dark Side of Camelot*, 208; Nixon, *RN*, 234; Stevenson, *The End of Nowhere*, 129.
296	"Laotian government"	Adams and McCoy, *Laos*, 160; *New York Times* (March 27, 1961).
296	"the armed forces"	Stacks, *Scotty*, 3–4; Schlesinger, *A Thousand Days*, 375; Kennedy, *Public Papers of President John F. Kennedy, 1961*, 533–534; Balfour, *West Germany*, 204–205; *New York Times* (August 19, 1961, and August 26, 1961).
297	"distant hope indeed"	Karnow, *Vietnam*, 265; Kennedy, *Public Papers of President John F. Kennedy, 1961*, 533–534; *New York Times* (October 12, 1961, December 12, 1961, and February 25, 1962); Guthman and Shulman, *Robert Kennedy in His Own Words*, 258.
298	"can be free"	*Time* (January 27, 1961); Reinsch, *Getting Elected*, 167–168; Eisenhower and Eisenhower, *Going Home to Glory*, 3–4; Ambrose, *Eisenhower: The President*, 616.
298	"Secret Service agent"	Ambrose, *Eisenhower: The President*, 610, 617.
299	"42 presidents"	*New York Times* (July 29, 1962); Ulam, *The Rivals*, 233; *New Republic* (May 9, 1983); C-SPAN website.
299	"Much worse"	Kennedy, *The Strategy of Peace*, 69; Hoffmann, *Theodore H. White and Journalism as Illusion*, 143; White, *In Search of History*, 403, 408; Sorensen, *Kennedy*, 178; Goodwin, *Remembering America*, 73–74.
300	"tell you that"	Ambrose, *Eisenhower: The President*, 603; Eisenhower, *Waging Peace*, 601–602; Beschloss, *Mayday*, 388; Oakley, *God's Country*, 433.

Bibliography

ORAL HISTORIES

The following abbreviations identify the sources of oral histories: AIC—Art Institute of Chicago; DDE—Dwight D. Eisenhower Presidential Library and Museum; HST—Harry S. Truman Library and Museum; JFK—John F. Kennedy Presidential Library and Museum; LBJ—Lyndon Baines Johnson Library and Museum; NASA—National Aeronautics and Space Administration; SHO—U.S. Senate Historical Office; UVA—University of Virginia Miller Center of Public Affairs.

Acheson, Dean (JFK)
Alsop, Joseph (JFK)
Armstrong, Neil (NASA)
Ashmore, Harry (UVA)
Bailey, John (JFK)
Barnett, Ross (JFK)
Bartlett, Charles (JFK)
Bissell, Richard Jr. (DDE)
Bray, William (HST)
Carpenter, M. Scott (NASA)
De Paulo, J. Raymond (JFK)
Dilworth, Richardson (JFK)
Doyle, James (JFK)
Eastland, James (LBJ)
Edwards, India (UVA)

Farmer, James (LBJ)
Finch, Robert (DDE)
Galbraith, John Kenneth (JFK)
Gates, Thomas (DDE)
Glenn, John (JFK and NASA)
Goldberg, Bertrand (AIC)
Goldwater, Barry (DDE and JFK)
Hewitt, Don (JFK)
Hodges, Luther (UVA)
Humphrey, Hubert (JFK and LBJ)
Johnson, Claudia "Lady Bird" (JFK)
Lawrence, David (JFK)
Marshall, Thurgood (LBJ)
McPherson, Harry (LBJ)
O'Brien, Lawrence (LBJ)
Robertson, A. Willis (UVA)
Schirra, Walter Jr. (NASA)
Scott, Dorothye (SHO)
Seigenthaler, John (JFK)
Shepard, Alan (NASA)
Smathers, George (SHO)
Stanton, Frank (JFK)
Stowe, David (HST)
Symington, James (UVA)
Valenti, Jack (JFK)
Voas, Robert (NASA)

Government Publications

Kennedy, John. *Public Papers of President John F. Kennedy, 1961*. Washington, DC: United States Government Printing Office, 1962.
National Center for Health Statistics. *Health, United States, 2009*. Washington: United States Government Printing Office, 2010.
United States Census Bureau. *Census of Population: 1950*. Washington: United States Government Printing Office, 1951–1953.
United States Census Bureau. *Census of Population: 1960*. Washington: United States Government Printing Office, 1961–1963.
United States Census Bureau. *Historical Statistics of the United States: Colonial Times to 1970*. Washington: United States Government Printing Office, 1975.

United States Congress. *Congressional Record*. 86th Congress, 2nd Session. Washington: United States Government Printing Office, 1960.

United States Department of State. *Background Notes on Laos*. Washington: United States Government Printing Office, 2009.

United States Environmental Protection Agency. *Municipal Solid Waste Generation, Recycling, and Disposal in the United States*. Washington: United States Government Printing Office, 2008.

United States Senate Select Committee to Study Governmental Operations With Respect to Intelligence Activities. *Alleged Assassination Plots Involving Foreign Leaders*. Washington: United States Government Printing Office, 1975.

Books

Abramson, Rudy. *Spanning the Century*. New York: William Morrow and Co., 1992.

Adams, Nina, and Alfred McCoy, eds. *Laos*. New York: Harper & Row, 1970.

Alexander, Charles. *Holding the Line*. Bloomington, Indiana: Indiana University Press, 1975.

Alexander, Edgar. *Adenauer and the New Germany*. New York: Farrar, Straus, and Cudahy, 1957.

Alinder, Mary Street. *Ansel Adams*. New York: Henry Holt and Co., 1996.

Allyn, David. *Make Love, Not War*. Boston: Little, Brown, and Co., 2000.

Alsop, Joseph. *I've Seen the Best of It*. New York: W.W. Norton and Co., 1992.

Ambrose, Stephen. *Eisenhower: The President*. New York: Simon & Schuster, 1984.

Ambrose, Stephen. *Nixon: The Education of a Politician, 1913–1962*. New York: Simon & Schuster, 1987.

Ambrose, Stephen. *Nixon: The Triumph of a Politician, 1962–1972*. New York: Simon & Schuster, 1989.

Anderson, Graham, and Ben Roskrow. *The Channel Tunnel Story*. London: Chapman & Hall, 1994.

Andrew, John III. *The Other Side of the Sixties*. New Brunswick, New Jersey: Rutgers University Press, 1997.

Asbell, Bernard. *The Pill*. New York: Random House, 1995.

Ashmore, Harry, ed. *Britannica Book of the Year 1961*. Chicago: Encyclopedia Britannica, 1961.

Ashmore, Harry. *Hearts and Minds.* New York: McGraw-Hill, 1982.

Ashmore, Harry. *The Other Side of Jordan.* New York: W.W. Norton and Co., 1960.

Ashmore, Harry. *Unseasonable Truths.* Boston: Little, Brown, and Co., 1989.

Baar, James, and William Howard. *Polaris.* New York: Harcourt, Brace, and Co., 1960.

Baker, Liva. *The Second Battle of New Orleans.* New York: Harper-Collins, 1996.

Balfour, Michael. *West Germany.* New York: St. Martin's Press, 1982.

Barber, James David. *The Presidential Character.* Englewood Cliffs, New Jersey: Prentice Hall, 1992.

Bartley, Numan. *The New South, 1945–1980.* Baton Rouge, Louisiana: Louisiana State University Press, 1995.

Bascomb, Neal. *Hunting Eichmann.* Boston: Houghton Mifflin Harcourt, 2009.

Bass, Jack, and Walter DeVries. *The Transformation of Southern Politics.* New York: Meridian, 1977.

Beach, Edward. *Around the World Submerged.* New York: Holt, Rinehart, and Winston, 1962.

Beach, Edward. *Salt and Steel.* Annapolis, Maryland: Naval Institute Press, 1999.

Bego, Mark. *Aretha Franklin.* New York: Da Capo Press, 2001.

Bellow, Adam. *In Praise of Nepotism.* New York: Doubleday, 2003.

Benfey, Otto, and Peter Morris, eds. *Robert Burns Woodward.* Philadelphia: Chemical Heritage Foundation, 2001.

Benson, Jackson. *The True Adventures of John Steinbeck, Writer.* New York: Penguin, 1990.

Berman, Edgar. *Hubert.* New York: G. P. Putnam's Sons, 1979.

Bernard, Richard, and Bradley Rice, eds. *Sunbelt Cities.* Austin, Texas: University of Texas Press, 1983.

Beschloss, Michael. *The Crisis Years.* New York: HarperCollins, 1991.

Beschloss, Michael. *Mayday.* New York: Harper & Row, 1986.

Blake, Peter. *The Master Builders.* New York: W.W. Norton and Co., 1996.

Bonazzi, Robert. *Man in the Mirror.* Maryknoll, New York: Orbis, 1997.

Bond, Peter. *Heroes in Space.* New York: Basil Blackwell, 1987.

Boorstin, Daniel. *The Americans: The Democratic Experience.* New York: Random House, 1973.

Bourne, Peter. *Fidel.* New York: Dodd, Mead, & Co., 1986.

Bradlee, Benjamin. *Conversations With Kennedy.* New York: W.W. Norton and Co., 1975.

Brady, Frank. *Hefner.* New York: Macmillan, 1974.

Branch, Taylor. *Parting the Waters.* New York: Simon & Schuster, 1988.

Brauer, Carl. *John F. Kennedy and the Second Reconstruction.* New York: Columbia University Press, 1977.

Bromberg, Joan Lisa. *The Laser in America, 1950–1970.* Cambridge, Massachusetts: MIT Press, 1991.

Brosnan, Jim. *The Long Season.* Chicago: Ivan R. Dee, 2002.

Brown, Seyom. *The Faces of Power.* New York: Columbia University Press, 1968.

Bruno, Jerry. *The Advance Man.* New York: William Morrow and Co., 1971.

Brunt, Stephen. *Facing Ali.* Guilford, Connecticut: Lyons Press, 2002.

Brzezinski, Matthew. *Red Moon Rising.* New York: Henry Holt and Co., 2007.

Burke, Larry, and Peter Thomas Fornatale. *Change Up.* Emmaus, Pennsylvania: Rodale, 2008.

Burns, James MacGregor. *Edward Kennedy and the Camelot Legacy.* New York: W.W. Norton and Co., 1976.

Cadbury, Deborah. *Space Race.* New York: HarperCollins, 2006.

Campbell-Kelly, Martin, and William Aspray. *Computer.* New York: Basic Books, 1996.

Cannon, Lou. *President Reagan.* New York: PublicAffairs Books, 2000.

Caplow, Theodore, Louis Hicks, and Ben Wattenberg. *The First Measured Century.* Washington: AEI Press, 2001.

Caro, Robert. *Master of the Senate.* New York: Alfred A. Knopf, 2002.

Caro, Robert. *The Path to Power.* New York: Alfred A. Knopf, 1982.

Carson, Rachel. *Silent Spring.* Boston: Houghton Mifflin, 1987.

Carter, Jimmy. *Turning Point.* New York: Times Books, 1992.

Carty, Thomas. *A Catholic in the White House?* New York: Palgrave Macmillan, 2004.

Chafe, William. *Civilities and Civil Rights.* New York: Oxford University Press, 1981.

Chichester, Francis. *Alone Across the Atlantic.* London: George Allen and Unwin, 1961.

Clifford, Clark. *Counsel to the President.* New York: Random House, 1991.

Clymer, Adam. *Drawing the Line at the Big Ditch.* Lawrence, Kansas: University Press of Kansas, 2008.

Cohen, Avner. *Israel and the Bomb.* New York: Columbia University Press, 1998.

Cohodas, Nadine. *Strom Thurmond and the Politics of Southern Change.* New York: Simon & Schuster, 1993.

Collier, Peter, and David Horowitz. *The Rockefellers.* New York: Holt, Rinehart, and Winston, 1976.

Crankshaw, Edward. *Khrushchev.* New York: Viking, 1966.

Cray, Ed. *Chief Justice.* New York: Simon & Schuster, 1997.

Crespi, Irving, and Harold Mendelsohn. *Polls, Television, and the New Politics.* Scranton, Pennsylvania: Chandler, 1970.

Crouse, Timothy. *The Boys on the Bus.* New York: Ballantine, 1974.

Cunningham, David. *There's Something Happening Here.* Berkeley, California: University of California Press, 2004.

Dallek, Robert. *Flawed Giant.* New York: Oxford University Press, 1998.

Dallek, Robert. *Lone Star Rising.* New York: Oxford University Press, 1991.

Dallek, Robert. *An Unfinished Life.* Boston: Little, Brown, and Co., 2003.

Darton, Eric. *Divided We Stand.* New York: Basic Books, 1999.

Davenport-Hines, Richard. *The Pursuit of Oblivion.* New York: W.W. Norton and Co., 2002.

Davies, Hunter. *The Beatles.* New York: W.W. Norton and Co., 2002.

De Witte, Ludo. *The Assassination of Lumumba.* London: Verso, 2001.

Donaldson, Gary. *The First Modern Campaign.* Lanham, Maryland: Rowman & Littlefield, 2007.

Donovan, John. *Pat Robertson.* New York: Macmillan, 1988.

Duiker, William. *Ho Chi Minh.* New York: Hyperion, 2000.

Edgerton, Robert. *The Troubled Heart of Africa.* New York: St. Martin's Press, 2002.

Ehrlichman, John. *Witness to Power.* New York: Simon & Schuster, 1982.

Eisenhower, David, and Julie Nixon Eisenhower. *Going Home to Glory.* New York: Simon & Schuster, 2010.

Eisenhower, Dwight. *Waging Peace.* Garden City, New York: Doubleday and Co., 1965.

Eisenhower, Milton. *The President is Calling.* Garden City, New York: Doubleday and Co., 1974.

Eisinger, Robert. *The Evolution of Presidential Polling.* New York: Cambridge University Press, 2003.

Ellis, Charles. *Joe Wilson and the Creation of Xerox.* New York: John Wiley & Sons, 2006.

Emerson, Rupert. *From Empire to Nation.* Cambridge, Massachusetts: Harvard University Press, 1960.

Ewald, William Bragg Jr. *Eisenhower the President.* Englewood Cliffs, New Jersey: Prentice Hall, 1981.

Ezra, Michael. *Muhammad Ali.* Philadelphia: Temple University Press, 2009.

Felser, Larry. *The Birth of the New NFL.* Guilford, Connecticut: Lyons Press, 2008.

Fine, Ralph Adam. *The Great Drug Deception.* New York: Stein and Day, 1972.

Finler, Joel. *Hitchcock in Hollywood.* New York: Continuum, 1992.

Fite, Gilbert. *Richard B. Russell Jr.* Chapel Hill, North Carolina: University of North Carolina Press, 1991.

Fox, Stephen. *The American Conservation Movement.* Madison, Wisconsin: University of Wisconsin Press, 1985.

Freedman, Estelle, ed. *The Essential Feminist Reader.* New York: Modern Library, 2007.

Freedman, Marc. *Prime Time.* New York: PublicAffairs Books, 1999.

Freeman, Martha, ed. *Always, Rachel.* Boston: Beacon, 1995.

Friedan, Betty. *The Feminine Mystique.* New York: W. W. Norton and Co., 1997.

Friedan, Betty. *Life So Far.* New York: Simon & Schuster, 2000.

Galbraith, John Kenneth. *A Life in Our Times.* Boston: Houghton Mifflin, 1981.

Gates, Gary Paul. *Air Time.* New York: Berkley, 1979.

Gellman, Irwin. *The Contender.* New York: Free Press, 1999.

George, Carol. *God's Salesman.* New York: Oxford University Press, 1993.

Gillon, Steven. *Politics and Vision.* New York: Oxford University Press, 1987.

Gipe, George. *The Great American Sports Book.* Garden City, New York: Doubleday and Co., 1978.

Gitlin, Todd. *The Sixties.* New York: Bantam, 1993.

Glenn, John. *John Glenn.* New York: Bantam, 1999.

Goldberg, Robert Alan. *Barry Goldwater.* New Haven, Connecticut: Yale University Press, 1995.

Goldman, Eric. *The Tragedy of Lyndon Johnson.* New York: Alfred A. Knopf, 1969.

Golenbock, Peter. *Dynasty.* New York: Berkley, 1985.

Goodman, Paul. *Growing Up Absurd.* New York: Random House, 1960.

Goodman, Walter. *The Committee.* New York: Farrar, Straus, and Giroux, 1968.

Goodwin, Richard. *Remembering America.* Boston: Little, Brown, and Co., 1988.

Gordy, Berry. *To Be Loved.* New York: Warner Books, 1994.

Graebner, Norman, ed. *An Uncertain Tradition.* New York: McGraw-Hill, 1961.

Greenfield, Robert. *Timothy Leary.* Orlando, Florida: Harcourt, 2006.

Greenstein, Fred. *The Hidden-Hand Presidency.* New York: Basic Books, 1982.

Griffin, John Howard. *Black Like Me.* Cutchogue, New York: Buccaneer, 1989.

Gunther, John. *Inside Europe Today.* New York: Harper & Brothers, 1962.

Guthman, Edwin, and Jeffrey Shulman, eds. *Robert Kennedy in His Own Words.* New York: Bantam, 1988.

Haig, Matt. *Brand Failures.* Philadelphia: Kogan Page, 2003.

Halberstam, David. *The Best and the Brightest.* New York: Ballantine, 1992.

Halberstam, David. *The Children.* New York: Random House, 1998.

Halberstam, David. *The Fifties.* New York: Fawcett Columbine, 1993.

Halberstam, David. *Ho.* Lanham, Maryland: Rowman & Littlefield, 2007.

Hampton, Henry, and Steve Fayer. *Voices of Freedom.* New York: Bantam, 1990.

Hansen, James. *First Man.* New York: Simon & Schuster, 2005.

Harvey, Robert. *The Fall of Apartheid.* New York: Palgrave, 2001.

Hayden, Dolores. *Building Suburbia.* New York: Pantheon, 2003.

Hayden, Tom. *Rebel.* Los Angeles: Red Hen, 2003.

Hayes, Harold, ed. *Smiling Through the Apocalypse.* New York: McCall, 1969.

Henderson, David. *'Scuse Me While I Kiss the Sky.* New York: Atria, 2008.

Hersh, Seymour. *The Dark Side of Camelot.* Boston: Little, Brown, and Co., 1997.

Hewitt, Don. *Tell Me a Story.* New York: PublicAffairs Books, 2001.

Heylin, Clinton. *Bob Dylan.* New York: Schirmer Books, 1996.

Higgins, Trumbull. *The Perfect Failure.* New York: W.W. Norton and Co., 1987.

Hill, Margaret Hunt. *H.L. and Lyda.* Little Rock, Arkansas: August House, 1994.

Hoffmann, Joyce. *Theodore H. White and Journalism as Illusion.* Columbia, Missouri: University of Missouri Press, 1995.

Horowitz, Daniel. *Betty Friedan and the Making of The Feminine Mystique.* Amherst, Massachusetts: University of Massachusetts Press, 1998.

Hughes, Emmet John. *The Ordeal of Power.* New York: Atheneum, 1963.

Humphrey, Hubert. *The Education of a Public Man.* Minneapolis: University of Minnesota Press, 1991.

Hurt, Harry III. *Texas Rich.* New York: W.W. Norton and Co., 1981.

Isaacson, Walter, and Evan Thomas. *The Wise Men.* New York: Touchstone, 1988.

Jackson, John. *Big Beat Heat.* New York: Macmillan, 1991.

Jackson, Kenneth. *Crabgrass Frontier.* New York: Oxford University Press, 1985.

Jamieson, Kathleen Hall. *Packaging the Presidency.* New York: Oxford University Press, 1996.

Jeffrey, Kirk. *Machines In Our Hearts.* Baltimore: Johns Hopkins University Press, 2001.

Jones, Howard. *The Bay of Pigs.* New York: Oxford University Press, 2008.

Jones, Howard. *Death of a Generation.* New York: Oxford University Press, 2003.

Jones, Peter, and Sian Kevill. *China and the Soviet Union, 1949–84.* New York: Facts on File, 1985.

Karnow, Stanley. *Vietnam.* New York: Viking, 1991.

Kendrick, Alexander. *Prime Time.* Boston: Little, Brown, and Co., 1969.

Kennedy, John. *The Strategy of Peace.* New York: Popular Library, 1961.

Keogh, Pamela Clarke. *Elvis Presley.* New York: Atria, 2004.

Kevles, Bettyann Holtzman. *Almost Heaven.* New York: Basic Books, 2003.

Khrushchev, Sergei, ed. *Memoirs of Nikita Khrushchev, Statesman, 1953–1964.* University Park, Pennsylvania: Pennsylvania State University Press, 2007.

Khrushchev, Sergei. *Nikita Khrushchev and the Creation of a Superpower.* University Park, Pennsylvania: Pennsylvania State University Press, 2000.

Kinsey, Alfred, Wardell Pomeroy, and Clyde Martin. *Sexual Behavior in the Human Male.* Bloomington, Indiana: Indiana University Press, 1948.

Kisseloff, Jeff. *The Box.* New York: Viking, 1995.

Klein, Herbert. *Making It Perfectly Clear.* Garden City, New York: Doubleday and Co., 1980.

Kluger, Richard. *Ashes to Ashes.* New York: Alfred A. Knopf, 1996.

Kramer, Michael, and Sam Roberts. *I Never Wanted to Be Vice President of Anything.* New York: Basic Books, 1976.

Kraus, Sidney, ed. *The Great Debates.* Bloomington, Indiana: Indiana University Press, 1977.

Krier, James, and Edmund Ursin. *Pollution and Policy.* Berkeley, California: University of California Press, 1977.

Ladenson, Elisabeth. *Dirt For Art's Sake.* Ithaca, New York: Cornell University Press, 2007.

LaFeber, Walter. *The Clash.* New York: W.W. Norton and Co., 1997.

Lally, Kevin. *Wilder Times.* New York: Henry Holt and Co., 1996.

Large, David Clay. *Berlin.* New York: Basic Books, 2000.

Larson, George, and Jay Pridmore. *Chicago Architecture and Design.* New York: Harry N. Abrams, 1993.

Lash, Joseph. *Eleanor: The Years Alone.* New York: W.W. Norton and Co., 1972.

Lassiter, Matthew, and Andrew Lewis, eds. *The Moderates' Dilemma.* Charlottesville, Virginia: University Press of Virginia, 1998.

Lau, Peter. *Democracy Rising.* Lexington, Kentucky: University Press of Kentucky, 2006.

Leary, Timothy. *Flashbacks.* New York: G. P. Putnam's Sons, 1990.

Lennon, John, Paul McCartney, George Harrison, and Ringo Starr. *The Beatles Anthology.* San Francisco: Chronicle, 2000.

Leslie, Anita. *Francis Chichester.* New York: Walker and Co., 1975.

Leslie, Richard. *Pop Art.* New York: Todtri, 1997.

Lewis, Richard. *Appointment on the Moon.* New York: Viking, 1969.

Lewis, Tom. *Divided Highways.* New York: Viking, 1997.

Lobel, Michael. *Image Duplicator.* New Haven, Connecticut: Yale University Press, 2002.

Lodge, Henry Cabot. *As It Was.* New York: W. W. Norton and Co., 1976.

Lodge, Henry Cabot. *The Storm Has Many Eyes.* New York: W. W. Norton and Co., 1973.

Lustick, Ian. *Unsettled States, Disputed Lands.* Ithaca, New York: Cornell University Press, 1993.

Lytle, Mark Hamilton. *The Gentle Subversive.* New York: Oxford University Press, 2007.

MacMillan, Margaret. *Nixon and Mao.* New York: Random House, 2007.

Maier, Charles, and Dan White, eds. *The Thirteenth of May.* New York: Oxford University Press, 1968.

Major, John. *Prize Possession.* New York: Cambridge University Press, 1993.

Malkin, Peter, and Harry Stein. *Eichmann In My Hands.* New York: Warner Books, 1990.

Manchester, William. *The Glory and the Dream.* Boston: Little, Brown, and Co., 1973.

Manchester, William. *Portrait of a President.* New York: Macfadden, 1967.

Maraniss, David. *Rome 1960.* New York: Simon & Schuster, 2008.

Maraniss, David. *When Pride Still Mattered.* New York: Simon & Schuster, 1999.

Marley, David John. *Pat Robertson.* Lanham, Maryland: Rowman & Littlefield, 2007.

Martin, John Bartlow. *Adlai Stevenson and the World.* Garden City, New York: Doubleday and Co., 1977.

Martin, John Bartlow. *Adlai Stevenson of Illinois.* Garden City, New York: Doubleday and Co., 1976.

Matthews, Christopher. *Kennedy and Nixon.* New York: Simon & Schuster, 1996.

Mazo, Earl, and Stephen Hess. *Nixon.* New York: Harper & Row, 1968.

McCullough, David. *Truman.* New York: Simon & Schuster, 1992.

McGillivray, Alice, Richard Scammon, and Rhodes Cook. *America at the Polls, 1960–2004.* Washington: CQ Press, 2005.

McKeever, Porter. *Adlai Stevenson.* New York: William Morrow and Co., 1989.

McLaughlin, Loretta. *The Pill, John Rock, and the Church.* Boston: Little, Brown, and Co., 1982.

Middleton, Drew. *The Duel of the Giants.* New York: Charles Scribner's Sons, 1978.

Miles, Barry. *The Beatles: A Diary.* London: Omnibus, 1998.

Miller, David. *Athens to Athens*. London: Mainstream, 2003.

Miller, Jeff. *Going Long*. Chicago: Contemporary, 2003.

Miller, Merle. *Lyndon*. New York: G. P. Putnam's Sons, 1980.

Mitchell, Greg. *Tricky Dick and the Pink Lady*. New York: Random House, 1998.

Moore, Winfred Jr., and Orville Vernon Burton, eds. *Toward the Meeting of the Waters*. Columbia, South Carolina: University of South Carolina Press, 2008.

Morgan, Murray. *Century 21*. Seattle: University of Washington Press, 1963.

Mosley, Leonard. *Dulles*. New York: Dial Press/James Wade, 1978.

Mullen, Megan. *The Rise of Cable Programming in the United States*. Austin, Texas: University of Texas Press, 2003.

Nash, Alanna. *The Colonel*. New York: Simon & Schuster, 2003.

National Party Conventions, 1831–2004. Washington: CQ Press, 2005.

Newfield, Jack. *Robert Kennedy*. New York: E. P. Dutton & Co., 1969.

Newhart, Bob. *I Shouldn't Even Be Doing This*. New York: Hyperion, 2006.

Nichols, David. *A Matter of Justice*. New York: Simon & Schuster, 2007.

Nixon, Richard. *In the Arena*. New York: Simon & Schuster, 1990.

Nixon, Richard. *RN*. New York: Grosset and Dunlap, 1978.

Nixon, Richard. *Six Crises*. Garden City, New York: Doubleday and Co., 1962.

Nolen, Stephanie. *Promised the Moon*. New York: Four Walls Eight Windows, 2002.

Oakley, J. Ronald. *God's Country*. New York: Dembner, 1986.

O'Brien, Lawrence. *No Final Victories*. Garden City, New York: Doubleday and Co., 1974.

Ochsner, Jeffrey Karl, ed. *Shaping Seattle Architecture*. Seattle: University of Washington Press, 1994.

O'Connor, Ian. *Arnie & Jack*. Boston: Houghton Mifflin, 2008.

O'Donnell, Kenneth, and David Powers. *Johnny, We Hardly Knew Ye*. Boston: Little, Brown, and Co., 1972.

Olson, Lynne. *Freedom's Daughters*. New York: Scribner, 2001.

O'Neill, Tip. *Man of the House*. New York: Random House, 1987.

O'Neill, William. *Coming Apart*. New York: Times Books, 1971.

O'Reilly, Kenneth. *Hoover and the Un-Americans*. Philadelphia: Temple University Press, 1983.

Parini, Jay. *John Steinbeck*. New York: Henry Holt and Co., 1995.

Parmet, Herbert. *JFK*. New York: Dial, 1983.

Parmet, Herbert. *Richard Nixon and His America*. Boston: Little, Brown, and Co., 1990.

Paterson, Thomas. *Contesting Castro*. New York: Oxford University Press, 1994.

Peirce, Neal. *The Pacific States of America*. New York: W.W. Norton and Co., 1972.

Peirce, Neal. *The People's President*. New York: Clarion, 1968.

Pelkonen, Eeva-Liisa, and Donald Albrecht, eds. *Eero Saarinen*. New Haven, Connecticut: Yale University Press, 2006.

Perret, Geoffrey. *Eisenhower*. New York: Random House, 1999.

Persico, Joseph. *Edward R. Murrow*. New York: McGraw-Hill, 1988.

Persico, Joseph. *The Imperial Rockefeller*. New York: Simon & Schuster, 1982.

Plimpton, George. *Truman Capote*. New York: Doubleday, 1997.

Pool, Ithiel de Sola, Robert Abelson, and Samuel Popkin. *Candidates, Issues, and Strategies*. Cambridge, Massachusetts: MIT Press, 1965.

Powledge, Fred. *Free at Last?* Boston: Little, Brown, and Co., 1991.

Powledge, Fred. *We Shall Overcome*. New York: Charles Scribner's Sons, 1993.

Pritchard, David, and Alan Lysaght. *The Beatles*. New York: Hyperion, 1998.

Railsback, Brian, and Michael Meyer, eds. *A John Steinbeck Encyclopedia*. Westport, Connecticut: Greenwood Press, 2006.

Reader, John. *Africa*. New York: Alfred A. Knopf, 1998.

Reedy, George. *Lyndon B. Johnson*. New York: Andrews and McMeel, 1982.

Reeves, Richard. *President Kennedy*. New York: Simon & Schuster, 1993.

Reinsch, J. Leonard. *Getting Elected*. New York: Hippocrene, 1988.

Reisler, Jim. *The Best Game Ever*. New York: Carroll & Graf, 2007.

Remnick, David. *King of the World*. New York: Random House, 1998.

Roberts, Chalmers. *The Washington Post*. Boston: Houghton Mifflin, 1977.

Roman, Antonio. *Eero Saarinen*. New York: Princeton Architectural Press, 2003.

Rotolo, Suze. *A Freewheelin' Time*. New York: Broadway Books, 2008.

Runyon, John, Jennefer Verdini, and Sally Runyon. *Source Book of American Presidential Campaign and Election Statistics*. New York: Frederick Ungar Publishing Co., 1971.

Rusher, William. *The Rise of the Right.* New York: William Morrow and Co., 1984.

Rusk, Dean. *As I Saw It.* New York: W. W. Norton and Co., 1990.

Rustow, Dankwart. *Oil and Turmoil.* New York: W. W. Norton and Co., 1982.

Sale, Kirkpatrick. *SDS.* New York: Vintage Books, 1974.

Saliga, Pauline, ed. *The Sky's the Limit.* New York: Rizzoli, 1990.

Salinger, Pierre. *With Kennedy.* Garden City, New York: Doubleday and Co., 1966.

Salisbury, Harrison. *The New Emperors.* Boston: Little, Brown, and Co., 1992.

Sampson, Anthony. *Mandela.* New York: Alfred A. Knopf, 1999.

Sampson, Curt. *The Eternal Summer.* Dallas: Taylor, 1992.

Sapolsky, Harvey. *Polaris System Development.* Cambridge, Massachusetts: Harvard University Press, 1972.

Scammon, Richard, and Ben Wattenberg. *The Real Majority.* New York: Berkley Medallion, 1971.

Schaller, Michael. *Altered States.* New York: Oxford University Press, 1997.

Schefter, James. *The Race.* New York: Doubleday, 1999.

Schickel, Richard. *The World of Carnegie Hall.* New York: Julian Messner, 1960.

Schlesinger, Arthur Jr. *Journals 1952–2000.* New York: Penguin, 2007.

Schlesinger, Arthur Jr. *A Thousand Days.* Boston: Houghton Mifflin, 1965.

Schoultz, Lars. *That Infernal Little Cuban Republic.* Chapel Hill, North Carolina: University of North Carolina Press, 2009.

Sevareid, Eric, ed. *Candidates 1960.* New York: Basic Books, 1959.

Shapiro, Michael. *Bottom of the Ninth.* New York: Times Books, 2009.

Shelton, Robert. *No Direction Home.* New York: William Morrow and Co., 1986.

Sherman, Janann. *No Place for a Woman.* New Brunswick, New Jersey: Rutgers University Press, 2000.

Shields, Charles. *Mockingbird.* New York: Henry Holt and Co., 2006.

Short, Philip. *Mao.* New York: Henry Holt and Co., 1999.

Shoumatoff, Alex. *The Capital of Hope.* New York: Coward, McCann, and Geoghegan, 1980.

Skeet, Ian. *OPEC.* New York: Cambridge University Press, 1988.

Smith, A. Robert. *The Tiger in the Senate.* Garden City, New York: Doubleday and Co., 1962.

Smith, Richard Norton. *Thomas E. Dewey and His Times.* New York: Simon & Schuster, 1982.

Solberg, Carl. *Hubert Humphrey.* New York: W. W. Norton and Co., 1984.

Sorensen, Ted. *Counselor.* New York: HarperCollins, 2008.

Sorensen, Ted. *Kennedy.* New York: Harper & Row, 1965.

Sounes, Howard. *Down the Highway.* New York: Grove Press, 2001.

Stacks, John. *Scotty.* Boston: Little, Brown, and Co., 2003.

Steel, Ronald. *Walter Lippmann and the American Century.* Boston: Little, Brown, and Co., 1980.

Steinbeck, John. *Travels with Charley.* New York: Viking, 1962.

Stern, Isaac. *My First 79 Years.* New York: Alfred A. Knopf, 1999.

Stevenson, Charles. *The End of Nowhere.* Boston: Beacon, 1972.

Stich, Sidra. *Yves Klein.* Stuttgart, Germany: Cantz Verlag, 1994.

Stone, Joseph, and Tim Yohn. *Prime Time and Misdemeanors.* New Brunswick, New Jersey: Rutgers University Press, 1992.

Strober, Deborah Hart, and Gerald Strober. *The Kennedy Presidency.* Washington: Brassey's, 2003.

Strober, Deborah Hart, and Gerald Strober. *The Nixon Presidency.* Washington: Brassey's, 2003.

Taubman, William. *Khrushchev.* New York: W. W. Norton and Co., 2003.

Thomas, G. Scott. *Advice From the Presidents.* Westport, Connecticut: Greenwood Press, 2008.

Thomas, G. Scott. *The Pursuit of the White House.* Westport, Connecticut: Greenwood Press, 1987.

Thomas, G. Scott. *The United States of Suburbia.* Amherst, New York: Prometheus, 1998.

Thompson, Neal. *Light This Candle.* New York: Crown, 2004.

Tillett, Paul, editor. *Inside Politics: The National Conventions, 1960.* Dobbs Ferry, New York: Oceana, 1962.

Tusa, Ann. *The Last Division.* Reading, Massachusetts: Addison-Wesley, 1997.

Tussman, Joseph. *Obligation and the Body Politic.* New York: Oxford University Press, 1960.

Ulam, Adam. *Expansion and Coexistence.* New York: Praeger, 1974.

Ulam, Adam. *The Rivals.* New York: Viking Compass, 1972.

Unger, Irwin. *The Movement.* New York: Dodd, Mead, & Co., 1974.

Valenti, Jack. *This Time, This Place.* New York: Harmony Books, 2007.

Van Dulken, Stephen. *Inventing the 20th Century.* New York: New York University Press, 2000.

Vare, Robert, ed. *The American Idea.* New York: Doubleday, 2007.

Vidal, Gore. *United States.* New York: Random House, 1993.

Wainwright, Loudon. *The Great American Magazine.* New York: Alfred A. Knopf, 1986.

Wallace, Doris, and Howard Gruber, eds. *Creative People at Work.* New York: Oxford University Press, 1989.

Wallace, Patricia Ward. *Politics of Conscience.* Westport, Connecticut: Praeger, 1995.

Walter, William. *Space Age.* New York: Random House, 1992.

Walton, Richard. *Cold War and Counterrevolution.* Baltimore: Pelican, 1973.

Walton, Richard. *The Remnants of Power.* New York: Coward-McCann, 1968.

Wasson, Tyler, ed. *Nobel Prize Winners.* New York: H.W. Wilson, 1987.

Weitekamp, Margaret. *Right Stuff, Wrong Sex.* Baltimore: Johns Hopkins University Press, 2004.

Whalen, Richard. *The Founding Father.* New York: New American Library, 1964.

White, Theodore. *Breach of Faith.* New York: Atheneum, 1975.

White, Theodore. *In Search of History.* New York: Warner Books, 1978.

White, Theodore. *The Making of the President 1960.* New York: Atheneum, 1961.

White, Theodore. *Theodore H. White at Large.* New York: Pantheon, 1992.

Wicker, Tom. *One of Us.* New York: Random House, 1991.

Williams, Charles. *The Last Great Frenchman.* New York: John Wiley & Sons, 1993.

Wilson, Charles. *Crossing Learning Boundaries by Choice.* Bloomington, Indiana: AuthorHouse, 2008.

Wilson, Robert, ed. *Character Above All.* New York: Simon & Schuster, 1995.

Witcover, Jules. *Crapshoot.* New York: Crown, 1992.

Witcover, Jules. *The Resurrection of Richard Nixon.* New York: G. P. Putnam's Sons, 1970.

Wofford, Harris. *Of Kennedys and Kings.* New York: Farrar, Straus, and Giroux, 1980.

Wolff, Miles. *Lunch at the Five and Ten.* New York: Stein and Day, 1970.

Woodward, C. Vann. *The Burden of Southern History.* Baton Rouge, Louisiana: Louisiana State University Press, 1993.

Wyden, Peter. *Bay of Pigs*. New York: Touchstone, 1979.
Zeilig, Leo. *Patrice Lumumba*. London: Haus, 2008.

Magazines and Journals

American Spectator
Art in America
Billboard
Booklist
Bulletin of the Atomic Scientists
Business Week
CA: A Bulletin of Cancer Progress
Chemistry and Industry
Chicago
China Journal
Computer Design
Cook's Illustrated
CPA Journal
Duke Law Journal
Economist
Entertainment Weekly
Ethics and Medicine
Forbes
Fortune
Good Housekeeping
Harvard Law Review
Historian
Historical Methods
History Today
Human Rights
Invention & Technology
Journal of African American History
Journal of Blacks in Higher Education
Journal of Public Policy and Marketing
Los Angeles
Maclean's
Middle East Policy
Nation
National Journal
National Review

New Republic
Newsweek
New Yorker
Pediatrics
People
Planning
Playboy
Polity
Popular Mechanics
Presidential Studies Quarterly
Security Distributing and Marketing
Smithsonian
Sports Illustrated
Technology Review
Texas Monthly
Time
Virginia Quarterly Review
Weekly Standard

Newspapers

Anchorage Daily News
Boston Globe
Boston Herald
Chicago Sun-Times
Chicago Tribune
Dallas Morning News
Greensboro News and Record
Hartford Courant
Investor's Business Daily
Kansas City Star
Los Angeles Times
New York Observer
New York Post
New York Times
Oklahoma City Daily Oklahoman
Philadelphia Inquirer
San Francisco Chronicle
Seattle Post-Intelligencer
Seattle Times

Toronto Globe and Mail
Wall Street Journal
Washington Post
White Plains Journal News

Websites

American Presidency Project at the University of California at Santa Barbara (http://www.presidency.ucsb.edu).
Avalon Project at Yale Law School (http://avalon.law.yale.edu).
Baseball Reference (http://www.baseball-reference.com).
Billboard (http://www.billboard.com).
Commission on Presidential Debates (http://www.debates.org).
C-SPAN (http://www.c-span.org).
Encyclopedia of Chicago (http://www.encyclopedia.chicagohis tory.org).
ESPN (http://sports.espn.go.com).
Museum of Broadcast Communications (http://www.museum.tv).
National Aeronautics and Space Administration (http://www.nasa.gov).
Pro Football Reference (http://www.pro-football-reference.com).
Pulitzer Prizes (http://www.pulitzer.org).
Roper Center for Public Opinion Research (http://www.ropercenter.uconn.edu).
United States Bureau of Labor Statistics (http://www.bls.gov).
United States Census Bureau (http://www.census.gov).

Index

About the Author

G. SCOTT THOMAS has written seven books: *Advice from the Presidents* (Greenwood, 2008), *Leveling the Field* (2002), *The United States of Suburbia* (1998), *The Rating Guide to Life in America's Fifty States* (1994), *Where to Make Money* (1993), *The Rating Guide to Life in America's Small Cities* (1990), and *The Pursuit of the White House* (Greenwood, 1987). He has been a journalist for more than 30 years, currently serving as an editor for American City Business Journals, and has written more than 100 articles for national magazines.